D1246787

Courtesy Mackinac Bridge Authority

Mackinac Bridge, built across the Straits of Mackinac

MICHIGAN

Yesterday and Today

By FERRIS E. LEWIS

HENRY FORD
COMMUNITY COLLEGE
DEARBORN, MICHIGAN

HILLSDALE SCHOOL SUPPLY
Publishers
HILLSDALE, MICHIGAN

1st Edition 1956

2nd Edition	1st Revision	1957
3rd Edition	2nd Revision	1960
4th Edition	3rd Revision	1961

Printed in U. S. A.

PREFACE

Michigan Yesterday and Today is really an extensive revision of *My State and Its Story,* which was first printed in 1937. Since that time *My State and Its Story* has gone through several editions and ten revisions. Much new material and many new pictures have been added to make the text more interesting and explanatory. This move is felt to be justified in view of the increased interest in Michigan history that has taken place since *My State and Its Story* first appeared.

Again I wish to express my thanks to the many people and companies for their help and cooperation in supplying information and pictures for this fourth revision in 1961. Each company has been credited for the pictures they so kindly supplied.

Ferris E. Lewis
Sept. 1961

TABLE OF CONTENTS

Chapter I

HOW MICHIGAN WAS FORMED

If you were to take a vacation trip through Michigan on our modern highways, you would soon learn that Michigan is not only a very beautiful state but that it has many natural resources. You would also find that the people who live here are employed in many different occupations. Perhaps these are some of the reasons people like to spend their vacations in Michigan, for few states have the scenic spots, natural resources, and varied industries and occupations that can be found within our state.

In some parts of the state, as you drove along, you would see farm lands. In these areas farming is the major occupation. You would soon learn that not only general farming and dairying are being carried on in Michigan, but crops which require special soils and climates, such as mint, chicory, sugar beets, and onions, are also being raised. In still other rural areas, especially on the western side of the Lower Peninsula, large orchards of cherry, peach, pear, and apple trees spread across the rolling countryside.

On your way you would soon come to one of the Great Lakes that form much of Michigan's border, for Michigan touches four lakes that are among the largest lakes in the world. If you are like most tourists who travel about Michigan, you would enjoy watching one of the large ore boats, carrying hundreds of tons of iron ore in its huge hold, as it steams quietly across the blue water leaving a hazy plume of smoke that slowly fades into the clear, blue sky above.

You would not go far before you would also discover that Michigan has many beautiful streams, lakes, and islands. Some of the time you would find yourself driving through forested areas where second-growth trees are slowly turning areas which only a few years ago were burned-over waste lands into pine and hardwood forests. Here you would meet and talk to people who are hosts to tourists and other travelers who come each year to spend their vacations in Michigan's forest and lake areas.

In the Upper Peninsula you would discover deep copper and iron mines. In other areas you would see quarries, large holes a mile or more across in the earth's surface where limestone or gypsum is being quarried for commercial use. In Detroit you would find a mine where rock salt is being taken from under part of the city. At other places along your way you would see the derricks, or pumps, of salt wells or oil wells.

In Grindstone City, at the tip of the thumb, you would be interested in visiting the place where grindstones and whetstones were made from Marshall sandstone. These stones were used for many years by farmers, lumbermen, and carpenters to sharpen tools.

Abandoned quarry at Grindstone City

Michigan has many large factories, where automobiles, furniture, drugs, heating units, rulers, buttons, chemicals, paints, and many other products are now being manufactured. Some of these industrial plants are so large that you could spend many hours visiting just one of them.

But, you might ask, as you rode along past weather-scarred mountains, sites of old Indian villages, and frontier posts, or as you watched the dark smoke drift slowly away from the stack of an ore carrier or a factory chimney, why does Michigan have so many kinds of soils and minerals which give rise to so many occupations for her people, and why and how have all these occupations developed here in Michigan?

If you would understand why Michigan is like it is today, you must begin with Michigan's story when the North American continent was first being formed. This interesting story can be found in the rocks that lie in and under our state. We call the study of the earth's formation, its early history, and the work of weathering agents the study of geology. People who have studied in this field of human knowledge are known as geologists. During the past hundred years, geologists have found out much about the early formation of our world and also what it is like today. Men carrying Geiger counters looking for uranium, oil drillers looking for new oil pools, men drilling to find salt brines, miners digging ores from the ground, and students studying rock formations are all adding more knowledge every day to what is known about the rocks and soils which lie under our feet.

The story of the earth's formation and early history has been learned by geologists who have studied the rocks from which our world is made. Sometimes rocks are called nature's great history book because, just as a history book is made up of pages that tell a story from beginning to end, the rock layers of our world tell the story of the things that happened long ago. Each of these rock layers is like a page of nature's book. In many places in the United States rock layers can easily be seen along the sides of river valleys, along a highway that has been cut through a rocky hillside, or along a railroad as it winds its way across a mountain side. In Michigan, however, these outcropping rocks can be found in only a very few places. Nearly all of Michigan is covered, as you will learn, by crushed and often powdered rock, called glacial till. This cover of glacial till hides the underlying rock layers from us and we can learn of them only by boring holes deep into the ground. Careful records kept by oil companies, salt companies, and geologists tell us how deep the layers are and how they fold and bend.

No doubt you have seen an old book, much used and worn, from which the cover has been broken off and the first few pages torn and crumpled from much usage. The date of publication is missing, but the rest of the pages toward the back of the book are still in good condition. Such is nature's book of the rocks. So old is this book and so weathered and beaten are the first pages that it is hard to tell just when the story of our world began and what happened in detail during the long ages of time.

The Archeozoic Age

About two billion years ago, according to geologists and our modern Geiger counters, the slowly cooling earth formed a crust of hard rock material called granite. This granite was formed from material which had once been so hot that it was in liquid form. Since it was the lightest material, it rose to the top, or the outside, of the earth's crust. Beneath the granite layer a thick layer of still heavier rock, called basalt, also formed. Still farther toward the center of the earth were hot, heavier materials. The forming of the granite crust on the earth marks the beginning of our first chapter in nature's book, which is called by geologists the Archeozoic Age. After that early time, ac-

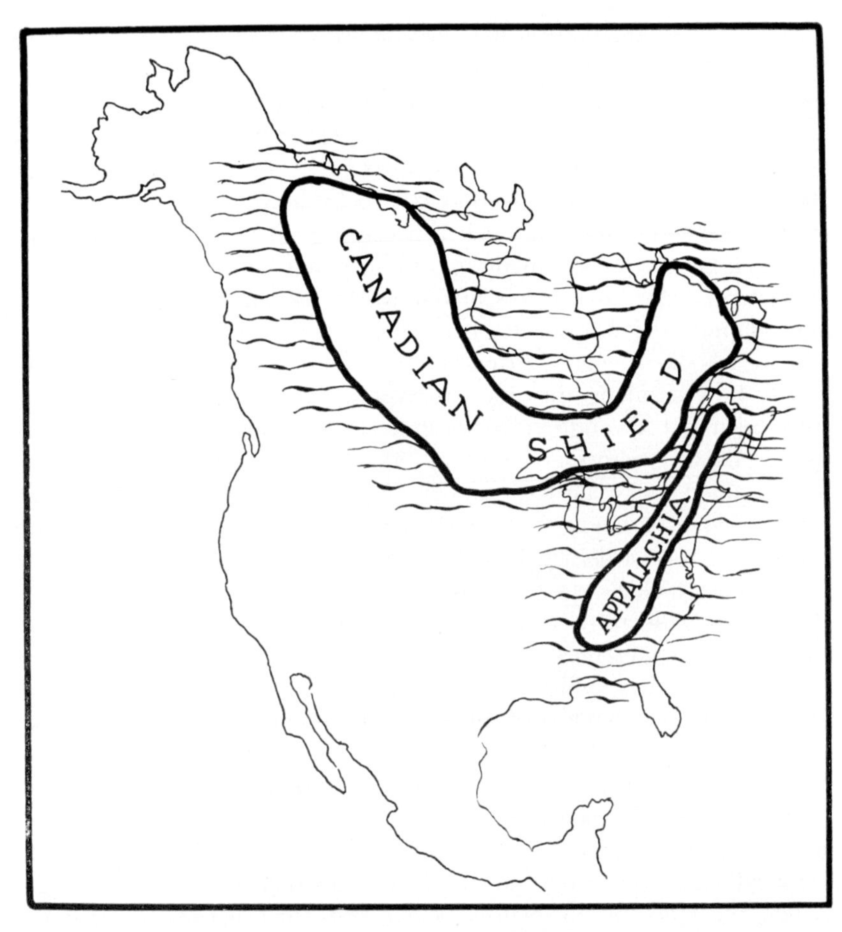

cording to geologists, the Archeozoic Age lasted a billion years or more. It is the longest and least-known period of our earth's history.

By the time the Archeozoic Age began, land masses had already formed and had risen above the seas that then covered the rest of the world. One of these first granite land masses formed is now known as the Canadian Shield or Laurentian Upland. It formed a huge U shape around what is now Hudson Bay, and spread from the Arctic Ocean in the northwest to Newfoundland and Labrador in the northeast. Today this Canadian Shield spreads across about two million square miles and covers half of Canada. In this Canadian Shield, uranium, iron ore, copper, nickel, and gold are now being found, and hundreds of recent mineral claims have been staked out.

Another land mass, now known as the Appalachian Mountains, was uplifted along what is now the eastern coast of the United States. All the rest of the continent of North America was then under the sea.

The Canadian Shield came as far south as northern Minnesota, northern Wisconsin, and the western half of the Upper Peninsula. The present rocky, northern shore of Lake Superior is made of the same granite rock which hardened into the Canadian Shield when the earth's crust was formed two billion years ago.

Very, very slowly the crust of the earth went on cooling and shrinking. At one time during this long era the granite of the Canadian Shield slowly folded upward and a huge mountain range, now known as the Laurentian Mountains, spread in a great U shape from the Arctic to Labrador. The roots of these weathered old mountains can still be seen in Canada.

During the millions of years of the Archeozoic Age there was day and night just as there is today. Cracks formed in the earth's crust, and volcanoes were born that poured out from their smoking cones hot basalt rock just as volcanoes still do today. Heat, cold, wind, sunshine, and running water very slowly wore away these ancient rocks just as these same weathering agents are wearing away rocks in our time. When the rains fell, the run-off water, going back to the oceans, carried little pieces of rock and minerals with it just as streams now carry sediment to the oceans. These little pieces of rock and mineral settled to the ocean bottom near the mouths of ancient rivers or were spread by waves and ocean currents farther out across the ocean floor.

Gradually, during long ages, these little pieces of rock and minerals became deeper and deeper until by their own weight they pressed the lower layers together to form a new kind of rock which geologists today call sedimentary rock. Sedimentary rock was thus formed from the sediment that had been carried into the ancient oceans by the winds and rivers. Sometimes these sedimentary rocks, because of heat and pressure, became very hard. Such rocks are known as metamorphic rocks.

It is by studying these layers of sedimentary rock, which are found over nearly all of the United States, that geologists have learned the story of how our land was formed. These layers of rock are the pages of nature's book. By reading the story of our earth from each of these pages, starting from the bottom, geologists have been able to tell us much about what happened long ago. To geologists, time is measured not so much by years as it is by what is found in the rock layers.

One sedimentary layer that was laid down during the Archeozoic Age contained many, many small pieces of iron ore. As we will later see, these deposits of iron ore became the basis of our present iron mining industry in Michigan and Minnesota. Now that our iron deposits are running low, this same layer of iron-bearing rock, called the Mother Lode, may become the basis of our future iron mining industry. Already large processing plants are being built to crush this hard old Archeozoic rock and get from it the iron ore that has lain there for over a billion years.

After about a billion years, say the geologists, the Archeozoic Age came to an end. It was a longer age than any single geologic period has been since that time. The new age that followed is known as the Proterozoic Age.

The Proterozoic Age

Thus begins the second chapter in nature's book. Although geologists start a new chapter here and give the next age a new name, we must be very careful to remember that there was no violent change in nature or nature's way of doing things. Nature went on just as it had for long ages past. The difference lies in this: Some time during the long Archeozoic Age life had begun on our world. No traces of this early life can be found except carbon. That is the only record in these early rocks which tells us of earliest life on the earth. But now, with the beginning of the Proterozoic Age, life had advanced far enough so that the little plants and animals began to leave their imprint in the sedimentary rocks which were then laid down. These little imprints of shells and tracks are called fossils. Only a few fossils of the early Proterozoic Age are found, and they are all of a very elementary form of life.

During the Proterozoic Age the earth went on cooling very slowly, eroding and shrinking just as it had been doing for millions of years. As it cooled and shrank, new, large wrinkles were pushed slowly upward, by great pressures, to form huge new mountain chains, even larger than those found in our western states today. One of these mountain ranges that were slowly pressed upward as the earth's crust folded and raised was a range of mountains that geologists now call the Killarney Mountains.

The Killarney Mountains ran in a general north and south direction through what are now the states of Minnesota, Wisconsin, and the western part of the Upper Peninsula of Michigan. Just how far south the Killarney mountains went we do not know. As one looks from the turn-out on Brockway Mountain Drive, near the northern end of the Keweenaw Peninsula in Upper Michigan, one can see even today the aged, worn edges of some of the upturned folds of the old Killarney Mountains. As one stands looking at these ancient, folded layers, it is still hard to realize that one is looking at one of the oldest parts of Michigan and some of the oldest rock to be found on the surface in any part of the world.

A rock outcrop of the old Killarney Mountains

For hundreds of thousands of years the Killarney Mountains raised their rugged peaks across the face of the land. At places along the range, volcanoes spilled lava down their slopes just as volcanoes do today. The Keweenaw Peninsula is the result of much volcanic action that took place during this time in the earth's history. There are some five hundred lava flows in the Lake Superior mineral belt. At one time the Killarney Mountains formed a shore line that ran roughly just west of a line from present-day Munising to Escanaba. All the rest of Michigan was still covered with water.

Little by little, as long periods of time passed, the hard old rocks of the Killarney Mountains were slowly worn away by frost, sunshine, wind, ice, and running water. The eroded material was carried to the sea by the rivers, and there it spread out and settled on the bottom of the ancient sea to give us our next rock layer, the Cambrian sandstone layer that lies upon the Archean rocks.

It was during this period that many of our mineral deposits were formed. As the iron-bearing layer of rock wore away, running water carried the little pieces of rock away and left the heavier ore behind. Thus, pockets of high-grade iron ore were formed in Minnesota and Michigan as the rock layers were worn away. In Minnesota and Michigan these iron deposits are often soft enough to mine with a power shovel. The rock layers, known as the Mother Lode, that did not fold and erode still contain large deposits of low-grade iron ore now called Taconite.* Other minerals were also formed for our use at this time. At Sudbury in Canada, just east of Sault Ste. Marie, a large deposit of nickel was formed.

Geologists tell us that as the Killarney Mountains slowly pushed upward they sometimes cracked under the great pressure. Into these cracks hot basalt rock oozed. In the holes in the lava and the cracks in the rock "native" copper was deposited.

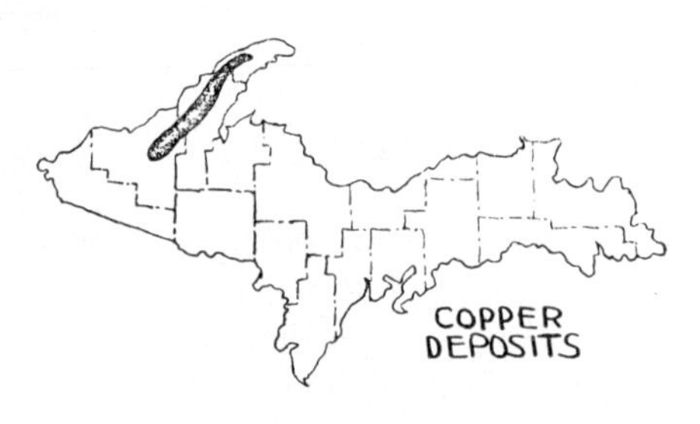

From Ontonagon to Copper Harbor, in the Keweenaw Peninsula, and on Isle Royale can now be found chunks of pure copper. To date only the best copper deposits, found in the old lava flows, have been mined. Many of the low-grade copper deposits still remain to be worked.

In Michigan, only the weathered stumps of the Killarney Mountains can now be found. These roots may be seen in the Porcupine Mountains, the Huron Mountains, in the old lava flows of the Keweenaw Peninsula, and in rock outcrops near Iron Mountain. Because the tops of these mountains have been worn away, the minerals left

Centennial Copper Mine at Calumet (1952)

*Called Jasper in Michigan.

An outcrop along US 2 west of Iron Mountain.

behind such as copper, silver, gold, and iron ore, which were formed during the Proterozoic Age, now lie near the surface of the land.

Following the folded rocks of the old Killarney Mountains, miners have dug native copper and iron ore from the hidden pockets of the mountain stumps.* We use the iron ore today to make steel for our railroads, boats, machinery, cars, and hundreds of other things. Copper is used in auto radiators, in shell casings, and in thousands of miles of copper wire that carry electricity to run our factories and to light our homes.

The Paleozoic Age

The third chapter in the book of geologic history is the Paleozoic Age. Up to this time there is little direct evidence of life found in the rock layers, but the layers beginning with this third chapter are found to contain many fossils. That is why geologists divide this period into a new chapter called the Paleozoic Age. Because different things took place during the Paleozoic Age, geologists divide this age into seven different parts which they call periods.

The Cambrian Period

The first period of this age is called the Cambrian Period. During the Cambrian Period most of the land area of Michigan, except the western part of the Upper Peninsula, was still under water much of the time. Large arms of ancient seas spread inland and covered the land. It is because of the sedimentary deposits which were laid down upon the bottom of these ancient seas that we now know so much about what took place so long ago in Michigan.

As ocean followed ocean, layer upon layer of debris was slowly laid down as one layer was covered by another. Today these former ocean bottoms that lie under Michigan and the nearby area are like huge saucers placed one inside the other. Each saucer, or layer,

*For the latest developments in iron and copper mining see chapter 19.

is a little smaller in size than the one in which it rests. All of them slope very gradually from their outer edges to the center of the basin. Each saucer was formed by the silt brought down into the seas by ancient rivers, just as debris is carried by the Mississippi River to its delta today, and by millions and millions of small sea plants and animals that then lived in the seas and left their bodies upon the bottoms of those ancient seas.

The first and deepest of these saucers, which is under most of Michigan, lies upon the Archeozoic rock bed. This layer is called the Cambrian Formation. This layer of rock, now known as Cambrian sandstone, was formed from the crushed and eroded rock that was carried into the seas by rivers as the Killarney Mountains slowly wore away during the Proterozoic Age. This Cambrian sandstone layer has

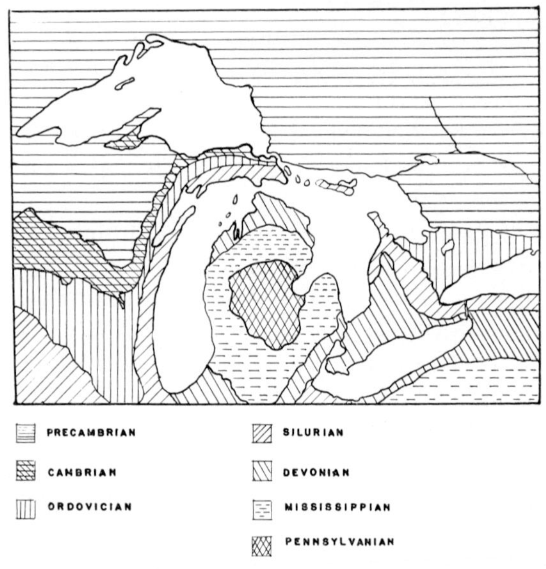

a reddish-brown color because of the iron ore that was deposited in it by the rivers as the small pieces of rock and iron ore were laid down upon the ocean floor. Today this Cambrian Formation outcrops in Michigan along the northern edge of the eastern part of the Upper Peninsula. It makes many of Michigan's beautiful waterfalls, like the Tahquamenon Falls, as the run-off water of some of the rivers of the Upper Peninsula, on their way to Lake Superior, spill over the northern edge of the Cambrian sandstone. The beautiful Pictured Rocks, which stretch along the southern shore of Lake Superior from

Munising to Grand Marais, are formed of this Cambrian sandstone. Wave action and ice pressures from Lake Superior, chewing at the northern edge of the exposed Cambrian Formation, have left cliffs along the shore some fifty to eighty feet in height. It is this rocky ridge that makes the rapids in the St. Mary's River at Sault Ste. Marie. When the first lock of the St. Marys Falls Canal was built at Sault Ste. Marie a hundred years ago, it was into this Cambrian sandstone that the workers had to cut to make the first lock. From the outcrop, reaching eastward from Munising across the Upper Peninsula, the Cambrian rock layer dips gradually down and under the entire Lower Peninsula. In the southern part of the state the Cambrian layer lies a mile or so below the surface of the land.

The Cambrian Period covers the time in the earth's history when the sedimentary deposits were made mostly of weathered rock being carried from the Killarney Mountains to the sea. There are, however, some fossils found in this Cambrian rock.

The Ordovician Period

The Cambrian Period was followed by the Ozarkian and Ordovician Periods. The sedimentary layers are now found to contain much less weathered rock and are made up mostly of the lime and fossils that were left by the little sea animals. The first known fish are found in these layers of rock.

At times during the Paleozoic Age the land rose and then the seas were driven from the land for long periods of time. Then again the seas came slowly creeping inland as the land settled into the water.

The Silurian Period

About four hundred and fifty million years ago the fourth period of the Paleozoic Age began. It is called the Silurian Period. During this period warm, shallow water advanced southward from the Arctic Ocean. Many small sea animals known as trilobites and squids lived in this shallow water. When they died, their shells left thick layers of limestone on the ocean bottom.

We know that the seas were warm, like those in the tropics, because coral grew in these ancient waters. Three coral reefs are now known to have been formed in the Silurian seas. One coral reef ran from present Bay de Noc, in the Upper Peninsula, to the north side of Drummond Island. The second reef ran along what is now the southern side of the Upper Peninsula to the southern side of Drummond Island. The third reef swung in a large half circle northward from Alpena to Petoskey. Today one can see the remains of this third coral formation in stones that are picked up near Petoskey and are known as "Petoskey stones." A thick deposit of several layers of salt was laid down in the area now reaching from St. Ignace and Muskegon south and eastward all the way to northwestern Pennsylvania and southeastern New York State. It is in this Silurian salt formation which underlies Detroit that salt miners today mine rock salt. During the Silurian period traces of land vegetation began to appear.

This limestone layer makes the Detroit River very shallow near its mouth. Today a large channel, called the Livingstone Channel, has been blasted through this rock layer on the Canadian side of the river so that large ore boats can pass through this part of the Detroit River.

Devonian Period

The Silurian Period was followed by the Devonian Period, which began about four hundred million years ago. By the time of the Devonian Period the size of the sea basin had become much smaller. Today the edge of the Devonian basin outcrops in Monroe, Wayne, Alpena, Cheboygan, and Charlevoix counties.

During this period, which lasted some fifty million years, the sea trilobites became fewer in number and the cephalopods became smaller in size. New forms of life came into the seas during the Devonian Period. Several kinds of fish began to appear. Fossil remains of these fish are now found in the limestone that is being quarried near Alpena. From these fossil remains we are able to know how fish and trilobites of this period looked.

Limestone formed in the Devonian Period is now quarried at Alpena and Rogers City. For several years, Sibley Quarry near Wyandotte produced limestone formed during this period which was used in making iron and chemical products. At Calcite near Rogers City is now found the largest limestone quarry in the world. Limestone quarried in this area is used to smelt over sixty per cent of all the iron ore mined in the United States.

During the Devonian Period, primitive evergreen trees, called seed ferns, grew on the land that was then above the water and formed the first known forests. In what is now Monroe County, a deposit of pure white sand was formed in the sand dunes that stretched along the edge of the sea. Today this pure white sand is used for making optical glass, plate glass, and table glassware. Some oil and gas were also formed. Shale and limestone from this period are now used in manufacturing cement at Alpena, Petoskey, and Dundee.

Courtesy Wyandotte Chemicals Corp.

Loading limestone at the Alpena Dock

The Mississippian Period

The Devonian Period was followed by the Mississippian Period. During this period, life was much the same as it had been during the Silurian Period. Trilobites became still fewer in number. More and more fish appeared in the seas. During this period most of Michigan's salt brine deposits were formed as the seas evaporated and left the salt behind. It is brine from these salt beds that the Dow Chemical Company at Midland uses in manufacturing its many products. Layers of sandstone were also formed during this period. It is this sandstone, which outcrops at Grindstone City, that was once used for the making of grindstones and whetstones.

The Pennsylvanian Period

As time passed by, the land that is now Michigan gradually rose, and the ancient seas that had left the thick limestone deposits retreated again from the land. What is now the Lower Peninsula then became a land of dense swamps and thick forests. Another period, called the Pennsylvanian Period, had begun. In the shallow, muddy pools of these swamps lived some of the earliest known reptiles. Some of these reptiles looked much like our present-day salamanders. In the air above the swamps were many large flying insects that made their homes in the dense, fern-like trees that then grew in the shallow water. Many reptiles, like our present alligators, crawled about in the shallow, swampy water and over the fallen, decaying vegetation. As the fern-like trees died or were blown down, they were often covered by the water in the swamps. Thus the trees, ground pines, and horsetail rushes that lived here at least two hundred and fifty million years ago were buried under the mud and have since slowly changed to peat. They now form a shallow bed of coal that lies under much of the central part of the Lower Peninsula from Jackson to Saginaw.

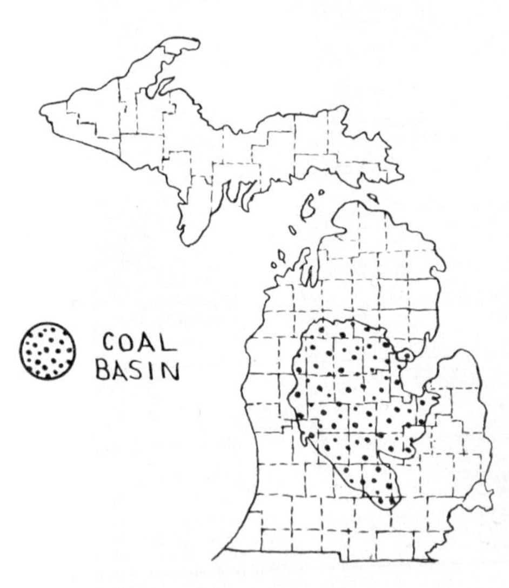

Permian Period

This period was the last period in the Paleozoic Age. In Michigan some animals left their remains on the shallow, swampy floor, but the layers of this period were made up mostly of plants, trees, sands, silts, and clays. What had been a swampy waste land became a dry area as the land rose higher. Salamanders and insects could no longer live here, but other larger animals, the first reptiles, now appeared as the Paleozoic Age came to an end.

The Mesozoic Age

With the coming of land animals the geologists begin the fourth chapter of their divisions of time as it is read from the rocks. This chapter they call the Mesozoic Age.

The area now known as Michigan had by then risen above sea level and has remained dry land ever since that time. Because of this, no rivers of any size left their story in their deltas and no sea animals left their remains on an ocean floor. Geologists know little about what happened in the next one hundred million years in Michigan. The sedimentary rocks laid down at this time in other areas of the world are all missing in Michigan because the land here was then above the sea.

The Cenozoic Age

The Mesozoic Age was followed by the fifth and last age, called the Cenozoic Age. This age is still going on today. What had once been a land of plant and animal life became a cold land of ice and snow. The weather slowly grew a little colder. What we now know as the last glacial age came on.

The glaciers were huge masses of snow and ice that formed far to the north and pushed out in all directions. These huge sheets of ice came down from Canada. They were thousands of feet in thickness and weighed countless tons. As each glacier slowly advanced, the animals of that time were pushed south ahead of it. Thus Michigan became at different times the homeland of the musk ox and the hairy elephant. Over one hundred fifty authentic records of these large elephant-type animals, called mastodons, have been recorded here in Michigan. Today a splendid specimen of a mastodon found near Owosso may be seen in the Museum of Natural Science at the University of Michigan.

In all, there were four huge ice masses that pushed one after the other over what is now Michigan. One would come, and then as the weather changed and became a little warmer, it would melt away, only to be followed by another. As each glacier pushed southward, it scoured and rubbed the land surface over which it passed. The ancient Canadian Shield between Hudson Bay and Lake Superior was scoured clean of the weathered rock and top soil that it then had. This soil was all pushed or carried southward as the glaciers moved slowly along. The ice and soil scraped over the weathered stumps of the Killarney Mountains but these old rocks were too hard for even the huge glaciers to tear completely apart. The ancient rocky folds pushed the ice upward as the glaciers scoured and scraped over them. Farther southward in the Lower Peninsula, where the seas of long ago had left their rocky limestone saucers, the glaciers scrubbed and rubbed on the saucers' rims. Much of the record of what had once happened in Michigan was thus destroyed by the grinding, pushing glaciers as they pressed down upon and rubbed across the land. Old rivers and their basins were wiped away, valleys were filled in, rocks were ground and crushed as the glaciers pushed slowly but steadily along. All the remains of the happenings which followed the Permian Period were thus ground and crushed and carried away by the moving ice. Five large valleys, which later became the Great Lakes, were formed. The glaciers advanced as far south as the Ohio and Missouri rivers. These present rivers were born as the ice melted on the southern edge of the glaciers and ran away.

About fifty thousand years ago the last glacier pushed down from the north. Then the land slowly became warmer again. The ice melted, and for the last time the water ran away. As it slowly melted, all of Michigan and the land far to the north was left uncovered. By this time most of the Killarney Mountains had been worn away. Only the hard stumps of the mountains still remained. Without this tearing away and breaking off by the glaciers, Michigan's copper and iron, which had been formed there long ago, might not have been found.

The basins that now hold the Great Lakes had been gouged out of the earth's surface. Thousands of smaller pockets, that were later to become smaller lakes, were scattered here and there across the glaciated surface of the land. Our soil, which the glaciers had brought to Michigan from north of Lake Superior, is known as glacial till.

As the weather gradually became more mild, plants and animals began to come north as they slowly followed the melting glaciers. Vegetable and animal matter mixed with the crushed rock and soil was slowly formed. Into this newly formed soil, seeds were blown by the wind and new types of vegetation sprang up.

Hardy arctic plants came first; next came willows, birches, pines, and such other trees as grow in the colder part of the temperate climate. Then came the harder woods such as oak, elm, hickory, walnut, and maple to take their stand in the better soils of the state.

Thus in a very general way the land and lakes of Michigan were first formed. It is a land of granite, sandstone, limestone, lakes, rivers, and transplanted soil. Today Michigan is an agricultural and industrial state. Many of its cities have harbors to which come large boats filled with ore, coal, grain, or limestone. All of this agriculture, industry, and shipping is built upon the geologic past of Michigan.

Geologic Periods in Michigan's Past

(See Chart Page 10)

ERA	PERIOD
I Cenozoic	A. Present Time
	B. Pleistocene
	C. Pliocene
	D. Miocene
	E. Oligocene
II Mesozoic	A. Eocene
	B. Cretaceous
	C. Jurassic
	D. Triassic
III Paleozoic	A. Permian
	B. Pennsylvanian
	C. Mississippian
	D. Devonian
	E. Silurian
	F. Ordovician
	G. Ozarkian
	H. Cambrian
IV Proterozoic or Algonkian	A. Keweenawan
	B. Huronian
	C. Timiskamingian
V Archeozoic or Archean	A. Laurentian
	B. Keewatin
VI Azoic Earliest stages of the earth as a planet.	

TEACHER'S NOTE. For a further breakdown and more material on each period see *Handbook for the Study and Teaching of Michigan History* written to accompany this entire text. Hillsdale School Supply, 1958.

Courtesy of the Detroit News

Courtesy of the Detroit News

Michigan shore line near Port Austin

Chapter II

THE GENERAL GEOGRAPHY OF MICHIGAN

Most of the state of Michigan lies in the center of the Great Lakes Region which forms a major part of the upper St. Lawrence River Valley. For that reason much of Michigan's history has been closely connected with the development of the St. Lawrence River system.

The St. Lawrence River system is one of the three large river systems that drain the North American continent. Beginning in the hundreds of small streams that flow into the Great Lakes, the water of this river system flows in a general northeast direction to the Atlantic Ocean. As it nears the ocean, the river valley narrows. Only a few people live in that area. On the north side of the valley the Canadian Shield forms a barren wasteland of weathered rock, while on the south side of the river the upper end of the Appalachian Mountain system presses in upon the narrow valley.

The St. Lawrence system is fed by several smaller rivers. Near the mouth of the St. Lawrence River can be found the Saguenay that flows from the Canadian Shield. Because it is the first large stream entering the valley, it became one of the first streams to interest the earliest white men who entered the valley to trade. At the mouth of the Saguenay a little Indian village called Tadoussac was located.

Farther up the St. Lawrence Valley the Richelieu River flows northward into the St. Lawrence, carrying the run-off waters of Lake Champlain. This river valley became of interest to the French settlers as soon as they founded their settlement at Quebec. Up this waterway Champlain went, in 1609, to fight the Iroquois Indians. Later, during the colonial period, the Richelieu River together with the Hudson River formed a main highway to the English settlements from Quebec.

Montreal in Canada now stands at the junction of the Ottawa and St. Lawrence rivers. This place was also of interest to the early Frenchmen. Here the St. Lawrence River has a rapids that stopped their little ships from going any farther inland. Here, too, a large stream, now called the Ottawa, enticed them farther to the west. Paddling up its rugged course the Frenchmen made their way on exploring expeditions.

Not far westward from Montreal lies the Great Lakes Region from which the St. Lawrence River draws most of its water. The Great Lakes form the largest fresh-water lake system to be found in any part of the world. In the Great Lakes, and the thousands of smaller inland lakes from Minnesota to Quebec, can now be found over half of all the fresh water in the world. Michigan lies in the center of this Great Lakes area, and from the earliest French fur traders to our modern ore carriers, Michigan's history has been closely tied to this water relationship.

These Great Lakes today form one of our nation's most important highways. During the shipping season, when the lakes are free from ice, large freighters carry iron ore, coal, limestone, cement, and wheat from one port to another.

The Great Lakes form the major part of the St. Lawrence drainage basin. All the rivers of northern Ohio, northern Indiana, northern Illinois, eastern Wisconsin, and northeastern Minnesota, many of Ontario's rivers, and all of Michigan's rivers except a few in the western part of the Upper Peninsula spill their run-off waters into the Great Lakes or connecting waters. From Lake Ontario this run-off water passes down to the Atlantic Ocean by way of the St. Lawrence River.

Near Montreal the St. Lawrence Valley expands outward as it pushes farther west. Today, in this expanded valley, can be found the Canadian-Ottawa Region, comprising southern Ontario, and the United States Great Lakes drainage area. These two regions, though separated politically, form one geographic region.

The Ontario Region is now the most heavily populated area of Canada. Over sixty per cent of Canada's people live in the area north of Lake Ontario and Lake Erie. This area is now the center of a large part of Canada's agriculture and industry. Here, too, can be found Canada's largest cities.

The United States Great Lakes drainage area is one of the most important drainage areas in this country. It contains the land of northern Ohio, northern Indiana, and northern Illinois, together with parts of Wisconsin and Minnesota, as well as nearly all of Michigan. It is now one of the major industrial and agricultural regions of the United States. Many people live in the area, and many large cities are to be found here, such as Cleveland, Toledo, Detroit, Flint, Grand Rapids, and Chicago. The Saint Lawrence Waterway has now made many cities on the Great Lakes ocean ports to which foreign ships can bring cargo or pick up cargo for foreign ports.

The St. Lawrence system, even from the earliest days of settlement, has shaped in many ways the pattern of historical development in the Lake Region. Its course leads directly to the markets of Europe, and even today, in our age of air transportation, the shortest route from Detroit to London lies along the St. Lawrence River Valley. Many planes follow this general course in going from the United States to Europe.

Then, too, the river provided the only direct route leading into the heart of North America from the eastern seacoast. What is more, the river provided easy access to other water systems. Only a short canoe portage took the early explorers from the St. Lawrence system to the Hudson River Valley, to the rivers of the Ohio and Mississippi watershed, and to many streams that flow north to Hudson Bay.

There were, however, many disadvantages to the St. Lawrence River system. During the winter the waters froze and shipping had to stop until spring came again. Ships leaving the river for Europe could sail only during the warm summer season. The Lachine Rapids at Montreal and other rapids in the St. Lawrence River between Montreal and Lake Ontario have made shipping difficult even from the earliest days of French settlement. Niagara Falls, also, was a hindrance to commerce to and from the West. The rapids in the St. Mary's River stopped, for many years, any real shipping into Lake Superior. Then, too, since the American Revolution, economic and international barriers stretching from Lake Superior to Montreal along the Great Lakes and St. Lawrence have hindered the valley's growth and kept in force the rivalry for commerce between the St. Lawrence and Hudson River systems.

Michigan has a land area of 57,980 square miles. This figure does not include the water area of Lake Erie, Lake Michigan, Lake Superior, and Lake Huron that is commonly shown on maps as belonging to Michigan. If this water area were added to Michigan's size, it would make Michigan the largest state east of the Mississippi River.

The land area of Michigan is formed by two large peninsulas and several small islands. The two peninsulas are separated from each other by the Straits of Mackinac. Some of Michigan's larger and better known islands are: Belle Isle, in the Detroit River; Bois Blanc Island

and Mackinac Island, in the Straits of Mackinac; Drummond Island and Sugar Island, between the Upper Peninsula and Canada; Beaver Island, the Manitou Islands, and the Fox Islands in Lake Michigan; and Grand Island and Isle Royale, in Lake Superior.

The land surface of Michigan is, for the most part, gently rolling glacial drift. In the western part of the Upper Peninsula, as was shown in Chapter One, the land is the rocky remains of what used to be huge mountains. In the Lower Peninsula the highest part is the area roughly bounded by Cadillac, Gaylord, and West Branch. This elevation is known as the High Plains Area. The soil is sandy and porous and easily absorbs the rainfall. In Oakland County and Hillsdale County the rolling hills reach up to 1,200 feet above sea level. The eastern part of the Upper Peninsula is gently rolling land like the Lower Peninsula, but in the western part, in Marquette, Iron, Baraga, and Gogebic counties, the land pushes upward to 1,600 feet. In Ontonagon County it reaches a height of 2,023 feet above sea level. This is the highest point in Michigan.

The average annual temperature varies from forty-nine degrees in the southern part of the state to thirty-nine degrees in the northern part. The growing season varies from one hundred eighty days in the southwestern part of the Lower Peninsula to only ninety days in Iron County and Crawford County. Michigan's summers are not so warm nor are her winters so cold as they are in the states lying west of Lake Michigan. Water warms and cools more slowly than does land, and therefore the Great Lakes have a cooling effect on Michigan during the summertime and a warming effect during the wintertime.

Michigan receives an average rainfall of thirty-one inches. The heaviest rainfall is in the extreme south central and southwestern parts along the Michigan-Indiana boundary line. In this area the rainfall averages thirty-six inches a year. In the Thumb area the average rainfall is only twenty-eight inches a year.

The surface area of Michigan is nearly all made up of materials that were pushed, or carried, down from north of Lake Superior and dropped as the glacier melted away. Therefore, every acre of Michigan soil is the result of ice work and running water. Large piles of glacial debris, called moraines and more commonly known as hills, stand today just where they were dropped as the last glacier melted away. These moraines cover some thirty to forty per cent of the state. They are not so large or high as they were when they were dropped as the last glacier melted, for as the running water ran away it carried some of the smaller pieces of crushed rock with it. As the running water slowed down, part of this load was dropped, and thus outwash plains at the sides of the moraines were formed. Sometimes this material was fine, and clay soils were thus formed. At other times sand and gravel were carried and deposited in valleys and in old lake bottoms. Sometimes the run-off waters from the glaciers left gravel deposits called kames or eskers. These gravel deposits are often used today for material with which to build roads.

At almost any place in the state one may find large chunks of granite that have been rounded on the corners as they were scrubbed along by the glaciers. These boulders, which have now been removed with great effort from farm lands, have sometimes been used in building foundations for houses, outside walls of houses, and fireplaces in homes and cottages.

Michigan touches four of the largest fresh water lakes in the world: Lake Superior, Lake Michigan, Lake Huron, and Lake Erie. Her shore line along these lakes extends some 3,251 miles and is the longest shore line of any state.* Along this long shore line can be found many beautiful spots that attract tourists and vacationers each year. Much of the shore line is sandy and often fringed with gaunt, wind-blown

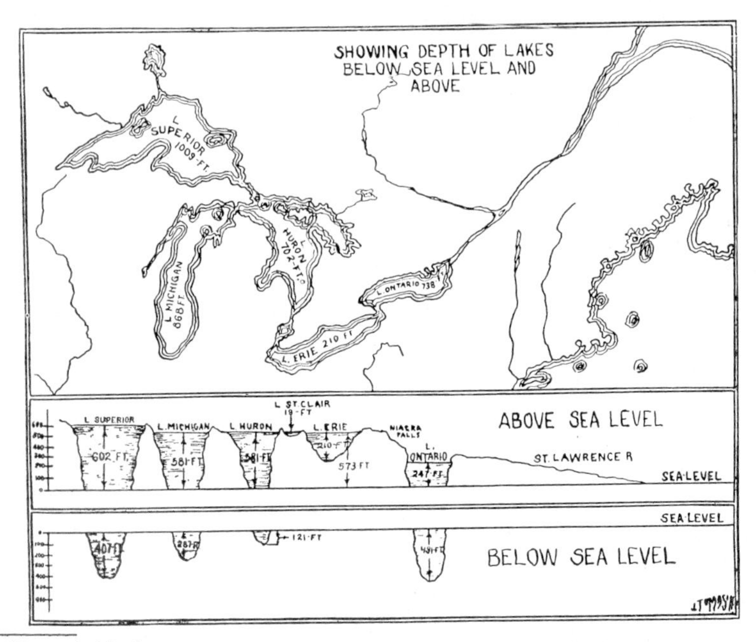

*Except Alaska.

trees which stand along the edge of the beach as though they were battered guardians of the forest lands. At some places large sand dunes, like Sleeping Bear in Leelanau County, have been formed by the winds and the waves. From Munising to Grand Marais the Cambrian sandstone, weathered and beaten by cold, rough Lake Superior, forms scenic cliffs and other huge and attractive formations in its reddish brown rock formation.

Lake of the Clouds

Michigan has over eleven thousand inland lakes. These lakes vary in size from very small ones to the largest one, Houghton Lake in Roscommon County. The size and location of Michigan's ten largest lakes can be seen in the following table:

Lake	Acreages	County
1. Houghton	20,044	Roscommon
2. Torch	18,700	Antrim-Kalkaska
3. Charlevoix	17,000	Charlevoix
4. Burt	16,700	Cheboygan
5. Mullet	16,630	Cheboygan
6. Geogebic	14,781	Gogebic-Ontonagon
7. Manistique	10,130	Luce-Mackinac
8. Black	10,130	Cheboygan-Presque Isle
9. Crystal	9,711	Benzie
10. Higgins	9,600	Roscommon

Most of Michigan's inland lakes have sand and gravel bottoms, but sometimes mud and soft ooze are found. Many of Michigan's lakes

Pre-Cambrian rock outcrop in the Porcupine Mountains at the Lake of the Clouds.

Brachiopods. Millions of these little sea animals, similar to present day oysters, lived in the Silurian and Devonian Seas. Their size can be seen by comparing them with the key.

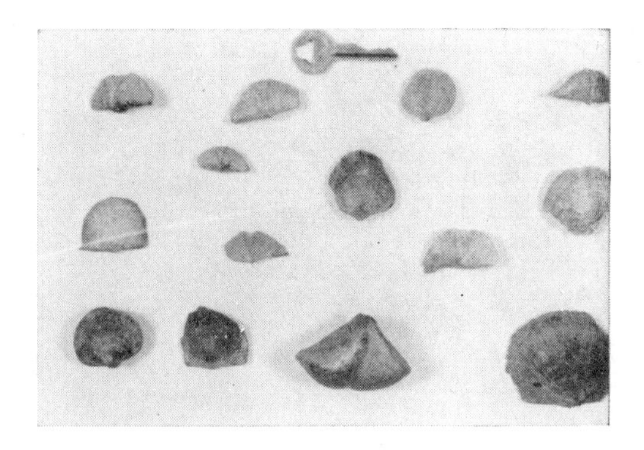

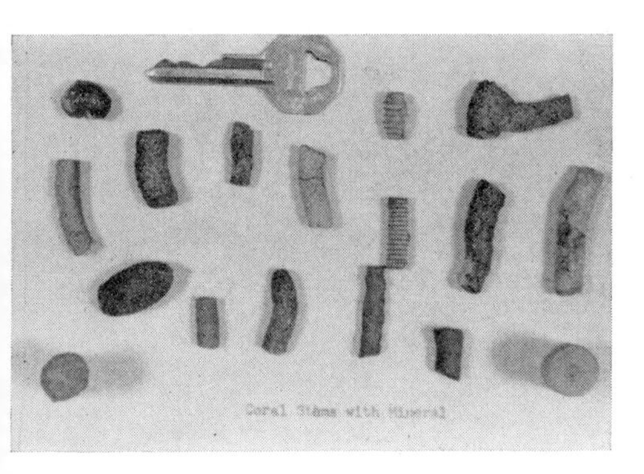

Crinoid or sea-lilie stems found in a modern limestone quarry. Such stems tell us much about life in the ancient seas.

Coral found near the shore of Lake Charlevoix in 1957. This is a Silurian fossil coral called "organ pipe."

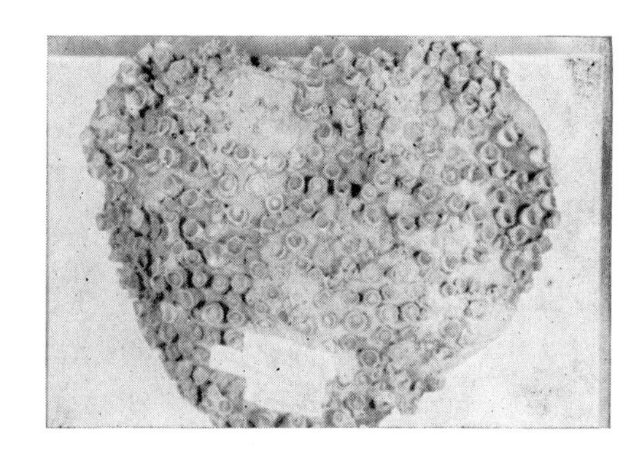

Fortune Lake open pit mine near Crystal Falls. During the late Proterozoic time water seeping through the rock left the iron ore and carried away the sedimentary rock.

Near Alabaster and National City gypsum is quarried. This picture shows how the glacial till has been removed so that the gypsum can be secured.

Port Inland, near Manistique. From this port much Silurian limestone is shipped to the steel mills at the southern end of Lake Michigan.

Marshall Sandstone quarry at Napoleon. Once this rock was used to make grindstones. Today it is used mostly for walks and in floral gardens.

have sandy, shallow shores and beautiful wood-lined borders. During the summer these lakes sparkle in the sunshine and reflect the passing clouds and the green, wooded shores. Thousands of wild ducks and geese settle on the lakes' surfaces as they pass north each spring and south each fall, going to and from their nesting grounds far to the north near Hudson Bay. In Michigan's lakes may be found many kinds of fish, plant, and animal life. During periods of heavy rainfall the lakes act as reservoirs which catch the run-off water and then let it flow slowly into the many streams.

From these lakes usually flow outlet streams which wind through farm or forest lands as the water runs to the Great Lakes. Once these lakes and streams were the source of furs, for on these streams beavers built their dams and lodges and reared their young. Here the musk-rats built their homes. To the lakes came the animals of the forest to quench their thirst and swim in the pure, cool water. Later, as we shall see, many of these streams were used to float pine logs to the sawmills. Today, Michigan's forests, lakes, and rivers, together with her long shore line, help to make Michigan one of the most popular tourist states in the Union.

Waterfalls near US 2 east of Iron Mountain (1952)

Most of Michigan's rivers are not very long. Because most of them flow over sand and gravel areas and because they are fed by lakes and springs, their rate of flow remains about the same throughout the year. In general they flow through long, shallow valleys. Because most of them flow through areas of glacial drift, there are many rapids but few waterfalls. In the Lower Peninsula there are only two natural waterfalls, Ocqueoc and Rainy River Falls, which are found in the area east and north of Onaway. In the Upper Peninsula, however, many of the streams flowing into Lake Superior flow over rocks and many waterfalls are found.

The St. Joseph River is one of Michigan's largest rivers. It starts

Courtesy Massey-Ferguson, Inc.

MF 35 Special Tractor and MF 66 Moldboard Plow. (1961)

in Hillsdale County and drains the southwestern part of Michigan. In the early Indian and French days the St. Joseph River was used as a part of one of the main river highways leading into the Mississippi Valley.

North of the St. Joseph River lies the Kalamazoo River. Rising in Jackson County, the Kalamazoo River runs through Calhoun, Kalamazoo, and Allegan counties. During the later part of the glacial age, both the St. Joseph River and the Kalamazoo River, as well as the Grand River, carried much more water than they carry today.

Still farther to the north in Michigan flows the Grand River. In some places this river flows over bedrock. At Grand Rapids the Grand River has a fall of sixteen feet in one mile. This drop formed a rapids which gave the city of Grand Rapids its name. The Grand River empties into Lake Michigan at Grand Haven.

North of the Grand River flows the Muskegon River. This river has its beginning at Higgins Lake. It is one of the longest rivers in Michigan. During the lumbering days, many pine logs were floated on this river to the busy sawmills at Muskegon. Today dams across the Muskegon River furnish water power for generating electricity.

There are no large rivers in southeastern Michigan except the Detroit and St. Clair rivers which run along Michigan's southeastern border. The run-off waters from Lake Huron pass first into the St.

Clair River, which carries the water to Lake St. Clair. From Lake St. Clair the Detroit River carries the water into Lake Erie. Several small streams drain the area. The Raisin River empties into Lake Erie. The Huron River drains parts of Oakland, Livingston, Washtenaw, and Wayne counties. The Clinton River flows into Lake St. Clair at Mount Clemens. The Black River flows into the St. Clair River at Port Huron.

The Saginaw River flows into Saginaw Bay. Many well-known streams empty into the Saginaw River. They are the Cass, the Flint, the Shiawassee, the Bad, and the Tittabawassee.

In the upper part of the Lower Peninsula may be found the Manistee, Sturgeon, Black, Thunder Bay, Au Sable, and Rifle rivers. All of these rivers, as well as the Muskegon River, have their beginnings on the High Plains Area and flow from there to the Great Lakes. During the lumbering days these rapidly flowing streams carried thousands of pine logs to the sawmills at their mouths. Today these same rivers attract thousands of people who come to Michigan each summer to spend a few weeks in cabins along the rivers' banks and to swim and fish in the clear water. Small power dams have been built on several of these rivers. These dams are used to generate electricity.

Most of the rivers of the Upper Peninsula are rather small. The Menominee, which forms part of the boundary between Michigan and Wisconsin, runs through much wild country and has many rapids and waterfalls. The Manistique River runs through a large swampy area in the central part of the Upper Peninsula. It empties into Lake Michigan at Manistique. Many other rivers such as the Black, Presque Isle, Ontonagon, Sturgeon, and Tahquamenon empty their waters into Lake Superior. Because these rivers pass over rocks, waterfalls are often found on them. The largest waterfall in Michigan is on the Tahquamenon River, a short distance east of Emerson on White Fish Bay. The Saint Mary's River carries the overflow from Lake Superior to Lake Huron. Today it is one of the busiest waterways in the world.

Before the white man came, nearly all of Michigan was covered with forests. For countless centuries the trees of Michigan grew almost untouched by man. From Copper Harbor, at the tip of the Keweenaw Peninsula, to the southern boundary of the state stretched one vast forest broken only here and there by lakes, rivers, little grassy plains, or prairies that were sometimes called "oak openings." Of Michigan's 37 million acres, 25 million were once covered with forest.

Many kinds of trees were found in Michigan. In general, the trees can be classed into two main groups, softwoods and hardwoods. Most of the softwoods grew north of a line drawn between Bay City and Muskegon. Most of the hardwoods grew south of this line. Where the various kinds of trees grew depended largely upon the kind of soil which the glaciers had left and upon the amount of moisture to be found in the soil.

In general the pine trees grew on the lighter, sandier soils. On the very best of the lighter soil grew the white pine. On the medium light soil grew the red, or Norway, pine. On the poorest of the sandy soil grew the little jack pines.

Replanting of red pine as it looked at Higgins Lake, 1948. Note that it is too dark for anything to grow under a thick pine forest.

The whole upper part of the Lower Peninsula and the eastern part of the Upper Peninsula formed one vast pine forest broken only by small areas of swamps or lakes, or by small stands of hardwoods which had driven the pine trees from the better land. The lower part of the Lower Peninsula and the western half of the Upper Peninsula were once covered with hardwoods.

The pine forests were made up of three kinds of pine trees. The most numerous trees were the Norway, or red, pines. You can easily tell a red pine because it always has two long needles in every sheath and when you bend a needle it breaks with a snap. Another type of pine, the one that the lumbermen wanted the most, was the white pine. You can tell this tree when you see it because it has five needles in every sheath. Thus you can remember that there are just as many needles in each sheath as there are letters in the word "white" or as you have fingers and thumb on one hand. The third type of pine that was found in Michigan was the jack pine. It was a smaller tree and lived on the poorest soil in the state. Because of its slow growth and small size it has been of little value.

The hardwood forests were made up of the trees that have broad, flat leaves. In the hardwood forests one could find such trees as beech, maple, ash, elm, white oak, and hickory.

Michigan's swamp forests grew in the moist soil found in swampy areas or near lakes or streams. In the swamp forests grew such trees as the tamarack, spruce, cedar, balsam, and birch.

In Michigan's forests there were small areas in which the trees would not grow. Near Grayling these areas were called "plains." In the southern part of the state these areas were spoken of by the early settlers as "oak openings." Oak openings were found mostly in Oakland County and, in the southwestern part of the state, in Berrien, Cass, and Van Buren counties.

Until the settlers cleared the land, much of Michigan was what is known today as a biological desert. Because large areas of the state were covered with vast forests which shut out the sunlight, small plants on which animals could feed did not grow on the deeply shaded forest floor. The animals that did live in Michigan lived in the swampy areas or near the rivers and lakes where sunshine could find its way to the ground and small plants could grow. Along the streams could be found such animals as beavers, muskrats, minks, martins, and otters. In the woods and swamps could be found deer, elk, wolves, and occasionally a moose or a buffalo.

Many minerals were found in Michigan. Most of these were discussed in the last chapter on geology. Many of them, such as salt, copper, iron ore, gypsum, and limestone, have had an important part in the industrial development of the state.

In many of the streams a fish known as the grayling could be found. Many birds such as ducks, geese, wild turkeys, passenger pigeons, and numerous varieties of small song birds came to Michigan each year. The grayling and the passenger pigeon are both now extinct.

Chapter III

THE INDIANS OF EARLY MICHIGAN

Exactly when the American Indians came to live in North and South America no one knows, for we have no records of their ancient wanderings. Students of history now think that the first American Indians came from Asia, by way of Alaska, and slowly worked their way downward across North and South America.

Not all the Indians of North America had reached the same stage of cultural development by the time the first white men came from Europe. There were many kinds of Indian cultures. Each group of Indians had developed its own culture, or way of life, adapted to the geography of the area in which it lived. Some tribes on the Great Plains of the West lived in tepees and made their living by following the buffalo herds as these large animals roamed across the broad plains in search of their food. Other tribes in the southwestern part of the United States lived in large houses made of clay and were farmers who made their living by raising food on irrigated land. Many other Indian tribes were forest dwellers. The Indians who were living in Michigan when the Frenchmen found them were a forest people living in a land of lakes, streams, and trees. Their way of life was one they had developed to best meet the needs of a people living in a forest land.

In this chapter you are going to read about how the Great Lakes Indian tribes lived before the white man brought European culture to them. The writings of the early French missionaries and traders tell us much about how the Indians used to live. Then, too, the Indians have left behind many interesting artifacts in their burial mounds and refuse pits. These remains of early Indian life have been carefully studied by people who have been interested in the culture of the Indians that once lived in Michigan.

The Indians living in the Great Lakes Region were divided into two large groups. The basis of their grouping is the Indian language which was spoken. One group is known as the Iroquois. Although their war parties sometimes came as far west as Michigan, the

Iroquois lived in what is now Ontario, Canada, and New York State. The Iroquois who lived in Ontario, Canada, were known as the Hurons, or Wyandottes, and had broken from the Iroquois tribes that lived south of Lake Ontario and were often at war with them.

The other and larger group of Indians is known as the Algonquins. This large group was composed of many tribes that occupied the lands all around the Iroquois. These tribes lived on the land all the way from the Atlantic Ocean to the Rocky Mountains. The Indian tribes that lived in Michigan belonged to this large Algonquin group.

When the Frenchmen came to live with the Indians, they found the Algonquins living in what we now call the Neolithic or New Stone Age. They knew how to make a fire and to chip stones for arrowheads and tools. They had also taken the first steps in writing their language. They had not yet discovered the wheel and had tamed only one animal, the dog, which they used for hunting, for guarding the village, and sometimes for food. Some plants, such as corn, squash, tobacco, and pumpkins, they had already domesticated. Socially they had begun to develop a home and family life. They practiced some farming, but most of their food was still secured by hunting.

Courtesy Newell E. Collins, Algonac, Michigan

Bowman carved on the Sanilac Stone, Sanilac County

Among the Indians there was a division of work just as there is among our people. The Indian men were known as braves. Most of their time was spent in hunting and fishing. To the Indians, hunting and fishing were not sports as they are for us today. Hunting was their chief means of getting food, and failure meant hunger and sometimes starvation for all.

For hunting and in war Indian braves used bows and arrows and stone war clubs. An Indian bow was large and strong and carefully made from one of the hardwoods, such as the ash. The ends of the strong, springy bow were bent toward each other and held there by a strong bowstring made from a tough piece of animal sinew or hide. Arrows were made from light, straight sticks, called shafts. Each shaft was tipped at one end with a pointed, chipped, flat stone called an arrowhead. On the opposite end of the shaft, feathers were skillfully fastened so that the arrow would fly straight to its mark. A plain, smooth arrowhead was used in hunting so that it could easily be removed from game that was killed. When on the warpath, however, the Indians often used barbed arrowheads which could be removed only with great pain and damage to the unfortunate warrior who had been hit by one.

Nearly all of the Indian braves' time was spent in hunting and fishing. Quietly they made their way through the forests in search of game. Here they found animals such as squirrels, muskrats, beaver, deer, elk, moose, bear, and sometimes a buffalo. These animals they killed with arrows or clubs. Sometimes they caught them in pitfalls, or carefully made deadfalls, or drove them into the water where other Indians in canoes clubbed them to death.

During the spring, summer, and early autumn the braves hunted waterfowl such as ducks and geese. In the lakes and streams the braves caught fish. Sometimes the fish were driven into shallow places and there they were grabbed by the hands of the hunters. Others were caught on bone or copper hooks to which was attached some animal sinew for lines. Others were shot with arrows or caught on spears having a stone or copper point. Still others were caught in crude nets. The Indians killed all this game so that they and their families might live.

Because of this endless search for game the Indians of Michigan lived in easily moved homes that they called "wigwams." These dome-shaped wigwams were made by covering bent trees, or poles, with pieces of bark or animal skins. These quickly made, and easily moved, shelters kept out some of the cold, rain, and snow. Near the center of a wigwam a small fire gave out some heat for warming the wigwam and for doing what little cooking the Indian family did. Most of the smoke from the fire passed out through an opening which had been left at the top of the wigwam. The Indians lived outside most of the time, but on rainy or cold days the family often gathered inside. Here they sat around the fire on animal skins or reed mats that had been placed upon the ground.

Among the Indians one could find skilled workers just as we can among the people living in Michigan today. In some places the remains of Indian workshops have been found. At these places broken stones and stone chips show that arrowheads, chisels, gouges, drills, and flint knives were once made there by Indian craftsmen.

Indian braves spent much time making traps and weapons. Spear handles were made from hickory or ash. Knives were formed from shells, antlers, teeth, or pieces of flint. Pipes of many descriptions were made. Some pipes were made of clay, others of wood, and still others from a soft stone called "pipe stone." No two pipes were alike. Some were made to look like birds, while others were shaped like turtles or other animals. With crude, handmade stone tools the Indians felled small trees, peeled bark from birch trees to make their

Courtesy Thomas E. Mackie, River Rouge, Mich.

Michigan barbed axes. Most of them have been found in Kent and Ionia counties. No other county shows more than one or two specimens. Few are found outside the state. No artifact is more representative of Michigan.

canoes, made bows and arrows, formed snowshoes, skinned and cut up animals, sewed their buckskin clothing, and cared for their little garden plots.

Some of Michigan's early Indians were also miners. On Isle Royale and from Ontonagon to Copper Harbor, in the Upper Peninsula, remains of their open pit mines have been found. These open holes and ditches from which the Indians once dug the native copper that lay buried in the rock tell us the story of this once important occupation of Michigan's Indians. In many of these little pit mines have been found charcoal and hundreds of stone hammers. From what has been left in these pits by the Indians, we now know something about how they did their copper mining.

Once the Indians had found where copper was, they set about getting it from the rock in which it lay. Fires were built to heat the rock. Then cold water was poured over the warm rock to make it crack and free the chunks of pure copper.

Remains of Indian forts and villages in the copper country seem to show that many Indians were once engaged in mining copper here in Michigan. Some of these Indian villages were located about where some of Michigan's mining towns are now located, for when the white man began looking for copper, some of the best mines were developed on the same pits that had long ago been worked by the Indians.

Only the smaller chunks of copper were of value to the Indians because they never learned to heat copper and thus to smelt it. Taking a piece of copper they patiently pounded it into the shape that they wanted. Thus they made knives, crude basins, hatchets, fish hooks, arrowheads, spear points, and jewelry. Because Michigan Indians had no gold and very little silver, copper was highly prized among them. Often it was carefully polished until the bright copper color would shine from it.

Pieces of native Michigan copper, as well as handmade copper objects, found their way by trade or capture over wide areas of North America. Early European explorers along the Atlantic found the Indians living there using copper jewelry and fish hooks that must have come from Michigan.

Copper is easily worked by pounding, and thus the Michigan Indians beat it into the shapes they wanted. Copper is soft, and they never learned to mix it with other metals to harden it as we do today. They did learn that pounding it makes it harder, and thus they formed the cutting edges of copper spears and hatchets.

We now have a few objects which the Indians made of iron, and from these objects we know that the Indians had some knowledge of this metal. If the white man had not come from Europe with his iron tools, perhaps the Indians would have developed the use of iron. With the coming of the white man the Indians soon stopped using their crude stone and copper tools and began to buy the iron ones made by the people of Europe.

There was little of what we call government among the Indians. Their constant wanderings gave them little chance to collect things or to develop village life as we know it today. Outside of their tribal customs each person was allowed to do much as he pleased unless he harmed other members of the tribe. There were no chiefs who received their titles from their fathers. The tribal leaders, known as chiefs, won their positions by being heroes and leaders in battle or around the council fire.

The Indians' ideas as to property values were far different from those we have today. Private property was almost unknown to them in their way of life. The Indians thought of most things as being owned by the tribe. The hunting grounds belonged to the tribe and were open to all for hunting and fishing. There were only a few small things that they thought of as personal property, such as birch bark dishes, bows and arrows, and jewelry. This lack of governmental development and private ownership made it hard for the Indians to understand the white man and his ways when he came to America.

Courtesy Newell E. Collins, Algonac, Michigan

Eagle Pipe

Because the Indians fought the white settlers who were taking their homelands away from them, the white men came to look upon the Indians as fearful warriors. It seems, however, that before the white men began pressing in upon the Indian lands, the Indians had spent long periods of time living in peace. But like the white man they sometimes went to war because of wrongs done to their tribes or to gain new and better hunting grounds. When on the warpath, braves were cunning, vengeful, and ruthless. All men, women, children, and even the aged then felt the brutality of the enraged warriors. Captive warriors were sometimes cruelly tortured, but captured women and children were often adopted into the winning tribe.

The Indian women were known as squaws. They stayed at home and did most of the work around the village and in the wigwam. When the braves brought home fish or animals that they had killed, it was the women who dressed the game and prepared it for food. Sometimes extra venison was cut up into small pieces about an inch square and strung on bark strings. This meat was then smoked and dried to cure it. This was called "jerked venison." These preserved pieces of dried meat were eaten when game could not be found. The women tanned deer skins to make buckskin for clothing. Tanning was a long, tiresome task. One squaw could tan only a few deer skins a year. A skin was first carefully scraped with a stone knife to get off all the flesh and hair. Then it was treated with tanning materials and buried in the ground for some time. Later the skins were dug up, treated again, and then buried again. When finished, doeskin and buckskin became a soft, pliable material for making clothing.

It was the women who gathered fallen wood from the forest to keep their little fires burning. They carried water for the family in birch bark pails from a nearby stream, spring, or lake. They gathered nuts, berries, and herbs. Now and then they found the eggs of some water fowl.

From birch bark the women made pails, dishes, and boxes. These they used for carrying water or nuts and berries and also for containers in which to keep various articles. Sometimes these birch bark boxes were decorated with brightly colored porcupine quills that had been tinted with dyes which were made from the juice of berries or plants. Sometimes they wove mats from reeds that they had gathered from marshy places. These mats were placed on the earth floors of the wigwams.

The Michigan Indian women were also basket makers. Long strips of clean, white wood were secured from black ash. First the log was pounded for hours to loosen the long fibrous strips. These strips were then cut to size by using a sharp stone. With these strips the Indian women wove baskets of many sizes and shapes. Sometimes the wooden strips were dyed bright colors so that their baskets would have bright designs. Sweet grass was often worked into the weaving of baskets or sewn onto birch bark boxes so that the boxes and baskets would carry the pleasing scent.

It was the women, too, who packed the family belongings and carried them to the canoes each time the Indians moved to another camping place. If they moved overland, the Indian braves, to guard the group, walked ahead of the women, carrying only their bows and arrows. Each woman followed behind in Indian file, carrying all her belongings and perhaps a papoose on her weary back.

The Indian women were also Michigan's first farmers, for they were the ones who planted the little clearings and cared for the gardens. In this land of forests the Indians found it difficult to prepare the land

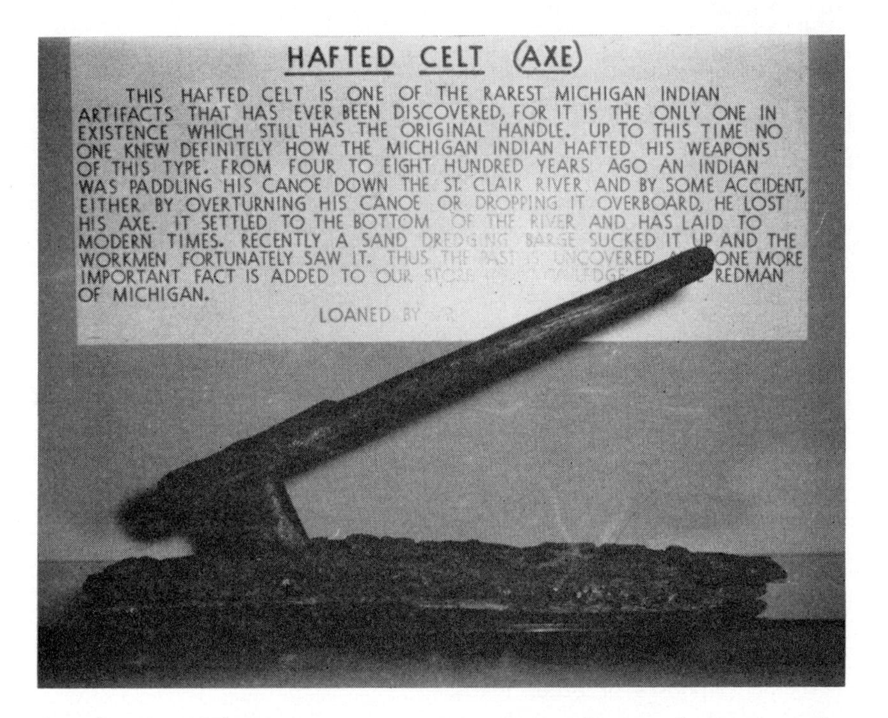

for planting. Their stone axes were too crude to clear away the larger trees. The Indians did, however, sometimes cut the bark all the way around some trees and thus caused them to die. This let more sunlight fall upon their little gardens, which often were planted among the dead trees if no clear ground could be found. Sometimes these dead trees, which had been girdled, were later burned and thus small clearings were made. In the southwestern part of the state and in Oakland County the Indians used the open spaces called "oak openings" for making their gardens.

Most of the seeds which the squaws planted were such as could be planted by merely pushing a hole into the ground with a sharp stick.

They planted beans, squash, melons, pumpkins, sunflowers, tobacco, and Indian corn, which they called maize. These plants, being either tall or of the running vine type, could thus seek out their own sunshine.

During the summer the women, girls, and a few of the old men hoed their gardens with little hoes made from flat stones, clam shells, or the shoulder blade of an animal. In the fall the women gathered the corn and stored it in baskets for the coming winter. The best Indian farmers in early Michigan were the Pottawattomies who lived in the southwestern part of the state.

In the fall the Indians who lived near Menominee gathered the wild rice that grew in the marsh lands near by. In the spring the Indians caught the sweet sap of the sugar maple trees in little birch bark cups. From this sweet sap the squaws made maple syrup and maple sugar for their families. This sweet syrup and, now and then, some wild honey were the nearest things to candy that Indian children ever had.

Today women spend much of their time doing the laundry and washing the dishes. Neither of these tasks was expected of the squaws. Indians did not know about soap. Birch bark or wooden dishes were used again and again without washing. Clothing was never washed as it is today, and no doubt it was as full of vermin as were the heads of the people who wore it.

Indian women usually wore their hair braided or wound on wood chips and pinned to the backs of their heads. In cold weather they wore animal skins to keep them warm. Loads were carried by means of a wide "carrying strap" that passed from one's back across the forehead and then again to the back. These straps were used for carrying papooses or other loads.

During the summer months the Indians wore little clothing. Bear grease was smeared on their bodies to help keep away flies, mosquitoes, and other pests. Sometimes they painted their bodies with dyes made from berries and roots. Soot was used for black to paint on their bodies and faces. During the wintertime they wore clothing made from the skins of animals. Large garments, like skirts and trousers, were made from buckskin. Soft-soled shoes, known as moccasins, were made from tanned skins. Often skirts, jackets, and leggings were decorated on their edges with dyed quills, or fringed with shells, stones, or animal teeth.

The lives of the Indians were filled with toil and hardships. They had few of the things that we call comforts today. By the time most of the women were thirty-five or forty years old, they were already old women.

The real highways of the Indians of the Great Lakes Region were the many lakes and their connecting river systems. This was a land of lakes and rivers, and traveling on them was much easier than tramping through forests and swamps. Indian canoes were well adapted for travel, and the Indians used them with both grace and speed.

Indian braves made canoes by putting green skins over wooden frames and letting them dry until the skins became taut, or by covering the wooden frames with birch bark. These Indian canoes should not be compared with the small pleasure canoes of today, for Indian canoes were usually much larger. Records left by the early missionaries and explorers tell us that the bark canoes of that time were usually large enough to carry an Indian family of five or six and all the possessions of the family such as bows, arrows, skins, and dishes for cooking.

In thinking of these early Indian canoes we must remember that we do not really know just how they looked before the Frenchmen came with better tools to make them. The Indians' tools were crude, and their canoes must have been rather roughly made because they had no saws, planes, glue, nails, shellac, or varnish with which to work. Whatever their shapes, they were used for hunting, fishing, and carrying the family and its supplies.

Bark canoes had several good points. Materials from which to make them and keep them in repair were easily found in the forest. They were very light and could be carried with ease by one or two braves across any of the many portages between the headwaters of streams, or where falls or rapids made it necessary to travel by land. They did not sink far into the water but rather floated lightly upon it. Because of this, it was possible to paddle canoes far up the smaller streams where larger boats, sinking more deeply into the water, could not have gone. This made it possible to greatly shorten the distance required in making portages from one river to another.

Although canoes had these very good qualities, they also had some faults that caused their users much trouble. Since they were made of bark and had light frames, they were often very short-lived. During the cold winter weather the bark often shrank and split open. Then too, the bark would often become brittle and peel. To keep canoes from shrinking and peeling they were sometimes buried in the moist sand beside a river or lake.

If you look closely at a large map of North America which shows the lakes and rivers, you will notice that the St. Lawrence River system and the Mississippi River system almost touch in a number of places. By going up these streams and from one river to another, the Indians, and later the Frenchmen, could make their way far into the continent.

In cold weather, when the winter snow lay deep on the marshlands, frozen lakes, and forest floor, the Indians, while hunting or on the trail, used snowshoes to keep their feet from sinking into the soft, white, fluffy drifts.

A few trails, or traces as they were called, the age of which nobody knows, ran through the ancient forest. No one could tell how they came to be. We can only surmise about their beginnings, but we do know that animals roamed the forests before man made his home here.

Buffalo, in their wanderings, pushed back the brush and trampled down small trees and, by some instinct known only to creatures of the wilds, marked with their pounding feet the easiest paths throughout the wilderness. Years later government surveyors, seeking the best places to run new roads across the land, found that the best routes often led along the same traces that the animals had made across the ancient land. No one knew all the turnings of these silent, mysterious paths where danger might lurk around any bend or spring from some nearby tree or stump.

Sometimes the trees were small and the trails led through leafy walls on either side. At other times the trails ran through forests where the ground was always damp and musty and where, in the summertime, tall trees held aloft their canopied tops and all was open underneath. Then one walked as if in a great cathedral.

Along lake shores and rivers and across swampy areas the flora often grew thick and dense and the traveler had to push his way through branches and undergrowth which blocked his path. Swamps, especially, were a problem to foot travelers. Often the soft, water-filled, boggy land would hardly support the weight of the traveler. Cattail marshes and long swamp grass gave little footing. Long black snakes and timber moccasins wriggled through the water and the long marsh grass. Here the smell of spruce and cedar blended with the stench of swamp muck and decaying grass and leaves.

At other times the traces ran across "oak openings" or open grassy plains among the jack pines. Here the traces were dry and firm. In the summertime the sun beat down and the June grass turned yellow along the trace. In the grass grew wild strawberries, deep red in color. So thick were these strawberries that they often stained the moccasins of Indians and the hoofs of animals.

Twisting and turning through shaded, silent woodlands, across oak openings and jack pine plains, past quiet blue lakes, up hill, down hill, across streams at fords, where the water ran wide and swift, went the traces or ancient forest paths. They were of little value even for the Indians because it was often very hard to push oneself through the forest, even without a pack on one's back.

One of these trails, now US 112, was known as the Great Sauk Trail. It ran across Lower Michigan from Detroit to the southern end of Lake Michigan. Another ran from Toledo, Ohio, to Kalamazoo, through Grand Rapids, and on to Mackinaw City. Another ran from Detroit to Saginaw and then to Mackinaw City by following the western shore of Lake Huron. Another ran from Saginaw to a spot near Higgins Lake. There it divided; one trail led to the Traverse City region while the other followed the present line of the railroad through Grayling and Gaylord to Cheboygan and Mackinaw City. Other trails ran across the Upper Peninsula. One ran from Sault Ste. Marie to St. Ignace and then on west to Escanaba. Others went north through the forests to Lake Superior.

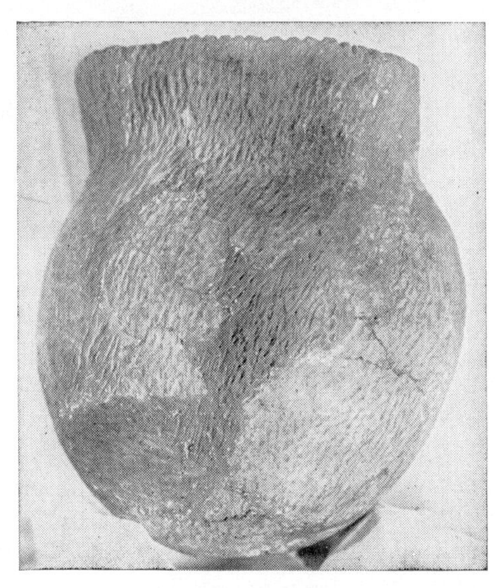

Courtesy Newell E. Collins, Algonac, Michigan

Indian pottery

Some of the early Indian tribes that lived in Ohio and southern Michigan were mound builders. In Michigan over six hundred Indian mounds have been located and recorded. Nearly all the Michigan mounds lie south of a line drawn west from Saginaw Bay. These mounds, which are really piles of earth and sand, were once Indian burial grounds. Michigan's Indian mounds were merely piles of earth, but some of the mounds in Wisconsin and Ohio were made in the shape of animals. One of the best known is the serpent mound in Ohio. In the Indian mounds have been found human bones; clay dishes; tools made of copper, stone, or bone; stone arrowheads; and crude pieces of jewelry made from animal claws, shells, or bits of copper. All these things tell us much about how the Indians of Michigan lived before the white man came to North America.

Courtesy Newell E. Collins, Algonac, Michigan

Rock Shelter, Sanilac County

Besides the mounds the early Indians left circular and irregular open spaces that seem to have been enclosed by banks of earth. These open spaces are known as "forts" and may have been used as such by the early Indians. Holes in the ground, known as "pot holes," present to students of this period another mystery. Were they used as root cellars for storing food, as places for cooking, or for fighting, as "fox holes" are used by our soldiers today? In some places low earth ridges have been found. These are known as "garden beds." Garden beds were of several shapes, but the most common shape was that of the spokes and rim of a wheel. Unfortunately for those who wish to learn more about Indian culture, nearly all the mounds, pot holes, and garden beds in Michigan have now been destroyed.

During the warm summer months the Indians of Michigan often gathered in small villages at places where hunting and fishing could support the people. The same tribe did not always occupy the same place. During the wintertime the Indians usually divided into smaller bands and went to winter hunting grounds so that the need for food would not be greater than the region could supply. In all, before the white man came, there were not more than fifteen or twenty thousand Indians living in Michigan.

Near Menominee lived the Wild Rice Indians, or the Menominees as they were called. They claimed as their hunting ground the land from Bay de Noc to Lake Superior and on west into Wisconsin. The Hurons, whose real Indian name was Wyandottes, lived east of Lake Huron in what is now Ontario, Canada. During the early days of New France this area was known as Huronia. They were really Iroquois by language though they had broken away from the Iroquois tribes. Later, as we shall see, the Hurons were driven from their homelands by the Iroquois and some of them settled in Michigan. The Miamis lived in the southwestern part of the state near St. Joseph, but about the same time that the white man came to Michigan, the Miamis moved eastward to northern Ohio and settled along the Maumee River in lands that had previously been claimed by the Eries. When the Miamis left the southwestern part of the state, the Pottawattomies from Wisconsin settled in their old homeland. The Sauk and Fox Indians once lived near present-day Saginaw. However, about the same time that the Miamis moved into the Maumee River area the Sauk and Fox moved to Wisconsin. The Ottawas and Chippewas, or Ojibways as they were called, lived in the eastern part of the Upper Peninsula and the upper part of the Lower Peninsula. Few Indians lived in the southeastern part of the Lower Peninsula along the Detroit River. The land there was later claimed by both the Pottawattomies and Iroquois. If there had ever been any tribes living in southeastern Michigan, they had been driven away by the fierce Iroquois that lived in New York State.

Although the Indians no longer possess the Lake Region, they have left many names to remind us of them. Many of our familiar names of Michigan places and rivers are of Indian origin, such as: Michigan, Michilimackinac, Cheboygan, Owosso, Petoskey, Munising, Ishpeming, Negaunee, Calumet, Tahquamenon, Wyandotte, Tecumseh, Tekonsha, Tittabawasse, Saugatuck, Muskegon, Escanaba, Menominee, and Pontiac. Today we use these words and seldom think of their Indian origin or meaning.

During the French and English Periods the Indians remained in possession of their ancient tribal homelands but with the coming of the Americans the land was gradually taken from them. Between 1796 and 1842 all the land of Michigan was ceded to the United States through a series of Indian treaties.

Today there are four small Indian communities or reservations in Michigan. The largest of these is the L'Anse Reservation in Baraga County. Here some 800 Indians live on a 15,000-acre tract of land. A small community in Menominee County, of some twenty-three families, live on a 3,400-acre tract known as the Hannahville Indian Community. At Bay Mills, west of Sault Ste. Marie, is another small settlement of about thirty-five families living on 2,200 acres of restricted land. The fourth Indian community is in Isabella County east of Mt. Pleasant. Here a small group of Indians live on about 450 acres of restricted land. In all there are about 25,000 acres of such restricted land in Michigan which is under the protection of the Bureau of Indian Affairs, Great Lakes Agency, Ashland, Wisconsin.

Besides these semi-reservations there are a few small communities that contain small groups of Indians such as Cross Village, Good Hart, in Emmet County, and at Peshwabestown, in the Leelanau Peninsula, on Grand Traverse Bay.

Very few Indians today are farmers. Many are skilled in the various types of woods work and find employment in Michigan's growing forests. Many have moved to the growing cities and have found employment in the expanding industries. Since June 2, 1924, all American Indians have been citizens of the United States and as such are entitled to vote. In Michigan all Indian children attend public or private schools. Because of the Indians' long association with European culture little of their original culture now remains among them. Some have married European stocks and many people living in Michigan today can name one or more Indians as one of their ancestors.

Chapter IV

FRANCE WINS AND LOSES THE GREAT LAKES AREA
(1608-1760)

When Frenchmen first began coming to North America we do not know. It is known that Frenchmen were among the first fishermen who came to North America to fish for cod on the Newfoundland Banks, for as early as 1506 French fishermen were fishing off Cape Breton Island and they had already given this name to that island.

French fishermen coming to the Grand Banks to fish soon learned that they could get valuable furs from the Indians in trade for things made in Europe. So before leaving the Grand Banks to carry their salted fish to Europe, the fishermen tried to find Indians with whom they could trade. Furs thus became a side cargo that was carried to Europe by the early fishing fleets.

As the years passed the French learned that beaver hair made a fine grade of felt, and more and more beaver furs were then demanded. In 1603 Champlain visited the St. Lawrence River area looking for a place to set up a fur-trading post. Because of the bitterness of the winters there, Champlain decided to locate his trading post a little farther to the south. The following year, 1604, Champlain with a few other Frenchmen came to the St. Croix River in present-day New Brunswick and built a little post on an island not far from the river's mouth. The following year the post was moved to Port Royal, and this settlement thus became the first permanent French settlement in North America.

Champlain searched the area for rivers leading into North America, but found none like the huge St. Lawrence farther to the north. As the local supply of furs was not large enough to meet the demand, Champlain decided to start a new post on the St. Lawrence. In the spring of 1608 he sailed from France to start a new settlement. The spot he chose was on the St. Lawrence River where the city of Quebec now stands. He chose this spot for several reasons. The high rock, now called Cape Diamond, would provide a good place for a fort. The river was narrow here and it could thus be more easily watched for passing ships. It would be easier to sail for France than if the post were located farther up the river.

Champlain was not only the founder of Quebec but also one of the first and most noted of the early French explorers. The first winter at Quebec was hard on the little colony, but in June, 1609, more men and supplies arrived from France. In the same month there also came to the little settlement at Quebec a band of some three hundred Huron and Ottawa Indians. These Indians were planning an attack upon their enemies, the Iroquois Indians who lived south of them in what is today New York State. The Indians wanted Champlain and his men to bring their strange guns and join the war party against the Iroquois.

On this island, near St. Johns, New Brunswick, Champlain and his men spent the winter of 1603.

As Champlain wanted to explore the region farther up the St. Lawrence River and also wanted to make friends with the Indians, he agreed to go with the warriors and to take eleven of his Frenchmen with him. This pleased the Indians very much, and after looking at the strange guns and armor of the white men they made ready for the raid by dancing the war dance and eating the battle feast.

Champlain and the Indians went up the St. Lawrence River to the mouth of the Richelieu River. There the Indians began to quarrel among themselves. About three fourths of them left the party and returned to their homes. In spite of this action on the part of his Indian allies Champlain did not turn back. With the few Indians that remained, the party went up the Richelieu River in twenty-four canoes and a small French sailboat. Later the sailboat and nine of the Frenchmen were sent back to Quebec.

On July 4, 1609, Champlain and his party came to a large lake of clear, blue water lying among beautiful green mountains. Since the lake had never before been seen by any white man, Champlain named it Lake Champlain in honor of himself. Although Champlain and his Indians tried to hide their movements, they were finally discovered and on July 30 a band of Iroquois made ready to attack them.

The Iroquois were strong, brave Indians and were always ready and willing to meet their old foe. However, just as they were getting ready to let fly their first shower of arrows, the loud report of a musket rang out through the woods. Champlain had fired upon the Iroquois. Three Iroquois warriors suddenly fell forward. One was badly wounded and two were dying. Never before had the Iroquois heard the report of a musket. Yet, true Indian warriors, they held their ground and let fly a flight of arrows at their enemies. Again a great noise was heard as Champlain fired his musket at the Iroquois. This strange loud weapon belching smoke and fire was too much for the Iroquois, and they fled in panic, only to be followed by the Hurons and Ottawas, who killed many of the Iroquois as they fled into the deep stillness of the forest.

This little battle, if it can be called even that, fought on the shore of Lake Champlain, was one of the main turning points in the history of New France.

It was not a large battle in which many men were killed. Yet it bound the Algonquin Indians in friendship to the French and made the Iroquois ever afterward their bitter enemy. Champlain had unknowingly made an enemy of one of the strongest and fiercest Indian tribes then living in all North America. The story of this defeat was handed down by the Iroquois from father to son. Several times during the years that followed, the Iroquois, in revenge for this defeat, attacked the little French settlements along the St. Lawrence and took many lives of the French settlers who came there to live.

It is one of the strange happenings of history that a Dutch sailing vessel sailed up the Hudson River just a few months after Champlain's battle with the Iroquois. It was the "Half Moon," the ship of Henry Hudson, an English sea captain then sailing for the Dutch. The "Half Moon" was followed by other Dutch trading vessels, and a strong friendship grew up between the Dutch traders who came up the Hudson River and the Iroquois, for the Dutch traders gave the Iroquois firearms in exchange for furs. This coming of traders into the Hudson Valley made it possible for the Iroquois to again meet their old enemies as equals in battle.

Tales of the coming of the Dutch traders soon were heard at Quebec, and the French quickly learned that if they were to push farther into the wilderness of the West they must do so by going up the Ottawa River, thus keeping away from the fierce Iroquois.

The silent, mysterious lands to the west of Quebec, where no white man's foot had ever trod, enticed the Frenchmen to go up the river and search out the secrets that lay hidden in the vast forest domain. Might there be another Indian empire like the ones the Spaniards had found in Mexico and Peru? Where did the massive waters of the St. Lawrence River come from? What kind of people lived along its banks? Might its source lie near the Pacific Ocean? Could the land be crossed and the way to the fabled East be found at last?

In order to find out about the Indians, their languages, their manner of life, and the nature of the lands in which they lived, Champlain sent young men into the wilderness to live with the Indians. One of these young men was Etienne Brulé, and some historians think that he was the first white man to reach the area now known as Michigan.

When only eighteen years old, Brulé may have journeyed with a party of Indians through the Sault Ste. Marie waterway. On his return to Quebec he startled the other Frenchmen there by showing them a nugget of copper he had secured in the Lake Region and by telling them of a large sea that lay to the west. Just where Brulé went is not known, but it is thought that he may have touched the shores of the Great Lakes as early as 1610. Other returning traders and explorers brought more stories of a large sea that lay far to the west of Quebec. Stories of this new discovery made Champlain eager to see the sea for himself, so in 1615 he made his way up the Ottawa River and crossed by way of Lake Nipissing to Georgian Bay, where he saw what is known today as Lake Huron. The lake was named the Lake of the Hurons after the Huron Indians who then lived on its eastern shore.

Because the Iroquois Indians lived near the upper St. Lawrence River, the Frenchmen did not dare to venture up the river. Instead, they turned more directly westward and following the Ottawa River thus pushed into the homeland of their Indian friends, the Hurons. From the Hurons they learned how to turn from the Ottawa up the little Mattawa and then to cross over to Lake Nipissing and by using the French River, to reach Georgian Bay on Lake Huron. It was at the mouth of the French River that the Frenchmen got their first view of the Great Lakes of North America. This water route into the wilderness was soon to become the main highway for the fur traders and missionaries of New France.

Not many years after the founding of New France, missionaries from France came to Canada to live among the Indians. In 1615 the Recollects set up a mission just south of Georgian Bay near the present site of Midland, Ontario, and began to work among the Huron Indians then living in that region. But they were a small order for so large a mission field. In 1625 the first Jesuits arrived in New France and soon were at work among the Indians.

In 1634 a young Frenchman named Jean Nicolet was sent out by Champlain to further explore the west. He followed the westward route along the Ottawa River and Georgian Bay until he came to Lake Huron. Nicolet perhaps went up the St. Mary's River to the place where the city of Sault Ste. Marie now stands. Returning south and west Nicolet discovered what is now the Straits of Mackinac. From here he went on westward across Lake Michigan to Green Bay. Just how far west Nicolet went is not known. He had no way of telling us, for as yet the lakes and rivers had no names. Some historians think he went almost as far west as the Mississippi River. Soon after Nicolet's return Champlain, the founder of New France, died on Christmas Day, 1635.

In 1641 two Jesuit missionaries, Fathers Raymbault and Jogues, left the Jesuit missions on Georgian Bay and went up the St. Mary's River, which they named after their mission in Huronia. Paddling up the river they came to the St. Mary's Rapids, which they called the "Sault." Here at the rapids they found an Indian settlement of about two thousand people who greeted the Jesuits with kindness and asked them to stay in their village. This the missionaries could not do, so after learning from the Indians of another large lake (Lake Superior), the two Jesuits returned to their mission on Georgian Bay.

After the journey of Fathers Raymbault and Jogues to the Sault, almost twenty years passed before the Frenchmen again came to Michigan. Cruel Indian wars raged between the Algonquins and the Iroquois, and traveling up the St. Lawrence River was dangerous for both traders and missionaries.

At first the French had been able to secure furs from the nearby areas. Not only that, but the Indians usually brought their furs to the ships or posts along the St. Lawrence River. In this way the Indians not only paid the cost of transportation but also took the risks of having their furs stolen or captured. As time passed, the local supply of fur-bearing animals grew fewer and fewer in number as the demand for more and more furs grew. As the local supply of furs in the St. Lawrence Valley and the Hudson River Valley grew smaller, both the Hurons and the Iroquois Indians wanted to act as middlemen between the tribes living farther to the west and the Europeans living in their own regions. This rivalry for the fur trade increased the old hatred between the Iroquois and the Hurons.

If the Iroquois could drive out the Hurons, they could then control both the St. Lawrence and the Ottawa rivers and carry the fur trade down the Hudson River to their friends, the Dutch and, later, the English. Armed with guns that they had bought from the Dutch traders, the Iroquois attacked the French and their allies, the Hurons, with a savage fierceness springing from years of bitter hatred and from the new rivalry that had developed in the clash for the position of middlemen in the fur trade.

Going up the Ottawa River, the Iroquois attacked the newly converted Christian Hurons. The Hurons were no match for the fierce Iroquois who burned their homes, killed and captured many, and drove the rest into the wilderness. The Iroquois cruelly tortured and killed some of the Jesuit missionaries and Huron Christians.

The French living along the lower St. Lawrence could give little aid to the Huron Indians because of the distance between them. Then, too, they were busy defending themselves from the Iroquois who also attacked their little settlements.

The missions in Huronia on Georgian Bay were then abandoned The Jesuit missionaries who had escaped the raids went back to Quebec. Some of the Hurons followed them to Quebec to there seek protection under the French guns. Others fled north and northwest into the wilderness on the southern shore of western Lake Superior.

By 1650 all of New France was in a state of siege, and Frenchmen had to keep very close to their forts and villages. The Iroquois, having destroyed the Hurons, then fell upon the Tobacco and Neutral Indians who lived in western Ontario, north of Lake Erie, and either massacred them or drove them away. The Iroquois then were in control of both the St. Lawrence and Ottawa routes.

No longer did the Hurons come down the Ottawa at springtime with canoes heavily loaded with fine furs. The trade in pelts for the French declined to a mere trickle and then stopped altogether.

Pushing west from their homeland, the Iroquois fell upon the Eries and Andastes, but they found these tribes to be more powerful. In 1653 a strong Iroquois war party was destroyed west of Lake Michigan. This defeat somewhat checked the war spirit of the Iroquois for a time, and they arranged a truce with the French which lasted until 1658.

The fur trade of the French could not be carried on while the Indian war lasted, but illegal traders, known as *coureur de bois*, were usually ready to risk capture for the large profits that could be gained from the fur trade. How many illegal traders went into the woods during this period no one can say, but it is known that two men, Radisson and Groseilliers, set out for the West in the year 1654. In the spring of 1656 they escaped the Iroquois and came back to Quebec with their canoes and those of their Indian friends heavily loaded with furs from the Far West. They also told of visiting some of the Huron Indians who were then living in the northern wilderness near the western end of Lake Superior where they had fled to escape from their enemies, the Iroquois.

In 1658 Radisson and Groseilliers again went to the West in search of furs. They followed the southern shore of Lake Superior and went as far west as eastern Minnesota. How much farther they went we do not know, but there is little doubt that they pushed even farther. Some records seem to show that they went as far as Hudson Bay. In 1660 these two men and their Indian friends returned to Quebec in sixty large canoes bearing many thousands of dollars worth of furs. Again they told about the Huron Indians who were then living in the wilderness on the western shore of Lake Superior.

The Jesuits were eager to again take up their missionary work among the Huron Indians, so in 1660 they chose one of their group, Father Rene Menard, to go west with the Indians who had come to Montreal with Radisson and Groseilliers, and search for the Hurons. Passing up the St. Mary's River with the returning Indians, Father Menard then followed the southern shore of Lake Superior to Keweenaw Bay. There he set up a mission, the first in the Old Northwest. The Ottawas near his mission were not very friendly to him and cared little for the Christian religion, so when spring came he set out again to continue his search for the Huron Indians. He became lost from his party, and what became of him is not known.

Radisson and Groseilliers made still another trip to the West, but when they returned in 1663, the governor of New France took most of their furs from them because they had been trading with the Indians without a license.

At last the mother country, France, came to the aid of her American colony. In 1665 the Marquis de Tracy arrived in Canada with over one thousand French soldiers. In 1666 this army, with some six hundred Canadians and their Indian allies, attacked and destroyed the villages and crops of the Mohawk Indians. Though not defeated, the war spirit of the Iroquois was weakened, and they were now willing to make an uneasy peace. New France at last could again push her trade and missionary work among the Indians to the west.

Father Claud Allouez was chosen by the Jesuits to take up the work of Father Rene Menard. In 1666 he joined a band of some five hundred Indians who had been to Montreal for the spring fair, and with them journeyed up the Ottawa River. Passing up the St. Mary's River, Allouez entered Lake Superior, which he named Lac Tracy. Following its southern shore, Allouez went westward as far as La Pointe, Wisconsin. There he founded a mission and built a little bark chapel. This church was the first to be built in what later became the Old Northwest.

Allouez returned to Quebec in the fall of 1667 to report on his missionary work and to ask for more Jesuits to help him. The Jesuits were pleased to hear his report and learn of the work that could be done in the region of Lake Superior among the Hurons who had escaped the attacks of the Iroquois. Others at Quebec who were not so interested in missions were very interested in the pieces of copper Allouez had brought back with him and in his stories of a great river, the Mississippi, that lay still farther to the west.

To find out more about the copper and to further explore the region, Jean Pere was sent westward in 1668. In 1669 a supporting expedition was sent west under the leadership of Adrien Joliet. Joliet and Pere spent the entire summer of 1669 searching the shores of Lake Superior for copper but they found only a few small pieces which could easily be carried back to Quebec in their bark canoes. Their interest, however, was aroused by stories of another large river that led to an unknown sea which lay to the southwest.

While at Sault Ste. Marie, Joliet rescued an Iroquois prisoner who was about to be burned at the stake by his Indian captors. In return for this the grateful Iroquois promised to take Joliet on a more southerly route when he went back to the French settlements on the St. Lawrence. Joliet's party, with the Iroquois as their guide, followed the western shore of Lake Huron southward, past Thunder Bay, Saginaw Bay, and at last entered what is now called the St. Clair River. Passing over Lake St. Clair they entered upon the Detroit River and followed it to Lake Erie. Turning east they followed the northern shore of Lake Erie almost to its eastern end. Then, fearing that the Iroquois Indians might attack them, Joliet and his men turned north and passed overland near the place where Hamilton, Ontario, now stands, and thus came to Lake Ontario. Joliet was thus the first white man to follow the southern route from Sault Ste. Marie to Montreal and Quebec. Because he turned north too quickly, he did not discover the Niagara River and Niagara Falls.

In response to Allouez's request for aid, two Jesuits, Father James Marquette and Father Claude Dablon, were sent into the region of the Upper Lakes to help him with his missionary work. Father Allouez returned to LaPointe while Father Marquette and Father Dablon started a mission at Sault Ste. Marie. Later this mission at Sault Ste. Marie became a French settlement. Thus Sault Ste. Marie was the first settlement in Michigan* and the first west of the Allegheny Mountains, except for the older Spanish settlements in the southwestern part of the United States.

In the fall of 1669 Allouez left LaPointe and went to Green Bay, Wisconsin. Here he founded a mission in response to a request from the Pottawattomie Indians. Part of his work was to try to keep the French traders from cheating the Indians. Marquette took Allouez's place at LaPointe while Dablon continued to work at the mission at Sault Ste. Marie.

Soon after Marquette took up Allouez's work at LaPointe, the Sioux, whom Marquette called "the Iroquois of the West," attacked the Ottawas and Hurons who lived near the mission. Many Hurons and Ottawas were killed, and those who remained fled into the wilderness for safety. Most of the Ottawa Indians took refuge on the Manitoulin Islands. The Hurons set out for Quebec and the protection of the French, but when they reached the southern part of the Upper Peninsula, near the Straits of Mackinac, they began again to fear the cruel Iroquois and so they went no farther.

When Father Marquette learned that the Hurons had gathered at Michilimackinac, he left his mission at LaPointe and started a new mission, which he named St. Ignace, on the Straits of Mackinac in

---

*It was abandoned in 1679 and remained without a resident for 80 years.

1671. This little mission was well located for carrying on missionary work among the Indians of northern Michigan.

Sixty years had passed since the first French settlement had been founded at Quebec. They had been years of hardship for the little French settlements along the St. Lawrence, but now, at last, the time had come when it was fairly safe to travel into the West. Both the fur traders and the Jesuits followed the Ottawa waterway into the strange unknown wilderness of the Lake Region. One came seeking furs and wealth; the other came to carry the message of Christianity to the Indians.

But though New France had opened the way to the furs of the West by way of the St. Lawrence-Ottawa route, she soon found this valuable trade endangered by the English who began sailing into Hudson Bay. For the next ninety years the two nations were rivals for the furs from north of Lake Superior and west of Hudson Bay.

Rapids in Ottawa River at Ottawa (1950)

Hudson Bay had been discovered by an English sea captain named Henry Hudson who had, just a few years before that time, discovered the Hudson River for the Dutch. England paid little attention to Hudson's discovery of the bay until the possibilities of the fur trade in that area were made known to the English by the two French traders, Radisson and Groseilliers. When the French authorities in New France had taken three fifths of their furs in 1663 because they had traded with the Indians without having a license, the two Frenchmen deserted to the English. They told the English of the profit that could be made by carrying on the fur trade along the shores of Hudson Bay where they had been.

King Charles II of England became interested in the story that the two French traders were telling. In 1669 ships were sent to the bay to trade with the Indians in that region. The ships came back loaded with furs. In the following year King Charles II granted a charter to "The Merchants of England trading into Hudson's Bay." This company, now known as Hudson's Bay Company, was to be the only fur trader permitted on the bay. The company was also given the ownership of all lands that could be reached by sailing west through Hudson Strait.

The formation of this trading company by the English was a threat to the growing western fur trade of New France, for furs could more easily be taken to Hudson Bay by the Indians than they could be carried to the French settlements along the St. Lawrence. What is more, English ships could carry goods to the trading posts on the bay much more cheaply than Frenchmen in canoes could carry them to the French trading posts in the West. England was now threatening France's fur trade from Hudson Bay as well as from the Hudson River area.

The French, kept from the lower lakes by the Iroquois, became very much interested in the Upper Lake Region which was then being opened and explored by fur traders and Jesuit missionaries. So far had the work of discovery progressed that by 1669 a fairly accurate map of the region had been made by two Jesuits. The French were eager to seize upon the friendship that was offered them by the Ottawas and other Indians of the region, and therefore made plans to take formal possession of the Upper Lake Region and thus to challenge the English who had started the Hudson's Bay Company in 1670 to carry on the fur trade from Hudson Bay.

The task of carrying out this formal ceremony fell to Simon Francois Daumont. With fifteen companions, Daumont made his way to Sault Ste. Marie, where he arrived in May, 1671. An invitation had been sent to the Indian tribes of the region asking them to come to the meeting, or council, which was going to be held. Fourteen Indian tribes sent members of their tribes to represent them. Indians, French officers representing the King of France, and the black-robed Jesuit priests all gathered for the ceremony. Father Allouez acted as the interpreter so that the Indians would know what the Frenchmen were saying. A large cross was erected and also a huge post upon which had been placed the arms of France. After the formal ceremony, Allouez told the Indians of the French king, whom he called "the greatest king in the world" and a "chief of chiefs." Thus France in 1671 took formal possession of the Upper Lakes Region and warned the English, who had begun trading from Hudson Bay, that the whole Northwest belonged to the King of France.

But for all its boasting, New France was still a weak colony. Only some 6,705 people lived in New France at the time. It was really but three small settlements—Quebec, Three Rivers, and

Montreal—which were strung along the St. Lawrence River. But it was growing in population and fast becoming one long struggling village spread along the St. Lawrence River's edge. What is more, there came to the colony in 1672 a new governor, Governor Frontenac. He was soon to prove himself to be the greatest of all the governors of New France.

The year after his arrival in the colony, Governor Frontenac sent Louis Joliet on an expedition to the West to search for the large river about which the French had so often been told. At the request of Joliet, Father Marquette, then at Michilimackinac, joined the expedition going to explore the West.

The two, Marquette and Joliet, went westward from the mission at St. Ignace, crossed the northern part of Lake Michigan, entered Green Bay, and then made their way up the Fox River. From this river they portaged (carried their canoes and supplies) to the Wisconsin River. Down this river they paddled until they came to the Mississippi River on June 17, 1673.

Pushing their bark canoes out upon the mighty river they began drifting slowly southward during the long pleasant summer days. On the way Marquette stopped to visit the Illinois Indians to keep a promise he had made to some of their tribe who had once visited him at his mission at LaPointe. He found them friendly but, although they desired that he stay with them, he and Joliet pushed on down the Mississippi as far as the Arkansas River. As they drifted along, their disappointment grew, for the Mississippi River ran steadily southward toward Spanish territory. Afraid to enter Spanish territory, they started the long journey northward back to the little mission in the wilderness at Green Bay.

When they reached the Illinois River they followed it northward and then passed over onto Lake Michigan. Following Lake Michigan's western edge, the party again came to the Jesuit mission at Green Bay. There Marquette and Joliet parted.

Joliet set out for Quebec to report his discoveries to Governor Frontenac. While going down the St. Lawrence River his canoe was upset at the foot of the Lachine Rapids, near Montreal. Two of the canoemen were drowned and everything in the canoe, including Joliet's records and charts, was lost in the water. Thus most of our knowledge of this expedition down the Mississippi comes from Marquette's journal which he wrote while staying with Allouez at Green Bay the following winter.

This circle of trees, known as the Indian Council Trees, stands on Greensky Hill, northeast of Charlevoix. Photo 1957.

Each of the council trees has been bent outward from the center. This is one of the best Indian relics in the state. Photo 1957.

Greensky Hill Indian Church located near the Indian Council Trees. It was built about 1860 and is still attended by a group of Indians. Photo 1957.

Indian cemetery, Pentoga Park, Iron County. The little wooden houses cover the graves of the Indians. Photo 1956.

The Mattawa River flowing east from the portage at the outlet of Lake Talon. Between its high rocky walls passed the French and Indians as they traveled to and from the Lake Region. Photo 1956.

The French River flowing west from Lake Nipissing. Westward along this rapidly flowing river came the French and Indians to Georgian Bay and the Lake Region. Photo 1956.

Restored Fort Michilimackinac at Mackinaw City. About 1740 the French moved the fort to this site from St. Ignace. It was here the English were massacred during Pontiac's Conspiracy. Photo 1957.

Back of this marker, on the St. Joseph River, once stood the little French fort of St. Joseph. Near the fort were several French cabins. Photo 1956.

When fall came again, Marquette set out to return to the Illinois Indians whom he had visited the year before. He followed the shore of Lake Michigan to its southern end. Here misfortune beset him and he became ill. His Indian friends deserted him. However, Jacques and Pierre, his French companions, stayed with him. Unable to go farther, the little group passed the winter of 1674-1675 near the place where Chicago, Illinois, now stands.

When spring came at last, the feeble Marquette again took up his journey to the land of the Illinois Indians. They received him with kindness and listened to him when he told them about the Christian religion. They asked him to stay with them, but Marquette was too ill and wished to return to New France. He promised them that he would return or send another missionary. With a sad heart Marquette set out for Quebec. Thinking that it might be a shorter way to reach Michilimackinac, the party followed the eastern shore of Lake Michigan. As they went northward along the shore of the lake, Marquette's strength failed him. He was carried ashore by members of his party and then, after saying mass at a crude altar, he died alone on May 18, 1675.

In a shallow grave near Ludington, Marquette was laid to rest in the vast wilderness that he had made his home. Two years later, friendly Indians brought his bones to the little mission of St. Ignace. There, beside the beautiful Straits of Mackinac, where he had labored among the Indians, his bones were buried beneath the floor of the mission chapel. The work of this wilderness missionary has not been forgotten. In his honor have been named a county, a city, a river, and a railroad. His grave at St. Ignace is now marked by a marble shaft. At Marquette, on the shore of Lake Superior, whose shores he helped to map and where he labored with the Indians, stands a bronze statue to remind us of this missionary and his work in the Land of the Lakes.

Soon after the death of Marquette, another Frenchmen, LaSalle, began his work of exploration. This man was then called a dreamer, but we today know that he really had good plans for New France. Although much of his work lay outside of Michigan, no history of this region can keep from telling something of LaSalle and his plans and work.

While at Montreal, LaSalle learned that to the south of Lake Erie there was a large river that flowed south and west to a large sea. So far away was this sea, said the Indians, that it took many moons to reach it by canoe, and so many were the dangers and hardships that few who undertook to reach it ever returned to their people. The sea! What sea? Perhaps this might be the passage to China for which explorers were still searching. LaSalle talked with the Indians and learned all he could from them about the river. Then, because the Iroquois were peaceful, he went south from Lake Erie with a friendly Shawnee who acted as his guide, and found the Ohio River, which he followed to the spot where Louisville now stands.

He dreamed of winning this vast area for New France. He would build ships to sail upon the Great Lakes and thus aid the fur trade and hold the English and Iroquois in check. He would enter the forests to the south and west and build forts upon the banks of the streams and thus hold the land for France.

LaSalle was not only a dreamer; he was also a hard worker. He tried to keep the Iroquois nations at peace. He had material for a sailboat, which he planned to build on Lake Erie, sent across Lake Ontario to the Niagara River. The materials for the boat were then carried across the twelve miles from Lake Ontario to Lake Erie, and there, on the shore of Lake Erie, the "Griffin," the first sailboat upon the Upper Lakes, was built. In the spring of 1679 the little vessel set sail upon the clear, blue water of Lake Erie. Westward she sailed across the lake. Turning to the north the "Griffin" passed up the Detroit River and on north into Lake Huron. At last, after a stormy voyage, she reached Michilimackinac, where she was welcomed by the Jesuits and *coureurs de bois* at the little mission of St. Ignace.

The "Griffin"

From there LaSalle sailed the "Griffin" to Green Bay, where the little boat was loaded with a cargo of furs. The "Griffin" was to return to Niagara Falls. After leaving her cargo there, her captain was to sail her back to the lower end of Lake Michigan, near the St. Joseph River, where LaSalle and his men would meet her.

After the "Griffin" had sailed east toward Niagara Falls, LaSalle and his men made their way down Lake Michigan to the St. Joseph River, where they began to build a little log fort which they named Fort Miami after the Miami Indians living in the region at that time. There LaSalle waited for the coming of Tonty, who was one of his helpers, and the return of the "Griffin." After some weeks Tonty and his men appeared. Eagerly the Frenchmen watched the blue water of Lake Michigan for the white sails of the little "Griffin."

Loaded with furs, the little boat had headed east across Lake Michigan for the Straits of Mackinac. Unlucky was this first voyage of the "Griffin," for she was never seen again. What happened to her is still unknown. Did she go down in a storm? Did the Indians capture and burn her?

Giving up hope for the "Griffin's" return and faced with the problem of getting ready for winter, LaSalle left Tonty at Fort Miami with a few men. With the rest he went south into the land of the Illinois Indians. There he stayed during the winter at another fort which he built and named Fort Crevecoeur (Brokenheart).

When spring came he sent some of his party on an exploration trip up the Mississippi. Then he and four men of his party made their way on foot across lower Michigan to the Detroit River and then to Quebec in quest of news of the "Griffin" and her crew. This is the first record of any white man crossing the Lower Peninsula of Michigan.

Three times LaSalle passed through Michigan. He was always dreaming of the great empire he would build in the wilderness. Later he started a settlement near the mouth of the Mississippi River. He tried to go from this settlement to Quebec, but he had not gone far inland when he was killed by one of his own men. Thus ended the life of the great empire builder of New France.

Other explorers, too, joined the long list of Frenchmen who journeyed into the Great Lakes Region to help hold it for New France. In 1684 DuLhut pushed as far west as Lake Nipigon. In 1686 he was the leader of a party of Frenchmen who built a fort on the western shore of the St. Clair River where Port Huron now stands. This new post was built to guard the river and thus keep the English and Iroquois from entering the French trading grounds from the south. DuLhut and his men stayed there during the following winter.

The post was abandoned the following spring, however, when DuLhut and his men were called east with their Indian allies to help fight the Iroquois.

In 1689 Jacques de Noyon went as far west as the Lake of the Woods. Farther and farther the Frenchmen ventured into the wilderness to win the friendship of the Indian tribes. In this way the Frenchmen hoped to keep the Indians from taking their furs to the English on Hudson Bay. Soon a highway of lakes and rivers which carried them to the Lake of the Woods area was known to the French. There, on the thousands of lakes and streams, lived the little animals whose skins the French wanted for the fur trade. Now French trading canoes were bringing the treasured furs along the waterway each spring to the posts at Sault Ste. Marie and St. Ignace. From Michilimackinac (St. Ignace) they were then carried in canoes to Montreal and Quebec.

If you look closely at a map of the Lake Region, you will soon see why Michilimackinac became the main post for the French fur trade. Its location gave it its importance. It was not far from the outlet of Lake Superior and it was near the route to the Ottawa River, which was then the main highway to Montreal and Quebec.

By 1690 the fur trade had greatly changed. The area near the French settlements no longer produced the furs as it had during the first years of French settlement. Furs had to be brought from farther and farther inland. Local traders gave way to large trading companies with offices in Montreal or Quebec. These trading companies had many men who worked for them in the woods as traders. The fur companies now had to risk the dangers of transportation and had to pay for having the furs brought from the Far West. Because the Iroquois were never friendly to the French, these trading companies never built ships on the Upper Lakes as LaSalle had tried to do. They contined to use the old route along the Ottawa River as their main highway.

Two kinds of traders sought out the furs. The *voyageurs,* or licensed traders, working with a government permit (*congé*) for one of the legal companies, carried on the legal fur trade. The profits from the fur trade were high and trading permits were hard to secure, so illegal traders called *coureur de bois* (forest runners) went into the woods and traded without a permit from the government. Often these illegally gotten furs were later traded to the English.

Only a few of the many names of these French traders have come down to us in the written records of that time. Who they were and where they went we today can only guess, but we do know many things about these early French fur traders.

On the whole they were a vigorous, daring, strong-limbed group of men. At the French settlements along the St. Lawrence River the traders loaded their bark canoes with articles, such as brandy, blankets, beads, guns, gunpowder, tomahawks, and knives, which they knew the Indians would like to get in trade. Then, bidding their wives, mothers, and friends good-by, they began, with their French companions and Indian friends, the long, hard journey to the West.

The Ottawa was rough and swift, but the Mattawa was even worse. Its current often came dashing and pounding between its rocky banks and over rough, jagged rocks which could easily have pierced the bottom of a bark canoe. It was necessary when going up these rivers to portage around many rapids and dangerous places. In all there were thirty-five portages before their canoes pushed out onto the smooth water of Georgian Bay. This meant that everything, including the canoes, had to be carried overland to a place on the river bank where the current was less swift and dangerous. Portages delayed the travelers and tired them as they toiled to get their canoes and goods around the portages. So slow was this river travel that it took several weeks to go from Montreal to Michilimackinac.

Traders going to the northwest went up the St. Mary's River to Sault Ste. Marie. At this point everything had to be portaged for a

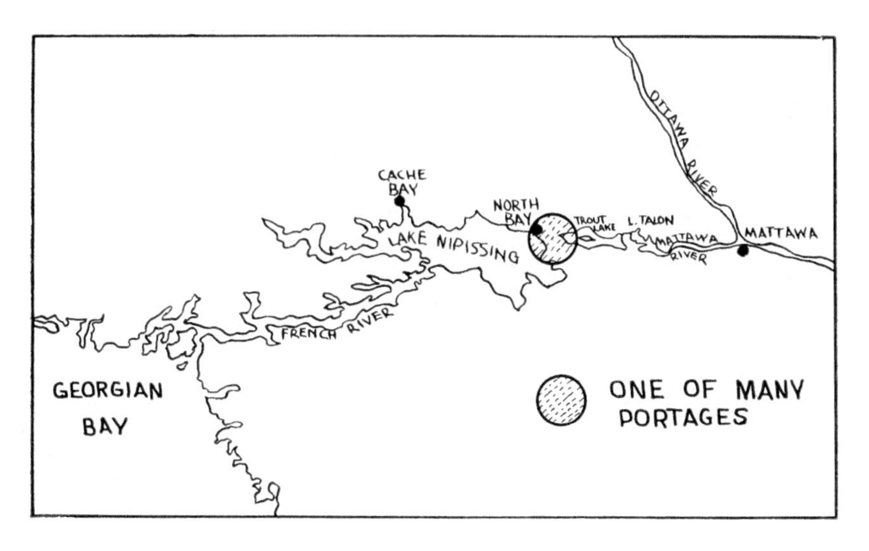

mile or more around the St. Mary's Rapids. When the canoes were again loaded, the traders followed the southern shore of Lake Superior. Traveling by canoe on Lake Superior was very dangerous. West of Grand Marais, in the area we now call the Pictured Rocks, the shore line was rocky and there was little chance to beach the canoes if a storm arose. Lake Superior is cold and deep. Storms, especially in the spring and fall, sometimes even now wreck our large modern freighters. Canoes were tossed about like little chips of wood on the mighty waves that came rolling from the west when a storm stirred up the icy water.

Farther to the west the traders came to Huron Bay and Keweenaw Bay. Huron Bay was easily crossed, but often bad weather on Keweenaw Bay forced the traders to paddle many extra miles along the shore. When they came to a point about ten miles from the head of the bay, they turned their canoes to the northwest and paddled eight or ten miles across the open water of the bay to the Keweenaw Peninsula, which juts out some fifty miles into Lake Superior. To paddle around this peninsula meant a hundred-and-ten-mile detour out into the lake. This detour was dangerous too, for the shore was often rocky and provided few places where the canoes could be beached without the risk of smashing them on the rocks.

To avoid this long, dangerous trip around the Keweenaw Peninsula, fur traders and missionaries followed the old Indian route now known as the Keweena Portage. This name was taken from the Chippewa Indian language and means a place where one walks across a point of land. From Keweenaw Bay to Lake Superior by way of the Keweena Portage was about twenty-five miles, and most of this distance could be traveled by canoe. After going up the Portage River for about six miles, the *voyageurs* entered Portage Lake. The next twelve miles of the way were across Portage Lake. At the northwestern end of the lake a small stream took the traders still farther across the peninsula. This little stream was so small, narrow, and crooked that canoes could pass along it only with great difficulty. Paddles were usually put aside and poles were used to push the canoes along the narrow, winding river. So narrow was the stream that marsh grass often brushed the canoes on both sides. So winding was the stream that the canoes could hardly make the turns in it as it meandered through the swampy land. When the *voyageurs* were within a mile and a half of Lake Superior, it became necessary to walk the rest of the way. The first half mile of the portage was across a swampy bog where the men, carrying their heavy burdens, tramped knee deep, and often belt deep, in the water and muck of the marsh. Then the trail reached firmer ground, and the portage path, for the last mile, wound through a pine forest to a little sandy slope on the western shore of the Keweenaw Peninsula.

The Keweena Portage was one of Michigan's most used portages. Nearly all early travelers, going along the south shore of Lake Superior, used it to keep from having to go around the Keweenaw Peninsula. Pierre Esprit Radisson crossed the portage in 1658-59. As late as 1820 Governor Cass and Schoolcraft passed along it on their way to the West. No doubt hundreds of unknown *voyageurs* used the same portage and waterway to take supplies to the West and bring the furs back to Michilimackinac.

Some portages were only a few steps. The longest one was known as the Grand Portage and was in northeastern Minnesota where the Pigeon River flows into Lake Superior. It was nine miles or more in length. All the goods of the traders, merchandise or furs, as well as the canoes, had to be carried over the portages. This was hard work for the *voyageurs* and required the hardiest kind of men for the task. All merchandise and furs were wrapped in bundles weighing about ninety pounds. When portaging, a *voyageur* would often carry two of these bundles on his back as he picked his way over fallen logs or along the rocky path of the portage trail. Bundles of furs and freight were carried by means of a tump-line that passed over the forehead and then back over the shoulders to the weight on the trader's back. Bending forward because of the weight on his back, the *voyageur* walked along the portage trail. Sometimes the trail was firm and ran over rocks and sand. At other times it ran through swampy places. Whatever its course, the trader, bending forward

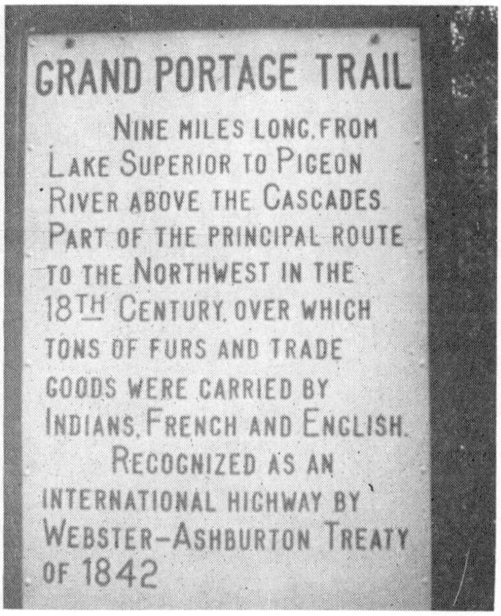

Marker near Grand Portage, Minnesota

against the tump-line, pushed on, around stumps, over fallen logs, and under low-hanging limbs, from one resting place to another.

Several trips along the portage trail were usually required before all the goods and the canoes had been carried across the land. Sometimes traders took their merchandise and canoes the entire length of a portage at one time. At other times, however, when the portage was a long one, they would divide the distance into one or more places of deposit. All goods and canoes were brought to one deposit before the traders moved on to the next one. Because of this practice, portage distances were often spoken of as so many "poses" or deposits in length.

In going to Rainy Lake from Grand Portage at the mouth of the Pigeon River, which now separates Canada from the United States on the far western shore of Lake Superior, it was necessary to make thirty-six more portages. If the *voyageurs* pushed on to Lake Winnipeg, they had to portage twenty-six more times. Thus, if furs were taken from Lake Winnipeg to Montreal, the *voyageurs* had to carry the furs and their canoes ninety-seven times.

Canoes used in the fur trade were known by two general names, "Montreal canoes" and "canoes of the North." The Montreal canoes were larger and were used on the trip from western Lake Superior to Montreal. When going farther to the west, the Montreal canoes were exchanged for the smaller *canots de Nord,* which were better adapted to the smaller streams and the winding portages of the rocky wilderness land northwest of Lake Superior.

The *canots de Nord* were usually about twenty-five feet in length and were paddled by six to ten men. They were small enough to be carried by one or, at most, two men when the party was making a portage in the wilderness. This the carriers did by turning a canoe upside down and placing it over their heads. They supported it on their shoulders by paddles which had been placed lengthwise in the canoe and tied in place along the cross bars of the canoe.

These French forest rovers became expert woodsmen and paddled their canoes as well and as far as could the Indians themselves. One man, known as the *avant,* stood or sat in the bow, or front, of the canoe. Behind the *avant* came the regular *voyageurs* who paddled the canoe. In the back, or stern, of the canoe sat the steerman, known as the *gouvernail.* It was his task to guide the canoe, as it sped along on the surface of the water, by using a paddle having a long handle. In the *gouvernail's* hands this paddle guided the canoe across lakes, down swirling streams, through boiling rapids, and past dangerous rocks which might easily have torn into the fragile bottom of the speeding canoe.

Sometimes the *voyageurs* were gone for months, and often they did not return for a year or two, or even three. They had little education, and often what little culture they did have was changed because their constant life with the Indian savages caused them slowly to adopt many of the Indian ways of life. Sometimes they almost forgot the ways of their French fathers. Some took Indian squaws for their wives, and it was not at all uncommon to see one of these traders surrounded by a group of half-breed children who came to be known as *bois brulés* (burnt wood).

Once in the wilderness the trader often lived like an Indian and did some of his own trapping. Then, too, he sought out the Indian, and on the wooded bank of some stream or lake he bartered his goods for the Indian's stock of furs. These he carefully wrapped in bundles weighing eighty to ninety pounds and put them in his canoe to replace the merchandise which he had bartered to the Indian. Everywhere north of the land of the Iroquois these roving Frenchmen went, ever seeking the Indian and his catch of furs.

At night he pulled his canoe on shore, cooked his simple meal, and made his bed beneath the trees and the stars. If it rained, he sheltered himself by crawling under his overturned canoe. When winter came he sometimes sought shelter in an Indian wigwam, a French fort, or a frontier settlement.

A thousand streams reached like outstretched fingers, always pointing into unknown, inviting lands. Farther beyond lay still more wilderness. There was always the great beyond to be explored. Each bend of the river or point of land along the shore of the lake hid new views of yet unexplored mystery.

The vast forest became the fur trader's home as truly as it was the home of his Indian brother. The land the French had discovered seemed to be too big for them. A few small groups settled here and there, but so vast was the spreading wilderness that their little posts seemed to have been lost in the silent depths of the forests which lay all about them. The Frenchmen were rovers, not settlers. They adopted both the Indian's homeland and his way of life. The fleur-de-lis flew above the little posts as a sign of possession and not of conquest.

Each spring the French traders gathered as many Indians with their furs as they could at the western posts. Then, in canoes loaded down with bundles of furs, Indians and traders set out for the French settlements along the St. Lawrence. Thus the Indian not only caught the furs but often had to deliver them all the way to Montreal, some one thousand miles away. Sometimes this spring flotilla numbered as high as four hundred canoes. Often it was midsummer before the Indians and the *voyageurs* arrived at Montreal and set up their huts on the river bank for the annual fair. Day after day more canoes laden with furs joined the others already on the river bank. Everywhere there was feasting and happiness. Naked savages from the western forests, *voyageurs, coureur de bois,* French merchants, and French nobility all joined in making the annual fair the one leading event of the year in New France.

The fair usually lasted from ten to fourteen days. Amid the drinking and carousing the merchants bartered their goods, which had just arrived in the ships from France, for the valuable furs of the Indians. Usually the Frenchmen got by far the better of the bargain. The Indians often gave valuable furs for a little brandy which increased their always-present weakness for a few cheap, bright-colored trinkets.

For some time the post at Michilimackinac (St. Ignace) was the leading fur trading post in the Lake Region. Other posts which spread farther into the wilderness helped to gather the furs that were carried to Michilimackinac and then to Montreal. One was built at Green Bay, Wisconsin. Another was on the St. Joseph River in the southwestern part of Michigan. Sault Ste. Marie also had its post. Others were started on the far western and northern shores of Lake Superior. They were all little log forts in a vast wilderness. The forts were made by standing logs upright in the ground. Each log was pointed at the top. These wooden walls around the fort were known as a palisade. Usually there was a priest or two at each post who conducted Christian services for the French settlers and tried to teach the Indians about Christianity.

The Jesuit missionaries and fur traders were often opposed to one another over the brandy trade. While the Jesuits gave their lives to help the Indians, the fur traders sold them guns and brandy. Brandy was the most wanted article in the fur trade. Often Indians would spend their entire winter getting furs and then get little more for them than enough brandy to allow the trader to cheat them out of the rest. Brandy often turned the Indians into raving madmen who did cruel things which they would not have done if it had not been for the brandy that was sold to them by the Frenchmen.

But once the brandy trade had been started, it could not easily be stopped. When Indians had tasted it they wanted more, and if they could not get brandy from the Frenchmen they could get rum from the English. What is more, the Jesuits feared that their Indian converts might pick up the Christian teachings of the English who were not Catholics.

Furs were the most important article sent from New France to the mother country. The Land of the Lakes with its many streams, wet prairies, swamps, and cold winters made an excellent homeland for wild fur-bearing animals, especially the much-sought-after beaver. Each winter, when the skins were most valuable, the Indians shot, trapped, snared, and clubbed many of the smaller animals in order that they might get their furs to trade to the French or English for the goods they were beginning to find necessary for their new way of life. Beaver skins were the most desired, but otter, martin, mink, and weasel were also killed for their furs. Some moose hides and buffalo skins were taken to Montreal, but they were bulky and of much less value.

When the French came to North America, the Indians were living a simple life and using only such things as they could find in their own little community. Seldom did they venture far from their tribal lands. The coming of the Europeans, however, suddenly changed the Indians from the stone age to the age of iron, and they became more and more dependent upon the white man's goods. Birch bark buckets were replaced by copper and iron pots. Blankets were soon used in place of skins to provide warmth. Bows and arrows were quickly discarded for the crude muskets of that day. Hatchets, knives, and needles became not luxuries but necessities of the everyday life of the Indians. To get guns, gunpowder, lead, brandy, and blankets the Indians had to trap animals, not to get food as they had in the past, but to secure furs for the French or English fur traders. This hunting for more furs did much to break up the old tribal locations and to break down the Indian way of life. They became greater rovers than they had been and were often found far from their native hunting grounds. Even though the Indian standard of life was raised by these material things, other aspects of European culture brought havoc to the Indian tribes. Brandy, rum, and strange diseases, like smallpox and measles, brought sorrow into many a native wigwam.

The French government knew that if New France was to become a permanent colony it would be necessary to send settlers who would found homes and turn the wilderness into good farms. At different times the French government offered to aid settlers from France if they would come to America and live. Yet, because of the political troubles at home and a poor system of colonization in America, French settlers did not come to New France in very large numbers. However, more and more French settlements gradually grew up along the St. Lawrence River and at a few scattered spots in the wilderness.

Their farms would seem very strange to you today. You are in the habit of seeing farms laid out in squares. The French farms differed greatly from this. They were long, narrow strips of land which ran straight back from the river or lake. Usually they were not more than three or four hundred feet wide, if that, yet they sometimes ran back into the land a distance of two or three miles. To go from one end of a farm to the other required much time. When a man died, these small strips of land were often divided among his children and thus the strips became smaller and smaller.

Along the river not far from the bank stood a row of French farmhouses. They were little cabins made of any materials which the French settlers could easily get. Usually they were plastered on the inside and out with a kind of mortar which was made by mixing mud and straw. Sometimes they were whitewashed, but seldom, if ever, were they painted. The roofs were made of bark and were often covered with moss. Few, if any, nails were used in building these homes, which were sometimes made from rough lumber produced in the settlement. Each house usually had around it a picket fence. Behind the houses, on still higher ground, ran a road which followed the river.

All the baking was done in a general community oven. A churn, a small number of wooden or leather buckets, and copper pots were the few household articles which were usually carried into the wilderness. When washday came, the women took the soiled clothes down to the river and washed them there.

Usually the farms were located near the forts. The forts gave the farmers protection and in a way provided a small market for the farmers' crops. Near these forts or villages there was often a strip of common land called "the commons" which was used for pasturing the stock of the settlement. Sometimes the field was large and sometimes it was small, depending upon the size of the community.

Farming was hard work. The land had to be cleared. Homes had to be built. The ground had to be tilled and the crops cared for. When a farmer finished his year's work he often had little to show for it because there was no place to sell most of his goods. Therefore he often wished to leave the farm and go into the woods and search for furs. However, this he was forbidden to do by very strict laws, for the fur trade was a large monopoly and its large profits usually went to only a few favored people who were friends of the king.

As the years passed, the small posts in the Great Lakes Region came to be more and more important. The constant demand for more and more furs caused the Indians and Frenchmen to push farther and farther west in their quest for new regions where game was more plentiful. Gradually better fortified posts were set up by the French government to hold the region for France and to keep the Indians in check.

Of all the posts in the Lake Region, that of Michilimackinac became the most important. There a fort named Fort Du Buade was built. It was surrounded by the usual wooden palisade for protection from the Indians, and it was sometimes garrisoned by as many as two hundred French soldiers. French settlers gathered there too. They lived in about sixty small wooden houses that were built along a single narrow street. The Huron Indians lived near the fort in houses which they had built.

In 1689 the first of four wars between England and France began. French raiding parties, made up of Frenchmen from New France and Indians from her western lands, went south and attacked English settlements in New England. The French were fearful of losing the friendship of their western Indians and so sent soldiers under Cadillac to St. Ignace to be stationed at Fort Du Buade.

Their time in Michigan was short-lived, however, for in 1697 King Louis XIV of France, at the request of the Jesuits, ordered all the traders, except those stationed at St. Louis, to leave the West. The Jesuits were to be the only persons who could teach and trade with the Indians. So the following year Cadillac and all the legal traders and soldiers in the West left their little posts and went eastward to the French settlements along the St. Lawrence.

But, though Cadillac left the area, he was soon to return. While at Michilimackinac, as commander of the troops stationed there, he had learned about a large river far to the south which is now called the Detroit River. Like La Salle before him, Cadillac was a man of vision. A post on the Detroit River somewhere near Lake Erie would act as a block and keep the English from coming north into the lands of the French with their rum to trade with the Indians.

From New France, Cadillac crossed the ocean to lay his plans before the king of France. In the court of the king, Cadillac found friends who listened to his plan and helped him to get permission from Louis XIV to start a little colony on the Detroit River.

The English, too, had a similar idea. Thinking that it would be wise for reasons of trade to build a fort upon the Detroit River, they entered into an agreement with the Iroquois Indians, who claimed the land, for permission to build a fort on the river. The Iroquois, thereupon, deeded the land to the English on July 14, 1701. The English, however, had acted too slowly.

Cadillac had already been given permission from the French government to found his new settlement, and he was then on his way from Montreal by way of the Ottawa route. On July 23, 1701, Cadillac and his followers made their way across Lake St. Clair and entered the Detroit River. As they paddled down the broad river, they scanned its banks for a good place to found the new settlement. They went as far as Grosse Isle, where they spent the night. On the following day, July 24, 1701, Cadillac and his party came back up the river and chose the spot where Detroit now stands as the best place to build the fort. At that point the river is the narrowest, and a small stream running into the river provided a point of land protected by water on three sides. There a palisaded fort called Fort Pontchartrain was built. Fifty soldiers, fifty traders and artisans, and two priests formed the white population. Before long, Indians—Hurons, Miamis, and Ojibways—began to gather near the little fort on the Detroit River. They came seeking protection from the Iroquois.

Although Cadillac had named his little post Fort Pontchartrain, in time it came to be known as the Village of the Straits (*ville détroit*). Later the word for village was dropped and the name became Detroit and means "of the straits."

It was Cadillac's plan to make his little post on the Detroit River a French settlement and not just a trading post. Cadillac's wife and Madam de Tonty, together with one of Cadillac's sons, James, came to Detroit from Quebec by way of Lake Erie. One of Cadillac's other sons had come with his father when Cadillac had come to start the settlement. These two French women, Madam Cadillac and Madam de Tonty, were the first French women to come to Michigan. Their coming meant that French family life was to be a part of Cadillac's new settlement.

Although Cadillac had good plans for his little settlement on the Detroit River, ill fortune followed him from the start. The fur trade had been given to him as part of his grant, but he had no sooner left France than the French king gave the same grant to a group of men known as the Company of Canada. To try to straighten out his trading rights and to try to get settlers to come west to his new settlement, Cadillac spent much of the next ten years at Quebec.

Unfortunately for Cadillac's small settlement, war again came between France and England in 1702. This war was called Queen Anne's War and lasted until 1713. The king of France was now too busy to be interested in Cadillac's little settlement on the Detroit River.

For a few years after Cadillac settled Detroit, the post at St. Ignace became less important. However, after Cadillac left for Louisiana, it again became the main trading center in the Lake Area.

In 1711, a band of Sauk and Fox Indians attacked Detroit. They had been told by their friends, the Iroquois, that France and England were at war, and they thought that it would be a good time to destroy Detroit and open trade with the English for their cheaper goods. Fortunately, although there were no soldiers in the fort at the time, the French traders were able to keep the Sauk and Fox Indians away until a band of friendly Pottawattomie Indians came to their rescue.

In 1713, Queen Anne's War came to an end and England gained in the peace treaty the control of Hudson Bay, Newfoundland, and Nova Scotia. New France was slowly losing out to the English, but New France still continued to hold onto her posts in the lake area and new ones were built. The little post on the St. Joseph River was restored. In 1721, when Charlevoix visited the St. Joseph area, he reported that a commandant and a small garrison of soldiers were there. Because of the "oak openings," good hunting, and fertile land, this area seems to have been well liked by both the Indians and Frenchmen. A mission seems to have been maintained there by the Jesuits during most of the period when France controlled the lakes.

Still another war, King George's War, was fought between England and France from 1744 to 1748. Although Michigan was too far to the west to take part in these wars, Indians from the Great Lakes

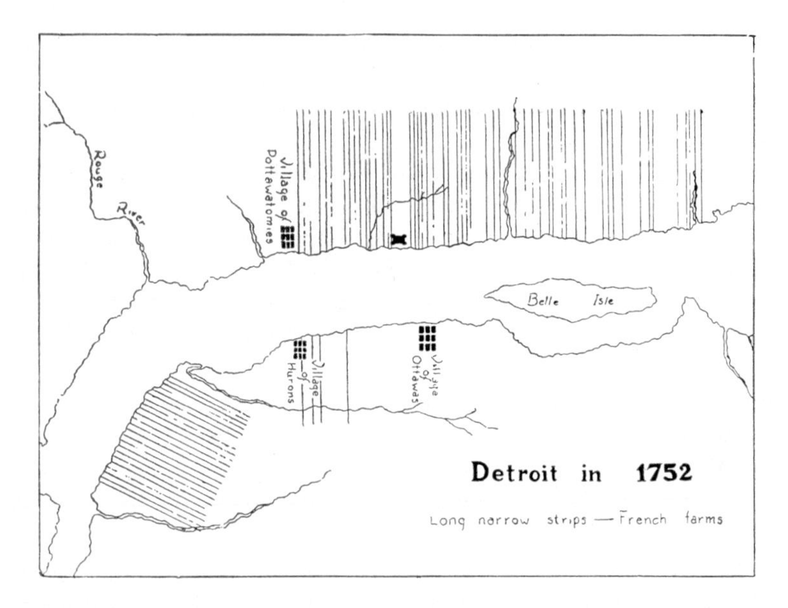

Area often went eastward to aid the French armies and to help defend the French settlements or to help attack those of the English. In 1748 the French seemed to sense their weakness and the growing rivalry between the French and English in America. In that year the French government tried to encourage settlers to come to Detroit by offering to provide them with a spade, an ax, a plow, a large wagon, a small wagon, a cow, a pig, and other grants. As a result of this offer some Frenchmen came from France to settle at Detroit the following year. France had waited too long to develop her agricultural resources in the New World.

English settlers were now eager to push into the Ohio Valley. In the same year that King George's War came to an end the Ohio Company was formed. New France learned of this threat from the English colonies against her land in the Ohio Valley and Pierre Celoron, Sieur de Blainville was sent into the valley the following year, 1749, to put up lead plates announcing France's title to the land. These lead plates were fastened to trees at important places, such as places where large streams flowed into the Ohio River. Other plates were buried in the ground. When Blainville's party reached the Miami River, they turned north. From this river they crossed to the Maumee and thus came to Detroit.

In 1756 war again came between France and England. Indians

and Frenchmen from Detroit and Michilimackinac again hurried eastward to help New France. Some of these men took part in the defeat of General Braddock. The lake posts were still too far away to enter into the actual struggle, but men from this area took part in most of the campaigns of the French and Indian War.

In 1759 General Wolfe's army scaled the heights at Quebec and, on the Plains of Abraham on top of Cape Diamond, they defeated the French general, Montcalm. Quebec, the key to New France, thus fell into the hands of the English. The following year English armies marched upon Montreal. The French surrendered and New France then passed to the English.

Like the Indians before them, the French explorers and settlers gave names to many places in Michigan. Here are a few of them: Presque Isle, "almost an island"; Belle Isle, "beautiful island"; Les Cheneaux, "the channels"; Sault Ste. Marie, "falls, or rapids, of the St. Mary's"; Bois Blanc, "white woods"; Grosse Pointe, "large point"; and Grosse Isle, "large island."

Bloody Run in Elmwood Cemetery in Detroit. Near here the Indians under Pontiac defeated the English soldiers led by Captain Dalzell. (1961)

Chapter V

EARLY YEARS OF ENGLISH RULE
(1760-1775)

To an English forest ranger, Major Robert T. Rogers, fell the task of reaching the distant French posts on the Great Lakes and telling the French soldiers that Canada had been captured by the English. With a small party of Englishmen and Indians, Major Rogers came westward along the south shore of Lake Erie and reached the outpost of Detoit late in the fall of 1760.

The French commandant at Detroit had not yet heard of the surrender of Canada by the French, but when he was shown the official papers which Major Rogers had with him, he gave up the fort to the English. He and his French soldiers were then sent as prisoners of war to Philadelphia.

In spite of the lateness of the season, Major Rogers planned to go on to the post of Michilimackinac, but because of the bitterness of the fall weather he changed his plans and remained at Detroit during the following winter. The other posts in the area were not occupied until the following year.

While Major Rogers was spending the winter at Detroit, things were happening at Michilimackinac. From that post a French settler and trader named Charles Langlade had gone east to the war at the head of a party of Indians from the region of Michilimackinac. It was he, in company with other Frenchmen, who led the French and Indians in the battle against Braddock at Fort Duquesne.

At the close of the war Charles Langlade and his Indians were at Montreal. The French commander, knowing that he must soon give up to the English and not wishing the Indians to be there, sent Langlade and his Indians back to Fort Michilimackinac. They had not gone very far when a messenger overtook them and told Langlade that Canada had passed to British control. Langlade continued homeward and upon reaching Michilimackinac, told of the passing of Canada to the British.

When Langlade reported the news to the French commander,

Beaujeu, the commander dismantled the little fort at St. Ignace. He and his soldiers then started for the French fort of Chartres which was located on the Mississippi River in what is now the state of Illinois.

Beaujeu and his men found the weather against them just as it was against Major Rogers. The Frenchmen were unable to reach Fort Chartres before the rivers froze over. Being unable to continue their journey, they were forced to spend the winter among the Indians. The following year Beaujeu and his soldiers arrived at Fort Chartres, where they remained for the next four years until the fort was abandoned in 1765.

The English fur traders were eager to get the profits that the French had been making from the trade in furs. Perhaps they were too eager. It was not long, therefore, before English fur traders began to appear in the Land of the Lakes. If a peace had been signed in Montreal in 1760, things might have been different, but the war continued in Europe, and it was not until 1763 that peace was finally made between England and France. It is no wonder then that the English soldiers and fur traders who had taken the lake posts soon became the victims of a French plan to regain the region for France.

Many causes have been given for the Indian uprising against the English which is known as Pontiac's Conspiracy. The English had failed to push into the Mississippi Region and take over the French forts located there. Frenchmen at these posts supplied the Indians with guns and ammunition and set afloat many rumors that aroused the war spirit of the Indians. Before the defeat of the French both the French and English had tried to keep the friendship of their Indian allies so that the Indians would not join the enemy. Now that the French had been defeated, the English did not feel that they had to try to win the Indians' good will.

By 1763 it was plain to the Indians that Englishmen were different from Frenchmen. They seldom married Indian women. They looked down upon the Indians and treated them as if they were beneath them. Moreover, the rivers did not flow with rum as the Indians had been told they would. In fact, it became hard for the Indians to get even the necessary supplies such as gunpowder and blankets upon which they had now come to depend. They grew dissatisfied with things as they were and willingly listened to the tales of the French who were still at Fort Chartres, their half-breed brothers, and *coureur de bois* who were eager for the profits of the fur trade. Rumors aroused hatreds. Hatreds bred plots. At last the well-planned Indian conspiracy of Pontiac was born.

Early in the spring of the year 1763 an Indian called Chief Pontiac, who lived on Peche Island, near Belle Isle in the Detroit River, held an Indian council on the Ecorse River near Detroit. To the council came many Indians and also several Frenchmen. The council reached its height with the speech of Chief Pontiac. Using all his force of words and character Pontiac clearly pictured to his Indian listeners how they had been misused by the English who had now come into their homeland. Then he aroused in their minds a glowing memory of the many kindnesses of their French brothers who had been driven away. Gradually, as a skillful speaker can, he excited the Indians by telling them of the ways in which the English had neglected their brothers, how they had driven the French from the country, and how they were only waiting for some excuse in order to drive the Indians from their ancient tribal hunting grounds.

Pontiac then held up a belt of wampum which he told his listeners had been sent to him by the great French king from far across the sea. He said that the long sleep into which the French king had fallen was now at its end, and that soon his large war canoes would be coming up the Mississippi and the St. Lawrence rivers to win Canada back for France.

Under the leadership of Pontiac the Indians planned to return to their homes and then, when a certain time arrived, each would attack the English post nearest him. Thus each of the English forts was to be attacked at about the same time so that the English soldiers could not help one another. When the forts were taken, all the Englishmen would be killed and thus the land would be rid of the hated English.

Of the forts located in the region of the northern lakes the one at Michilimackinac was the largest and best garrisoned. By the time of Pontiac's conspiracy it had been moved from St. Ignace and was then located on the south side of the Straits of Mackinac at what is now Mackinaw City. It was at that time under the command of Captain Etherington. Only ninety-two soldiers made up the entire garrison.

Although Captain Etherington had been warned by friendly French and Indians of the danger of an Indian attack, he paid little attention to the Indians when they began to gather about the fort, for they acted in a manner very friendly to him and his men.

On one of the first days in June, 1763, the Indians invited the

English soldiers to see a game of lacrosse which was going to be played between two rival Indian tribes. As it was the king's birthday, the soldiers were already in a holiday mood. Carelessly they straggled out of the palisade which surrounded the fort and sat down in the shade to watch the Indians as they tossed the ball back and forth from one side to the other.

For some time the game of lacrosse continued. Back and forth flew the ball as each group of braves tried to win for their tribe. Meanwhile many squaws, one after another, passed into and out of the fort through the open gate. None of the English had noted their careless but well-planned actions. About noon one of the players threw the ball high into the air so that it would fall well within the pickets of cedar which surrounded the fort.

This was the signal for the Indians to attack the post. As if still in friendly play, the Indian braves dashed in through the open gateway of the fort in one mad rush as though they were all eager to get the ball. Once inside, the Indian warriors raised the war whoop and were quickly given tomahawks which the squaws had carried into the fort well hidden beneath the heavy folds of their blankets.

Where all had been peace and friendly play, all was now excitement. Tomahawks flew and many of the Englishmen were killed. Before they had time to act, over half of the little company had been struck down. Captain Etherington and the remainder of the soldiers and traders were then taken prisoners. After weeks of cruel suffering, they were finally freed.

Thus fell the fort at Michilimackinac (Mackinaw City) before the crafty Indian attack. The Indians then wandered through the fort and took whatever they wanted. Then they burned the fort.

But what about the other forts? Were the Indians as successful there?

Fort St. Joseph, at present-day Niles, was attacked by a band of Pottawattomies on May 25. The small garrison there was wiped out except for Ensign Schlosser and three men. These four were later taken to Detroit where they were exchanged for Indian prisoners then held by the English.

The attack on the fort at Detroit was led by Chief Pontiac. The crafty chief with a band of his trusted Indian followers planned to hold a council with Major Gladwin who was then in command of the post. On May 7, 1763, Pontiac and sixty of his warriors entered the fort and were greeted in a friendly but stern manner by the

English commander who had his soldiers on duty and ready for quick action.

For some time the Indians talked with the English officers. At last Pontiac rose to make a speech. The Indians had planned that, as their chieftain talked, he was to present a belt of wampum and at this signal the Indians were to take their sawed-off guns from under their blankets and make an attack on the officers while their brothers were to attack the fort and the soldiers stationed there.

It looked for a time as if the Indians' plans would succeed. The guns, whose barrels had been sawed off, were actually there, hidden beneath the blankets of the warriors. But a strange thing happened just as Pontiac was about to present the wampum belt. Drums rolled, a door opened, and there stood a group of English soldiers ready for the Indian attack should the braves try to carry out their plan. Then one of the Englishmen stepped forward and pulled back the blanket of an Indian and uncovered his hidden gun.

The Indians were taken by surprise. They now understood why the English soldiers had all been at their posts when they entered. Someone had told the English that the Indians were planning to capture the post.

Pontiac finished his speech very quickly but he did not present the wampum belt. When he had finished, Major Gladwin arose and spoke to the Indians. He told them the English would be friends to the Indians as long as they were peaceful, but if they took the war path they would soon feel the mighty power of the English king.

How had the English at Detroit learned of the Indians' plans? Many stories have tried to explain the mystery. One story tells that women saw the Indians filing off their gun barrels. Still another tells that Major Gladwin was warned by an Indian maiden who came to sell him a pair of Indian moccasins. A study of the records shows that there were many Frenchmen who were loyal to the English, and it was probably they who gave warning of the coming Indian attack.

On May 9 Pontiac and a band of warriors again tried to gain entrance into the fort in order, they said, to smoke the peace pipe with the commander. Major Gladwin told Pontiac that he and a few of the Indian chieftains might enter but the rest of the Indians must stay outside the stockade.

This action on the part of Major Gladwin angered the Indians, and they no longer tried to keep the false face of peace. They set up a war whoop and fell upon the luckless Englishmen who happened to be outside the palisade of the fort. Not far away lived an old lady and her two sons. These the Indians killed and scalped. Going to Belle Isle, they attacked Mr. Fisher and his family who were living there. Mr. and Mrs. Fisher were killed and their two children were carried away.

English traders were no longer safe in the woods. Everywhere they were in danger of being robbed and murdered by the Indians. More than a hundred English traders were killed by the Indians during the summer of 1763.

On May 10 Pontiac and his Indians moved their camp across the river to what is now the American side near the Belle Isle Bridge. Then began the Indian siege of Detroit. It is one of the few sieges to be found in all Indian history. English sentries had ever to be on their guard lest they expose themselves to the gunfire of one of the Indians who lay hidden just outside the walls of the palisade.

As the days passed, the English soldiers learned, little by little, the fate of the English soldiers who had been stationed at the other frontier posts. Nearly always the story was the same: cruel treachery, murder, and the smoldering remains of what had once been a British post. Such news was disheartening, and gloom settled over the little post on the banks of the Detroit River.

But help would surely come. In fact, they were expecting supplies from Fort Niagara to arrive at Detroit about the last of the month. Could Major Gladwin and his soldiers hold out that long against the Indians? Eagerly the English sentries watched the river for the coming of the canoes that would bring aid to the imprisoned garrison. On May 30 a shout of joy ran through the fort. A fleet of canoes could be seen coming up the river from Lake Erie. All rushed to the pickets and watched anxiously to see what would happen. Would the Indians attack the canoes? Did the soldiers in the canoes know that the Indians were attacking the fort?

Steadily the canoes came on up the river. Why did the Englishmen not return the salute from the fort? Why did they keep to the far side of the river? Suddenly the war whoop of the Indians rent the air and the little garrison at the fort knew what had happened to the supply expedition. Their friends were prisoners of the Indians. The Indians had captured them while they were camped on the north shore of Lake Erie. Now the Indians were forcing the Englishmen to paddle the canoes for them. A few of the Englishmen tried to break away and reach the fort. Two did reach it, but most of those who tried were killed by the Indians. Up past the fort the flotilla of canoes went, twenty-three canoes filled with provisions and powder for the fort.

At the Indian camp the party landed. Then began one of the most cruel happenings ever to take place in Michigan. For the pleasure of the squaws and children and to the horror of the soldiers, the English prisoners were put to cruel Indian torture and death.

On July 29 two hundred and eighty men with supplies did reach Detroit. Captain Dalzell had made his way up the Detroit River under the cover of a heavy fog. The arrival of more men and supplies brought new hope to the soldiers in the little fort, but hope lingered for only a short while.

Captain Dalzell was not a seasoned Indian fighter like Major Gladwin. Captain Dalzell thought that the Indians could easily be defeated if their camp were attacked by surprise. Unwillingly, Major Gladwin finally gave permission to Captain Dalzell to make an attack on the Indian camp.

On July 31 at two-thirty in the morning the English soldiers marched quietly out of the gate of the little fort beside the river. Up the River Road (now East Jefferson Avenue) they marched toward Lake St. Clair. On their right flowed the Detroit River. On its surface came two boats, the "Michigan" and the "Huron," armed with guns. It was hoped that the boats with their guns could aid the soldiers, or that they could at least help to cover a retreat should the men be driven back toward the fort.

Silently the English soldiers marched in the darkness of the early morning hours. French farmhouse after farmhouse was passed. On they went until they had gone about two miles from the fort. Then they came to a bridge where the River Road ran over Parent's Creek just before the little stream entered the Detroit River.

As the leading soldiers of the English column reached the bridge, the Indian war whoop and heavy musket fire came from three hundred hidden savages who had been waiting in the darkness for the English soldiers to arrive. The surprisers were thus themselves surprised. All quickly became confusion in the inky darkness of the early morning. Then the English began their retreat to the fort. Back along the road from house to house the fight went on as the retreat continued. Slowly the English gave ground before the Indians' attack. Several English soldiers were killed as they tried to save their wounded comrades from the Indians. Captain Dalzell was thus killed while trying to save an English sergeant. By eight o'clock that morning the English soldiers who were left had struggled, weary and beaten, into the shelter of the little fort.

The siege of Detroit lasted from May until October. During this time the garrison had little touch with the outside world. Fortunately there were two sailboats, the "Huron" and the "Michigan," which were stationed just outside the fort. These boats aided the garrison in many ways. Their gunfire helped to protect the side of the fort next to the river. Then too, they sailed down the Detroit River and across Lake Erie and brought back supplies from Niagara.

The Indians tried many times to get rid of these boats. At one time they made large rafts, loaded them with material that would easily burn, and sent them floating down the river in hopes that the flaming rafts would pass near enough to the fort to burn the boats.

As the summer passed, the Indians' hopes, patience, and ammunition grew smaller and smaller. Some wandered off into the forest in search of winter hunting grounds. Yet Pontiac held on even though his warriors grew fewer and fewer in number. In late October Pontiac received a letter from the commandant at Fort Chartres telling him that he could no longer expect aid from the French in Illinois.

Pontiac began to understand that he had been made the tool of crafty planners. No war canoes from France were to come up the Mississippi or the St. Lawrence River. Defeated and humiliated, he left Detroit. At first he planned to return again the following summer and take up the siege. This, however, he did not do. When he did return, he asked for peace.

In the same year, 1763, that the Indians of the West had tried to drive the English from the West, France, which had now been fighting England for seven years, gave up the war and accepted defeat. In the peace signed in 1763 England gained most of France's colonies throughout the world. Canada and all of New France east of the Mississippi River were given to England by the treaty. France was allowed to keep only two very small islands near Newfoundland, St. Pierre and Miquelon, to serve as a base for her fishing fleet.

England thus claimed, after 1763, all the land from her West Indies Islands north to the top of Hudson Bay and east of the Mississippi River. This vast colonial possession in America brought with it many new problems of government for England.

What should be done with the new unsettled land to the west of the Atlantic colonies was one of the major problems. Many of the colonial charters had stated that the colonial grants ran from sea to sea. Thus each colony would have to deal independently with the Indian problem. The English government, however, disregarded the wishes of the colonies in regard to the western land and passed what is now known as the Proclamation of 1763 in an attempt to settle the Western Indian problem for a time. This act forbade the colonial governments to grant land to settlers west of the head waters of rivers flowing into the Atlantic Ocean, and ordered any settlers already west of this line to return to the East. It was hoped that such an act would help the Indians to give up their war-like practices against the English and that the fur trade of the Lake Region would be kept for English traders.

This act of the English home government greatly angered the colonists and, though unable to get title to the land, they began pushing into the Upper Ohio Valley. Wheeling and Pittsburgh soon became permanent settlements. Other settlers in 1768 began settling the Upper Tennessee Valley. In 1774 they began coming into the center of Kentucky, and in the following year, when the Revolution began, Daniel Boone and others cut a road from the Cumberland Gap to Boonesboro. Englishmen thus began their expansion into the West, and the Indians soon were beginning to see their hunting grounds taken from them and turned into farm lands.

In 1774 England passed an act that made the colonies very angry. It was known as the Quebec Act. By this act the colony of Quebec was to extend west to the Mississippi River and south to the Ohio River. This large area took in lands that the colonies claimed as theirs. The Quebec Act said that all Frenchmen living in the area must swear allegiance to the English king but that they could keep their religion, language, and way of life. This act did much to help the French people in Canada keep their French customs.

Chapter VI

REVOLUTION AND CHANGE
(1775-1796)

In 1775, as you know, thirteen of England's American colonies began a war against their mother country. England's other colonies in the West Indies and Canada remained loyal to her. The thirteen colonies tried to win the good will of the Indians from the English, for each side knew that the Indians would be useful allies. However, the colonies failed to lure the Indians away, and most of them remained loyal to England during the struggle.

The Quebec Act of 1774 had made the Lake Region a part of Quebec. Under provision of this act, four local governors were sent into the area of the Lakes and the Illinois country. Col. Henry Hamilton was appointed lieutenant-governor at Detroit and Capt. Patrick Sinclair was appointed to the post at Michilimackinac.

When Colonel Hamilton arrived at Detroit on November 9, 1775, the Revolutionary War had already begun and the task of keeping the Indians loyal to the English cause became the most important one.

At that time Detroit had only a little over 1,300 people, not including the soldiers stationed at the fort. The little fort was in a bad state of repair, so Colonel Hamilton set to work immediately to replace the pickets of the stockade so that it would be in a better condition to hold out against a colonial army and the Indians, should they try to attack the post. At best, it could hardly be called a fort because it had no earthworks or cannon. But, small as it was and located in the vast expanse of forests, lakes, and rivers, it was the headquarters for the Indian Department in the West and for the fur traders and rangers operating in the Great Lakes Region.

Michilimackinac, now Mackinaw City, was only a small settlement of some four hundred people. The stockade there was still just about the same as it had been when it had been captured by the Indians in 1763. Sault Ste. Marie was very small and so was the little post of St. Joseph. The old French fort, Fort Chartres, on the Mississippi had been undercut by the Mississippi River and had been abandoned.

On the Wabash River was the old French settlement of Vincennes, while on the Mississippi River were the settlements of Cahokia and Kaskaskia and the new post of St. Louis that had been started in 1764 in Spanish territory.

To keep the friendship of the Indians, the English gave them many presents such as kettles, tobacco, vermillion, knives, tomahawks, guns, gunpowder, and blankets. Thus Detroit and Michilimackinac became centers of war activity far behind the enemy lines.

Plans were soon under way to use Indians and rangers to strike at the colonies from the West. This the English felt would not only bring war to the colonies but would also weaken the colonial armies because they would have to send soldiers to aid the western settlers against the Indians and rangers. Before long, raiding parties made up of whites and Indians were leaving Detroit to go on raids against the frontier settlements in New York, Pennsylvania, West Virginia, and Kentucky. Other parties left Michilimackinac and went to Montreal to aid the English armies stationed there.

Going south from Detroit through the vast wilderness of Ohio and Kentucky, these raiding parties of English and Indians fell upon the backwoods settlements. Such havoc was done in these raids in the year 1777 that the American settlers came to call that year "the year of the three bloody sevens." Just how many of these raids there were, or where the raiding parties struck, no one will ever know, for many times no one was left to tell of the war whoop that came so suddenly from a silent, midnight forest or of the death and destruction that lay behind as the raiders vanished into the gloomy wilderness. We do know, however, that these war parties, often led by white men like Simon Girty, covered vast areas and brought fear and death to the whole colonial frontier.

Mutilated bodies with scalps gone, smoldering ashes of what had once been cabins on the frontier, tales of horror and massacre—these were the signs that marked the bloody trail of the Indian raiders. Many settlers and their families thus perished from the guns, tomahawks, and scalping knives of the Indian war parties.

Sometimes the settlers' women and children were spared by the Indians and brought as captives to Detroit. Only a few men were that lucky, although Daniel Boone and some of the other frontier Indian fighters whom the Indians admired for their cunning and bravery were brought to Detroit.

Little mercy was shown to the Indians' prisoners as they made their way to Michigan with the returning rangers and Indians. Should one of the prisoners become ill or too tired to continue the journey, he was often speedily put to death with the tomahawk or a club and only the scalp continued the journey.

When a returning war party reached Detroit, the people turned out to greet it. With a savage pride, supported by an inner feeling of justice in fighting for their homeland, the Indians showed their prisoners and the strings of scalps which they had taken from their enemy, the Kentucky "Long Knives." To them, scalps were badges of bravery and signs of loyalty to show to their English brothers.

But what of the women and children who had been forced to come with their Indian captors to Detroit? Sometimes they were forced to become members of an Indian tribe. Many small children thus learned to live like Indians and lived out their lives as brothers of the red men. Sometimes the women and children were bought from the Indians by the settlers living at Detroit. To arouse the feeling of the settlers for the white captives and thus increase their willingness to pay, the Indians often tortured their captives as they paraded them around the streets of the little town.

But the year 1777 was not all bad for the colonies. In the fall of that year General Burgoyne, with his Indian allies, was defeated as he pushed down the Lake Champlain-Hudson River water route. Then too, in that year France joined with the colonies in their fight against England. This move on the part of France, together with letters to the French living in the Northwest, made many of the French settlers willing to quietly side with the colonists against the English.

In order to check the raids on the frontier, the government of Virginia planned a military campaign that would strike at the French settlements in the Illinois country and at Detroit. Such a campaign would carry the war into the Indian country from which the raiders were coming.

George Rogers Clark, a frontiersman, was granted permission to raise a band of volunteers for this campaign. With a war party of only about one hundred seventy-five men, dressed in their frontier coonskin caps, buckskin shirts with fringed edges, leather leggings, and moccasins, he floated down the Ohio River to a point about sixty miles from its mouth. From this point on the Ohio River he marched with his men overland to Kaskaskia. That little French post, and Cahokia, then held by the English, gave up to the Americans without a fight. Vincennes, on the Wabash, also surrendered to Clark's men without a struggle. But by then cold weather was coming on and besides, Clark had far too few men to push on to Detroit where the Indians were then more friendly to the English.

News of Clark's raid on the Illinois settlements soon reached Lieutenant-governor Hamilton. At this time Hamilton was in danger of losing his office because of his actions at Detroit. In hopes of winning back the western posts and keeping in favor with his superiors in Canada, Hamilton quickly gathered a few troops and some Indians and set out for Vincennes by way of Lake Erie, the Maumee River, and the Wabash River. More Indians joined the war party on the way.

Vincennes was easily taken because it was guarded by only a captain and one soldier. Then Hamilton settled down to spend the rest of the winter at Vincennes before moving further against Clark and his men.

But Clark had no desire to wait with his little band until spring came and Hamilton would be able to rally the Indians to help him. So in mid-February, 1779, Clark and his men set out to cross the flooded prairies that lay between him and Hamilton at Vincennes. Hamilton had not suspected such a bold move by Clark and so was caught unprepared and was forced to surrender.

Though it had been Clark's plan to march on against Detroit, he never had the men or supplies which would have been necessary for such a campaign. But small as his force was, it was still large enough to keep the English and Indians from driving him from the posts he had already taken.

The year 1778 was a busy one at Detroit. Not only had it seen Hamilton's party off to Vincennes, but also several raiding parties, with which a number of Frenchmen were "ordered to go," had left the post to attack the frontier. In that summer also the Indians captured Daniel Boone and Simon Kenton and brought them with other prisoners to Detroit. Simon Kenton escaped while at Detroit and made his way back to Kentucky. Although a large reward was offered for Daniel Boone, the Indians would not release him to the English. He was taken back south to Chillicothe, Ohio, where, upon learning that the Indians planned an attack upon Boonesboro, he escaped and reached it in time to warn the settlers.

Hamilton had no sooner left for Vincennes than Captain Lernoult, then in command at Detroit, began the building of a new fort on the spot where the Detroit post office now stands. The old palisade by the river was much in need of repair, and if Clark and his frontier fighters had reached Detroit and placed even small cannon on the higher ground overlooking the old palisade, there would have been no way for the English to defend the town. For this reason, settlers, soldiers, and prisoners were all put to work to build a new fort and to dig a moat which was to surround the fort on all sides.

When finished, the fort occupied the higher ground and a picket fence or palisade, somewhat like a large V, ran down from it to the water's edge and enclosed the old village of Detroit, the cemetery, the parade ground, and the gardens of the garrison.*

On May 8, 1779, Spain joined France and the colonies in their war against England. At Detroit work was still being pushed on the building of Fort Lernoult. On October 4, 1779, Patrick Sinclair, after much delay, arrived at Michilimackinac to take up his post as lieutenant-governor in that area. The English post at that time was still on the south side of the straits where a new palisade had been built to replace the one destroyed by the Indians in 1763. It stood close, too close, to the sandy shore of the Straits of Mackinac. As it had no cannons, its only defenses were small arms and a vast, spreading wilderness, in which lived savage Indians and which any raiding party of Americans must cross before reaching the fort.

Sinclair, therefore, during the same fall in which he arrived at

Old Fort Mackinac

*See page 98.

Michilimackinac, began work upon a new and better fort on Mackinac Island. To build a fort so far back in the wilderness was no small task. Laborers were always scarce, and skilled workmen were even harder to find. But Sinclair kept his men building the fort all through the year of 1780. In the summer of 1781 the Indians deeded Mackinac Island to the English for $12,500. The old post at Mackinaw City was abandoned and the garrison was moved over to the new fort on Mackinac Island. The general plan of the new fort was just about the same as it appears to tourists visiting the island today. The fort was to be known as Fort Mackinac, but the post was still to be known as Michilimackinac. This name it kept until the Americans occupied the island in 1796, and then both the fort and the post became known as Mackinac.

On January 1, 1781, a small party of Spanish and French with some Indian allies made their way across what is now Illinois and Indiana to the little fort at St. Joseph (now Niles, Michigan). This advance was made through country that was inhabited by Indians who had been loyal to England but whose loyalty had weakened after Clark had captured the French settlements in Illinois. The little post of St. Joseph quickly fell to the raiders. The Spanish flag flew from the fort for a few hours. Then the post was looted and burned by the raiders. After spending a few days at the post, the Spanish raiders went back to St. Louis carrying with them the captured English flag. The little post of St. Joseph was not rebuilt.

Indian raids continued through 1781 and 1782 and border fighting took place in what is now Ohio and Kentucky, but the Revolutionary War was coming to a close. The colonies, together with their European allies, were winning the long struggle.

In March, 1781, when the Articles of Confederation went into effect, the colonies which had claims to western land gave up their claims and turned the entire land area over to the new confederation government. Thus the vast area lying between the Appalachian Mountains and the Mississippi River became the possession of the new Continental Congress. From it new states were to be formed that later would join the union of states then fighting against England.

In Ohio at this time there lived a tribe of Delaware Indians. These Indians are known to us today as the Moravian Indians because of the work some Moravian missionaries did to convert them to Christianity. When the war began, these Indians, because of their Christian teaching, did not wish to take either side in the struggle. Unfortunately for them their homeland lay along the path of the raiding parties from Detroit. Both sides began to mistrust these Indians and wish them out of the way.

In 1782 a group of Virginians cruelly killed several of these Indians after taking their arms away from them and promising to take them to safety. The rest fled to Detroit and the protection of the English. Until the war was over these Moravian Indians lived on the banks of the Clinton River near Mt. Clemens. Here they built the first Protestant church in Michigan. When the war was over, some of these Indians returned to their homeland in Ohio. Others, still fearing the Kentucky "Long Knives," crossed over to Canada and founded the settlement of Fairfield on the banks of the River Thames. Many of their descendants still live in that area.

By 1783, when peace was made between England and the thirteen American colonies, England was sick to death of the war. Power politics soon entered the peace negotiations and England tried

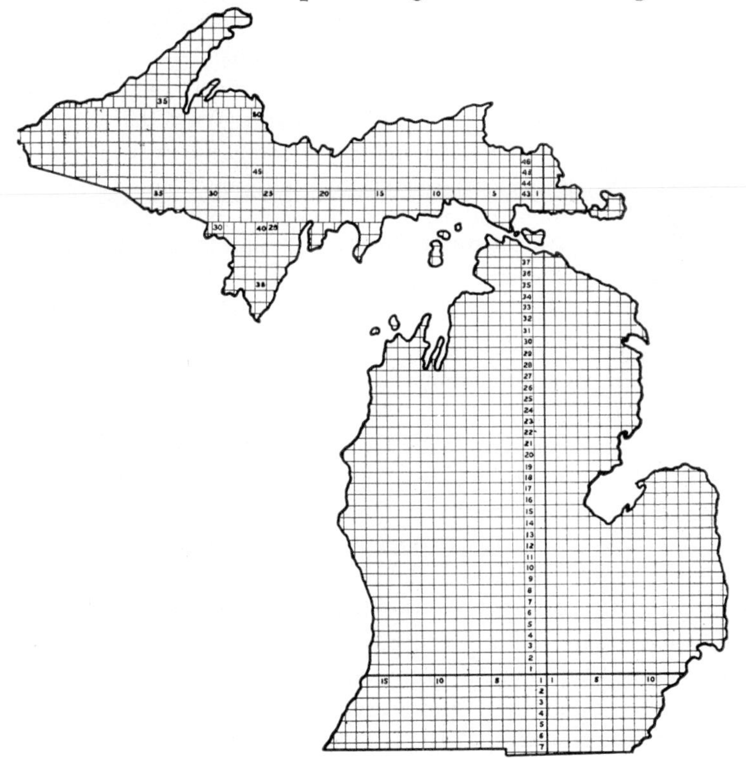

Map showing congressional, or geographical, townships

to keep some friendship with her colonies even if it meant being indifferent to her Canadian colony which had no representative at the conference. At first the American delegates asked for all of Canada to the Arctic Ocean but later two northern boundaries were considered in earnest. One proposed boundary was to begin at the St. Croix River and run to the height of land and then west along the forty-fifth parallel to the Mississippi River. The second was to follow a middle line through the Great Lakes and connecting waters to the Lake of the Woods, and then west to the Mississippi River. This later line was accepted as being a little more definite though many years were to pass before a definite boundary line was finally settled between Canada and the United States.

In accepting this line much of what had been New France was lost to the St. Lawrence settlements. England seems to have forgotten that just a few years before, in the Quebec Act, she had given the land north of the Ohio River and east of the Mississippi to Canada and that Canada needed this area for her economic development. Also England seems to have forgotten that Canada had been loyal to her during the war. In so doing England ruined the Montreal fur trade and also abandoned the Indians in the West that had fought for both England and their homeland during the war. Detroit and Mackinac had not been conquered by the Americans. These factors were seen soon after the peace was signed and a few years were still to pass before England finally turned the Great Lakes area over to the Americans.

Although England still had her soldiers stationed in the Northwest, the Continental Congress went ahead with plans for the sale of the land and the settlement of the area.

In order to give each settler who moved into the Northwest Territory a clear title to his land, the Continental Congress in 1785 passed the Grayson Land Ordinance. This Ordinance made a plan for a general land survey of the entire area. According to it, all the Northwest Territory was to be divided into congressional townships each six miles square. This would make a map of the area look somewhat like a huge checkerboard. In Michigan these squares, called congressional, or geographical, townships, were to be measured east and west from a prime meridian that runs north and south through the state at 84 degrees, 22 minutes, and 24 seconds west longitude. They were to be numbered north and south of a base line that now forms the Eight Mile Road, or the northern boundary of Wayne County, and

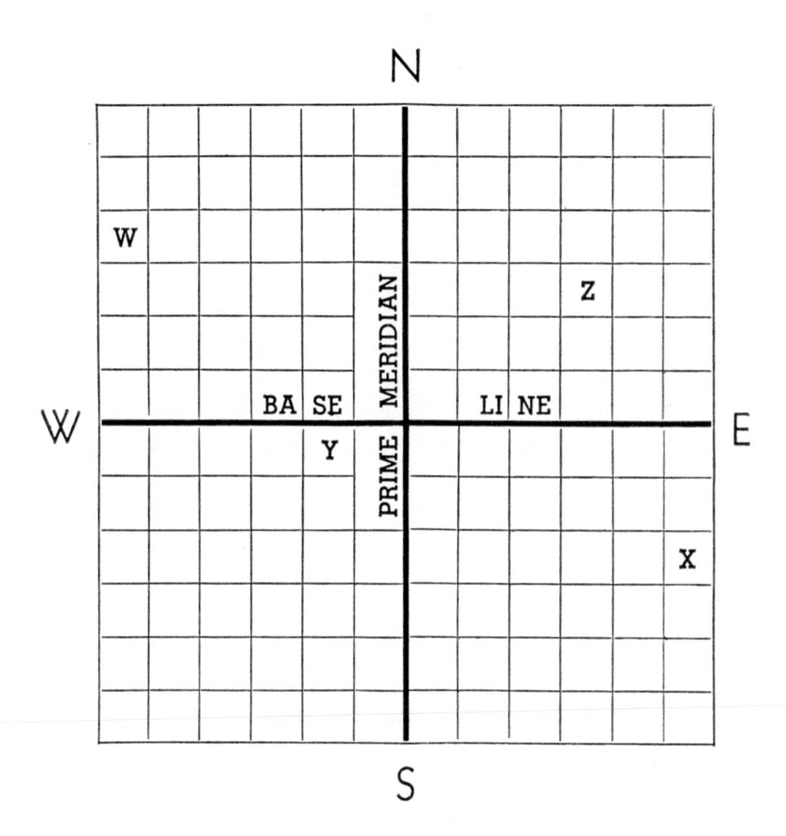

is located at 42 degrees, 26 minutes, and 30 seconds north latitude. If you look at a map of Michigan you will see that this line forms the northern boundary of the second row of counties.

If a farmer settled on land in township W his title would be described as being in township 4 North, Range 6 West. No other township in the state can have this same location. Township X would be described as 3 South, Range 6 East; Y as 1 South, Range 2 West; Z as 3 North, Range 4 East.

To locate a township was well but a township six miles square in size contains 36 square miles and many acres of land—23,040 in all. The early settler in the West grew farm produce and usually forty or eighty acres of land was all that a man could work with the agricultural tools then to be had.

In order to locate more specifically these little pieces of land each township was again divided into thirty-six smaller parts like a smaller checkerboard in this manner:

6	5	4	3	2	1
7	8	9	10	11	12
18	17	16	15	14	13
19	20	21	22	23	24
30	29	28	27	26	25
31	32	33	34	35	36

A Congressional Township

Each township is six miles square and contains thirty-six square miles called sections. These sections are numbered like the sections shown above.

Thus the entire Northwest Territory was divided into areas of one mile square. Each of these square mile blocks is called a section. It takes thirty-six of these sections to make one township such as W, X, Y, and Z, or any other township in the state. Each of these sections contains 640 acres of land, and can be divided in the following manner to locate smaller pieces of land.

A is described as N. ½ of Section (1, 2, 10, 36) or any other section of a definite township and contains 320 acres more or less.
B is described as N. ½ of the SW.¼ (80 acres more or less).
C is described as S. ½ of the SW. ¼ (80 acres more or less).
D is described as NW. ¼ of the SE. ¼ (40 acres more or less).
E is described as NE. ¼ of the SE. ¼ (40 acres more or less).
F is described as N. ½ of the SE. ¼ of the SE. ¼ (20 acres more or less).
G is described as SW. ¼ of the SE. ¼ of the SE. ¼ (10 acres more or less).

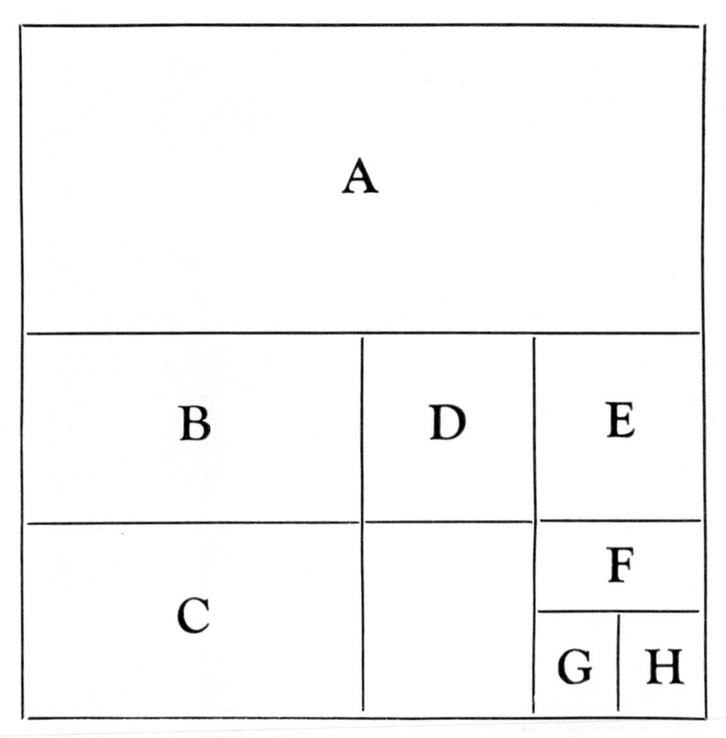

H is described as SE. 1/4 of the SE. 1/4 of the SE. 1/4 (10 acres more or less).

Let us suppose that this section drawn is section 21 of Township 4 North, Range 5 West. The title to the 320 acres marked A would read: north 1/2 of section 21, township 4 North, Range 5 West and contains 320 acres more or less.

This would give a settler who chose that area a definite title to his land that could not be duplicated by any other settler coming into the region. The system of land survey provided by the Grayson Land Ordinance of 1785 was much better than the one then in use in the East, for it made it possible to exactly locate land anywhere in the area.

According to this ordinance the land was to be sold for one dollar an acre, but the purchaser must buy at least one square mile of land or six hundred forty acres. Few settlers had the six hundred forty dollars in cash to spend for western land. If they possessed that amount of money there was little need in their having to find a new home for themselves in the wilderness. Speculators thus became the

Courtesy Burton Historical Collection

Detroit—July 24, 1794

principal land buyers. They bought the best land in large amounts and after the price had advanced resold it in smaller parcels to the incoming settlers.

Although this was the general system of land survey and title granting, some areas of the state were already claimed by the older practice of "meets and bounds." Such areas as those that had been granted by the French and English before the Americans came were not granted under the land survey system, but rather described by natural markers such as a river, a tree, a large stone or other objects.

Then, too, some of the early traders had secured titles to lands from Indian chiefs and friendly tribes. Many of these titles were written deeds bearing the totems of the Indians then living in the area. These private claims did much in early days to confuse treaty making and the granting of land to new purchasers.

In 1787 the Continental Congress, in one of its last acts, passed what has since come to be known as the "Ordinance of 1787" to provide a government for the area north of the Ohio and east of the Mississippi River. Under the ordinance, the government of the territory was to be carried on by a governor, a secretary, and three judges. Later the area was to be divided into states and the people were to be allowed to carry on their own government. The Ordinance of 1787 contained six very important articles. They provided for the area: (1) freedom of worship; (2) a bill of rights; (3) "religion, morality, and knowledge being necessary to good government and the happiness of mankind, schools and the means of education shall forever be encouraged"; (4) all states formed from the area were to remain in the union as part of the United States; (5) not less than three states nor more than five were to be made from the area; and (6) slavery and involuntary servitude were not to be allowed in the territory or any of the states made from it except as a punishment for crime.

Settlers were soon coming over the mountains to Wheeling, West Virginia, and from there floating down the Ohio on flatboats to take up new homesteads in the Northwest Territory. Soon the Ohio Valley and the valleys of the streams flowing into the Ohio River were covered with settlements. However, northern Ohio and Michigan had few settlers because there was no way for them to send their goods to market. Then, too, the Indians of the area were not friendly at that time, and their lands had not yet been taken from them by treaty.

But England, too, had plans of civil government for the area. In

1788 the District of Hesse was created. This included all the area west, northwest, and southwest of Long Point on Lake Erie.

In 1791 the Canadian Constitutional Act divided the old province of Quebec into two parts along the Ottawa River, thus separating the older French settlers from the new Loyalists who had moved into the area north of Lake Erie and Lake Ontario. Lower Canada, still known as Quebec, contained the major part of the French settlers, while Upper Canada, later called Ontario, contained the English Loyalists. In 1792 Detroit had her first popular election and chose representatives to the Parliment of Upper Canada.

Meanwhile the new constitution of the United States of America had come into being and George Washington had become president in 1789. This new and better government was interested in its claims to western land, and campaigns against the Indians were soon under-way. Generals Harmar and St. Clair both led unsuccessful expeditions into the Ohio country. Then the command fell to Gen. Anthony Wayne. After careful preparation Wayne pushed into northern Ohio and in 1794 defeated the Indians under Little Turtle in the battle of Fallen Timbers in the Maumee Valley not far from Toledo, Ohio. Although this battle was fought in Ohio, it was so near the boundary line and had so much effect on the later development of Michigan that one can almost call it a Michigan battle.

In 1795 a treaty was signed by the Indians which gave the Americans the claim to the post at Detroit together with a strip of land six miles in width, from Lake Erie on the south to Lake St. Clair on the north; Mackinac Island; a small tract of land at the northern tip of the Lower Peninsula; and the county about St. Ignace in the Upper Peninsula.

Chapter VII

THE FIRST YEARS OF AMERICAN RULE
(1796-1815)

As soon as Jay's Treaty was signed with England in 1795, the Americans sent troops to occupy the forts in the Northwest Territory. Stopping at Monroe, the Americans raised the first American flag to fly over Michigan. The following day, July 11, 1796, two boats, the "Weazell" and the "Swan," carrying sixty-five United States soldiers and Captain Moses Porter, docked at the foot of what is now Griswold Street in Detroit. The American soldiers then marched up to Fort Lernoult and replaced the English garrison. Two days later Col. John Francis Hamtramck came with some five hundred more soldiers. The following month General Wayne also arrived in Detroit.

The Americans changed the name of Fort Lernoult to Fort Shelby. The English flag no longer floated over the post; in its place now was seen the Stars and Stripes, the flag of the new United States of America.

Up to the year 1796, the Detroit area on both sides of the Detroit River had always been one single community, but the coming of the Americans now made the Detroit River an international boundary line. Separate communities began to develop on each side of the river. The English had to move to the other side of the river and build a new fort there. For the location of their new fort the English chose a spot on the Canadian side near the mouth of the Detroit River not far from Lake Erie.

Fort Malden, as the new fort was called, was to have five sides, bastions, a dry moat, and a naval yard. Part of the buildings were made at Detroit and then, in sections, floated down the Detroit River to the new fort. Besides this, the English took all the timbers then in the navy yard, some 2,000 pickets, and all of their supplies at Detroit.

For some time there was a friendly feeling between the two forts. Sometimes the commanders even loaned supplies to each other. Both

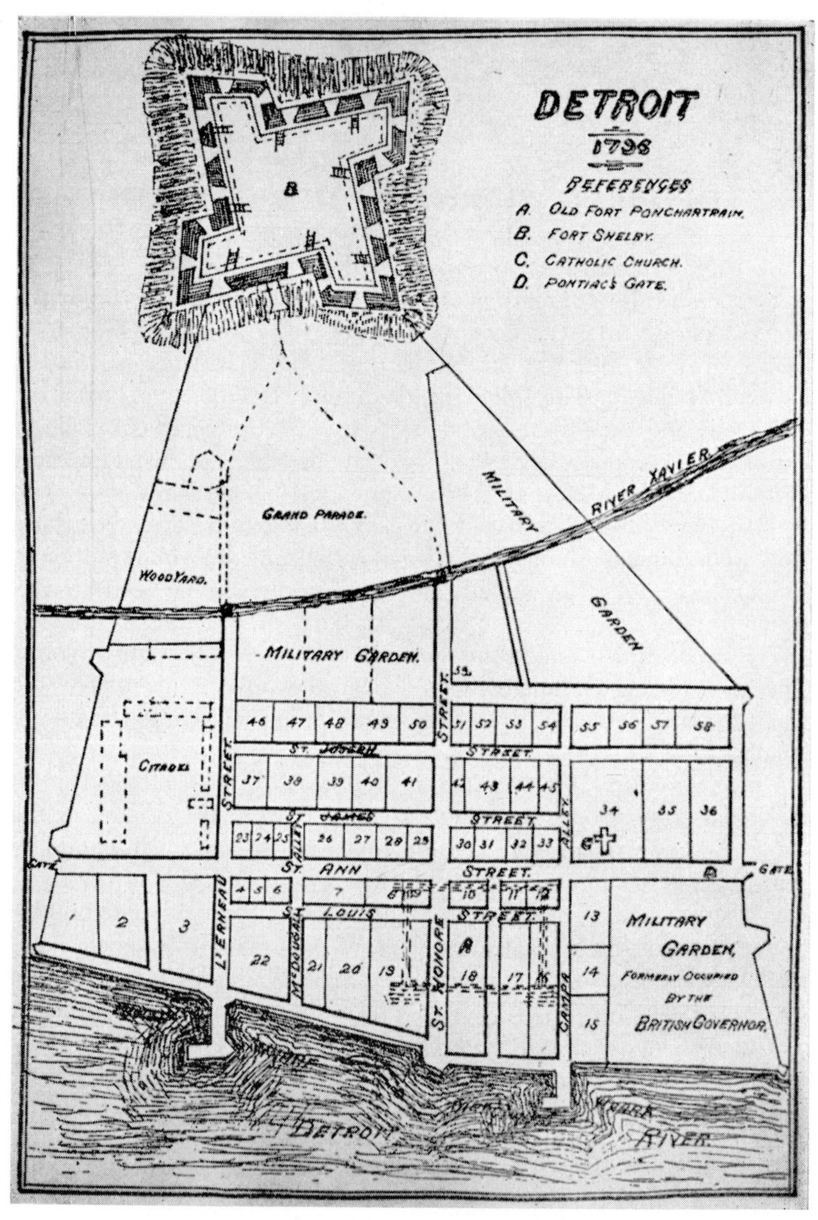

Courtesy Burton Historical Collection

Ruins of bastion and moat at Fort Malden (1929)

the English and the Americans tried to win the friendship of the Indians who made social calls at both forts to collect the free gifts of each government.

In 1796, the year that the Americans came to Detroit, Detroit was still a small French frontier village. Most of the people living there were descendants of the early trappers and settlers. The little log houses were now old and weathered. Men and animals still walked in the muddy, narrow streets that had been laid out by Cadillac nearly one hundred years before. To the north, on the second rise of ground, stood Fort Lernoult which the English had built during the Revolutionary War. This fort and its garrison were the main features of the little frontier post. A wooden picket palisade ran down from the fort like a large V spreading out from the fort to enclose two sides of the village. Another palisade ran along the waterfront just below West Jefferson Avenue. Several gates opened into the palisade. Most of the business of trading and shipping was done near the river in the old French village. French farm houses sat along both sides of the river. The little ribbon farms behind the houses pushed back only a short way from the river. Just beyond the farm land, the spreading forest began. No roads ran into the heavy stands of hickory and white oak; only Indian trails led into the vast forest that reached out in all directions. Indians could always be seen in the village or encamped in the nearby forest.

The fort on Mackinac Island was occupied by Americans in the same year as the fort at Detroit. Michilimackinac at this time had a population of about five hundred people. They were mostly Canadian French and half-breeds who fished, farmed, and traded with the Indians. The English occupation had had very little effect upon the people living there. When the English left the fort on Mackinac Island, they built a new one on St. Joseph's Island.

One of the first tasks of the Americans was to start a new government for the area. On August 15, 1796, the first county in the area, Wayne County, was formed. The new county included all the area of what is now Michigan and parts of Wisconsin, Illinois, Indiana, and Ohio. Soon a court system was organized.

Some of the people then living at Detroit did not think they would like to live under the new government of the Americans, so they moved across the river and settled on land which the English government gave them. Thus Detroit lost part of its population.

In December, 1798, the people of Detroit elected three men to represent Wayne County in the Legislative Assembly of the Northwest Territory which at that time was meeting at Cincinnati, Ohio.

In 1800 the Northwest Territory was divided into two parts by a line which ran between what is now Ohio and Indiana and which continued northward through Michigan. The Lower Peninsula was thus cut in half. The eastern part remained as a part of the Northwest Territory but the western half and nearly all the Upper Peninsula went to the newly created Territory of Indiana. This change had little effect on the people living in Michigan at the time as most of them lived in the Detroit area. In 1802 the Legislative Assembly for the Northwest Territory passed an act making Detroit a town. This act gave to the people of Detroit the right to choose a board of five trustees and other town officials to regulate local affairs.

During these years many settlers came into the Ohio Valley to start new farms and villages. Soon there were enough people living in what is now the state of Ohio to let the area qualify for statehood, so in 1803 the state of Ohio was formed. Unfortunately, Ohio's northern boundary was not settled at this time, and later Michigan and Ohio were to have a dispute as to just where this boundary line was to be. When Ohio was made a state, all of Michigan was placed under the Territory of Indiana.

The people of Michigan did not like this. The new capital was at Vincennes, and it placed them once again back under the rule of a governor and judges. What is more, Vincennes was far away to the southwest and was difficult to reach in a time of canoe and snowshoe travel.

Fortunately for the people of Michigan, Congress created a new territory called Michigan Territory in 1805. The southern boundary of the new territory was to be an east-west line starting at the most southerly point of Lake Michigan and running due east to Lake Erie. All of the Lower Peninsula and the eastern part of the Upper Peninsula were included in the new territory. Detroit became the capital on July 1, 1805. An old Revolutionary War soldier, Gen. William Hull, was chosen to be the first governor of the new Michigan Territory. He reached Detroit in July, 1805, and found the little town in ashes.

The old town of Detroit had disappeared in one day. The day of June 11, 1805, was a tragic one for Detroit. It was one of those windy June mornings in late spring. A baker named John Harvey needed to get some flour from the grist mill on May's Creek, located near the place where the New York Central depot now stands. Going to his stable, he hitched his little French pony to a small two-wheeled cart. Before climbing upon the seat, he stopped to knock the ashes from his pipe because the wind was blowing sparks from it into his face. As the lighted tobacco dropped from the pipe, it was caught by the strong wind and blown through the open doorway and into the barn. There it was scattered among some dry hay which it quickly caught on fire. Before Harvey could put the fire out, the whole pile of hay was a roaring blaze. The cry of "fire, fire" rang through the town. Men and boys seized buckets and axes to stop the fire but it kept on spreading before the strong wind. The century-old timbers of the early French settlement were too dry to be saved.

By three o'clock in the afternoon what had once been houses were but smoldering remains with gaunt, smoke-blackened chimneys standing among the glowing embers. Here and there a mother could be seen gathering her children about her and watching sadly over what few household things they had been able to snatch from their little cabin before it was burned by the advancing fire. Fortunately the homes of the settlers along the river had not caught fire. Many of the homeless people from Detroit soon found shelter there among their friends or relatives. Not only their homes but also their food had perished. Father Gabriel Richard, then pastor of Ste. Anne's Church, was quick to see the need of the people. Under his leadership canoes were sent up and down the river to call on the farmers for supplies such as corn meal, eggs, and milk.

Old Detroit with its little cabins had vanished. Would it ever be rebuilt? Some of the settlers left and went south to Ohio and took up farms there. The land was good and the fear of the Indians in that region was now almost gone. Yet hardly had the fire ceased before some people were talking of a new and better city to be built upon the charred ruins of the old. Judge Woodward drew up the plans for the new city. He made his plans similar to those of the city of Washington, D.C., which was then being built as the nation's capital. The city was to be laid out in a manner which was to be a combination of the checkerboard and spider web plans. Had the plans of Judge Woodward been carefully followed, downtown Detroit would today have wide streets. But the men of his day could not see any sense in making the streets of their little village so wide.

After the lots of the new city had been surveyed by Thomas Smith, they were given out by lot to those who had owned property in the old town.

Before settlers could come into Michigan to start new homes more land had to be secured from the Indians. In November, 1807, Governor General William Hull held a meeting at Detroit with chiefs and warriors of the Pottawattomies, Wyandottes, Chippewas, and Ottawas. At this meeting a treaty, known as the Treaty of Detroit, was signed with the Indians. In it the Indians agreed to give up more land in southeastern Michigan. A western line was run due north from a point about twenty miles west of the western end of Lake Erie to the southern end of Lake Huron. From this point the line ran northeast to White Rock on Lake Huron. For this land the Indians were to receive ten thousand dollars cash and two thousand four hundred dollars each year thereafter.

Not many years after this, Detroit and Michigan became once again the center of military activity. Europe was being torn by the cruel wars of Napoleon. For years the new United States had remained out of the European struggle, but at last it was drawn into the war on the side of France against England.

To the aid of the English cause in America came a famous Indian warrior and chieftain named Tecumseh. Tecumseh was a chief of the Shawnee Indians and lived not far from where Springfield, Ohio, now stands. Tecumseh was glad to aid the English against the United States. He looked upon the English as the friends of the Indians, for they had not taken the hunting grounds from his Indian people. To him the Americans, as the people of the United States now began to be called, were enemies. It was they who were ever pushing farther and farther into the West and taking the land from the Indians and driving away the game.

Tecumseh, like Pontiac before him, was a good speaker and a great leader of his Indian people. In reply to his messengers, bands of Indians came to his wigwam to talk with him and make plans against the Americans. Some of these bands also visited Fort Malden on the Detroit River. The British gave the Indians many presents and encouraged the Indians to strike against the Americans. The hatreds born in the last war were not yet dead, and the fact that the Astor Fur Company, which had been started in 1809 and was using Mackinac Island as its center of trade, was taking much business from the English fur companies kept alive the feeling of bitterness.

Gradually the Indian menace in the West grew stronger and stronger. Large bands of hostile Indians began to gather around the frontier posts as they had done under the leadership of Pontiac. The people of the West became fearful of an Indian plot and asked Congress to come to their aid by sending more soldiers to protect them.

In reply to this hostile attitude of the Indians, General Harrison advanced with an army of men into the region and on November 7, 1811, defeated the Indians in the battle of Tippecanoe. Although Tecumseh was not present at the battle, his spirit was aroused to still greater bitterness against the Americans. In the year following the opening of the War of 1812, the Indians joined themselves to the English and again fell upon the frontier American settlements.

General Hull was then governor of Michigan Territory. Fearing a united English and Indian attack upon the western posts, he went to Washington to secure more military aid for the territory. This was granted to him, and on June 1, 1812, with about twelve hundred soldiers, he began the long march through the wilderness from Dayton, Ohio, to Detroit.

There was no road from Ohio to Michigan at that time, so a road across the great swamps of northern Ohio had to be made. To do this meant the clearing of a roadway and the building of bridges across many streams.

When the party reached the mouth of the Maumee River near the place where Toledo now stands, their supplies were put on a little schooner named the "Cuyahoga" which, with another smaller vessel, was sent on ahead to the fort at Detroit. When the little vessels came into the channel of the Detroit River opposite Fort Malden, they were stopped by the British and taken as prizes of war along with Hull's supplies which were on board.

Meanwhile Hull, who had not yet learned that war had been declared, pushed on to the Raisin River. While building a bridge so that his army might cross the river, General Hull learned of the fate of his boats and supplies, and he also learned that war with England had been declared.

Though the English and Indians knew that war had been declared and that Hull was advancing on Detroit with soldiers, they did not attack him. When the American soldiers reached Detroit, they urged their commander to cross the river and attack Fort Malden and recapture the boats and supplies. General Hull, however, feared to make such an attack. At last, on July 12, in response to repeated urging, he sent a large force of men across the river to the Canadian side as though an attack on Fort Malden were to be made.

Had Hull made a strong attack on Fort Malden, the fort would probably have fallen because there were then few men there to defend it. Hull, however, hesitated. He sent out a scouting party, captured a few supplies, and then recrossed the river to the American fort.

Hull then received word that Captain Henry Brush was on the way to Detroit with two hundred and thirty men, one hundred head of cattle, and other needed supplies, and that he was being attacked near the Raisin River by Tecumseh and his Indian allies. Col. Thomas Van Horne was sent with a force of two hundred men to Brush's aid. While going down the river road, two of his scouts were surprised and scalped near Trenton. A little farther on, the whole relief party walked into an ambush at Brownstown. Van Horne slowly retreated toward the fort. Although he asked for aid, none was sent to him.

While Hull dallied at Detroit, the British and Indians were active. News of the declaration of war had been sent to the English commander on St. Joseph's Island, and he at once gathered a force of nearly one thousand men and prepared to attack the fort on Mackinac Island, which was then held by the Americans. Lieut. Porter Hanks was at that time the American commander of the fort. Hanks and his men did not yet know that war between England and the United States had been declared. They awoke at sunrise on July 17, 1812, to the sharp report of a cannon being fired. The startled American garrison was taken by surprise. During the night the English had landed on the north side of Mackinac Island at a place since known as

"British Landing," and had placed their guns on the north side of the fort so they could shoot down into it. All was now in readiness for their attack upon the fort, but no attack was made. Hanks, so greatly outnumbered, was forced to surrender. Thus the post on Mackinac Island again passed into the hands of the English.

At Detroit things changed little. Six hundred fifty French Canadians joined Hull against the English but still no attack was made, for Hull imagined the English and Indians to be far stronger than they were. A party was at last sent from the fort to the aid of Brush and his men. At Brownstown they defeated a party of English militia and a band of Indians under Tecumseh.

Although General Hull had by far the larger force, he still delayed attacking Fort Malden. Meanwhile General Brock had made his way from Fort Niagara to Fort Malden with three hundred militiamen and thirty English soldiers. No sooner had General Brock arrived at Fort Malden than he decided to attack Detroit, although his forces were much smaller than those under the command of General Hull. On the day after his arrival General Brock advanced up the Canadian side of the river to Sandwich, Ontario, across the river from Detroit. There General Brock placed his cannon in a basement which had been dug for a new house and began firing at the American fort across the river.

In the morning of the following day the English crossed the river and began to advance upon Detroit. Halting outside, Brock sent a messenger to General Hull demanding Detroit's surrender.

Although General Hull had more men than the English had, he ordered his outposts to retreat into the fort. Without asking advice from anyone, Hull ordered the American flag lowered and a white tablecloth raised as the sign of his surrender.

The soldiers, the people, and the French allies were all very angry with this sudden action of General Hull. In the fort at that time there were forty barrels of powder, hundreds of rounds of ammunition, one hundred thousand ball cartridges, twenty-four thousand stands of arms, and five cannons. Yet not a shot was fired.

General Hull was later tried at Albany. Although he was declared innocent of treason, the court found him guilty of other charges that were placed against him and General Hull was sentenced to be shot. This order, however, was not carried out, for he was later pardoned by the President because of his services during the Revolutionary War.

Where the city of Chicago now stands there then stood a little fort named Fort Dearborn. General Hull ordered Captain Heald to abandon the post and to go with the other Americans to Fort Wayne, Indiana. When hostile Indians began gathering around the post, Captain Heald told them that he was going to leave and that the Indians could have everything in the fort. The night before he left the post, Captain Heald had the powder of the fort emptied into the creek and the liquor poured into the well. The Pottawattomie Indians discovered this trickery of Captain Heald when they went to the river the next morning. They, however, kept their anger to themselves.

Captain Heald with the soldiers and settlers then set out on the road to Fort Wayne. They had gone only a little way along the lake shore when they were attacked by the enraged Pottawattomies led by Shavehead and other chiefs. Nearly all the Americans were killed and scalped. Thus the Great Lakes Region again passed into the hands of the English. General Brock, now in command of Detroit, made it his headquarters in place of Fort Malden. Soon Colonel Henry Proctor was made civil governor.

No sooner had the Americans lost the Lake Region than they began preparing for its recapture. Men from Kentucky and Ohio joined General Harrison. A series of raids on the Indian settlements was soon begun. When spring came in 1813, General Harrison was at Sandusky, Ohio, ready to advance into the region of Michigan.

In January, General Harrison sent Colonels Lewis and Allen with five hundred men to Frenchtown (Monroe) to give protection to the people living there. These men advanced upon Frenchtown on the ice that covered the swamps south of it. When they reached the stockade, they drove the British from it and took over the town. Soon Lewis and Allen were joined by General Winchester and two hundred fifty other men.

At that time the Detroit River was frozen over and English soldiers from Fort Malden with their Indian allies could easily cross on the ice and make an attack upon Frenchtown. General Winchester was warned by the Navarres, a French family then living at Frenchtown, that the English were crossing on the ice and soon would attack the Americans, but General Winchester paid no attention to the friendly warning of his French friends.

The night of January 23, 1813, was bitter cold. The American sentries at Frenchtown grew lax and gathered around their fires to warm themselves and sleep. When morning came, the British, who had worked through the wintry night, were ready for action. Their guns had been placed within three hundred yards of the American position. General Winchester was aroused from his sleep in the Navarre home. He hurried, half-dressed, to the fort and fell an easy prisoner to the English and Indians. Two Kentucky Indian fighters, Graves and Madison, in spite of General Winchester's surrender, continued to hold their ground against the surprise attack of the English and Indians. They surrendered only when Colonel Proctor promised that there would be no massacre or violence from the Indians.

The able-bodied prisoners were then lined up and made ready for the march across the frozen river to Fort Malden. The wounded were to be left behind in the town. Some of them were taken into private homes, but the greater part were placed in two large buildings which were used at that time for storing furs.

Monument marking the massacre at the River Raisin (1929)

Soon after the English and Indians left Frenchtown with their prisoners they came to Stony Creek. There Colonel Proctor kept the promise he had made to his Indian allies. A barrel of rum was smashed open. Most of the Indians stayed behind and started drinking. As the fiery rum in the barrel grew less and less, the Indians' spirit for bloodshed rose. A few Indians followed the English across the ice and quickly killed and scalped any of the American prisoners who fell behind the main party.

Most of the Indians returned to Frenchtown. In spite of angry words from some of their leaders, who tried to guard the wounded Americans, they began their bloody work since known in American history as the Massacre at the River Raisin.

A few of the less seriously wounded Americans had left the warehouses. These were seized, killed, and scalped. In their eagerness for American scalps the Indians set fire to the buildings to drive out the wounded Americans. Driven out by the increasing heat, the wounded men made their way through the door only to be killed and scalped and to have their bodies thrown back into the flames.

Meanwhile the English with their prisoners arrived at Fort Malden. There the Americans were turned into the open stockade of the fort and left to suffer in the bitter January weather.

News of the terrible happenings at Frenchtown soon reached Detroit. Everyone was shocked to learn of the cruel neglect on the part of Colonel Proctor. Fearing the prisoners at Fort Malden would be turned over to the Indians, a party from Detroit made its way to Fort Malden and asked if the prisoners could be ransomed from their captors. Thirty prisoners were brought out by the Indians and four were quickly killed to increase the bidding. The rest of the prisoners' lives were spared when money and presents were given to the Indians.

Other battles were fought in northern Ohio and more prisoners were brought to Detroit by the Indians. To save them from cruel torture, the people bought them from the Indians, usually paying between ten dollars and eighty dollars for each. Before long, some of the people at Detroit had spent all they possessed. However, they still tried to save the lives of the wretched prisoners by offering to the Indians blankets and other articles from their homes. This action on the part of the people at Detroit angered Colonel Proctor, and he had some of the leading persons driven from the country.

The Massacre at the River Raisin aroused the Americans to a greater war spirit. "Remember the Raisin" became their battle cry. Frontiersmen flocked to General Harrison to help rid the land of the Indians and their savage ways. But the Americans could not have hoped to win the Lake Region again as long as the Great Lakes were controlled by British boats. They knew that American boats must be built for use upon the lakes and a naval battle won. This would allow the Americans to better transport supplies and weaken England's strength in the region.

Where Erie, Pennsylvania, now stands, the Americans began the building of some boats in the spring of 1813. The work was pushed as rapidly as possible. Commodore Oliver Hazard Perry, of Rhode Island, was sent to take command of the little fleet which had been quickly made from unseasoned timbers. Slipping out of the harbor where the boats had been built, Commodore Perry sailed his boats to the western end of Lake Erie. Here he met General Harrison. Together the two made plans for a naval victory that would bring the Great Lakes under American control.

Making his headquarters at Put-in-Bay on Lake Erie, Perry planned and waited for the English attack that he knew must soon come.

On the morning of September 10, 1813, the British boats under Captain Barclay sailed away from Fort Malden and down across Lake Erie to attack the new American fleet commanded by Commodore Perry. Tecumseh and other Englishmen and Indians interested in the success of the English fleet followed the English boats along the Canadian shore as far as they could until they reached the mouth of the Detroit River. There they stood and watched the little boats of the English sail slowly south upon the surface of the lake until even the sails finally disappeared from sight. In the early afternoon the roar of guns could be heard from across the water. Anxiously Tecumseh and the others waited, watched, and hoped as they stood there on the shore. Would the English fleet return or would the Americans win the victory?

The coming of the English fleet was reported to Commodore Perry by an American lookout. Everything was in readiness, so Commodore Perry sailed out to give battle to the English squadron. The boats moved slowly toward each other, for there was little wind on the lake that day. For some time the two fleets sat watching each other just out of gunshot. A little after twelve o'clock the American boats came within the longer range of the English guns. Soon the battle was on in earnest.

About two-thirty that afternoon Commodore Perry left his flagship, the "Lawrence," which had been badly damaged, and was rowed in a small open boat to the "Niagara," which up until that time had taken little part in the battle. A slight change of wind favored the Americans and the boats closed in for final action. Although the English guns were of longer range, the American guns were heavier and so, as the boats came closer together, the American guns raked the English boats with a heavy fire. The English were forced to surrender. Commodore Perry treated the wounded British and prisoners with all the courtesy possible. He also sent a message to

General Harrison which said, "We have met the enemy and they are ours; two ships, two brigs, one schooner, and one sloop."

As the day closed, hope dropped in the hearts of Tecumseh and the others who were still watching from the Canadian shore. The distant roar of the guns had ceased, but no boats came sailing back from out upon the lake. Each knew what had happened without having to be told. The Americans had become the masters of the lakes.

Now that the Americans controlled the lakes, Colonel Proctor knew he could no longer hold Fort Malden. Therefore he quickly abandoned it and set out by land for Fort Niagara. This action on the part of Colonel Proctor angered Tecumseh, and he upbraided Colonel Proctor, saying that he could at least have left the arms and supplies for the Indians if he did not have the courage to stay and fight for his Indian allies.

General Harrison made use of his opportunity. The little fleet carried the Americans to the Canadian side on September 27. They advanced upon Fort Malden, but no battle took place. The Americans found the fort deserted and partly burned. Proctor had gone.

General Harrison then pushed on up the Canadian side of the river. The next day General McArthur was sent across the river to take command of the fort at Detroit. Once more the Stars and Stripes floated over Fort Shelby at Detroit.

Joined by new troops, General Harrison pushed on into Canada and defeated Colonel Proctor and Tecumseh at the Battle of the Thames in October, 1813. Only the Indians tried to hold their ground before the Americans' attack. During the battle Tecumseh was killed. This was a sad blow to the Indians, for Tecumseh was one of their greatest chiefs and he was in many ways a remarkable man even when measured by our present standards of thinking.

In the summer of 1814 Lieutenant Croghan was sent to recapture Mackinac, but his attack was not a success and the British retained control of that fort until the end of the war when it was returned to the Americans in the spring of 1815.

For a short time after the War of 1812 the fur trade was carried on as it had been in the earlier days. A new company known as the American Fur Company now became the leader in the fur trade. The American Fur Company was owned by John Jacob Astor. Mr. Astor was a German immigrant who had come to the United States in 1784. In 1809 he received a charter for the American Fur Company from the state of New York. In 1811 the American Fur Company bought out the British merchants that were then known as the Mackinac Company. Mackinac Island became the main trading post for some time for the American Fur Company. Here Mr. Astor sent bookkeepers and traders to carry on his business. In the Astor House on Mackinac Island the furs that the brigades of the company brought in were stored and packed for the fur trade. In 1815-1816 the Congress of the United States passed a law keeping all foreigners trading in furs out of the United States. This was a great help to the American Fur Company. But romantic as were the days of this company on Mackinac Island, the days of the fur trade were coming to an end. Settlers were soon to come pushing into Michigan to take up land from the government. This meant that the small game animals on which the fur trade depended would be driven away. Before long the Astor company moved to the West where the fur trade could still be carried on. At the present time efforts are being made to restore the Astor House on Mackinac Island so that visitors going to the island can see how the fur trade, which was for so long Michigan's major industry, was once carried on.

Courtesy Pennsylvania History Commission

The "Niagara"

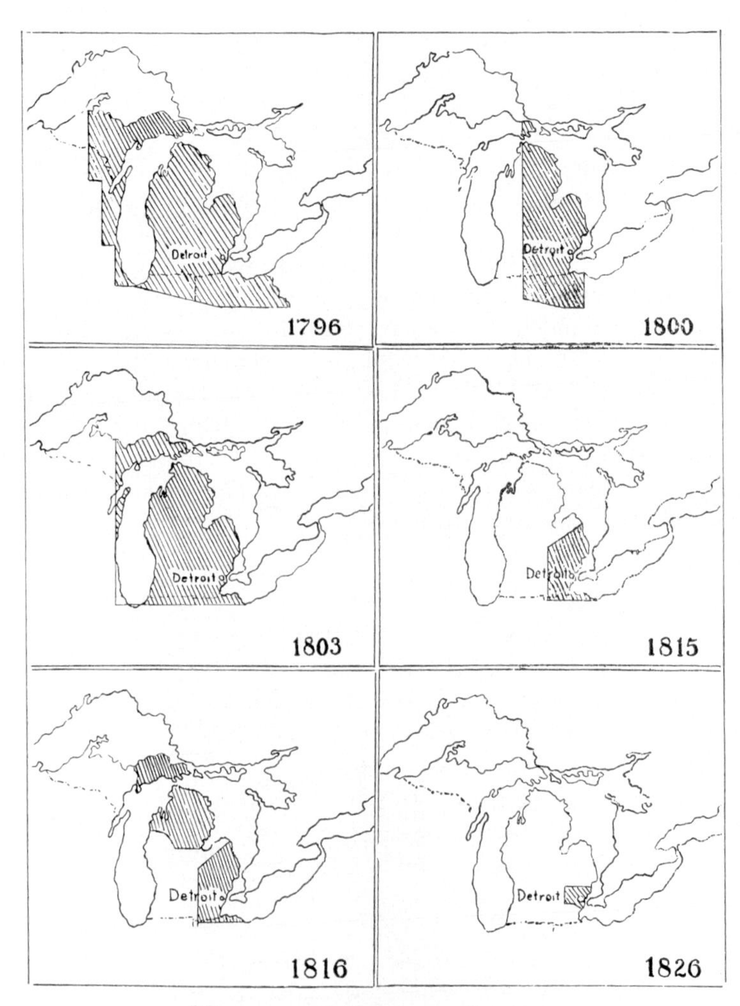

History of Wayne County

Chapter VIII

THE SETTLEMENT OF SOUTHERN MICHIGAN

After the War of 1812, Lewis Cass was made governor of Michigan. Lewis Cass had come to Michigan with General Hull's army just before the War of 1812. Cass stood among the main political leaders in American history of that time, and his leadership did much in developing the new territory. He not only aided in exploring the territory but also made several treaties with the Indians for their land. For eighteen years Lewis Cass was territorial governor. He then became Secretary of War in President Andrew Jackson's cabinet. Later Cass served in another President's cabinet, spent twelve years as a United States senator, was our minister to France, and ran for President of the United States in 1848.

It was during the early years of Cass's term as territorial governor that settlers began coming to Michigan in large numbers. After the War of 1812 many people from the eastern states began to go west to take up new lands in the wilderness. For many years the Ohio River had been the main road to the West. Enough settlers had pushed down the Ohio River and settled in southern Ohio to enable Ohio to become a state in the year 1803. Enough settlers had taken lands in southern Indiana to allow Indiana to become a state in the year 1816. Illinois followed and became a state in 1818. But the area around the Great Lakes was too far off the path of westward advance (down the Ohio River) to interest settlers. There was still no easy way to reach the land or to send crops from it.

Because of this lack of transportation, Michigan was not settled as soon as the area along the Ohio River. Only a few places had little settlements by 1825. As early as 1780, some French traders had set up a trading post near the mouth of the Raisin River. Later other Frenchmen came to this area and Frenchtown grew up on the north side of the Raisin River. It was here that the massacre of the War of 1812 had taken place. Later, Americans settled on the south side of the river and the name for both places was changed to Monroe, after President Monroe who visited Michigan soon after the War of 1812. French settlers laid out ribbon farms along the Rouge River just west of Detroit, but no village was begun in that area. About 1785 French settlers had begun a little village at St. Clair on the St. Clair River. In 1809 a trading post had been set up, which later became Ypsilanti, so that trade could be carried on with the Indians living farther up the Huron River.

Hull's treaty of 1807 with the Indians had opened the land of southeastern Michigan to settlement but, as the land had not yet been surveyed, title to it could not be given to settlers. In 1815 Mr. Edward Tiffin was hired by the government to survey a small area of land near Detroit. This was the first survey of land that was made in Michigan. The report of the survey stated that Michigan land was not suited for farming because it was swampy and sandy and had scarcely one acre in a thousand fit for cultivation. No doubt this report of Mr. Tiffin kept many a settler from coming to Michigan during the next ten years.

Life in Michigan at that time was crude and hard. There were no mills in the area, and grain had to be ground by hand in crude grinders which were made by burning a hole in one end of a log and then setting it upright. In these grinders, corn was crushed by pounders that were attached to spring poles thirty or forty feet in length.

Fish was a principal item of food, and the mouth of the Detroit River was one of the favorite fishing spots for miles around. To it the Indians, with their families, came to catch fish, which they dried for their winter food supply. One writer of the time, in speaking of this area, said, "This river afforded more fish and in greater varieties than any other river of fresh water in America, and perhaps in the world. The most numerous and valuable were the wall-eyed pike, the muskallonge, catfish, bass, and many other kinds, amounting to thirty or more varieties. The fishing was done with hooks, spears, and dip nets. The fish were so numerous, it was quite common for Indians to spear from one to three at one stroke, at some stages of the water, particularly when roily."

To reach this wilderness land at that time one had to come across Canada, by boat across Lake Erie, or come up from Ohio along the road that led through the Black Swamp south of where Toledo, Ohio, now stands. Those who came by way of Lake Erie faced the dangers of storm and shipwreck, and those who came by way of the Black Swamp were often obliged to wade through water, mud, and ice, and to provide their own quarters for the night. It is no wonder that settlers preferred to drift leisurely down the Ohio and leave the Lake Lands to the Indians and French who were more at home in its forest area.

Even the shores of the lakes and rivers, with the exception of the old French settlements, were still as wooded as nature had made them. The islands in the Detroit River, too, were still all heavily timbered and untouched by the settler's or woodsman's ax.

The little Canadian settlement near Fort Malden was a small wilderness village where a fort with a breastworks, barracks, and warehouse was still maintained by the English. Each year the Indians gathered at the fort for their annual gift of presents.

On sailing up the Detroit River in 1817, one passed through pretty, heavily timbered lands where the mighty forests stretching to the water's edge were broken only by the French farm houses which, being whitewashed, contrasted markedly with the dense woodlands' heavy green of summer or golden brown of fall. Here and there on prominent points where the breeze was strong stood little windmills which were the only markers for sailors since there were then no lighthouses or buoys along the inland waterways.

Indian canoes still glided across the blue water of the river. French bateaux passed by. Now and then a sail on one of the few lake boats billowed out with the wind. As yet, the lakes knew no steam-powered boats; however, even then one was being built near Buffalo. The following year, 1818, its paddle wheels began to churn the waters of the river and its wood smoke commenced to drift over the forest land beside the river.

Such was southeastern Michigan in the year 1817. But all was soon to change, for back east in New York state Judge Rutherford, on July 4, 1817, turned the first shovel of earth on the new Erie Canal at Rome, New York. This new canal, as we shall soon see, placed Michigan on the best direct highway to New York and the East.

At this time about the best way to explore the lands around Detroit was still to use the rivers. People began pushing up the Clinton River and, in 1816, started a little settlement at Rochester. Pontiac began just two years later, in 1818, when some men from Detroit purchased two square miles in that area. Mt. Clemens was also started in that same year. Settlers pushing up the rivers from Detroit usually looked for a waterfall so that water power could be used to run gristmills and sawmills.

Some French settlers were still farming the little ribbon farms along the Detroit, Rouge, and Huron rivers, but as yet no farm land was offered for sale. Perhaps this is one of the reasons why settlers did not come into the area. However, in 1818 some of the land that had been surveyed three years earlier was put up for sale and auctioned off to the highest bidder. Some of it, near Wyandotte, sold for as much as forty dollars an acre.

A new land law, passed in 1820, made it possible for a person to buy eighty acres of land at $1.25 an acre in cash. Thus for one hundred dollars a man could become the owner of an eighty-acre farm. Today an eighty-acre farm seems small, but in those days of hand tools and hand farming eighty acres was a good-sized farm.

In 1818, the same year that public land was put up for sale in Michigan, the first steamboat on Lake Erie docked at Detroit on her first trip from Buffalo. Steamboats were just starting to be built. At that time Fulton's "Clermont" and other new steamers were already carrying people between New York and Albany on the Hudson River. As early as 1811, steamboats had appeared on the Ohio River.

At Black Rock, on the Niagara River, the "Walk-in-the-Water" was built for use on Lake Erie. This new boat was called the "Walk-in-the-Water" after what one Indian had said about Fulton's "Clermont": "She-walks-in-the-water." As it was the only steamboat on the lakes at that time, it was usually called "The Steamboat" by the white men, and the white man's "Big Canoe" by the Indians.

The "Walk-in-the-Water" was modeled after the clipper ships which were then being built on the Atlantic coast. She was made of white oak which was cut on the land where Buffalo, New York, now stands. She was one hundred thirty-five feet long, thirty-two feet wide, and eight feet six inches deep. On each side of the boat, at its center, was a large paddle wheel which was turned by a steam engine. A wood fire was used to make steam in the boiler. Bass wood, pine, or hemlock, split fine and well seasoned, were, the firemen soon found, the best wood to burn. Their quick fire made a hot blaze that kept up the steam in the boiler. From her funnel came the smoke of the burning wood, and sometimes flying sparks.

You would think the "Walk-in-the-Water" a strange steamship if you could now see her. Her funnel, or stack, was like a large stovepipe. There was no pilothouse. The paddle wheel on each side was in plain view. To aid the steam engine, two masts were erected on the "Walk-in-the-Water." One mast was in the bow and the other in the stern. Upon these masts the usual sails were rigged and used whenever the wind was favorable. As the current in the Niagara River was very swift, the little steamer could not force her way against it. Twenty oxen were therefore used to tow the vessel up into the still waters of Lake Erie. These oxen were jokingly spoken of by the people of that time as the "horned breeze."

"Walk in the Water"

The "Walk-in-the-Water" began making regular runs from Buffalo to Detroit. On the way she stopped at Erie, Pennsylvania, and Cleveland and Sandusky, Ohio. Sometimes, if the weather was fair, the vessel ran in close to the shore and, as there were few docks, the passengers and freight were often carried to the land on the backs of sailors who waded to shore through the water. During stormy weather the vessel stopped in deeper water or not at all. On board was a small brass cannon, a four-pounder. This cannon took the place of a whistle. It was fired to announce the vessel would leave in half an hour, or on nearing a port it was fired to announce her arrival.

At Detroit a new dock was built at the foot of Bates Street for the steamboat. To go from Buffalo to Detroit and back sometimes took about two weeks, for lack of steam, shortage of fuel, and bad weather often delayed the little vessel. The fare from Buffalo to Detroit was eighteen dollars in the cabin and seven dollars if one traveled steerage.

The life of the "Walk-in-the-Water" was a short one. On October 30, 1821, she started from Buffalo on her last trip. The threatening weather soon turned into a gale, and before the little boat had gone many miles the captain had her turned around and headed back toward Buffalo for shelter. The storm grew worse and, fearful lest the "Walk-in-the-Water" run aground during the gale, anchors were dropped. The strain on the anchors was too great for the boat, and soon the hold of the vessel began to fill with water. Near morning of the following day, the anchors were cut loose and the ship was allowed to drift ashore in the darkness of the storm. The waves tossed her upon a sandy beach where she leaned over on one side. Later a line was run from the boat to the shore and all the passengers were saved.

Although the "Walk-in-the-Water" thus came to an early end, it nevertheless began a new age in lake travel. More steamships were soon built. The engine and boiler of the "Walk-in-the-Water" were used to drive two other boats before they were finally scrapped. A path was cleared through the forest from the wreck and the machinery was brought overland and placed in a new vessel called the "Superior." In 1835, when the "Superior" was turned into a sailing vessel, the old engine was again placed in a new boat called the "Charles Townsend."

The second steamboat was the "Superior." She left for Detroit on her maiden voyage April 23, 1822. Two years later, in 1824, another steamer was built and named the "Henry Clay." Still another early boat was the "Pioneer."

By 1818 the horrors of the War of 1812 were being forgotten and things around Detroit were getting back to normal. The Indians were again at peace. In order to keep the Indians satisfied, Governor Cass thought it best to get a new and larger land grant from the native owners of the land. This was a real task. The Indians were still friendly to the English who had not threatened to take the Indians' land from them as the Americans were now doing. Nevertheless, Governor Cass thought that the time had come for action, and in 1819 he went to Saginaw to make a treaty with the Indians for more of their land.

Arrangements for the treaty-making council, to be held at what is now Saginaw, were made by Louis Campeau, a French settler then living there and running a trading post. He and a group of traders cleared a space in the wilderness three hundred by one hundred feet. Over this cleared space a roof of boughs and bark was fastened to the trees along the edge of the clearing. Under this temporary roof, seats were provided by placing logs in rows across the meeting enclosure.

Governor Cass sent his brother, Captain C. L. Cass, by boat to Saginaw with a company of soldiers, three thousand dollars in silver, and such trinkets as they thought the Indians would like. Governor Cass then set out overland to the meeting place.

The Indians met with Governor Cass in the council house. Governor Cass then proposed to them that they should give up their land and all leave Michigan and settle beyond the Mississippi River. His message was then repeated by the Indian interpreters to the tribes. Of course this plan was not pleasing to them, and some of them left the council in disgust.

Then the usual means was used to bring the Indians to terms. They were given liquor to drink. At last it was agreed that the Indians would give up about six million acres of land for the three thousand shiny silver dollars lying on the table and five barrels of rum. The tribes were also to be paid one thousand dollars in silver coin every year thereafter.

Five barrels of rum were then opened. This Governor Cass knew would be a safe amount for two thousand Indians. Louis Campeau, however, had not been pleased with the deal that had been made because the Indians owed him much money. He therefore went to his own warehouse and brought out ten barrels of his own whisky which he gave to the Indians. Soon the Indians were nearly out of control, and General Cass and his troops were almost scalped. Peace was then made with Campeau and he quieted the Indians.

This treaty gave the Americans, for three thousand dollars and five barrels of rum, the land east of a line drawn roughly from Kalamazoo, in Kalamazoo County, to Lewiston, in Montmorency County. The Indians knew that the white men were going to get the land anyway and therefore thought to make the most of a bad bargain.

In August, 1821, Governor Cass and Solomon Sibley, acting for the United States, and fifty-five chiefs and leaders of the Pottawattomies signed another treaty at Chicago. This treaty gave the Americans a large section of land in southwestern Michigan.

What Michigan lacked was a better system of communication with the older settlements back East. There was still no good route for settlers to use in coming to Michigan from the East. Moreover, once crops were raised in the Great Lakes area there was no way to send them to the markets in the East. If New York City was to get any of the growing western commerce, she must provide a route to the West that would compete with the National Road and the Ohio River. Yankee businessmen proposed that the state of New York build a canal reaching across the state of New York from Albany to Buffalo along the route followed by the old Genesee Road.

"Clinton's Ditch," people jokingly called the new canal, as men and mules began to excavate the three-hundred-and-sixty-mile canal from Albany toward Buffalo on Lake Erie. There were then no large machines as there are today to do the work. It was man power, horse power, and mule power which dug the canal steadily toward the West and the Great Lakes. Many men died from swamp fever, from accidents, and from exposure, but the project went on.

The Erie Canal had been started in 1817. Soon it was opened from Rome to Albany. By 1819 it was opened to Utica. Smoke hung over Lake Erie as the steamer "Walk-in-the-Water" ran from Buffalo to Detroit. A new era was coming to shipping on the Great Lakes.

During the years 1820, 1821, and 1822 the canal lengthened. Straining men, mules, and oxen moved wheelbarrows and wagons. More men with axes cleared a sixty-foot-wide path farther and farther into the forest toward the West. New machines brought from Europe ripped the tree stumps from the earth. Newly designed plows with sharp edges cut through the trailing roots ahead of the lengthening canal. Four feet deep, forty feet wide at the top, and twenty-eight feet wide at the bottom, the workmen made the water highway for the settlers and goods that were soon to move through the canal.

All through 1823 and 1824 the men and horses worked on. With pick, shovel, and black blasting powder the canal was cut farther and farther toward Lake Erie. Then, in 1825, the Erie Canal was completed.

The Erie Canal had been built in eight years. Now it lay like a long, narrow ribbon stretching some three hundred and sixty miles across New York State from Buffalo, on Lake Erie, to Albany, on the Hudson River. Seventy-two locks carried the Erie Canal waters up and down. One of America's most important early highways of commerce had been built at a cost of about eight million dollars. This all-water route from the Great Lakes to New York City was soon to change the course of westward expansion. No longer would freight have to be dragged along muddy roads at excessive cost. Freight rates from Buffalo to New York dropped from $100 a ton to $15 a ton, and the time for the trip between these two cities was cut from twenty days to only eight days.

In the West, thirty-cent wheat rocketed to one dollar a bushel. The golden grain, harvested from the rich lands of the Great Lakes area, was soon being carried eastward along the canal. More and more land was cleared along the southern shore of Lake Erie in northern Ohio. Land values in northern Ohio shot rapidly upward. Boom times hit the Lake Erie Region. Towns along the Erie Canal grew rapidly. New York City doubled its population by 1830, thus passing Philadelphia in size and becoming America's largest city and seaport. Buffalo, Cleveland, Toledo, Detroit, and even far-away Chicago all soon felt the effects of the Erie Canal.

Boats of thirty tons which did not sink into the water more than four feet could now easily be pulled along the canal. Later the canal was made seven feet deep and canal boats carrying two hundred and forty tons could pass through it. The canal brought the Great Lakes Region to the very front door of New York City and the Atlantic Ocean, and it served as the main highway to and from the Great Lakes until the coming of the railroads some twenty-five or thirty years later.

The canal made possible good dependable transportation from early spring until it froze over in late fall. Farm crops and lumber from the Great Lakes area could now be economically shipped to the markets of the East and to the markets of the world. Soon provisions in large quantities began to be shipped east along the lake route and the Erie Canal.

Captain Samuel Ward sailed a small schooner from Detroit to Buffalo. There he lowered the schooner's masts so the little boat could clear the bridges of the canal. He then had the boat towed along the canal to Albany. At Albany he again raised the ship's masts and sailed it down the Hudson River to New York City, thus making the first voyage from the Great Lakes to the Atlantic Ocean. Before long as many as twenty thousand canal boats passed along the canal in a summer season.

The price of farm products dropped sharply in the East. Farmers living on the poor stony lands in New England could not receive enough for their crops to pay their expenses. The value of their farms went down. Farming the worn-out lands of New England was no longer worth while or profitable. Therefore many farmers began to seek work in the new factories then beginning in New England. Others set out with their families for the West to begin farming once more on more productive land.

In 1826 the general survey of Michigan lands began. Later, this land survey became a geological survey as well. As the surveyors staked out the land, they collected samples of minerals and rocks and sent them to Washington with their papers. A land office had been established at Detroit in 1804 and another was established at Monroe in 1823. Until 1824 only 61,919 acres of land had been sold, and it was nearly all in the Detroit area.

Michigan now needed better roads so that people coming west by way of the Erie Canal could reach their claims in the vast wilderness. The French and English made no effort to make roads in this undeveloped wilderness. Thus when the Americans began to come, only the Indian trails led across the state.

The problem of building roads near Detroit was a difficult one at best. The region around Detroit for about twenty miles in any direction is an old lake bottom. The land surface is mostly clay of a very sticky kind. Moreover, the whole region was covered with forests, bushes, "oak openings," and marshes. The water drained away slowly and seeped into the clay, making it a heavy paste. The bogs and marshes could be crossed only with great difficulty.

The first road in Michigan was what is now East Jefferson Avenue in Detroit. It was made during the French period and was merely a muddy path running behind the row of French houses along the river.

When General Hull came north from Dayton, Ohio, just before the War of 1812, his men cleared a road from Dayton to Detroit. This road, however, was poorly located and poorly built and passed through the Black Swamp near or in the area where Toledo, Ohio, now stands.

One early settler at Ann Arbor says, "Soon after I came to Detroit I made a contract to carry the mail from Detroit to Ann Arbor for four years, and all that time I forded all the streams, never once crossing a bridge, for there were none to cross. During the winter of 1825 and 1826 my son Lucius and I carried the mail on horseback, and often in fording streams and rivers in high water we were obliged to secure the mail bag on the top of the saddle, grasp the horse's mane, and swim him over.

"On the first day of March, 1826, I began to cut a road from Ann Arbor to Detroit, on the Indian trail running by my present residence. I got all the help I could, and in sixty days completed a wagon road through from Ann Arbor to Plymouth. On the first day of May, 1826, I took a light two-horse wagon and three Indian ponies, and went to Detroit one day and back the next. This was a great wonder in those days."

Before settlers could come into the newly ceded lands, better roads than this had to be built. Soldiers stationed at Fort Shelby were put to work cutting and improving a road to Toledo. About this time, too, a company was hired to cut and corduroy a road north of Detroit. This road has since become Woodward Avenue in Detroit. The company was to receive $1,000 a mile for building the road north of Detroit. The area past the six-mile road was found to be too swampy for a highway. Later a road was constructed there with great difficulty. Most of the way to Royal Oak the road had to be cribbed and corduroyed.

In 1824 Father Richard was elected to Congress from Michigan Territory. As a representative he became active in getting Congress to grant money for road construction in Michigan. By 1825 it was enacted, for military purposes, that several roads leading into the state from Detroit should be built. One of these roads was to follow the old Sauk, or Pottawattomie trail, and run from Detroit to Chicago. At first Congress granted only three thousand dollars for building the road, but two years later it added twenty thousand dollars to the original grant. This road, for many years called the Chicago Road, was under construction for ten years. When finished, it was a typical turnpike of the time. From Detroit the road ran west through what are now Wayne, Ypsilanti, Saline, Clinton, Jonesville, Quincy, Coldwater, Sturgis, and White Pigeon. This old Chicago Road is now known as U.S. Highway 112. Another road was put through the second tier of counties and was known as the Territorial Road.

Further grants by Congress provided for a road from Detroit to Saginaw Bay, and from Detroit to Fort Gratiot (Port Huron). A later grant was made for road construction from Detroit to the mouth of the Grand River.

These new trunk roads led in a fan-shaped arrangement into and from Detroit. Bridges were soon built over the streams and rivers, making the roads, in a way, reasonably passable. To the forest the settlers turned for a better road and from it they cut thousands of poles to make corduroy roads. By 1836 the first twelve miles toward Pontiac had been corduroyed. These roads gave wagons and stage-coaches a bumpy motion that made riding very uncomfortable. Yet these humble beginnings were the forerunners of our splendid road system today.

As early as 1827 a stagecoach line was opened between Detroit and Toledo. A stagecoach ran three times each week between the two places. Another coach line soon began to run between Detroit and Romeo. When the Chicago road was opened, still another stage began running three times a week between Detroit and Chicago.

Behind the four or six horses came the coach bouncing the tired passengers up and down and from side to side. During dry weather the ride was hot and dusty. During wet weather the coach had to be actually dragged through the mud. When a bad mud hole had to be crossed, the driver often called down to the passengers, "Lean to the left, gentlemen." This would help keep the coach from tipping over. So poor were these early roads that often only fifteen or twenty miles could be covered in a day. Traveling was done mostly during the daylight hours, for the traveler on the highway at night was always in danger of being robbed.

Because of the many delays in travel, inns or taverns sprang up at short intervals along the road. Often these inns were the beginnings of some of our modern towns and cities such as Dearborn, Wayne, Ypsilanti, and Ann Arbor. Where the stage stopped there was trade and people settled.

When the stage arrived at an inn, there was much excitement. If the coach were to continue, the tired horses were changed for fresh ones. The mail, as well as the wants of the passengers, had to be cared for. If the coach stopped for the night, the passengers made themselves at home in the inn. Some stayed in their rooms, if they were lucky enough to get them; others sat in the living room and talked of their journey with their traveling companions or with the owner of the inn and his family. The passengers were served their meals from the inn's kitchen where the food was cooked in a huge fireplace.

Most of the early settlers took up farm lands in or near Wayne County. Gradually the old flat lake bottom around Detroit was cleared and drained. Fields of grain appeared where only a few years before had stood dense forests of virgin hardwood. With the opening of the

Courtesy Ford Motor Co.

Wayne County farm land, showing Henry Ford's birthplace on the southeast corner of Ford Road and Greenfield. (1937)

Erie Canal this grain began to move eastward to feed the new industrial centers that were then growing in the East. The increase in the grain supply caused the price of grain to fall in the East.

The growing number of settlers wanting to come west caused lake traffic to boom even more than it had previously. In 1825, the year the canal was opened, there were seven side-wheelers (steamboats) running to Detroit from Buffalo. In 1827 the first steamboat steamed down Lake Michigan to Chicago. By 1833 there were eleven steamboats on the lakes. In 1845 there were two hundred and seventeen sailing vessels and forty-five steamboats on the lakes.

During the long, warm summer days, when the canal and lakes were free from ice, the busy steamers and sailing vessels left the bustling, crowded port of Buffalo carrying hundreds of settlers and their families westward across Lake Erie to Toledo, Detroit, and as far west as Wisconsin, and Chicago in northern Illinois.

The great surge of people to the new West by way of the lakes was on. Ann Arbor was founded in 1824, Adrian in 1825, Niles, Jackson, and Kalamazoo in 1829, Battle Creek and Grand Rapids in 1831, and Coldwater in 1832. In the year 1830, two thousand four hundred immigrants arrived at Detroit in one week. In that same year also the first steam ferry boat started to run between Detroit and Windsor, Ontario. In July, 1831, settlers were passing through the booming port of Buffalo at the rate of one thousand a day. As many as two thousand landed at Detroit in one week. In 1833, after the cholera scare in 1832, twenty thousand arrived at Chicago. In 1834 nine hundred arrived in one day at Detroit. In May, 1836, ninety boats arrived at Detroit during the month of May and docked at the wharves along the Detroit waterfront.

The steamers grew in numbers and spread their smoke along the horizon where it contrasted with the ever-growing number of white sails as steamers and sailing ships hurried back and forth across Lake Erie to carry the ever-swelling numbers of settlers to the western lands.

The little frontier village of Detroit was now a busy place during the summer shipping season. From the crowded decks of the steamers and sailing boats came an almost endless flow of Yankees who were going west to start life anew in the lands which the Indians had so recently ceded to the Americans.

By the 1830's a new Detroit, built after the fire of 1805, stood on the site of the old French settlement. Many of the new buildings that had been built by the French gave the little village an odd look to the Yankees coming from the more settled parts of New York and New England. Among these buildings of the older French settlers stood others of more recent and different designs that had been built by the immigrants from back East. These new houses stood out plainly from the older French ones and gave a glaring notice that a new group of people was already at work in making the area American.

Jefferson Avenue was then the main street. East of Woodward, the muddy road ran along the river behind the houses of the French farmers, then meandered on along the river and up along the shore of Lake St. Clair. West of Woodward it ran as far as Cass Avenue, where the old Cass house then stood on a high bank overlooking the Detroit River. One settler coming to Detroit in 1834 has this to say about Jefferson Avenue: "I went up Jefferson Avenue; found some brick buildings, barber poles, wooden clocks or large watches, big hats and boots, a brass ball, etc. I returned to the hotel, satisfied that Detroit was actually a city, for the things I had seen were, in my mind, sufficient to make it one."

There were at that time some six or more blocks of brick buildings, but there were no large buildings of any kind. The streets were muddy and gave the whole town a primitive appearance. But the slippery, impassable mud of the streets did not seem to stop the steady stream of ox teams and wagons that passed along them.

Four hotels and a few small inns cared for the steady stream of settlers if the newcomers had any money to spend. Of these hotels, the most fashionable was the Mansion House which was followed by the Steamboat Hotel, the Eagle Hotel, and the United States Hotel.

The capitol of the territory stood far out on the commons and away from the other buildings on a spot in present-day Detroit now called Capital Park at Griswold and State streets. Where the Detroit Post Office now stands stood the remains of old Fort Shelby which General Hull had surrendered to the British during the War of 1812. On the southeast corner of Jefferson and Woodward avenues stood a one-story wooden building in which was a saloon. Across the street stood a market place. One block below, toward the river, was a dry goods store.

Many of the people were still French, and the soft French language was often heard along with the noisy English of the Yankees. Many Indians and half-breeds mixed with the French and Americans. Some were still clothed in their native dress. With mixed feelings they watched the Yankees pour into the city on their way west to take up farms in areas that up to then had been their hunting grounds.

The ring of axes increased in the forests. Huge trees, centuries old, came crashing to the ground. Little log cabins and log barns nestled in small clearings amid the forested area. Towns were platted on drawing boards. Village lots, where as yet no man had stood, often sold and resold for fancy prices, but no surveys were ever made of them while other villages were mushrooming in the wilderness. Marine City began in 1831, and Port Huron, which had been a lumbering center since 1827, was laid out in 1835.

Along the new roads leading from Detroit in an ever-widening circle, little frontier villages were springing up. In 1834 lumbering operations began on the Saginaw River at Saginaw. In that same year a little stock of goods was offered for sale at Jonesville. This was the first store west of Tecumseh.

By 1836 a change had already taken place in the huge fan shape of settlement around Detroit. The frontier was already passing from the area near Detroit, and culture from the East was coming in. Land values had already skyrocketed, and farm land along the Chicago Road was now selling for $20 an acre.

New land offices were established in order to take care of the increasing demands of the settlers for lands. One was located at White Pigeon in 1831, another at Kalamazoo in 1834, and another at Grand

Courtesy Detroit Historical Museum

The Detroit River—1838

Rapids in 1836. In 1836, 1,475,725 acres of land were sold in the Detroit district alone while in the territory as a whole about four million acres passed from the government to the settlers.

Settlers following the Chicago Road began settlements at Saline, Clinton, Jonesville, Coldwater, Sturgis, and Mottville. Others taking the Territorial Road, that ran west through the second tier of counties, settled Lima, Grass Lake, Jacksonburg, Sandstone, Marshall, Battle Creek, Comstock, Kalamazoo, and St. Joseph.

The area of southwestern Michigan had been of interest to trappers and missionaries since the time of La Salle, and a settlement at Niles had been in existence since the time of Father Allouez. Now this area was to attract a new type of men, the American settlers. Here in southwestern Michigan were to be found what were then known as prairies or "oak openings." These small plains were open spots, some being as large as five miles across. They were, as it were, meadows in a forest land. Heavy grass and thick sod spread across them. In the springtime they were bright with flowers. Wild strawberries grew among the grass and flowers, and their red juice stained bright red the feet of deer, ox, or man that wandered across the prairies.

The Pottawattomies had found the open prairies good for farming and had long made their gardens in the fertile prairie soil. The land did not have to be cleared and was better for farming than the acid soil of the forest lands.

The Treaty of Chicago, signed by Cass and Sibley in 1821, had promised the Pottawattomie Indians that a mission worker would be sent among them. In response to this promise to the Indians, Rev. Isaac McCoy came by wagon from Fort Wayne, Indiana, in 1822 to the south bank of the St. Joseph River, not far from present-day Niles, and there set up a mission for the Indians. Several acres of land were cleared, some buildings were built, and a school for the Indians was started. For a short time the mission was successful, but disease, whisky, and the coming of white settlers to the area forced the mission to close in September, 1830.

As early as 1823 a family by the name of Thompson settled in Berrien County. The Putnum family settled in Cass County in 1825, and in 1829 the Morris family came to live in Van Buren County. Most of the early settlers in southwestern Michigan came over the route from Fort Wayne, Indiana, and were southerners from Ohio and Indiana. At first there was no link that joined them to the settlements growing near Detroit, but with the coming of the Chicago Road about 1834, the western settlements of southwestern Michigan were more closely joined to the expanding eastern settlements. Soon easterners from New England were coming west along the Chicago Road to join the settlers coming north from Fort Wayne. In 1840 a new road was cut from Hastings to Battle Creek and thus new areas were opened for settlement.

The settlers pushing into southwestern Michigan were thus beginning to settle upon the tribal lands of the remnant of the only strong tribe in southern Michigan, for at this time the Pottawattomies were still living there and in northern Illinois. The Pottawattomies living on the plains in northern Illinois were called Pottawattomies of the plains. Those living in Michigan were known as Pottawattomies of the woods.

Father Marquette had found the Pottawattomies of his time living in lands near Green Bay, Wisconsin, and La Salle tells us that the Miamis were living in southwestern Michigan when he built his little fort on the Miami River (St. Joseph) in 1679. As was explained in Chapter Three, about 1700 the Miamis seemed to have moved eastward and settled in northern Ohio around the western and southern shore of Lake Erie. Some historians seem to think that the Pottawattomies and Ottawas drove out the Miamis and took over their land. The Pottawattomies seem to have settled in the St. Joseph and Kalamazoo River valleys while the Ottawas occupied the valley of the Grand River. Others seem to think that the Pottawattomies were driven southward into the land left by the Miamis by the stronger Menominees who moved into their old lands at Green Bay, Wisconsin.

As early as 1712 a Jesuit mission was started among the Pottawattomies near Niles. In that same year the Pottawattomies helped to defend Detroit against the Sauks and Foxes. In their earlier days they were a strong war-like nation. They joined Pontiac in hopes of driving the English from the land. They helped defeat General Harmar and General St. Clair. Their great chief Topinabee was one of the signers of the Treaty of Greenville after the battle of Fallen Timbers. At this treaty the Pottawattomies gave up, for the first time, lands claimed by the tribe. They, too, signed the treaty of 1807 that ceded southeastern Michigan to the Americans. Topinabee and his warriors were in the defeat at Tippecanoe. When Tecumseh led his warriors in the War of 1812, the Pottawattomies were part of the band. They took part in the massacres at both River Raisin and Fort Dearborn (Chicago). Pottawattomies, too, were fighting along with

Tecumseh in the Battle of the Thames. Each June from 1812 to 1834 both the Ottawas and the Pottawattomies went to Fort Malden, over the Indian trail that led eastward to Detroit, to receive their annual gift of presents as payment for their services to the English.

Topinabee had been their chief for over forty years and had led them on many of their war parties. Two other leaders of this tribe should be mentioned, Shavehead and Pokagon. Shavehead was the older of the two and no doubt got his name from the manner in which he wore his hair, for it was his habit to draw his hair upward and then tie it on top of his head with a string. Into this top lock he usually thrust a feather or two. He was a sullen man and had a great hatred of the white men who were coming into his tribal lands. Tradition says of him that he had ninety-nine white men's tongues strung on a strip of bark and that he wanted one more to make it an even hundred. He played a leading part in the massacre at both River Raisin and Fort Dearborn, and his scalp locks showed that he spared not even women or children. By the time settlers began to move into the area he was an old Indian living on Shavehead Prairie in what is now Cass County. Time, war, and whisky had made him a poor, despised old man. Like Tecumseh, with whom he fought, his death is hidden in several conflicting stories.

Pokagon was far different from either Topinabee or Shavehead. He, too, was at the massacre at Fort Dearborn but by now had become a friend of the white men. He signed the Treaty of Chicago in 1821. He was a man of high intelligence and understanding, and though he had little education himself, his son became one of the best-educated Indians of his time. Pokagon was a man of temperance and tried to get the other Indians to follow his example but he had little success. Furs were growing more and more scarce and, as they did so, whisky flowed more and more freely as the competition between traders grew. This competition for the fur trade, plus the fact that many Pottawattomies had died in the cholera plague of 1832 and in the smallpox epidemic of 1837, no doubt helped to reduce the once powerful Pottawattomies to a miserable little band and led to the failure of Reverend McCoy's Mission.

With sad hearts the Pottawattomies watched the settlers push into their tribal lands. With each passing year, more prairie sod was ripped open by the white men's plows and more trees fell from their swinging axes. Most of the Pottawattomies who still remained were living on a little reservation on Prairie Nottawa Seepe in northern St. Joseph County. Once they had been a powerful nation of warriors. Now they were reduced to a little band. But even this little area of land was soon to be taken from them, although they had been granted it by the Treaty of Chicago. Why this should happen the Indians could not understand. As one chief in council said, "You have more lands than you can use, so why do you want more? You have much; we have little; why do you want our little?"

But the white man did want even the little. That it had been the land where these Indian people had played as children, where they had sat by the council fire, or danced the war dance with braves that never returned from battle made no difference to the settlers. Even the graves of the Indians had little meaning for them. The land would be better without the Indians around.

By another treaty, signed in 1833, the Pottawattomies agreed to give up all of their remaining lands and to move west of the Mississippi River as General Cass had wanted them to do in 1819. Governor Cass was then Secretary of War in the President's cabinet. He sent Reverend McCoy with Chief Noonday, of the Ottawas, and five other Indians west to find a place where the Pottawattomies would be less under the influence of the whites.

The Pottawattomie Indians were called together in 1838 so that they could be taken to new reservations west of the Mississippi. Bands from the north, Ottawas and Chippewas under military escort, joined the saddened Pottawattomies. Escorted by federal soldiers and military wagons carrying supplies, the unfortunate, helpless Indians began their westward journey to strange lands beyond the Mississippi. The soldiers had little regard or respect for these old warriors and their families that had fought them in years past and so had little sympathy for their sufferings and hardships. There was much malaria that year, and many of the Indians who started never finished the westward journey. A few Indians escaped to the woods along the way, but most of these and other stragglers were rounded up the following year and sent westward to join the band. At first they were settled in Missouri. Two years later they were moved to Iowa. From there the few that remained were taken to Kansas and then to Indian Territory (Oklahoma). Only Pokagon, the friend of the whites, and a few of his Christian followers remained of the once proud war-like Pottawattomies.

Michigan had hardly begun making roads when a new and better means of transportation began in the state. Railroad building began in Michigan even before Michigan became a state. In fact, the first railroads and locomotives in the Old Northwest were in Michigan. The first railroad to be chartered within the limits of the Old Northwest was the Detroit and Pontiac Railroad. This road was chartered on July 31, 1830. By this charter a group of men was granted permission to build a railroad from Detroit to Pontiac. This first company, however, laid no track.

Courtesy of the Henry Ford Museum, Dearborn, Michigan

An early train

Among the first railroads to receive a charter in this area was the Erie and Kalamazoo. The charter for this road was granted in 1833. According to the charter the company was to build a railroad between Toledo and Adrian. Although this charter was granted after the Detroit and Pontiac Railroad Charter, the Erie and Kalamazoo was the first railroad to begin active service. The line opened on November 2, 1836. The Erie and Kalamazoo Railroad is still in existence and is now part of the New York Central System under terms of a perpetual lease.

At first the cars on this road were pulled by horses which ran along ahead of the cars on a path between the rails. The horses were changed every four miles. Horses, however, were not used very long, for in

January, 1837, the first steam locomotive to be used in Michigan arrived at Toledo and began pulling cars behind it.

The early railroads were far different from the ones that may pass near your home today. The tracks upon which the trains ran were at first made of wooden rails. Long timbers, about one foot thick, were laid lengthwise of the track on top of ties that had been hewn flat on three sides. On the long stringers were later placed long iron strips upon which the wheels of the engine and cars ran. Sometimes,

Courtesy Michigan R. R. Association

Early engine on the Flint and Pere Marquette R.R.

with the changes in temperature, these iron strips broke. When the trains passed over them they suddenly curled upward. This would cause the next wheel to run under the iron strip instead of on top of it. This forced it upward and forward, thus breaking it off. Sometimes these bended strips tore a hole through the bottom of a car and injured the passengers. Occasionally passengers were killed by these "snake heads" as the bent rails were then called.

The engines were small and usually had only one pair of driving wheels. Behind the engine came a car that looked like a wagon. On this car was piled four-foot wood which the fireman used to heat the water in the boiler of the engine to make steam. It also carried barrels of water for use in the boiler. To aid the fire, these early engines had a large smokestack. Sometimes these smokestacks were almost as large as the boilers. With each puff of the little engine, huge glowing sparks from the fire went flying up the stack much to the dislike of the passengers and the people living along the railway. Fires were often started by these flying sparks. To stop this, laws were passed requiring that wire screens be placed over the tops of the engine stacks to keep the burning wood from flying out.

Behind the engine came the little cars. They were not much more than stagecoaches put upon the rails. Sometimes the seats ran lengthwise of the coach while in other coaches they ran crosswise. Often half of the passengers rode backwards in these seats. The freight cars and passenger cars had only four wheels each. For springs on these early cars white ash wood was used. The wheels on the engines and coaches were the same distance apart as were the wagon wheels of that day. That distance became known as "standard gauge" (four feet eight and one-half inches), and even today our railroad rails are laid the same distance from each other.

In 1834 permission was granted to another group of men to build the Detroit and Pontiac Railroad. In April, 1836, work on this railroad was started. Building this road proved to be a real task, for when the workers reached the Six Mile Road, just a short distance out of Detroit, they came upon a boggy region which was then called a "quaking prairie." The ground, although it had the appearance of being solid, would not hold up the weight of even the lightweight trains of that day. Trees were cut, dirt was hauled, and at last, after great delay and expense, the line reached to Royal Oak. Train service between Detroit and Royal Oak began in 1838. Later the road was built to Birmingham and service to Birmingham was started on August 16, 1839. In 1843 the little line was pushed north as far as Pontiac.

At first the trains, or cars, of this railroad were pulled by horses, but in the summer of 1839 the "Sherman Stevens," the second railroad engine to arrive in Michigan, was put to work pulling the little cars on the Detroit and Pontiac Railroad. In 1858 the name of this engine was changed to "Pontiac," and it was then used to haul cars on the Port Huron and Owosso Railroad.

For a time the Detroit and Pontiac Railroad ran its line into Detroit on what is now Gratiot Avenue. The depot for the road was then located where Kern's store now stands in Detroit. People living along the tracks soon complained that the trains made too much noise, frightened their horses, and set fire to their houses. A group of angry citizens twice tore up the downtown tracks of the Detroit and Pontiac Railroad. Then the depot was changed to a new location.

Still another early railroad was the Detroit and St. Joseph Railroad. Plans were made as early as 1830 for this road which was to run from Detroit to St. Joseph on Lake Michigan. In 1832 a charter for the road was granted. Because of the military advantages of the new line across the state, the War Department aided its building by surveying the route to be followed. By 1836 the line was graded as far as Ypsilanti.

When Michigan became a state in 1837, she was very railroad-minded, and the new state legislature soon voted fifteen million dollars for building railroads that were to be owned by the state. It was then planned that three roads should be built at state expense: the Michigan Northern, the Michigan Central, and the Michigan Southern.

The Michigan Northern was to run across the state from Port Huron to Grand Haven on Lake Michigan. The Michigan Central was to run across the state from Detroit to St. Joseph. This line had already been chartered and was being built as a private line under the name of the Detroit and St. Joseph Railroad. The road was bought by the state and renamed the Michigan Central. By January, 1838, the line was opened for service from Detroit to Dearborn. The following month it was opened to Ypsilanti. In 1838 it reached Ann Arbor; in 1844, Albion; in 1845, Marshall and Battle Creek; and in 1846, Kalamazoo. At that time the tracks of this railroad ran down Michigan Avenue in Detroit, and the depot for the road was located where the old Detroit City Hall now stands.

The Michigan Southern was to run from Monroe to New Buffalo on Lake Michigan. All of these roads were to be built and operated by the state. The fact that the state had little money at that time seems to have made little, if any, difference. It was felt that the money could easily be borrowed on the state's credit.

The bonds were printed and delivered to the Morris Canal and Banking Company of New Jersey. Part of the money was received, but before it was all paid to the state that company and its bank went bankrupt and Michigan found herself with a few miles of poorly built railroads, some worthless paper money, and a debt of $5,000,000.

Michigan's railroad building program was part of a wild speculation in western development that brought on the panic of 1837. So large were Michigan's undertakings that for a time it looked as though even the state would be forced into bankruptcy.

In addition to the railroad program there had been extensive plans for building many canals to join the rivers so that traffic could be carried on across the state by canals, such as the Erie Canal in New York and the canals in operation in Ohio. Unable to carry out her huge program because of financial troubles, the state abandoned the idea of constructing canals. This was just as well, for the days of canal transportation were already passing. Railroads were to become the new means of transportation for reaching the interior part of the state.

In 1846 Michigan was ready to sell her interests in the state-owned railroads. Accordingly, the Michigan Southern, which had been built from Monroe to Hillsdale, and the Michigan Central, which then ran from Detroit to Kalamazoo, were offered for sale. The Michigan Northern had been graded for some distance west of Port Huron but, because no tracks had been laid, the road was abandoned.

Buyers were found and the railroads then passed into private ownership. The Michigan Central was sold to the Michigan Central Railroad Company with the understanding that the new company would extend the line to Lake Michigan as rapidly as possible. This they did, and the Michigan Central reached Lake Michigan.

The road did not go to St. Joseph as had been originally planned but went to New Buffalo on Lake Michigan. From New Buffalo the Michigan Central Railroad began to run passenger and freight boats across Lake Michigan to Chicago. Also, by 1849 the old strap-iron rails of the road had been replaced by the T rails made of iron.

Under private control the Michigan Southern, like the Michigan Central, soon began to pay its owners a profit. In 1849 it leased the Erie and Kalamazoo Railroad and began to push rapidly west toward Lake Michigan. Great rivalry developed between the two railroads as to which would be the first to reach Lake Michigan and then Chicago. Both wanted the traffic of that rapidly growing city.

When the two rival roads wanted to extend their lines through northern Indiana and Illinois, they found their plans blocked by the legislatures of those two states which had railroad plans of their own. By agreements with roads in those states the two railroads finally reached Chicago. The Michigan Central made an agreement with the Illinois Central, and even today the two roads use the same station in Chicago.

Both the Michigan Central and Michigan Southern reached Chicago in 1852, and so great was the rivalry between the two companies that the Michigan Southern reached Chicago only one day after the Michigan Central.

As the years passed, settlers from Europe joined those of New England in the Michigan wilderness. After the revolutions of 1830 and 1848, many Germans left the Old World and came to the United

States to live. Some of these immigrants settled here in Michigan. Today the children of these German immigrants form a large part of our rural population.

Many Irishmen, too, found their way here from Ireland during this period. The potato famines of Ireland caused poverty and starvation among the Irish people. By the hundreds they came to America. Few of them had any money left after they arrived in New York City, and so they sought work in the growing number of factories in the East. A few came west and worked as laborers or started farming on new and better lands than they had had at home.

Among the settlers who came to Michigan from Europe were many people from Holland. These people in many ways were very similar to the earlier Pilgrims who came to America in 1620. The Pilgrims came here to escape religious persecution, and so did the Hollanders, or Dutch, from Holland. Both were people from the middle classes that were suffering from political and economic conditions unfavorable to them.

The Holland government had set up a state church which some ministers like Rev. Van Raalte and Rev. Vander Meulen and their followers did not like. The same potato blight that brought suffering to the Irish had also caused poverty and starvation among many of the middle-class people of Holland. Because of high taxes, famines, and religious persecution, many people left Holland and came to America and settled in Michigan, Iowa, Wisconsin, and Minnesota.

The first group of these Dutch settlers in Michigan came here under the leadership of their pastor Rev. Van Raalte. On October 2, 1846, Rev. Van Raalte, his wife, and their five children, together with fifty-seven other men, women, and children, left Rotterdam and sailed for New York. In November the party reached New York, where they met others who had sailed from Holland on other ships. From New York the immigrants went to Albany and then to Detroit.

Rev. Van Raalte had planned to take the group to Wisconsin to settle, but, since the freezing of the lakes had closed the season of navigation, the party was forced to stay in Detroit for the winter. A large warehouse then sheltered many of them during the winter that followed. Many of the men found work at Detroit while others found work in the St. Clair shipyards.

Rev. Van Raalte, not yet fully decided as to the best place to settle, studied maps of Michigan and the Great Lakes area and discussed his plans with several people. He and a few of his friends went to

Kalamazoo and that winter they set out from there by dog sled to explore the area in Allegan County near the shore of Lake Michigan. Day after day in snow and cold Van Raalte and his party explored the forest-covered wilderness until he was sure that the area would make a good homeland for his followers and their children. Then, kneeling in the snowy cold of the silent forest, he thanked God for leading him to this fertile area.

Courtesy Department of Conservation

An old Witness tree as it looks today to a modern surveyor (1953)

This area he had selected because it had not yet been settled and because there was room enough for farms for all of his followers and they would not have to mix with the other settlers. This would keep their church strong and also let them help one another. Because of Lake Michigan the area would be good for growing fruit. The open lake also would provide fisheries and good transportation to the eastern markets. Black Lake could become a fine harbor from which ships could sail not only to Lake Huron and Lake Erie but also to the growing number of Wisconsin ports and to Chicago, Illinois.

Several thousand acres of this wilderness land were then purchased for the settlement. Early in February, 1847, Rev. Van Raalte and a small group of his followers came to the spot they had chosen near the mouth of the Black River and began cutting trees and making cabins. Soon the others followed from Allegan, Detroit, St. Clair, and New York. Another group of Hollanders, seeking a place to settle, came up from New Orleans and joined the group under the leadership of Van Raalte.

Still another group, four hundred and fifty in all, under the leadership of Rev. C. Vander Meulen came from Zeeland, Holland, and founded a Michigan settlement called Zeeland in 1847. Another group settled at Vriesland in August, 1847. Still other groups settled south of Black Lake, at Kalamazoo, and at Drenthe.

Sickness struck the group during the first summer and many died. The first fall was beautiful, and the first winter was rather mild. By the time winter came again, the thrifty Dutch settlers were better prepared for it. Heavy rains in 1851 together with rodents, which attacked what little crops there were, again brought misery to the settlers. In 1856 dysentery struck the settlement. Some families lost two or three children. In one school district forty-five of the one hundred and twenty-three children died during the summer.

These early Dutch settlers cleared the land and farmed during the summer.

Like the Pilgrims before them, these settlers were a stern, religious people. They read their Bibles daily and carefully taught their faith to their children. Their little log meeting houses were filled each Sunday by a happy people who had found freedom to worship as they chose in the wilderness of Michigan.

Today the descendants of these settlers from Holland form the largest group of people of Dutch descent to be found in America. Their farms cover some five thousand square miles of some of the best farming land to be found in Michigan.

By 1860 the southern part of the Lower Peninsula had become a settled area. Thus, in just thirty years, the spreading wave of settlers had turned Michigan from a wilderness to a land where one could find homes, churches, schools, railroads, highways, and farmlands.

Chapter IX

PIONEER LIFE IN SOUTHERN MICHIGAN

Settlers coming to Michigan could choose one of three routes. Some of them drove their teams from New York across Ontario to Windsor and then crossed the river to Detroit. Others came south of Lake Erie along the roads of northern Ohio and entered the Lower Peninsula along its southern side. Most of the settlers, if they could afford it, came westward along the Erie Canal to Buffalo. Those who could not ride on the canal drove their teams, or walked, along the Genesee Road across New York to Buffalo on Lake Erie.

Each summer during the 1830's and 1840's canalboats on the Erie Canal moved endlessly back and forth from Buffalo to Albany, New York. Straining, sweating horses and mules, followed by drivers with whip in hand, wore a deep groove in the towpath along the side of the busy canal. Freight boats with wagons and supplies and packet boats crowded with tired passengers came westward in a never-ending line along the narrow, blue ribbon of water.

On warm summer days some of the passengers sat lazily in deck chairs on the flat roofs of the canalboats. They passed the little cabins of the lock-keepers, the farmhouses of the settlers in the wilderness of western New York State, straining horses pulling wagons along the Genesee Road, new and growing cities fed by the commerce of the canal, and the green foliage of the forest wilderness. Heads all bent low at every bridge.

Other canalboats coming east from Buffalo were always passing by. These boats carried goods from the growing West. Some were filled with wheat; others carried corn; still others carried barrels of cider, salt pork, bags of corn meal or flour that had been ground in the little gristmills on western streams, crates of eggs, hams and bacon from farm smokehouses, hogs grunting and squealing; others carried cattle; and still others transported salt, ashes for making lye, lumber, or cement. What could have been more amusing to travelers than to pass a canalboat going east loaded with turkeys, ducks, and chickens. All were passing eastward to markets along the busy canal.

All day the boats moved endlessly along. Regular packet lines had horses stationed every few miles. At these stations the tired horses rested while others took up the task of keeping the packet boats moving. Some lines carried their extra horses with them on the boat. One team would pull while the other rode along.

When night came, the passengers went into the cabin. Tables and chairs were pushed aside and beds for the passengers were dragged from storage closets. Women slept up in front, while the men slept in the room at the rear of the canalboat. No curtains gave personal privacy. Beds were narrow and hard, and usually the passengers had to furnish their own bedding. Some boats docked for the night; others pushed steadily along. When morning came, all the passengers were aroused. The berths were put away for the day, chairs and tables appeared, and the pleasing aroma of breakfast drifted through the packet boat.

So the immigrants came westward into the Land of the Lakes—single men, young couples, middle-aged men with their wives and children, and elderly ladies and men who could not be left behind. All followed the canal as the boats moved westward toward Buffalo.

At Buffalo the settlers changed to lake steamers, or schooners that would carry them westward across Lake Erie. The fare for the passage from Buffalo to Detroit was about five dollars and there were special rates for families. Those with money could get cabins while the others had to fare the best they could. All streamed aboard. Wagons were driven on deck. There the wheels were taken off and tied securely to the boat so that they could not roll around and cause damage if the boat should run into a storm. The wagon boxes, still sitting on their axles, were placed on deck, and the families often lived in them during the voyage westward across the lakes.

All summer long little passenger steamers and schooners plied back and forth across Lake Erie on a somewhat regular schedule. The brightly burning fires of the steamers always called for more and more wood. Whenever they stopped along the northern shore of Ohio, cords of firewood, later called "propeller wood," were hastily thrown aboard so that the boilers could be kept hot. Farmers then settling in northern Ohio hauled the wood to the docks in their wagons and got cash for it so that they could buy such things as sugar, flour, salt, guns and gunpowder, axes, and other tools.

Steaming across Lake Erie was far different from crossing it today. There were no weather warnings, no lighthouses, no buoys or charts to guide the boats. Sometimes the steam pressure got too high for the boilers, and then they blew up, killing many passengers. At other times storms blew across the lake and many settlers found this part of the journey the most difficult of all. Some were drowned and others became seasick and were sure that the little boats were going to sink.

But hour after hour the little boats pushed westward across Lake Erie, and the turning paddle wheels left a foaming track in the blue water behind. Sparks flew upward from the smokestacks and hot ashes drifted down upon the deck and passengers, but the steamers moved steadily on to the new lands of hope along the shores of the Great Lakes.

As the boats left the broad expanse of Lake Erie and steamed up the wide mouth of the Detroit River, past Fort Malden and Grosse Isle, on their second or third day out of Buffalo, the passengers gazed in wonderment at the green-forested shores on either side as the boats slipped quietly along on the pure, blue water of the silent, steadily flowing river. To the majesty of the forest was added the quaintness of the Indian villages on the western shore, the white-washed French cabins, and the spreading wings of the French wind-mills that stood out so brightly along the river bank.

When the boats docked at Detroit the horses, mules, and oxen were led ashore. People, boxes, and bundles all spilled from the holds of the boats along with babies, older children, axes, shovels, and pieces of cherished furniture and cooking utensils.

Among the confusion along the waterfront where settlers were getting their families, teams, and wagons ashore were criers who called out the names of one of the local hotels or inns for which they were drumming up business. Cries of "American," "Mansion House," "Eagle Hotel," and others were heard as the drummers tried to get some of the settlers to seek rest in one of the frontier inns where roughly dressed men sat around in small groups passing the time of day in talking, drinking, and squirting brown streams of tobacco juice on ground, floor, stove, or any other handy target.

When the wagons were assembled, and fixed at the local smithy if needed, and all the family was loaded amidst the assortment of luggage, the settlers were ready to continue their journey into the wilderness. Leaving the busy docks at the foot of Woodward Avenue, the straining teams of horses or oxen hauled the wagons up the hill to the place where Jefferson Avenue and Woodward Avenue cross and where stood the town market of that day. Then dipping down-

Courtesy of the Henry Ford Museum, Dearborn, Michigan

The village blacksmith shop

ward the wagons crossed the little Savoyard River and passed on out through the town. Mothers, not used to the roughness of a frontier town, clutched their little ones close to them and urged their sons and husbands to hurry and get on their way.

Long black-snake whips cracked with snapping stings that stung the backs of horses and oxen. Men shouted at their straining teams. Slowly the lumbering wheels of the mud-stained and weathered Conestoga wagons turned in the oozing mud as the straining horses or oxen dragged the wagons out of Detroit along one of the main roads leading into the forest-covered land. Indians standing along the way watched the newcomers move into their old homelands.

Immigrant wagons were of various kinds, sizes, and construction. Usually they were drawn by one, two, or three teams of oxen. The more prosperous settlers drove teams of horses, but horses were not then considered as good for frontier work as oxen. Most of the wagons had open boxes, but a few were covered with crude canvas tops of unsimilar designs.

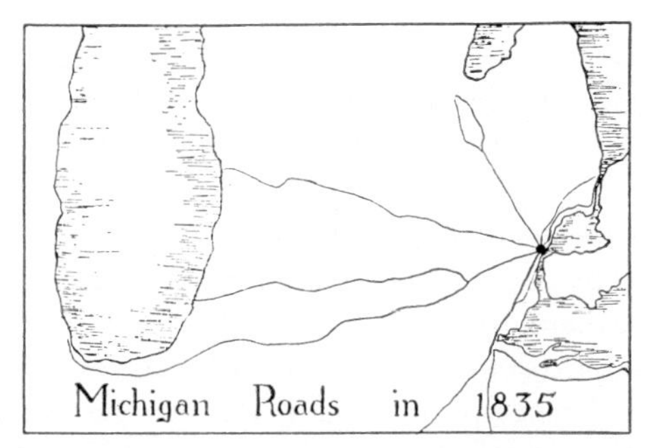

Wagons, wagons, wagons—one every five minutes from daylight until dark during the summer of 1836 left Detroit for points north or west. Most of them went west out Michigan Avenue and followed the road toward Chicago or branched off to the Territorial Road that ran west in the second row of counties. All were loaded with boxes of precious household goods and supplies. The larger boxes were usually placed on the bottoms of the wagons. Onto these were piled smaller ones with the smallest ones on top. The rest of the settlers' belongings, not easily lending themselves to box transportation, were often fastened here and there where best they could hang on the sides of the wagons.

In the front of the wagons on the only seat rode the settler and his wife. However, the men often walked along beside the oxen. Among the various boxes, crates of chickens, ducks, and a small pig or two could be seen the curly heads of children covered with caps or sunbonnets. Behind, tied securely to the wagon by a piece of old rope, came "Old Crumplehorn," the family cow. Other stock usable to settlers was often driven by boys of all ages. Many settlers brought a cat or two to catch rats, field mice, and squirrels. Under the wagon box, in the shade, often ran a lean, panting hound or two. Now and then the hound ran off into the forest, hot on the trail of some animal that had chanced to cross the road a short time before.

Courtesy Henry Ford Museum, Dearborn, Michigan

A Conestoga wagon. These wagons were the freight trains of their day.

Thus, the settlers left Detroit and took the new turnpikes to new farmlands deep inside Michigan. Back east, far across Lake Erie, lay their former homes and loved ones. To many of the settlers it seemed as if they were still going away from home and not getting closer to one.

Soon the little village of Detroit lay behind and all about them were trees, for all of Wayne County was then heavily timbered. Trees, trees were everywhere—elm, ash, oak, hickory, black walnut, and maple. So thick were these hardwood forests, especially in Oakland County, that the trees often reached upward to a height of one hundred fifty feet.

Overhead, a huge green summer canopy of broad leaves shut out the bright sunlight, thus leaving a dark and dusky gloom beneath the trees where the road lay. Huge tree trunks, standing clear of underbrush, closed any distant view except in places where clearings had been made by settlers.

This was truly a forest area. It lay like a great, deeply napped green carpet stretching on and on across the gently rolling hills of Michigan. Through this forest the slowly moving settlers struggled along the little turnpikes like a column of tiny ants wriggling and straining through tall grass.

From Detroit the flat and often swampy land stretched away in all directions for a distance of twenty miles or more. Long ago this area had been a part of the bottom of a large lake that has shrunk in size to present-day Lake Erie. This old lake bottom is mostly heavy clay soil. Scarcely a stone of any kind is to be found in the area.

Crossing this area was for the settlers often one of their greatest problems, especially in wet weather. There were days when a steady drizzle fell for hours. Then the trees, bushes, and roads became soaked with water. Horses and oxen became wet, as they plodded faithfully along. Little streams of water ran off their backs and down their legs. Men covered themselves with oiled leather jackets and splashed along beside the teams through the slippery mud.

Sometimes all sought shelter in the covered wagons or in little temporary camps that the settlers set up along the road. Clothing and bedding picked up the moisture and grew clammy, soggy, and cold. Dry wood for their fires was hard to find in the wet, dripping forest. Little pools of water gathered in the wagon tracks, in the ditches along the way, and in the low, swampy places in the woods. Streams rose and flooded marsh lands, thus making both the marshes and streams harder to cross.

Wet clay was churned and mixed by the feet of horses, oxen, men, and the slowly turning wheels of the pioneers' wagons as they moved along. It oozed up through the cloven feet of oxen, sheep, and swine and was sucked downward with a sticky sound as men or horses raised their feet from the slippery paste. It stuck to the slowly turning wheels and sometimes filled the spaces between the spokes until the wheels looked almost solid.

At times the weary travelers wondered where the water was the deepest and the ground most firm: in the center of the crisscrossed mass of wagon tracks or in the watery ditches along the side of the road? Wagons mired, horses and oxen strained forward as they tried to pull, only to slip in the clay. Men secured poles from the forest and helped the teams by pushing or prying the wagons.

If unable to go on, the settlers and their families waited until others going along the road came to them. New friendships that often lasted many years began at many of the mud holes along the roads to the West. Teams were then doubled, or even tripled, and the little wagons rolled on.

During the summer season mosquitoes, in dense clouds, buzzed in the air and in the evening settled in black masses on humans and animals alike. Deer flies bit with a nasty sting.

When the hot days of summer came and the rains fell less often, the clay roads began to dry. The yellow paste became thicker and thicker until at last it was baked into solid ridges and ruts by the summer sun. Old water holes stood empty and dry, and where once had been wagon tracks filled with dirty, muddy water, there stood huge ridges of baked clay. Horses and oxen picked their way across the pattern of ridges and holes. Wagons and stagecoaches rattled, bumped, and shook along behind.

Travelers pushing west on the Chicago Road found on the bank of the River Rouge Ten Ecyk's inn that he had built to care for weary travelers after a hard day's journey from Detroit. Just past the inn, in what was soon to be the center of Dearborn, they came to the Detroit Arsenal which the Federal Government had started to build in 1833 to care for troops and supplies needed in the Detroit area. At Eloise there were two cabins covered with one roof and named the Black Horse Tavern. At Wayne, then known to travelers as Derby's Corners, stood another inn that had been built by Mr. Stephen G. Simmons in 1825. At Clinton stood the Clinton Inn which was built in 1832 and which has now been reconstructed in Greenfield Village by Mr. Henry Ford.

Courtesy of the Henry Ford Museum, Dearborn, Michigan

Clinton Inn now at Greenfield Village. For many years this inn stood at Clinton, Michigan.

Of such inns one early pioneer said, "The emigrant was supposed to stop two nights at a tavern—the night he reached it and the first night after he left it, as he could not get far enough from it in one day." Many humorous stories were told about these crowded little frontier inns. One pioneer says, "The landlords would stow away at night all the beds would hold, and then wait until they were asleep, when he would take them from the beds and stand them up in the corners, until all were put to sleep. The great trouble with this method was personal identity in the morning."

Now and then as the settlers pushed out on the roads from Detroit they passed little clearings in the forest where sat tiny log cabins from which smoke sometimes wafted gracefully upward until it drifted off among the forest trees and disappeared in the blue sky far above. Around the cabins, amid "girdled" trees, grew little patches of wheat or potatoes half lost in the debris that littered the half-cleared ground. Now and then a settler's dog barked at the passing wagons, some settler waved a hand, or children's voices called out to the newcomers as they passed along the road.

When the straining teams had pulled the wagons about twenty or thirty miles from Detroit and the rolling, hilly land was reached, the clay often changed to sand. During rainy weather these roads were fairly good, but warm dry weather dried out the golden sand until it slid from the sharp angle of the turning rims of the wheels and fell back in a steady flow.

Steep hills were hard to climb. When going down them the loaded wagons often pressed hard upon the teams. Men sometimes stopped their rapid descent by tying a log on the back of the wagon or pushing a stick into the spokes of a back wheel, thus keeping it from turning.

Rivers were a never-ending source of trouble for the westward pushing pioneers. Sometimes the settlers were fortunate enough to find a "ford" where the water was shallow and the river bed firm enough to allow the team and wagon to cross. Sometimes, during flood seasons, settlers often had to wait for days before they could get across. Some rivers could not be crossed at all in this manner, so bridges had to be built. From the forests the travelers cut piles, braces, and girders for the bridges. Over these wooden spans they placed logs or planks hewn from the forest near by.

Scattered here and there along the way were poles and rails that had been cut from the forest to use as pries by men when their wagons had mired. Old wagon wheels, broken wagon tongues, and broken-down wagons that could go no farther were strewn here and there along the way telling of the troubles encountered by others who had gone on before. These pieces of equipment had often been searched for spare parts to repair the wagons that had followed, for there was no chance to get new parts to replace the broken ones. Everything was used as long as it could be, and then when it no longer was of value it was abandoned by the wayside. Like the dead ashes of the campfires, the discarded articles told the story of a people who were then coming into the wilderness.

Thus day after day the settlers toiled along the muddy or dusty roads. Some, with money to spend, stayed at the new log-cabin inns that were springing up in the shadow of the forests along the way. Others, closely saving the little money they still possessed, slept in their wagons or on the ground around little campfires beside the road. Fires glowed along the road at evening time, and their flickering lights cast weird shadows on the trees along the way. In battered and dented kettles and pans the settlers' wives cooked the evening meal.

The timid deer on their nightly forage stopped and looked from their forest cover, with big soft eyes, at the curious invaders who were coming in ever-increasing numbers to their ancient land. The slinking bobcat, attracted by strange new odors arising from the cooking kettles, crawled, with belly pressed close down, to sniff again the odors that came drifting down wind on the evening air. Distant howls of wolves broke the starry silence of the summer night. The howls grew closer and closer until at last shining eyes glowed in the bushes along the road and the rattle of dry leaves not far distant in the forest told of their presence. Horses or oxen pawed the ground and pulled at their tethers. The settlers threw another stick of wood upon their fires.

But the settler was a realist, and along with his troubles he found pleasures as well. In the inns and along the road he found friends and swapped stories far into the night. He discovered that the land was far from being the great swamp which had been pictured a few years before. The vast forests, the many streams, the "oak openings," the hills, the prairies, and the bright blue, sparkling lakes along the way added charm and variety as they slowly passed by. But best of all, somewhere—not now too far ahead—lay a new farm that would be their own.

Many of the new settlers could not afford wagons and had to depend upon their own feet for transportation. Often these foot travelers walked five or six hundred miles before they drove in their stake, recorded their claim, and jokingly told in after-years that they had come to Michigan on the "Foot and Walker Line." As the wagons rolled along, these less fortunates walked along with the slowly moving wagons. Most of them had little but a dream and, in their pockets or in a bag slung over their shoulder on a stick, what few worldly possessions they had carried all the way. Journey's end found nearly all very weary and almost, if not, penniless.

The sick, suffering, and dying struggled along as best they could, and when the rigors of the journey proved to be more than their health would stand, their fellow travelers, relatives, and friends, in simple frontier fashion and often without the aid of a minister, lowered them into shallow lonely graves along the wayside.

Thus the settlers, spreading outward in the shape of a growing fan, kept pushing into the wilderness out past the latest settlements. The spreading frontier lay just a mile or so from the traveled roads. As the settlers neared their journey's end their problems of transportation often increased because there had been fewer people ahead of them. Often as they came near the place where they were to settle, they had to make the first road through the forest. Trees had to be cut, "down timber" had to be pushed aside, bridges had to be built. But the turning wheels moved slowly on.

At last, after many trials and hardships, the long journey from the East came to an end. Weary children no longer asked how much farther they had to go. The worn oxen were perhaps as happy as the family that the journey had come to its end. Where the settler and his family stood probably no white man had ever stood before. The sound of strange English voices, foreign to the ancient land, re-echoed from the trees. Their feet now trod ground that had known no other footprints than those of soft-padded feet, the split hoofs of animals, or the soft press of an occasional moccasin as an Indian had chanced to pass by while hunting. The nearest settler's cabin might be close or it might be miles away.

Few of Michigan's early settlers had a home to come to. When they arrived on the spot that they had chosen for their home, most of them found themselves in the midst of the ancient wilderness. Sometimes a family continued to live in the wagon, while others built crude shelters in which to stay for the first few weeks. A few of the more fortunate ones were able to stay with neighbors.

Once the spot had been selected and the proper title to it had been granted by the nearest land office, the settler and his family began the task of building a little log cabin that they would soon call their home.

A good supply of pure water for the family and stock was a necessity, so if possible the settler chose as the site of his cabin a place near a spring or stream. Then, taking his ax, he began the task of felling the trees to make his cabin. The larger trees were of no use to him because they were too heavy to be handled by men or oxen. Logs for the cabin must be about a foot in thickness. So for days the settler worked, cutting and trimming logs. When enough logs had been made ready, he set out to tell the neighbors that he was ready to put up his cabin, or log house, as it was called. On the day set the men from all around, perhaps as far away as ten or fifteen miles, came to the "house raising bee," as the frontier people called it. If any had oxen, they brought them along to "snake" the logs from the forest to the place where the cabin was to be built. Sometimes even Indians came to make, as they said, the white man's wigwam.

The earlier French cabins in Michigan had been built by placing logs upright in the ground. This method was not followed by the early English settlers of Michigan. Their cabins were made by laying the logs parallel with the ground. Four logs were thus placed on the ground on the spot where the little cabin was to stand. Upon these the others were placed with their rough ends sticking out to form the corners. Men known as "corner men" skillfully notched each log where it overlapped at the ends. The first few logs were not hard to put up, but as the little building grew in height, it became more of a task to raise the heavy logs. Slanting poles were then placed from the top log to the ground, and up these slanting poles the logs for the cabin were rolled. Sometimes oxen were used to pull chains that passed over the building and rolled the logs upward into their places. If oxen were not to be used, men used long poles called "hand spikes" or poles having a crotched end called "moleys" to pry and push the logs up the slanting poles into place on the wall.

An early hewn log cabin at Dixboro (1955)

Pioneer cabins were usually very small, only about twenty feet square in size. When the logs had reached the height of about seven feet, the workmen began to make the roof. The two ends of the cabin were "cubbed" or "cobbed" up. That is, each log was cut shorter and shorter until it came to a point at each end of the cabin. From point to point of the cubbed-up ends, a pole, called the "ridge pole," was placed. Onto this the roof rafters, other small poles, were placed. More poles were placed lengthwise of the cabin on these rafters. These poles were held in place by pegs or springy strips of wood called "withes" which tied the poles to the roof. Onto these poles were placed marsh grass or hand-split shingles called "shakes." Long poles, held in place by pegs or withes, held the shakes in place. Although these roofs kept out the rain and most of the snow, they also let out most of the heat. During the storms of the winter, the wind often blew small flakes of snow through the cracks between the shakes. These flakes settled down onto everything in the room.

A door was cut into one side. Usually there were no windows. A fireplace was cut into one end of the cabin and built up on the outside with smaller sticks to form the fire box and chimney. The inside of the fire box and chimney were then plastered with a mixture of sand and clay to keep the wood from catching on fire. Each night before going to bed, the settler would have to look up the chimney, after the fire had burned low and been banked for the night, to see if the chimney had caught on fire as it often did when the clay coating cracked open.

At best the cabin was only a secondary house for the settler. Like the Eskimo, he kept his body warm by wearing warm clothing day and night during the long, cold winter.

At first the settlers used oak shakes for shingles. These were followed by oak shingles. Still later pine or cedar shingles were used. At first there were no floors in the little cabins. Later oak logs were cut in half and hewn smooth on one side. These pieces, laid round side down into the dirt, served as flooring. Later, when sawmills came, lumber could be used for floors and building material. Each cabin door swung on wooden hinges. It had a wooden latch with a string which could be pulled inside to serve as a lock. Usually, however, the latch string hung on the outside as a sign of welcome to any who might chance to come that way. Not a nail or piece of iron was used in building these early pioneer log cabins.

Between the logs the pioneers drove grass, mud, and chips called "chinkers." These helped to keep the wind and rain from coming in between the logs. To keep the cracks filled required repairs from time to time as the mud fell out and the chinkers then came loose.

If a settler had oxen or horses, a little log barn similar to his log house was built to protect the animals from the cold storms of winter as well as from the wolves and bears that came prowling around the buildings during the night.

At first there was little furniture in these tiny cabins. Now and then a few choice pieces had been brought from back East, but wagon transportation greatly limited the carrying space. The article most commonly brought was the spinning wheel, and this was more of a necessity than a piece of furniture. At first blocks of wood served as chairs. Beds were built into one corner of the room by using small poles and wooden pegs. As almost every settler had an auger, he soon began making chairs with legs. Where boards could be secured, other and better pieces of furniture were often made. Clothing was sometimes stored in trunks that the settlers brought with them as they came west.

The years of settlement were the years of the age of wood. From wood the settlers made pitch forks, shovels, ax handles, carts, wagons, houses, barns, machine parts, dishes, bowls, ladles, boxes, barrels, roads, bridges, pails, furniture, spinning wheels, and looms. Moreover, it was the fuel with which they cooked their food and heated their cabins.

To the new settler, the spreading forest about him had little value. There was too much of it. He had come to farm and not to lumber. Every one, except those settling on the oak openings, had timber or could take what he needed from nearby lands still belonging to the government. So the next big job for the settler's family was to clear the land.

Most people today, second or third generation descendants from these early settlers or children from more recent immigrations, are used to seeing open farmlands and well-paved and ordered streets with trees selected and arranged in orderly fashion. Unless one has been in the woods where trees are being cut, it is difficult for one to realize the extent of debris and toil that went with clearing a forest land to make it into farming land suitable for even a single plow and swinging scythe.

Only a few of the early settlers had good tools with which to work. Good grades of steel were scarce and tools were easily broken. An ax was the most common and useful tool. Its constant thud, thud, thud was the battle sound of the struggle between the forests to remain in possession of their age-old lands and the new settlers to claim it for themselves and their children. Axes, swung by muscles that had grown strong from daily toil, bit through the rough outer bark of the trees and then with each stroke sank deeper and deeper into the moist, clean, sappy wood beneath. White, damp chips snapped out with each swing of the ax and fell among the dead leaves and decaying twigs around the foot of the trees. Clearing the land was a task that took long hard days of toil, and fortunate was the settler who, at the close of the year, had the trees down on as much as five acres of land with the stumps still left standing.

To cut these huge trees with merely an ax was a huge task and one that could not be done in a single season. Yet food had to be planted so the family could live through the following winter. But food could not grow in such heavy shade as the forests made. To let the sunlight in, settlers often "girdled" trees by cutting a wide band in their bark. Then the uprunning sap, checked in its rise, oozed out and went running back onto the ground from whence it had come. The green leaves, high overhead, curled up, shriveled, turned brown, and finally came drifting gently downward to the ground, finding their places of rest before their time.

Even when the trees were down the settler's clearing problems were far from over. A felled tree was one thing; cleared land was yet another. Hours of toil were often required to cut the branches from the fallen trunk. Some of the branches were cut into firewood for the coming winter. The rest were gathered into piles, and when they had lain long enough to dry a little, they were burned. The stumps and trunks still remained to be cleared.

To get rid of the huge tree trunks was a seemingly endless task, often requiring more strength than a single settler could provide. At first the tree trunks had to be chopped into logs, but later with the coming of cross-cut saws the trunks could more easily be cut. Once a tree trunk was cut into logs it was still far from being destroyed. If a settler were fairly prosperous, he might have the help of a team of oxen or horses, but many settlers had no such luxury.

Because the large logs were too heavy for one man to handle alone, the settlers often helped each other in getting rid of the logs. When a settler had felled his trees and cut them up into logs, his neighbors came to his farm to help him. These gatherings were known as "logging bees." If a settler had a team of horses or oxen, he brought them along to help drag the logs close together so that they could be burned. With pries, made from small poles, the men rolled the logs into piles three or four high. Over these log piles dry branches were placed and then the whole was set on fire. It is safe to say that the clearing fires of the settlers destroyed as much good timber as ever came from the sawmills of Michigan as lumber.

Hardwood stumps rot out in a few years, and so they were sometimes left to slowly decay. To chop and dig them out was hard, tiring work that gave little sign of the hours of toil which a settler spent upon them. Besides his ax, the settler had another force to put against the stumps and that was fire. When the stumps had dried out and the oozing sap no longer came from the ground, the settler tried to burn them. With his spade he dug a hole under the dried roots. Into the hole he pushed dried twigs and chips. These he then set on fire. The little flames grew and crept upward. Brush was piled on. Then the stump caught fire and burned for a time. Sometimes a settler had to do this several times before the entire stump was burned.

So the early settler farmed as best he could around the stumps. If he had a plow, he ran his furrows in curves around the stumps and across his half-cleared land. If he had no plow, he dug up the fresh earth with his spade and planted his crops for food for the coming winter.

Other settlers came and soon the thud of more axes sounded just beyond the settler's line. Curling smoke, rising skyward, showed plainly that another family had arrived and was busy changing woodland into open farmland where a good man could with a plow run a true straight furrow from one side of his field to the other. The sound of voices broke the silence of the wilderness: voices of men at work, voices of mothers calling for their children, voices of children at play. Strange new smells, too, blended with those of the flowers and trees. The greasy smell of frying bacon, the warm, pleasing aroma of fresh baking bread or biscuits, the dark smoke drifting lazily from the smokehouse where bacon and hams were being cured—all mingled with the smoke from the smoldering clearing fires as the forest land changed to farmlands.

The blue, hazy smoke, like a soft, misty vapor, rose from the ever-increasing number of clearing fires, where roots, logs, stumps, and rotting debris of the forest were burned to clear the land. Dry brush and limbs burned quickly with an intense flash that sent the crackling flames high into the air. Rotten logs and old stumps burned slowly. Sometimes they smoldered on for days or even weeks before they were consumed. Blue smoke drifted upward among the tree tops, or hung like a thin blue haze in the valleys between the higher green ridges. The clean, fresh air of the forest took on a new odor, the odor of burning wood.

The hardwood lands yielded easily to the plow once the trees were down and the stumps and roots removed, but the prairie land was hard to break on the first plowing. Prairie land did not have to be

Courtesy of the Henry Ford Museum, Dearborn, Michigan

Plows like this one were brought to Michigan by the early settlers

cleared, but the sod was so tough that it usually took from two to six teams of oxen pulling together to "break" the land. A large plow called a "bull plow," made entirely of wood except for the "share" and "coulter," was used for the first plowing of prairie land. The standard price for plowing the tough prairie land was five dollars an acre.

Fences were a problem for the early settlers too, but the fields had to be strongly fenced to keep horses, cattle, and pigs from wandering off into the woods where they would be caught by the wolves. To fence their fields, settlers split fence rails from the forest trees. In fact, rail splitting became a regular employment for some men. By means of a large wooden hammer, called a "beetle," and wedges and gluts, smaller oak logs were cracked lengthwise into fence rails. A good workman could make about one hundred fence rails a day.

A few of the settlers who lived near the Great Lakes were able to sell some of their timber as cordwood for the early steamships. Others who happened to have farms along the early railroads drew the cordwood to a "wooding station" along the tracks, where they sold it for sixty-five cents a cord. To cut this cordwood was hard work, but it did give some early settlers a little cash money with which to buy a few things like salt, flour, and gunpowder.

Getting and keeping a fire was always a problem to a pioneer family, for they had no matches as we have today. Sometimes live coals were brought from a neighbor's fire. At other times "punk" (a soft, rotten wood from maple trees), a flint stone, and a piece of steel

Courtesy of the Henry Ford Museum, Dearborn, Michigan

An early settler's home

were used to start a fire. By striking the flint stone with the steel, a spark could be thrown against the dry punk. Careful blowing would cause the spark of fire to spread. Fine, dry "whittlings" were then placed on top. Before he went to bed, a settler carefully banked his fire for the night by covering it with ashes. In the morning the ashes were carefully removed, and by means of a "bellows" which blew air onto the coals, the fire was again started.

As the settlers prospered, the old wooden fireplaces gave way to better ones made of stones or bricks. Until the coming of stoves, the fireplace was still used for doing all the cooking. Potatoes were baked in the glowing coals. Fresh corn from the fields was roasted. Sometimes "bake ovens" or "bake kettles" were placed over a bed of coals and thus biscuits, bread, and johnny cake were made. Large frying pans, called "spiders" in Michigan, standing on three or four legs could be placed over a bed of coals and used to fry bacon or pancakes. From the side of the brick or stone fireplaces later hung a swinging iron bar called a "crane." The bar could be pulled out in front of the fireplace or pushed back in over the fire. Onto this bar were fastened "pot hooks" which held the iron "pots" or "kettles" in which the foods were stewed or boiled. Other mechanical devices called "spits" allowed an iron bar to be pushed through a roast of meat or fowl and then turned slowly so that the meat would be evenly cooked on all sides. Some spits were turned by hand, others had a clock arrangement with a weight that kept the spit slowly turning. Some later fireplaces had a brick oven built in at one side of the fireplace opening. These were slow to heat, but once hot, they stayed warm for a long time and were used for much of the baking that was done by the family.

When bread was baked, some of the dough called "emptins" was saved for starting the next batch of dough. There was no way to buy yeast and thus some dough was always saved to start the next batch of bread. Cider was used to make homemade vinegar. Into the fresh cider the settler's wife placed some "mother" from old vinegar. This would cause the cider to ferment and turn to cider vinegar.

The fireplace was the center of family life, especially during the wintertime when the family gathered indoors. On cold days a bright fire in the little fireplace bade welcome to strangers and the cheer and comfort of home to father and boys as they came in from doing the chores or from the hunt. In the evening the glowing coals lit up the family circle. Before it mother and the girls sat and knit, or patched the family clothing, while father and the boys cared for their guns, shoes, and other outdoor equipment. All lived together before the open fire and thought mostly of one thing—how could they make a living in the wilderness?

Almost everything the pioneers ate came from their own farms or the nearby woods. The first year or two, until the crops were harvested, were often hungry years for many settlers and their families. But food could be had if the settler had a gun. Wild turkeys, bears, deer, ducks, passenger pigeons, geese, and rabbits could be found in the forests and marshes. Wild berries too could be gathered. Fish were then plentiful in the lakes and streams. Wild honey was found in bee trees and used for a table sweet. When a settler found a bee tree, he chipped it with a mark or put his initials on the tree, thus marking it as his property. No Indians or other white men would then touch it.

There was very little fruit other than wild berries to be had by the early settlers, but from their farms soon came wheat, corn, potatoes, and many kinds of vegetables. Lean, tough pigs fed in the forests on the mast that lay beneath the trees. Sheep furnished wool for clothing and food for the table. Chickens, ducks, and geese were raised by every settler. Cows became common and milk could be found on most tables. Oxen provided draft animals and also meat. Bears and wolves often raided the farmer's stock and killed pigs, sheep, calves, and chickens. Poultry was hard to keep because of the foxes and hawks that liked to carry off the birds. Because tea, coffee, and butter were costly, they were rarely seen on the settlers' tables. Sometimes substitutes for coffee, such as crust coffee or browned grains, were served. Tea leaves were saved and used again and again in order that young folks could have their fortunes told. Baked and boiled potatoes were common, as were johnny cake and milk gravy, which was made of milk, flour, salt, and bacon grease Salt was scarce and costly for many years.

Courtesy Henry Ford Museum, Dearborn, Michigan

Looms like this one were used for making cloth. This loom has a flying shuttle. One of the boxes into which the shuttle flies can be seen just to the left of the warp threads. The shuttle is thrown back and forth by the ropes which this boy holds in his left hand. His right hand is on the beater.

Though the food was plain, there was usually much of it from the fertile lands and people ate heartily. Many developed what was jokingly called the "Michigan appetite," and as one settler said, there was "nothing but the dishes left after the meal."

Maple syrup and maple sugar furnished the settler his only sweet except wild honey. The art of gathering maple sap and making maple syrup and sugar had been learned from the Indians. Early each spring, just as the snow was leaving the ground, the settlers gathered maple sap and boiled it. "Sugaring off" as they called it was a jolly time when candies and sweets made up part of the social occasion.

Clothing such as we know it today was scarce in the early settlements. Children sometimes went barefooted all winter. Some buckskin jackets like the Indians had were worn by the men, but wool was the most-used item. This the settlers got from their sheep. The women carefully cleaned, carded, and spun the wool into yarn on the spinning wheel that could be found in every home. Often the skeins of yarn were dyed with colors made from nuts, berries, or roots. Pioneer women spent much of their time knitting. They knitted sweaters, socks, mittens, and shawls. The yarn was also made into cloth called "homespun" and then made into suits or dresses. There was little store clothing before 1880.

Hooked rugs fashioned from discarded cloth or clothing were made to cover the floors. By 1840 carpets could be found in some of the settlers' homes.

Bedding was important to the early pioneers, for their houses were cold at night after the fire had been banked. There were no springs on their beds. Rope crossed at right angles served in place of springs. Onto this was usually placed a tick filled with straw or marsh hay. In the wintertime a feather tick was placed over the straw tick. A feather tick was a big bag made of "ticking" just the size of the bed and filled with goose "down" that had been plucked from the live geese. Feather ticks were soft and warm.

Over them the settlers put "comforters" or large quilts. Making quilts took long hours of work for the women and girls. They were made by placing a thickness of cotton or wool between two layers of cloth. The wool or cotton in the center was held in place by threads which passed from top to bottom every few inches. Putting these threads and knots in a quilt was called "tying it." Quilts were carefully made and skillfully stitched by hand. Sometimes the stitches were spaced almost as evenly as they are now done by machines.

The women and girls made all the soap used by the family. All the ashes from the fires were carefully saved. Water was then allowed to drip through the ashes. This water then contained lye. To it were added old fats that had been saved from day to day. After boiling the fats and lye together, the liquid was allowed to jell. Thus soap was made.

Doing the family washing was a hard task for the women and girls. Water had to be heated and poured into wooden wash tubs. Then each article to be washed had to be scrubbed by hand. It took long hours of tiring work.

As the cows increased in number, butter was more often seen on the settlers' tables. Fresh milk was placed in pans and left to stand overnight so that the cream would rise to the top. This rich, yellow cream was then skimmed off and placed in an upright churn. The churn was usually a tall crockery one, or one made of wood that looked like a tall wooden pail. On top there was a cover with a hole in the center. Through this hole went a round stick like a broom handle. To the lower end of the stick was fastened a round, flat piece of wood or two crossed sticks that splashed in the cream as the handle was raised or lowered. Up and down, up and down, up and down went mother's arms each time the ladle splashed in the churn. At last the golden butter came to the top of the liquid in the churn. Skimming it off with a wooden "butter ladle," she put the freshly churned butter into a wooden bowl and then worked it with the ladle into a yellow lump. The liquid that remained in the churn was called "buttermilk." Sometimes this was drunk by the family. If there was more than the family wanted, it was added to the skimmed milk, milk from which the cream had been taken, and fed to the pigs.

Candle-making was another household task. Tallow was carefully saved and then melted and poured into candle molds through which a piece of string had been stretched. These candles, Betty lamps, and the fire in the fireplace were the only sources of light during the hours of darkness. Tallow candles, however, were not so good as our candles today. They burned rather quickly and gave off a black, greasy smoke.

Brooms were made by hand, as were ox yokes, sleighs, carts, and many of the farm tools.

At first many of the settlers' cabins had no windows, but before long small pieces of window glass began to be put into little window frames. This made the cabins lighter and better, and, since the danger of Indians looking into the open windows was past, the settlers were glad to have glass windows.

Sickness was a dreaded thing to the early settlers, for many of them were ill much of the time. Malaria, or the "fever and ague" or "ager" as they called it, was common among them. One of the first questions they often asked a newcomer among them was, "Have you had the fever and ague yet?" If he said No, they knew that he had not lived in Michigan very long. This dreaded disease, carried by mosquitoes that lived in the swampy lands, caused the early settlers much suffering and loss of work. One day they would be burning with fever and the next day cold and shaking all over even if the weather was warm and bright. Gradually, as the land was drained and the breeding places of the mosquitoes were made much smaller, the cases of fever and ague became fewer and fewer.

Cholera, a type of dysentery, was another disease that visited the settlements almost every summer. Many people, especially children, died after having it only a few hours. Sometimes whole families died in two or three days. Typhoid, pneumonia, diphtheria, and smallpox were other diseases dreaded by every family. Though there were often many children in these early pioneer families, many times only a few lived to become men and women.

Doctors were few and often miles away. Sometimes before the doctor could be brought to the house, the sick were already dead. The women did the best they could to care for the sick. Every summer they gathered herbs and dried them for medicines. Sassafras was used for boils, boneset for fevers, lobelia for measles, sage for worms, and elder blossom tea or catnip tea for upset stomach.

Barn raisings, house raisings, and logging bees furnished occasions for mutual help and community gatherings. Then there were dances, too. A violin or two, and sometimes an accordion, provided music for the dances. Square dances were popular at that time, and all present entered into the fun and spirit of the gay occasion. The pioneers found pleasure also at the corn husking bees. When fall came they gathered for the husking. What fun there was when someone found a red ear of corn! The lucky finder had the right to kiss any girl at the bee—that is, if he could catch her.

Harvest time was a busy time for the early settlers. The sun shone and the little fields of grain ripened. Men and women looked and were glad. There would be bread next winter and feed for the chickens and the stock. There would be some to sell, too, and that would bring money for salt, gunpowder, and a few things from the local stores that were beginning to appear at the crossroads.

But the grain had yet to be gathered. At first little sickles were used, and gathering in grain was a very slow, hard task. Later scythes were used, and the grain could be cut faster. Scythes and sickles were carefully sharpened, because the harvesting had to be done by human muscle power.

Early dawn found the farmers starting across their fields with scythes well sharpened on a hand whetstone. With a swinging rhythm, developed by days of toil, the long blades of the settlers' scythes mowed through the standing grain, and the golden blades of the wheat fell back into the cradles. The filling cradles swung back and forth with the scythes as they were carried by muscles as strong as steel.

Each cradle full was carefully bound and stacked. Every now and then the working men stopped to whet their scythe blades with a whetstone that they carried in their hip pockets.

The sun rose higher. The day grew warm. Sweat broke out upon the men as they moved slowly across their golden fields. Shirts grew dark with perspiration. Great beads of water rolled down cheeks, necks, and brows and dripped from noses and chins. Sweating arms and moist shirts gathered the flying dust and chaff.

Across the fields came children carrying jugs filled with water—clear, cool water from the spring—for their fathers. Sometimes a beaten egg, ginger, salt, and pepper were added to the water. The toiling men paused. Taking one of the jugs, they tossed it up into the air and brought it to rest upon the elbows of their bent arms. The cool water ran gurgling from the brown jug into thirsty dry mouths.

At last the grain was cut and gathered in. Then it was "flailed" or "tromped" and "winnowed" and hauled by wagons to the nearest railroad or port, where it began its journey eastward to the markets of a hungry world. The great golden stream of wheat had begun its flow from the West to the East along the busy Erie Canal. At first it was only a small trickle started forward by tired human arms gathering it from dawn to dusk, for as late as 1830 the entire grain supply of the world was still being gathered by hand with no better tools than the sickle, scythe, and cradle.

But these days of toil were soon to pass. In 1831 the first successful reaper cut a field of six acres. In 1834 Mr. Cyrus McCormick was granted a patent on his new machine, but he did not sell a reaper until 1840. In 1846 Mr. McCormick moved his business to Chicago and in the following year sold seven hundred reapers. By 1849 his business had more than doubled, and by 1860 his company was selling more than four thousand reapers a year. Along with the sewing machine and the steam engine, the reaper helped to lessen the hours of human toil. Many reapers were sold in Michigan, and for many years these machines helped to make Michigan a leading wheat-producing state.

At first it was hard to get grain ground for home use. Sometimes the settlers had to grind it by hand. As the settlements increased, small gristmills, run by water power, appeared on several of the streams in the southern part of the state wherever enough water fall could be found in the streams to turn a water wheel. Mills run by water power were few in number, however, because most of the rivers did not permit enough fall to turn a water wheel.

To these early mills the settlers took their wheat and corn to be ground. From the bins above, the wheat or corn ran down into the center of two burrstone grinding wheels. One stone, the bottom one, was held firmly in place while the upper one turned slowly upon it. As the grain passed outward from the center of the stone, it was crushed between the two stones into flour or meal. Then the ground material was sifted, or "bolted," through a "bolting cloth." This bolting process removed the outer husk of the grain which could not pass through the cloth. These early flours did not keep as long as our present-day flours because they retained the heart or germ of the grain and all the materials nature had stored in the wheat.

The gristmills also ground corn, rye, and buckwheat for both human use and animal feed. Corn was commonly used among the Michigan pioneers as a food. From corn meal they made cornmeal mush, spoon breads, and johnny cake. Cornmeal mush was eaten as a cereal with milk or cream and a little maple syrup. Johnny cake was eaten with maple syrup. Later some butter was also used. Buckwheat flour was used for making buckwheat pancakes.

Later, steam-driven gristmills were built in places where water power could not be found. With the coming of the large flour mills in the West, during the latter part of the nineteenth century, most of the little gristmills in Michigan disappeared. However, a few throughout the state are still grinding grain just as it was ground over a hundred years ago. One of these early gristmills is now in operation at Greenfield Village in Dearborn. Today at the Village you can see grains being ground just as they were in the days when the settlers took their grain to the gristmill to be ground into meal or flour.

To keep his other crops such as carrots, potatoes, and turnips from freezing during the winter, the settler often stored them carefully away in a place called a root cellar. This was usually a cave dug into the side of a hill and packed with straw to keep the food from freezing.

Not only did the settler have to put away supplies for himself and his family, but he had to put away hay and grain for his livestock as well. Often hay was stacked in the open barnyard.

Chapter X

EARLY CULTURAL DEVELOPMENT

(1815-1875)

Settlers coming to Michigan after the War of 1812 were often poor and sometimes lived far apart. Most of them were Protestants from New England or from the southern states. At first there were no churches in the settlements. Sometimes an itinerant preacher stopped for a day or two in a settlement, preached a sermon, said a few words over the grave of one of the settlers who had been buried by the family, and then passed on to another settlement. Within a few years little churches began to appear in the wilderness. In the spring of 1818 the first Protestant church to be built in Michigan after the American occupation was built by a group of Methodists on the banks of the River Rouge just west of where the Ford Rouge Plant stands in Dearborn today. At that time there were just ten people who were members of this little church.

During the years from 1820 to 1830 other little log churches began to appear in the Michigan wilderness. These early log buildings were later replaced by newer churches made of lumber. To these little churches the early settlers went on Sunday mornings. Those who lived close by walked to church, but others who lived farther away often came in buggies or wagons that were drawn by horses or even by oxen. At first the horses were tied to trees near the church while the church service was being held. Later, back of most churches there was a long shed where horses could be sheltered from storms as they waited during the time of the service.

The church played an important part in the settlers' lives. The weekly church meetings not only cared for their spiritual needs, but also gave them a chance to meet their neighbors and friends. At the church they met and visited with their neighbors and often invited them home for Sunday dinner. Picnics, too, were common on Sunday afternoons after church when the weather was warm. Huge tables, spread with all the best cooking of the women for miles around, drew young and old.

Because many of the settlers came from New England, they were Congregationalists or Presbyterians. A Presbyterian church was started at Monroe in 1820, at Pontiac in 1824, at Farmington in 1825, and at Ann Arbor in 1826. A Mormon church, more correctly called a church of the Latter-day Saints, was started in Pontiac in 1834. Many of the settlers were Methodists, and soon many Methodist churches could be found in southern Michigan. In 1855 people of the Seventh-day Adventist faith began settling in the area near Battle Creek. Lutherans who came from Germany and the Scandinavian countries started Lutheran churches in their communities. A few Quakers came to Michigan from Pennsylvania. About the time Michigan was settled, there was a religious awakening in America. The rapid spread of churches across the southern part of the state was a part of this general movement that spread across America in the years before the Civil War.

Marker erected at Dearborn in 1954 on the site of the oldest continuing Protestant church in Michigan.

As the population of Michigan grew larger, there began to be a need for banks. In 1819 the first bank in Michigan was started. It was known as the Bank of Michigan and was located in Detroit. Two more banks were started in 1827. One of these banks was the Farmer and Mechanics Bank of Detroit. The other new one was the Bank of Monroe. In 1834, banks in Michigan were allowed to set up branch banks. Branch banks appeared in that same year at Kalamazoo and St. Joseph. During the next three years these banks were kept very busy because of the land speculation which was going on at that time. A new law, passed in 1837, made it easier to establish banks. Many new banks quickly sprang up. Most of these new banks had little capital, and some of them were in places that were hard for the bank examiners to find or to visit even after they once found out where they were located. These banks are usually written about in your history as "wildcat banks." Many of them had little cash. Some of them had only land as security, and sometimes the land was just swamp. When the Panic of 1837 came, several of these early banks failed and many of Michigan's early settlers lost all their money. This panic and the failure of these banks hurt the early economic advancement of Michigan. Later better banking laws were passed and safer banks were started.

As early as 1817 there was a feeling among many of the people then living in Michigan that the state should have a university. In that year the governor and the judges of the territory passed an act founding a university. It was called the University of Michigania. There were to be thirteen professorships in the new university. This means that thirteen men were to be appointed as heads of the thirteen departments. When the excitement died away and the search for these thirteen men began, they were not to be found in the territory. Rev. John Monteith, the Presbyterian minister at Detroit, was made president of the new university and given seven professorships. The remaining six, as well as the vice-presidency, were given to Father Gabriel Richard. Thus Michigan's first university began in Detroit on what is now Bates Street, between Larned and Congress. This little university was not very successful. The main reason for its failure was that there were few qualified students to enter it at that time. What Michigan needed was a system of public schools that would prepare students to enter a university. Such a system was started a little later because the settlers felt strongly the need for their children to have a chance to get an education.

The Ordinance of 1787 had stated that "religion, morality, and knowledge being necessary to good government and the happiness of mankind, schools and the means of education shall forever be encouraged." But such high phrases did not pay the bills for educating the settlers' children. The settlers were busy clearing land and trying to raise enough crops to feed their families. What is more, children were needed around the home to do what work they could. Although many of the settlers realized the need for schools, they did not feel that they could afford the expense such schools would require.

As early as March 26, 1804, the Congress of the United States had started a long-time plan to aid education in the United States. According to the act passed on that date, section sixteen of every congressional township was to be set aside as the school section and the funds received from the sale of the school sections were to be used for education. During the years before Michigan became a state, this money was often spent by local school districts to pay teachers. Some districts received more money than did others because of this grant.

Some section sixteens were good land and were sold at a good price, but other section sixteens were poor or even swamp land and therefore brought in little or no money. Because of this, all districts did not share alike in the amount of money each received from the sale of these public lands.

In 1827 the territory passed a law that made each township responsible for the schools in its area. Most townships, however, had little money to spend on education, and most of them sent out what were known as rate bills to parents who had children in school. Besides these early schools there were some private schools and academies. The first fully organized school district in Michigan seems to have been started at Raisinville, on the River Raisin, in 1828.

In 1829 further funds were raised for education by placing a tax on property belonging to people who did not live on it. A law of that same year divided the townships into smaller school districts that were nearer to the homes of the children going to school. As yet Michigan had no organized school system.

When the settlers began to come into Michigan in greater numbers, there developed a demand for newspapers. The first newspaper ever printed in Michigan was published at Detroit by Father Gabriel Richard and was known as the *Michigan Essay* or *Impartial Observer*. It was a four-page paper that was printed once a week. Most of it was printed in English, but usually a page or so was printed in French so that the French-speaking people in Detroit could read the news.

The *Detroit Gazette* was started in Detroit in 1817. At first part of this paper was also printed in French, but this practice was soon given up. This little weekly that now gives us much information about early Detroit came to an end in 1830.

Another paper, the *Michigan Sentinel,* was started at Monroe in 1825. In 1829 the *Northwestern Journal* appeared at Detroit and the *Western Immigrant* began publication at Ann Arbor. In 1830 the *Detroit Courier* appeared in Detroit and the *Oakland Chronicle* in Pontiac. In 1831 there appeared at Detroit the *Democratic Free Press* and *Michigan Intelligencer.* This paper, known today as the *Detroit Free Press,* is Michigan's oldest newspaper that is still being printed. In 1833 another paper appeared at White Pigeon. This paper was moved to Kalamazoo in 1837, and the name was then changed to the *Kalamazoo Gazette.* In 1840 still another paper, the *Monroe Advocate,* was started. This paper is also still published and is known today as the *Monroe News.*

These early newspapers, though small and often very political, were the first of many to be published later throughout Michigan. During their first years they usually were printed only weekly, but after 1840 some of them began to be printed as daily papers. As there were no means of rapid communication then as there are today, most of the news was of a local nature. Any outside news that was printed was usually several days old before it appeared in any of the local papers. As settlers pushed farther and farther across the state, many other papers were started. For many years these newspapers did much to mold the way people thought about public issues. No doubt much of Michigan's anti-slavery stand can be traced to the fact that many of Michigan's early papers were very much against slavery.

Commandant's headquarters of the old Detroit Arsenal. Now the Dearborn Historical Museum.

Soon after the abandonment of Fort Shelby in 1827, plans were made for the building of an arsenal near Detroit. This need for a handy supply of guns and powder was shown in the fear that swept across southern Michigan at the time of the Black Hawk War. The site chosen for the new Detroit Arsenal was about ten miles west of Detroit at Dearbornville. This arsenal consisted of eleven buildings located along the outer edge of a square some four city blocks in size. A wall twelve feet high and three feet thick ran around the entire square. Two other buildings, the powder magazine and the hospital, were located outside the wall. All the brick used in building the Detroit Arsenal were handmade brick from the area. The timbers were hand-hewn or hand-sawed. Two of these buildings are still standing and are now used as historical museums in Dearborn. These buildings, with their pegged beams, wrought ironwork, and original fireplaces, are good examples of pioneer skill and industry.

When Governor Lewis Cass was appointed Secretary of War in

Andrew Jackson's cabinet in 1831, General John T. Mason, then Secretary of Michigan Territory, became the new governor. The office passed to his son, Stevens T. Mason, that same year. As Stevens T. Mason was not yet twenty-one years of age, he is usually called the "boy governor." It was under Mason's leadership that Michigan became a state.

Michigan had grown rapidly during the twenty years from 1815 to 1835. In 1835 the people of Michigan Territory made ready for the admission of Michigan into the Union as a state. On April 4, 1835, delegates were chosen by the voters of Michigan Territory to draw up a constitution for the new state to be presented to Congress along with a request that Michigan be admitted as a state. The delegates to the Constitutional Convention met at Detroit on the second Monday in May. A constitution for the state was then drawn up and later submitted to the people for their approval. On the first Monday in October, 1835, the people of the state accepted the new constitution and at the same time elected their first state officers. Stevens T. Mason was chosen as the first governor. In November, 1835, the newly elected legislature met and chose two senators to represent Michigan in the Congress of the United States. Thus Michigan made ready to be admitted as a state into the United States. Michigan, however, was not to be accepted as a state for two more years.

As Michigan began making plans for admission into the Union, a dispute arose between the State of Ohio and Michigan Territory over the location of the boundary line between the two. When Ohio had become a state in 1803, the northern boundary of Ohio had not been definitely fixed. Now both the State of Ohio and Michigan Territory claimed the twenty-mile strip of land that lies just south of Michigan's present southern boundary.

Michigan claimed, under the Ordinance of 1787, all the land north of a line drawn east from the southernmost bend of Lake Michigan to near where Port Clinton, Ohio, is now located. This strip of land included some good farm land and also the growing city of Toledo, Ohio. What is more, Ohio had built a canal from Toledo to Cincinnati by going up the Maumee River and then down the Miami River. If the territory around Toledo should go to the new state of Michigan, it would mean that the canal would run through Michigan territory for a few miles near Toledo. The people of Ohio, therefore, felt that Michigan might hinder commerce over the new Ohio Canal. Michigan's claims to this land aroused the people of Ohio, and in 1835

Governor Lucas of that state laid claim to the strip, and the Ohio state legislature then organized it into the county of Lucas.

Governor Mason of Michigan Territory was also active and sent the Territorial militia to Toledo to keep Ohio from seizing the strip of land. Although a few shots were fired, no one was harmed. The battle over the Ohio strip was mostly one of words.

Because there would soon be a presidential election, a compromise favorable to Ohio was proposed to Michigan. This was done so that Ohio's electoral votes would not be lost in the coming election. According to the compromise, the southern boundary of Michigan was to be drawn where it is at present. In return for the loss of this strip of land, Michigan was to be given the Upper Peninsula. Many people then living in Michigan thought of the Upper Peninsula as a land of swamps. What did Michigan want with the Upper Peninsula? What good was it, anyhow? Nevertheless, a convention held at Ann Arbor in December, 1836, voted to accept the terms of the compromise. This convention was called the "frostbitten" convention. Congress accepted its work, and on January 26, 1837, Michigan became the twenty-sixth state to enter the Union.

Detroit was to be the capital of the new state. The state capitol building was then located in Capital Park, which is now but a little, busy, bus-loading station in downtown Detroit. This location, however, was to be only a temporary one, for the new state constitution stated that the state legislature should give the state capitol a permanent location by the year 1847.

At that time there were two well-educated men who lived in Marshall. As early as 1834 they saw the need for better education for Michigan's children. On many summer afternoons these two men, Rev. John Davis Pierce and Isaac Edwin Crary, discussed the future of education in Michigan as they sat in the shade of an old oak tree that has since become known as the "educational oak."

When Michigan became a state, the new state constitution accepted public education as a state duty. The general plan of state education suggested by Crary and Pierce was adopted. The state legislature was to provide a school system that would be open to all children for at least three months each year. The cost of paying for these public schools, however, was still to be paid by the local school districts. The state at the same time changed the method of collecting and spending the money derived from the sale of public land in the school sections. Now all the money received from the sale of such land was to be kept by the state. The money thus secured was to be known as the Primary School Fund. This money was spent by the state for other purposes. The state was to pay interest to the school districts each year on the money the state had borrowed.

Each year since that time the state has paid interest to the school districts on the Primary School Fund money that it then borrowed. The state never pays back any of the Primary money. The annual interest paid by the state to the school districts is known as the Primary Interest Fund. To this amount is now added other moneys such as taxes on railroad companies, telegraph and telephone companies, money that escheats back to the state from unclaimed estates, and part of the money received by the state from inheritance taxes. This Primary Interest Fund money is divided among the school districts in proportion to the number of children enrolled in each school district. Although this has proven to be wise planning on the part of Congress and our state legislature and aids education today, it was some time before the Primary Fund was collected from the sale of all the land, and the state did little to pay the cost of early elementary education.

When Michigan became a state, the new state constitution provided for a State Superintendent of Public Instruction whose duty would be to develop a public school system for Michigan. In 1838 Governor Stevens T. Mason appointed John D. Pierce, of Marshall, to this new state office. Under the leadership of John D. Pierce the beginnings of our public school system were started. Under the plan of public education which Mr. Pierce set up, a system of state schools was to be organized whereby a child could progress upward through the primary grades, the grammar school, the high school, and then enter the state university at Ann Arbor. However, it was several years before this plan was actually put into practice in the entire state.

When we think of schools in Michigan as they were before the Civil War, we should not think of them as large brick buildings such as they are in the state today. Schools in those days were usually little log cabins. Often they had just one room about eighteen feet by twenty feet in size. Some of them were better than others, but at best they were far from modern standards. These little log schoolhouses usually were built on one of the four corners where two roads crossed. Thus children could walk to them from any one of four directions. At other times the little schoolhouse sat proudly beside the road on the brow of a hill.

At first, these one-room buildings often had no windows. Sometimes, as in homes, scraped deerskin was used to let in some light. Later glass windows were used. At best, these little log schools were small, dark, and often cold and drafty in the wintertime. Chinking between the logs kept out some of the cold and snow in the winter and some of the flies and bugs in the summer. The schoolhouse door and the floor were usually made of rough planks. Later some schools were lined on the inside with boards. In the first schoolhouses small fireplaces gave out the only heat. Later, when stoves were made, a large heavy iron stove usually sat in the center of every rural schoolhouse. Although twenty to thirty children often met in these little schoolhouses, there was still plenty of fresh air for all, as usually there was plenty of it blowing in through the cracks between the logs. Screens were unknown, so flies and mosquitoes often made life miserable for everyone.

In these schools there were no desks or other school furniture such as we are familiar with today. Long planks that served as one long desk were sometimes pegged into two sides of the room. In front of these long desks the students usually sat, facing the wall, on a long bench that ran the entire length of the room on each side. No one then ever thought of playgrounds. Children got plenty of activity walking to and from school and doing the chores around the farms each night and morning. Though they had no special playgrounds, the children did have fun in the fields and woods that stood near their little schoolhouses. The teacher and some of the older children did the work done by janitors today. Either the teacher or one of the older boys came early on winter mornings and built a fire so that the schoolroom would be warm when the little ones arrived. Wood for the fire was often furnished by one of the parents as all or part of the cost of teaching his children.

Teachers were often not well prepared, and received only a small amount of pay. Men got as much as fifteen dollars a month, but women often were paid not more than five dollars a month. Both men and women were expected to be able to thrash any of their students should such treatment be needed. Sometimes the students were older and larger than the young ladies who taught them. Teachers usually boarded around at the homes of the children. They would spend a few days at the home of one child and then move on to live for days at the home of another.

To these schools the pioneers' children went when possible, but during the winter there was deep snow, in the spring there was planting to do, during the summer the crops had to be cared for, and in the fall came the work of the harvest. Thus there was often little time left for school. The winter months were not so busy and then the children were sometimes sent to school. However, there was no law which made them go. Because the settlers were usually scattered, small children often had to walk long distances from their homes to the little log schoolhouses. This was hard for them when the snow was deep and the weather cold.

As theirs was not a complex society such as ours is today, the children were taught only such subjects as reading, writing, arithmetic, and spelling. Sometimes geography and grammar were also taught. Because there were few, if any, books, lessons were sometimes learned orally. All the children repeated the lessons at once. For this reason these early schools are sometimes called "blab schools." Long hours were spent in teaching the alphabet. Spelling was a favorite subject. Most of it, because of the lack of materials, was oral spelling. Spell-downs were a part of everyday school life. In fact, so popular were spelling bees that our pioneer forefathers often held them at picnics, especially on the 4th of July, and at evening parties, just for the fun they gave the people.

Paper was often too expensive for school children to use, but most scholars had a slate on which they wrote and figured. Pencils and steel pens were unheard of at that time. For writing on slates, school children used slate pencils. If paper was used, people of that time wrote on it with a quill pen and homemade ink. One of the tasks of the teacher was to sharpen the quill pens of the students. Penmanship was stressed, and children spent long hours learning to make the letters like they were in the copybook. To own a textbook or reader was to possess a rare prize. There were few books then, but the few that did exist were read and reread again and again and then passed on to younger children. In those days students measured their progress by the reader they were using. When a student had mastered one reader, he passed on to the next harder reader. Yet in those early schools many of our finest citizens secured their education and later planned better schools for boys and girls, like the ones that you attend today.

There were a few colleges in Michigan before the Civil War. Many of the early colleges such as St. Philip's College, at Detroit; Marshall College, at Marshall; and St. Mark's College, at Grand Rapids, did not last long. In 1829, Kalamazoo College was started by the Baptists

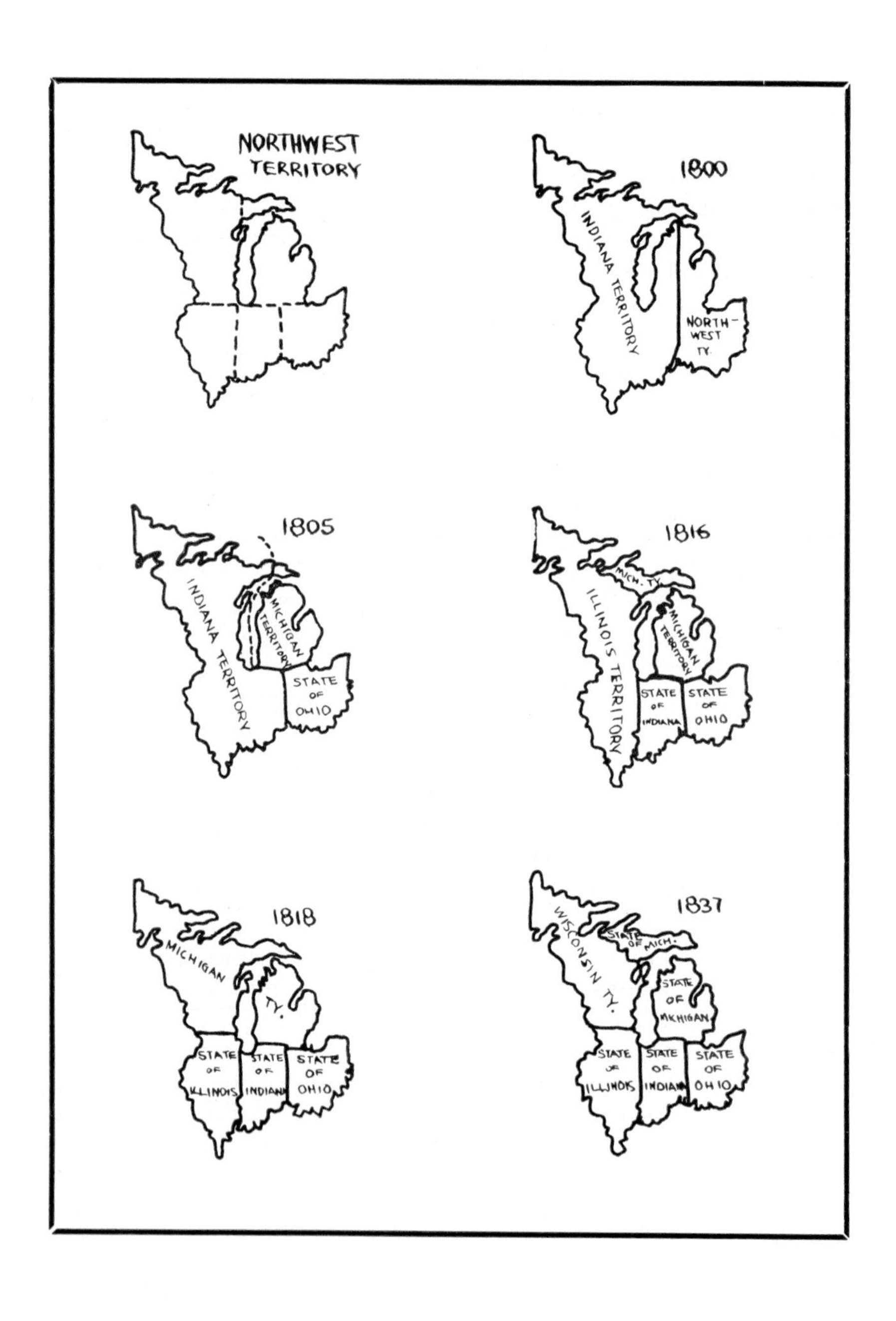
NORTHWEST TERRITORY
1800
INDIANA TERRITORY
NORTH-WEST TY.
1805
INDIANA TERRITORY
MICHIGAN TERRITORY
STATE OF OHIO
1816
MICH. TY.
ILLINOIS TERRITORY
MICHIGAN TERRITORY
STATE OF INDIANA
STATE OF OHIO
1818
MICHIGAN TY.
STATE OF ILLINOIS
STATE OF INDIANA
STATE OF OHIO
1837
WISCONSIN TY.
STATE OF MICH.
STATE OF MICHIGAN
STATE OF ILLINOIS
STATE OF INDIANA
STATE OF OHIO

at Kalamazoo. This college was granted a charter by the state in 1831, and is, therefore, the oldest continuing college in Michigan.

Albion College is a Methodist college that was founded in 1836. It was started so that men could be educated as ministers for the Methodist Church. At first classes were held in the local Methodist church, but in 1844 the college moved into the first of its new buildings. According to its early history this college accepted "gentlemen, Indians, ladies." At first there was a school for men and a school for women. These two colleges were combined in 1861. During the past century this college has developed in many ways. As its list of subjects has increased, so has the number of students attending the college.

The following year, 1837, when Michigan became a state, the present University of Michigan was started by the new state government. This university was to be the successor of the earlier university that had been started in Detroit in 1817. The site of the new university was to be at Ann Arbor rather than Detroit. Because it was hard, in those days, for the students to reach Ann Arbor and as there were still no high schools, the university established preparatory schools in Detroit, Kalamazoo, Monroe, Niles, Pontiac, Tecumseh, and White Pigeon. In these preparatory schools young people were prepared to enter the university. At that time there was only the College of Literature, Science and Arts. The first class consisted of six students. There were two professors on the faculty. By 1844 the teaching staff had been increased to three professors and three assistants, while the number of students had increased to fifty-three. About 1850 many of the old classical college subjects that had been taught in universities up to that time were dropped, and the student body soon became larger. In 1850 the university started a Medical School. The Law School was started in 1859. By 1860 there were five hundred nineteen students enrolled at the university. Since that time the University of Michigan has grown to be one of the largest and best known in the country. However, at the time the university was founded, there was much discussion as to whether higher education should be controlled by the churches or by the state. Some people at that time favored the university, while others gave their support to the church colleges which were then being built.

The charter for Adrian College was granted in 1839. At first the college was located at Marshall, but from there it was moved to Lenoi in 1845 and was then known as the Lenoi Theological Institute. In

1859 it was moved to Adrian. This time it was chartered as Adrian College. This early college, also supported by the Methodists, became coeducational in 1861.

The public schools of Detroit were made into a separate school district in 1842, and the city was allowed to lay a tax of not more than one dollar a child for the support of the city schools. By 1842 over one third of the school districts still had no school at all. There was not yet any law saying that children must go to school. However, the district was to receive no money from the state if it did not keep school for at least three months. The main question facing the schools of the time was who should pay for the cost of education. As yet people had not been taught to accept the idea that education is a public duty and that the public in general, rather than only the parents of children going to school, should pay for the schools.

In 1843 were started what we today call graded schools. Children were to pass upward by grades rather than by readers. From the primary grades they were to pass to the middle school. This took them through what is now our eighth grade. That is as far as tax-supported schools went in those days. This left a four-year gap between the eighth grade and college. Private schools filled this gap if one wished to go on to college. When the University of Michigan was first formed, it found it necessary to start a few high schools as feeder schools to supply the University with students. The University soon found this too expensive, and the feeder schools were dropped one by one.

In 1844, Michigan Central College was started by the Baptists at Spring Arbor, in Jackson County. This college was the first coeducational college in Michigan. In 1853 the college was moved to Hillsdale and the name was changed to Hillsdale College. In 1844 the Congregationalists started a little college at Olivet called the Olivet Institute. In 1859 the name of this college was changed to Olivet College.

St. Mary's Academy was founded at Monroe in 1845. This college was the first to be founded in Michigan to provide for the higher education of women. This college later became St. Mary's College. In 1927 the college was moved to the corner of McNichols Road and Wyoming in Detroit and was renamed Marygrove College. Marygrove College is a girls' college and is taught by a group of Catholic sisters.

Unfortunately for the plans of Michigan's early state-supported schools, they did not progress as well as some people had hoped they would. The same year that Michigan became a state, the Panic of 1837 upset the economic life of the people. Banks failed, farmers could not sell their crops and thus they could not pay for their farms, prices fell, and land went down in value. It was hard for the settlers to provide for their families, and there was little or no money left during the panic years for schools. But in 1845 the state took another step in bringing better education to Michigan's children. In that year the state placed a tax of one mill on each dollar's worth of property evaluation. This money was to be used to support public education. The law further stated that schools, if they were to get their primary money, were now to remain open five months a year instead of three.

As the time drew near for choosing a permanent location for the state capital, a struggle developed between several cities and villages. The people of Detroit wanted the capital to remain in their city. Others, outstate, however, objected to this. They said that Detroit was too near Canada and English power. It would be too easy to disturb the officers and records in case of another war with Canada. Then, too, Detroit was too far from the center of the state. They reasoned that the state capital should be nearer the center of the state so that it could be more easily reached by all the people of the state.

Nearly all the cities of any size tried to influence the state legislature to locate the capital in their locality; Ann Arbor, Albion, Battle Creek, Charlotte, Dexter, Eaton Rapids, Flint, Marshall, Owosso, and other places tried to get the capital located there. All of these places received some votes but not enough to bring the capital to them.

At last section sixteen, the school section, in the township of Lansing, in Ingham County, was selected as the location for the new state capital. In the fall of 1847 men began clearing away the forest for the building of a new city which was to be called Michigan. Enough land had been cleared to permit the building of the new capitol building by December of that year. This first capitol building was made of wood. In 1854 this first wooden building was replaced by a new one made of brick. The name Michigan, however, did not last long, for the legislature changed it back to Lansing the following year. Although Lansing is perhaps well located now for the state capital, it nevertheless was difficult to reach at that time. There were no railroads, and its only link with the rest of the state was by means of poor, muddy, swampy roads.

The first state constitution that had been adopted in 1835 was not long-lived, for in 1849 the people voted in favor of a new convention to draw up another constitution for the state. The delegates to this convention met at Lansing on the first Monday in June, 1850, and drew up a new constitution which was adopted by the voters in November of that year. Many democratic advances were made in this new constitution, but one amendment—to give Negroes then living in Michigan the right to vote—was defeated by a vote of almost three to one.

The year Michigan became a state, the people living in Canada, across the Detroit River, had a political uprising known as the "Patriot" war or rebellion. There was some unrest along the border, and there were a few clashes between Americans and Canadians. Because of this feeling between the two countries, people felt that Detroit should again be fortified against any attack that might come from Canada. The Detroit Arsenal at Dearbornville was not a fortification. It was only a place for repairing and storing arms and other military supplies. Thus in 1840 plans were made by the United States government to build fourteen forts along the Canadian border. One of these forts was to be built at Detroit. The following year the Congress of the United States provided the needed money, and a new fort was started in 1843. The site chosen for the new fort was in Springwells township, on the southward bend of the Detroit River about three miles west of Detroit. This new fort at Detroit was completed in 1849 and named Fort Wayne after General Wayne. No troops, however, were stationed there until 1861. Fort Wayne, though a good fort for its time, was never really armed or used as a fort. During the Civil War, troops going south to join the Union Army used it as a meeting and drilling place. It was also used as an induction center during World War II and is still used for that purpose. In 1949, just one hundred years after it was completed, Fort Wayne was turned over to the City of Detroit for use as a historical museum.

In order to prepare teachers for Michigan's new growing educational system a college for training teachers was founded at Ypsilanti in 1849. This college, known for years as Ypsilanti Normal College, is the oldest of Michigan's four teacher training institutions. At the time it was founded it was the first normal school west of Albany, New York. For over one hundred years students have been prepared by this college to teach in Michigan's public schools. Today it is known as Eastern Michigan University.

As a further aid to public education the Congress of the United

States granted 5,838,775 acres of land to the State of Michigan in the year 1850. The money received from the sale of this land was added to the Primary Fund. Interest at the rate of five per cent on this money was to be paid by the state each year. This money was added to the Primary Interest Fund. Another step toward better education for all was taken in 1854 when a school for the blind and deaf was started in Flint. Later, in 1880, the students of this school were divided, and a new school for the blind was started at Lansing.

The Dutch people who settled at Holland were eager to have their children have the benefits of a college education. In 1851 they began the "Pioneer School." In 1866 this school became Hope College. This college was largely the work of the Dutch Reformed Church. Hope College is one of the largest of the denominational colleges in the state today.

The first teachers' association in Michigan was formed in 1852 and met that same year at Ypsilanti. This association of teachers was known as the Michigan State Teachers Association. Since that time the name has been changed to the Michigan Education Association. This new association made a strong effort, in 1858, to have the rate bills abolished and the schools put on a better financial footing. In 1859 at least two thirds of the public school districts were still charging parents tuition for their children. Yet progress was being made toward public support of education, and in that year the state legislature passed a law allowing school districts to tax for the support of high schools as well as grammar schools. Finally rate bills were done away with by an act of the state legislature in 1869. People were gradually coming to believe that education is a state responsibility and that state and local taxes should pay for public education. In that same year the legislature also made a law saying that in school districts where there were more than eight hundred children, school would have to remain open nine months of the year. In districts of thirty to eight hundred children, school must be kept open for five months. In all other districts of thirty or less children, there must be at least three months of school.

The early settlers of Michigan realized the need for training in agriculture. In 1855 the state legislature established a State Agricultural College. This same legislature also provided $40,000 and set aside twenty-two sections of land for the building of the new agricultural college. This new agricultural college, one of the first of its kind in the nation, opened in 1857 in what is now the city of East

Lansing. At that time the new brick buildings of the college were surrounded by stumps and forest. To reach the college, students had to travel over muddy roads and across long stretches of marsh land.

By the time settlers began coming to Michigan, the North and the South were already becoming divided over the question of slavery. As many of Michigan's early settlers were from New England, they brought to Michigan the anti-slavery feelings of the North. Some settlers in the old Northwest were Quakers, and this group especially was against slavery. Before many years had passed, several men developed an organization, known as the underground railroad, so that they could help slaves reach the northern states where they could have their freedom. Many escaping slaves were even taken to Canada, where they no longer needed to fear the men from the South that came into the northern states looking for runaway slaves.

Once an escaping slave reached one of the stations on the underground railway, he received much help on his journey to the North. Stations were usually people's homes where the runaway slaves were hidden until they could be passed along to the next station. Negroes were hidden in the woods, in barns, under hay, in attics, and in cellars during the daytime. When night came, farmers or townsmen hitched up their horses, hid the Negro, or Negroes, under straw, blankets, or bales of hay, and drove him to the next station on his way north. Sometimes the white friend and the Negro merely walked north along back fence rows or through a woods to the next station. From this station his new friend passed the escaping slave along to still another. At last the escaping Negro crossed into Michigan or even into Canada. As the years passed, regular routes, called lines, developed on the underground railroad. Slaves were passed along from the Ohio River through Ohio, Indiana, and Illinois to Michigan or western New York State. Battle Creek became a central station for the lines coming north from Indiana and Illinois. From Battle Creek, slaves were passed along to Detroit or to Port Huron, and from there they often were taken to Canada. Many of the present villages and cities in southern Michigan were once stations on the underground railroad.

Several times trouble arose between men from the South who were looking for slaves and the people living in Michigan. One of the best known of these cases took place at Marshall, Michigan, in 1847. An escaped Negro family by the name of Crosswhite was living at Marshall at that time. There were six in the family, Mr. and Mrs. Crosswhite and their four children. There were also other free

Negroes and escaped slaves living in Marshall. Mr. Crosswhite feared that men from the South might come at any time and try to take his family back into slavery. It was agreed between Mr. Crosswhite and his neighbors that should Southerners come to take him and his family back into slavery, Mr. Crosswhite was to fire a gun as a signal to his friends. When men from Kentucky did come to his house, Mr. Crosswhite gave the signal that they had agreed upon. Soon a group of friendly people, both black and white, gathered around the Crosswhite home. The Kentuckians were arrested by the sheriff for breaking into Mr. Crosswhite's house. Meanwhile the Crosswhite family was quickly taken to Canada. The case entered the courts, and after many months the court ruled that the people of Marshall were to pay for the escape of Mr. Crosswhite and his family. This case aroused much attention at that time and helped to raise the public feeling that resulted in the passing of Henry Clay's Fugitive Slave Law in 1850, by the Congress of the United States.

In the years immediately following the Crosswhite case, the anti-slavery feeling grew in the Michigan area and in the adjoining states. While the Congress of the United States compromised with slavery and the courts of the nation upheld the property rights of the southern slave owners, there grew up a feeling in the area around Michigan that there could be no more compromise with slavery. Old political party lines broke down as more and more people came to feel strongly against slavery and its further extension into more of the new territories of the West. A meeting of anti-slavery people was held at Ripon, Wisconsin, in February, 1854. This meeting was followed by another at Jackson, Michigan, on July 6, 1854. Many leading men in Michigan business and politics were at this meeting in Jackson. So large was the crowd of people which gathered there on that date that their meeting had to be held out in a park at the edge of Jackson. There, "under the oaks," men pledged themselves to drop their old political parties and join the new Republican party that would devote itself to the stopping of the further extension of slavery in the United States. Many farmers in Michigan and the other nearby states soon joined the new Republican party. Protestant ministers also lent their support to this new moral crusade. Abraham Lincoln once came to Michigan and addressed a meeting of this new party at Kalamazoo on August 27, 1856. Because of the rising feeling against slavery in the North, the Republican party grew rapidly. The movement was also strengthened because of the Dred Scott decision handed down by the Supreme Court of the United States in 1857.

When President Lincoln issued his call for troops for the Civil War, many men from Michigan joined the Union Army. The state legislature met and voted $1,000,000 for raising and equipping an army. They also voted $15 a month for the support of families who were left dependent because of husbands or fathers going to war. From the farms, the colleges, and the high schools men came to join the units preparing to leave for the fighting front. Units were formed at several places in the state, such as Grand Rapids, Kalamazoo, and Detroit. Some of these men trained at Fort Wayne near Detroit, while others trained at other places in the state. Michigan men took part in almost every major campaign of the Civil War. It was the 4th Michigan Cavalry that captured Jefferson Davis at the end of the war.

During the Civil War, President Lincoln signed what is known as the Land Grant College Act. Under this act a state legislature in any state having an agricultural and mechanical college could accept a land grant from the United States for the support of such a college. To any state applying, thirty thousand acres of land were to be given for each senator and representative it then had in Congress. Under this Morrill Act of 1864, Michigan State College added engineering to its program in 1865 and thus received 24,000 acres of government-owned land for its support. Because this act was passed during the war years, military training was required of all male students attending colleges that accepted government land under the act. That is why military training is still required of all male students attending Michigan State University.

Another bill of this same year, 1862, was the Homestead Act. This law, passed by Congress, gave a quarter section of public land, 160 acres, free to any man twenty-one years or older who was a citizen of the United States or to any alien if he had taken out his first papers. All one had to do to receive title to the land was to live on it for five years and show that he was improving the property. Many acres of land in northern Michigan were homesteaded by farmers who claimed their land under this new Homestead Act.

After the Civil War the population of Michigan grew rapidly. In fact, between 1860 and 1880 Michigan doubled her population. Many new railroads were built. Many foreign immigrants came to Michigan and found work in the woods, mines, and new industries. Better homes in both the country and city were being built. Horse-drawn streetcars

This little white rock in Lake Huron marked the northern boundary of the Indian land given to the Americans in 1807. Photo 1956.

These two old cannons at Gibraltar, near the old River Road to Ohio, mark the site where Maj. Thomas Van Horne was attacked during the War of 1812. Photo 1956.

Pokagon Indian Cemetery. This little Indian cemetery sits on a hill southwest of Niles. Photo 1956.

On this ground, west of Niles, once stood the Carey Mission to the Indians. Photo 1956.

Replica of the little mission built on Old Mission Peninsula in 1839. The bell is the original mission bell. Photo 1956.

Making good log houses required good axemen. A man who could cut the corner fitting was called a corner man. One way the logs were joined together can be seen in this picture. Photo 1952.

This old inn, still standing at the junction of US-127 and US-112, was once an important stopping place along the old Chicago Road. Photo 1955.

Now the Ross-McFadden Museum in Dearborn, this old building was once the powder magazine of the old Detroit Arsenal located at Dearbornville. Photo 1961.

were appearing on the city streets. Eighteen sixty-eight saw the beginning of what later became the Detroit College of Medicine and Surgery.

In 1871, Michigan passed her first compulsory school attendance law. This law required that all children between the ages of eight and fourteen must attend school at least three months each year. In 1873 the time was increased to four months. Slowly people were accepting the idea of tax-supported public schools. There were still some, however, who felt that people who did not have children should not be taxed to help pay for the education of other people's children. In 1872 there appeared in the Michigan courts the now famous "Kalamazoo Case." Action was brought against tax-collecting officers to stop them from collecting the state tax for the support of high schools. The case was taken to the State Supreme Court, and that court upheld the tax. This was a great victory for public-supported education, and in the twenty years that followed, high schools and high-school attendance both grew rapidly in numbers.

Michigan's third capitol building, the present state capitol building in Lansing, was begun in 1873. Unfortunately for Michigan planners, their plans were again upset by another depression. The Depression of 1873 caused many of Michigan's banks to fail. The market for lumber dropped, and hundreds of woods and mill workers were unable to work. Railroad building was slowed down. Many of the iron furnaces and mines shut down or worked only a few days a week. But work continued on the new capitol building. The new state capitol building, made of Ohio sandstone, was finished in 1879.

An early horse-drawn street car. Now at Greenfield Village.

Chapter XI

THE EARLY DEVELOPMENT OF WATER TRANSPORTATION ON THE GREAT LAKES

As has been told to you in an earlier chapter, the Indians' canoes were the first known boats on the Great Lakes. When the Frenchmen came to the Great Lakes area, they adopted the Indians' canoe and made it larger and stronger than it had been before.

If you had visited this region during the French period, you would not have been at all surprised to have seen a flotilla of forty or fifty canoes come up to the beach in front of you, for in such large groups the French *voyageurs* and Indians often journeyed through the wilderness. These parties often traveled forty or fifty miles in a day. Distance at that time was not measured in miles but rather in "smokes" or "pipes." If you were to inquire the distance to any point, you would be told that it was so many "pipes" or "smokes" away. This custom came from the practice of resting every two or three miles for three or four minutes. During these brief rest periods, every man lighted his pipe and smoked. Such brief rests were greatly needed, for the French *voyageurs* and Indians paddled their big canoes in earnest. Often they paddled at the rate of forty strokes a minute. To the smooth, even motion of their paddles they often sang together the popular tunes of the day. As they paddled away down the river, their singing grew fainter and fainter as the canoes got farther and farther away.

For carrying larger loads, the French settlers sometimes built a kind of boat called a pirogue. A pirogue was but a dugout which they split in half and made wider by fastening planks between the sides. The true pirogue was a canoe-shaped boat which had been made by hollowing out a large log. Such a dugout was often forty or fifty feet long and was capable of carrying a war party of thirty or forty men. Although the pirogue had some advantages over the canoe, it had one quality which made it almost useless. It was too heavy to carry over a portage.

Another French boat quite widely used was called a bateau.

These were flat-bottomed boats with sharp-pointed ends. They were usually forced along by four or five men and occasionally a sail. Sometimes, if the currents were too swift, they had to be pushed along by means of poles. Sharp-pointed boats began to be called Mackinaw boats. Sometimes in fair weather small sails were used on these Mackinaw boats.

Sailboats appeared on Lake Ontario soon after the French settled in the St. Lawrence Valley, but none reached the Upper Lakes until La Salle built the "Griffin." The story of her building and fate you already know. Only a few sailboats were built during the French period, and none of these were used on the Upper Lakes.

When the English took over the region, they built two sailboats on the Upper Lakes, the "Huron" and the "Michigan." These boats are sometimes called the "Gladwin" and the "Beaver." It was the work of these two vessels that did so much to save Detroit during the siege by Pontiac. Because of their size and speed, they could face the Indian attacks and go to Niagara for supplies. In 1764 three more boats, the "Victory," the "Boston," and the "Royal Charlotte," were built. Soon after this, the first sailboats appeared on Lake Superior. They were used in carrying men and supplies to the Keweenaw Peninsula, where in 1771 Alexander Henry tried to start the first copper mine in Michigan.

During the time the English controlled the lakes, nine sailing vessels were launched. In all there were about thirteen before the period of the Revolutionary War. The building of sailing vessels on the lakes was prohibited, unless they belonged to the king or were sailed by naval officers. Thus the English tried to limit the trade in furs and discourage illegal trade and settlement. In 1800 there were only three schooners and six sloops on the lakes.

In 1796 the first American boat appeared on Lake Erie. It was a war vessel named the "Detroit." The following year it was wrecked near Erie, Pennsylvania. Between 1800 and 1805 six schooners and three sloops were built.

The early settlement of Michigan is closely tied to the opening of the Erie Canal and the development of shipping on the Great Lakes. Up to the War of 1812 there were only a few boats on the Great Lakes. During that war, as you will remember, the Americans hastily built a few small boats of unseasoned lumber. With these, Perry won his victory over the English on Lake Erie. These were the last of the fighting craft to appear on the Great Lakes, for in the

Treaty of Ghent, signed in 1815 at the close of the War of 1812, and in the Rush-Bagot agreement, signed two years later, both England and the United States agreed not to build fighting boats on the Great Lakes. What is more, they agreed that the long border stretching west between the two countries of Canada and the United States should never be fortified. For that reason the story of lake shipping after the War of 1812 is the story of freight and passenger boats.

The push of settlers into the area after the War of 1812 caused an increase in shipping on Lake Erie. By 1820 there were some thirty small sailing boats, averaging in weight about thirty tons, sailing on Lake Erie. Both sailboats and the newly developed steamboats competed for the growing commerce of the lake trade.

Courtesy "Steelways," published by American Iron and Steel Institute

The brig "Columbia." This brig brought the first load of iron ore through the "Soo" locks.

Abundant supplies of white oak and pine made boatbuilding Michigan's first major industry. The increasing carrying trade demanded more and more sailboats. Because they were of a very small size, shipyards for building them were not necessary. Later, the building of larger steamers required shipyards, and such yards were built at Marine City, Detroit, and at other ports on the lower lakes where materials and skilled workmen were available.

In the early sailboat days, however, lake captains often built and sailed their own boats. Some of these lake captains like Samuel Ward and E. B. Ward soon had several boats of their own and became wealthy from the early carrying trade. The Wards began their boatbuilding at Marine City, on the St. Clair River, where white oak lumber could be cut for the holds of the boats and pine for masts could be brought down from the area near what is now Port Huron.

Others wishing to build sailboats chose a good launching place along the Detroit, St. Clair, or Saginaw River and then began the building of a vessel. Ship carpenters and their helpers sawed out by hand the timbers and planks to be used in building the sailboat. Sometimes beams or square timbers were hewed by using a broad ax. Making lumber in this manner was cheaper than buying it from the little sawmills. This hand-sawed or hewed lumber was then left to cure in the open air. Large braces, called "knees," were cut out with axes and allowed to dry with the lumber. Other pieces of oak, called "ribs," were also carefully cut out and dried. When the oak had properly seasoned, the little sailboat was then built.

To a large oak beam, called the "keel," the ribs were fastened. Onto the ribs the oak planking was fastened to form the sides of the hold of the vessel. Then the masts were put in place and the deck built. No nails were used. All the pieces were held together by making joints and fastening them together with wooden pins driven into holes which had been bored with an auger.

Native white oak was the cheapest and best material for boat construction, and was used until about 1870 when the supply of oak trees became scarce and more expensive. Oak was replaced first by iron. When steel became abundant, it replaced iron for boat construction.

The War of 1812 had shown the superior maneuverability of the schooner, and although many other craft were still sailing the lakes by 1846, over eighty per cent of the 407 sailing vessels on the lakes were schooners.

Wouldn't you have liked to have gone sailing on one of these early sailboats? Overhead was a clear, blue sky, while beneath was the cold, blue, sparkling water. Against your cheek would come the breath of air that filled the white, billowing sails above your head. In the hold of your boat you would have carried furs, grain, lumber, or perhaps passengers. The Great Lakes, with their spreading waters, appealed to the youth of that day, and many boys and men took up the life of a sailor on the inland waterways.

Sailing had its bitter side as well as its pleasant one. At times severe storms suddenly arose. Then the wind whistled through the sailboat's rigging. The waves grew high. Then the sailors reefed their sails and rode before the storm, hoping that their staunch craft would ride out the fury of the gale. Sometimes their boats were broken by the storms or driven upon the rocks along the shore, and then crew and boats were lost. The stories of the lakes tell of deeds just as heroic as those that happen on the high seas.

Sailing on the Great Lakes in those days was much different from today. There were few harbors where boats could take refuge in case a storm arose. There were at first only a few of the modern aids that help the sailors so much today. After 1831 the Federal Government began to improve shipping conditions on the Great Lakes. A few lighthouses, with lights that burned whale oil, began to be built at dangerous points along the water's edge. Harbors and channels were deepened in a few places. But there were no buoys or beacon lights to warn sailors of the sand bars and shoals or to guide them through the narrow channels that connect the lakes. Most of the entire coast line of the lakes was still a wilderness where the forests crept down to the water's edge. There were no lifesaving stations. In fact, there was no one upon the shore, and sailors had to depend upon their own resources. Failure meant shipwreck and often death. The sailors of that day were a hardy lot, and they learned from one another the winding courses through the channels and into the many harbors.

Fur trading companies built small schooners to carry the furs across Lake Superior. The "Discovery," "Recovery," "Invincible," "Mink," and "Otter" had all ended their days of sailing on Lake Superior by 1830. Four had gone to the bottom of Lake Superior. The "Recovery" had been sent through the rapids of the St. Mary's River and was by that date sailing in the carrying trade on Lake Erie.

In 1835 boats larger than canoes again came to Lake Superior when the "John Jacob Astor" was launched. Soon several boats from the Lower Lakes were hauled around the St. Mary's rapids in the wintertime and began their part in the carrying trade of Lake Superior.

At only a few places along the lakes were there docks for these early boats. Sand bars often kept the boats from entering the harbors at the rivers' mouths, and it was many years before these bars were removed so that boats could go into the harbors. Freight and passengers were often carried to and from land in small boats. Horses and cattle were pushed overboard and allowed to swim to land. Such loading and unloading not only was unhandy but also caused much delay, for often the water was too rough for small boats to leave the shore.

With the increase of western traffic, sailing vessels soon became too slow for people who were eager to hurry westward to start life anew. The new steamboats such as the "Walk-in-the-Water," which has already been described, answered this demand. Soon several steamers were running across Lake Erie each summer on a somewhat regular schedule. By the time the Erie Canal opened, there were four steamboats on Lake Erie and soon others were added.

Traffic on the Great Lakes grew very rapidly. From the East came an increasingly steady stream of passengers, while from the West began to flow a steady stream of furs in even greater volume than ever before. In 1833-1834 the number of skins shipped out ran into the thousands. With this fur trade there began to appear shipments of what were then called "Ohio fur." Ohio fur was white oak barrel staves and barrel heads that were then used to make flour barrels and pork barrels. To these items were soon added such others as wheat, corn, flour, whisky, salt-pork, dried fruits, cider, and jerked beef.

At first freight rates were high. Passenger rates ran something like this: It cost six dollars to go from Buffalo to Cleveland. From Buffalo to Detroit the fare was eight dollars. Twelve dollars was charged to go from Buffalo to Mackinac Island or to Sault Ste. Marie. The fare was twenty dollars from Buffalo to Green Bay or Chicago. Of course, these fares are only general, as they varied from boat to boat and also with the type of room and service.

Courtesy Henry Ford Museum, Dearborn, Michigan

An early steamboat

In 1835 a boom in land prices swept the East, and many people, as we have seen, came westward seeking new homes. In that year there was much cheap money in use, and everyone seemed to be getting rich. Many people thought they saw good opportunities in the Great Lakes carrying trade, and in 1835 and 1836 several new boats were built and others were being built when the panic of 1837 hit the country.

With the coming of the steamboats on the Great Lakes there arose a new demand for more and more firewood. Fuel was needed to fire the boilers of these boats to make steam. Thus all the early steamboats became markets for wood. Until about 1850, wood for the roaring fires was plentiful, cheap, and easy to secure. Farmers living near the fueling points could thus get ready cash for wood that other farmers, living farther inland, just burned in their clearing fires. The supplying of fuel for steamboats became a regular business for many people. Because wood is bulky, each steamer usually wooded up at every stop. The roaring boiler fires called endlessly for more and more wood. The run from Buffalo to Chicago usually took about one hundred fifty cords of wood. Many wooding stations sprang up along the northern shores of Lake Huron and Lake Michigan. For this wood the steamboat lines usually paid from a dollar and a half to two dollars a cord. On long trips the boats' wood bunkers were filled and sometimes huge piles of cordwood were even stacked above deck. This bulky fuel cut into the cargo space of the early steamers and greatly reduced the steamboat's cargo, unless wood could be easily picked up from time to time as the steamboats made their way along the lake shore.

As the near supplies of fuel along the lake shore were cut, wood had to be brought from farther and farther inland. The supplying of this fuel wood for steamers running on the lakes became a regular business for many men and helped in the settling of many new areas. Frenchmen living along the Detroit and St. Clair rivers began to run what were known as "wooding scows" as well as wooding docks. These scows, loaded with firewood which later came to be called "propeller wood," met steamers passing up or down the two rivers and "wooded" them up as the steamers went along on their way. This practice of using wooding scows saved time for the passing steamers. When the scows were empty, they returned to dock where they were again loaded with firewood and thus made ready to meet the next passing steamer.

By 1839 there was regular passenger traffic between Buffalo and Chicago. Eight steamers were making this their regular run. This meant that many of the goods that had been transhipped at Detroit for Chicago were now taken directly to Chicago. At that time there was not as yet a harbor at Chicago. Vessels arriving there were not able to find a harbor until after 1854, when a twelve-foot channel was cut through the sand bar at the river's mouth. Up to that time all boats had to anchor outside on the lake and send passengers and freight ashore in small boats. In the long run, however, this passenger traffic to Chicago was to aid Michigan, for the settlers pushing out onto the western plains were soon to demand more and more lumber from Michigan to build their homes.

By 1840 there were more steamboats on the lakes than were needed to carry the passenger traffic. Soon some began to reduce their rates in order to secure the passengers of the other boats. At that time it was not at all uncommon to see two steamers racing into port, each trying to get there first so that she could get the passengers before the other boat arrived.

In 1841 a new type of boat appeared on the lakes, the screw propeller. Before this time all the steamboats had been driven by paddle wheels on their sides. The screw propeller was a new development and was turned by a shaft which jutted out from the stern of the boat just below the surface of the water. This new method of driving a steamboat has now come to be used on all the boats now on the inland lakes except one old railroad car ferry operating between Detroit and Windsor.

By 1850 the mineral resources of the Upper Peninsula began to be developed. This new traffic called for better transportation than sailboats could supply. In 1845 a group of mine owners bought a little propeller steamship, called the "Independence," for use in transporting ore on Lake Superior. To get the new boat to Lake Superior was a difficult task. They sailed her up the St. Mary's River as far as she could go and then they hauled her around the portage and across the snow on rollers. It took seven weeks to get her around the rapids. In 1846 the "Julia Palmer," a side-wheeler, was also hauled around the rapids.

There were three lines running ships between Buffalo and Chicago by 1845, and as many as 200,000 people crossed the lakes westward bound in that one year. Even though steamboats had gotten well under way, the great bulk of the freight was still being carried by sailboats.

In 1847 the Michigan Central tried to gain more traffic for its line by running steamships to Buffalo, at the western end of the Erie Canal. In 1849, the year that the railroad reached Lake Michigan, the Michigan Central launched the "Mayflower" for passenger service across Lake Erie. This was one of the finest passenger boats ever to steam across our inland lakes. Eighty-five staterooms cared for the people traveling on her. So large was she that three hundred steerage and three hundred cabin passengers could be carried.

By 1850 it was becoming harder for the Michigan Central to get business. To increase its traffic, the Michigan Central in 1853-

1854 built two new steamers called the "Western World" and the "Plymouth Rock." Fine steamers were these, both in size and in comfort, but the age of passenger traffic on the lakes had already begun to pass. In 1857 the two new boats were kept in port, tied up at Detroit. Soon they were sold and taken apart. The hulls of these huge liners were for some years used as dry docks, one at Bay City and the other at Buffalo. The engines were used for a time near New York and later they were used on the coast of China.

Courtesy of the Henry Ford Museum, Dearborn, Mich.

The "Western World" built by the Michigan Central Railroad in 1853-54. Note the walking beam in the upper part of the center of the boat and also the long wooden arch that gave support to the wooden boat.

Although the days of heavy passenger traffic on the lakes were fast passing, the best days of lake shipping were still ahead. With the opening of the "Soo" Canal, the attention of the shippers turned to hauling the vast cargoes of lumber, wheat, iron, and coal in place of passengers.

One might ask what caused this change in passenger traffic on the lakes. The answer lies in the fact that the steam train gradually cut into part of the commerce of the Great Lakes. In 1852 a railroad line was built across northern Ohio from Toledo to Cleveland. This new line, together with the New York Central, made a through route from New York City to Chicago. Running along the southern shore of Lake Erie, these combined roads began to get much freight and passenger traffic that had before gone by boat across the lake. Even the new liners of the Michigan Central were no match for this through traffic on the new railroads.

The "J. T. Wing" at Belle Isle (1951)
(See page 267)

Chapter XII

THE SAWMILL COMES TO MICHIGAN

As the years passed, the crude little pioneer log cabins of the settlers were replaced by better and warmer houses. Up to the time of the Civil War, lumber was still a luxury in Michigan and only a few people could afford to build homes or barns with such expensive material.

Some of the settlers, however, had broad axes and with these they began to hew round logs into square timbers. These hand-hewn beams, or square timbers, were used in making the houses, barns, and boats of that time. Even today in many old houses and barns the skillful ax work of those early craftsmen can still be seen and admired.

In hewing a log the worker first snapped a chalk line along the length of the log to show where the cut was to be made. Then taking a regular ax, a "square timber" man, as he was then called, stepped up onto the log. With the common ax he "score-hacked" away the largest part of the curving part of the log, thus removing most of the unwanted material. Then as he neared the chalk line with his ax, he changed to a "broad ax." This tool was similar to a regular ax but had a broader face, or cutting edge, and the handle was off-set about two inches. With swings of this ax a good "broad ax" man could hew well to the line leaving a flat cut on the side of a log. Having thus "faced" one side of a log, it was rolled over onto the flat face and the same manner of cutting was repeated until all four sides were faced and the square timber was finished and ready for

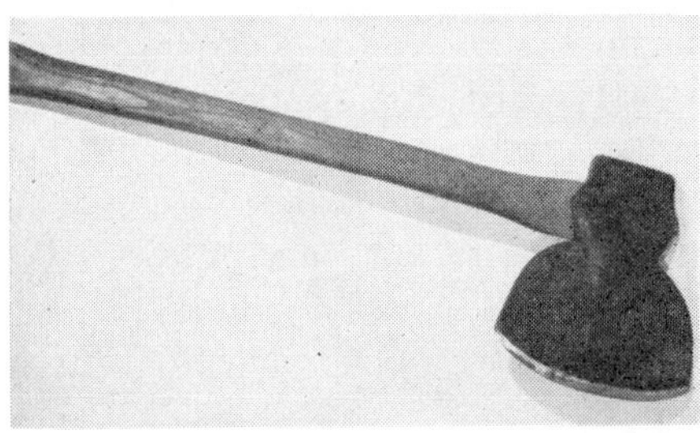

Courtesy of the Henry Ford Museum, Dearborn, Mich.

A broad ax. These axes were used to make square timbers or to hew planks.

use. A good "square timber" man was as proud of his straight line and flat-hewn surface as any craftsman could be.

Soon whole cabins were being built of these hand-squared timbers. They were called "block houses." By placing one square timber on top of another, the amount of space between the logs was made smaller and thus the houses were made much warmer. The ends of the square timbers were cut flat with the corner and thus a square corner was made on the house. A few log cabins of this block house type can still be found in Michigan today. As lumber became more abundant and cheaper, the block houses were replaced by houses made from mill-cut lumber.

As early as 1749, during the French period, Michigan's first sawmill was built on the St. Clair River to cut pine boards from the logs coming from a pinery near Lake Huron. Little is known of this early mill except that from it came clear pine and cedar lumber for the little French homes at Detroit and along the river. This little mill was probably driven by animal or windmill power, and its output was very small. After the fire of 1805 hewn timbers from this same pinery, as well as hand-sawed boards, were floated down the Detroit River for the rebuilding of Detroit.

As more and more people came to settle in Michigan and on the plains of the West, the demand for lumber grew. Settlers needed window sashes, doors, wagons, buggies, roof boards, barrels, churns, wooden pails, and furniture. At first boards for lumber and barrel staves were made by hand. Lumber was supplied by human labor in a process called "pit sawing" that was centuries old. To cut lumber in this manner a log was placed on a rack over a pit, or raised upon a strong wooden frame. A line was marked along the top of the log where the cut of the saw was to be made. One man called the "sawyer" stood on top of the log and pulled the saw up and guided the cut along the line on the downward stroke. Another man, called the "pitman," stood under the log in the pit and pulled the saw on its downward stroke.

The saw that was used was called a "whip saw" or "pit saw" and was often stretched tight in the center of a wooden frame or "gate." These saws usually measured from five to seven and one-half feet in length and were usually tapered from the back, or upper end, to the point. The teeth were hooked and set for ripping with the grain on the downward cut. As it was pulled downward, all the sawdust came with it, and much of it fell on the man standing in the

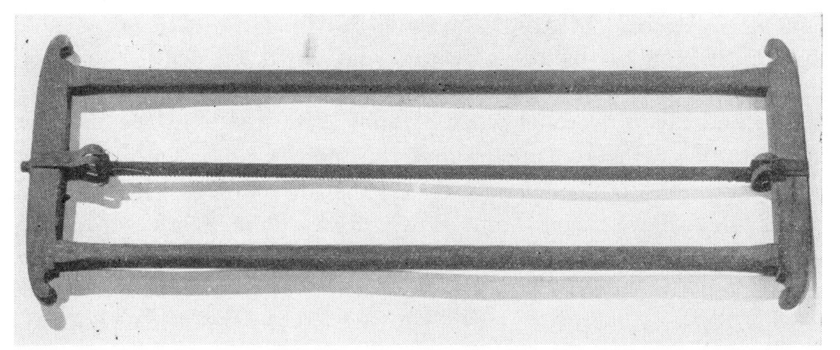

Courtesy of the Henry Ford Museum, Dearborn, Mich.

A whip-saw. Saws like this one were used to make lumber. They were used by two men. Note the two handles on each end where the men held the saw. This saw is also called a pit-saw.

pit. Because such sawing was hard work, only the softer woods such as pine, cedar, whitewood, and basswood were cut into lumber. The hardwoods that spread across the settlers' lands were then considered useless for lumber and so were usually destroyed by burning.

Pit sawing was not only slow, hard work but expensive as well. Yet as slow, hard, and tedious as this labor was, many an early house and sturdy sailboat was built from lumber cut in this manner.

Pit sawing in the early colonial days in the East had been followed by little sawmills that were run by water power. The first sawmill in the United States had been built at Pisotaga on the line between Maine and New Hampshire as early as 1634 and began cutting logs from the large pine forests of Maine. Two hundred years later, mills of this same type were built in Michigan. Both overshot and undershot water wheels were set up at places along Michigan's streams where waterfalls offered such power. In 1817 a little sawmill was set up on the Black River near present-day Port Huron. Another was built on the middle branch of the Clinton River some thirty miles from Detroit. Others were later built at Ann Arbor, Ypsilanti, Tecumseh, Sharron Hollow, and at other places where enough water power could be had to turn a water wheel.

Such early mills were at best, by modern standards, crude affairs. The slowly turning water wheel turned a set of gears made by placing wooden pegs in a wheel. These gears in turn worked on an arm, called a "pitman," which slowly raised and lowered the saw. The saw then used had an upright blade, similar to the whipsaw, held in position by a heavy wooden frame, called a "gate," from which was derived the name of "gate saw." As the gate raised and lowered it brought the saw blade up and down and held it firm for the downward cut as the gate dropped with the pitman. Thus water power had taken over the work of human muscles, but the method and rate of sawing remained about the same.

A feed of the ratchet variety edged the log along as the saw rose in the cut. The carriage crept slowly forward on a track made of wooden ribbons. The "gig wheel," the "shafts," and the "cogs" were all made from wood. The "head blocks," which held the head of the log securely in position, were heavy oak blocks fitted with the old-fashioned "brail dogs."

The saw was not allowed to cut the entire length of the log, but was stopped about four inches before the cut was finished to keep

Gate saw (left) and wooden gears on an early saw. Spoffard Mill, Greenfield Village.

the saw from running into the iron "brail dogs" at the rear end of the log. The uncut end was called the "stubshot." After sawing, the stubshot had to be removed by an ax or adze. Because of the remaining stubshot, it became customary in those early days to cut all logs three or four inches longer than the desired length of the finished board.

From daylight until dark the heavy gates and the crude saws went up and down. Men pulled, pried, and strained to move the heavy logs. The earth shook as the gate came down and the teeth of the saw bit farther into the log. For a hard day's toil such a mill produced a cut of only about two thousand feet of lumber, but crude as were these early mills they were better for making lumber than was hand sawing in the pit.

The heavy gate saw was replaced by the lighter "muley." The

muley saw was an upright saw like the gate saw, except that the heavy frame which had been drawn up and down to carry the older gate saw was taken off. The muley was fastened at the bottom while the upper part slid up and down in a groove. The blade was still the same upright saw and cut as it made the downward stroke. A muley saw was about six feet long and ten inches wide. It took a two-foot stroke and cut a one-fourth-inch kerf, thus wasting much good timber. The teeth marks that the saw left on the lumber were still the vertical marks instead of the curved ones soon to be made by the newer whining circular saws. The carriage upon which the log rested was still pinched along with a pry as the log was pushed into the saw.

A raceway and sawmill were built at Fort Brady at Sault Ste. Marie as early as 1822. This mill burned in the summer of 1826 but was soon rebuilt and continued in operation for over thirty years.

In 1826 a little mill was erected at Schwartsburg, Nankin township in Wayne County, on the bank of the River Rouge. On the Thread River at Grand Blanc a mill was built in 1828-1829. There appears to have been a mill at Waterford at the time, but twenty miles was too far to haul lumber over the roads of that day. The Grand Blanc mill, however, proved a failure because of its poor construction and the lack of a good pinery from which to get logs, and was soon abandoned. Another mill built about the same time and four or five miles north of the site of the other sent downstream the first raft of lumber ever floated on a tributary of the Saginaw River.

The year 1832 saw still more mills come into operation. In that year a little sawmill was built near Jonesville and still another appeared there in 1835. In 1832 a mill was also built across the river from Menominee on the Wisconsin side. Another mill was built at Grand Rapids on what is now called Indian Creek. Here an undershot water-power-driven wheel furnished power to run a saw that cut about two thousand feet of lumber a day. In this same year a mill was built on the Black River at Port Huron. Still another was built at Detroit on a strip of river frontage at the foot of Hastings Street. The builder of this mill in Detroit was Harvey Williams who was a prominent blacksmith and steam engine builder of the time.

In 1834 this same Harvey Williams built a steam sawmill at Saginaw. To run this first steam-driven sawmill Mr. Williams used the old engine that had once been used to drive the "Walk-in-the-Water." Though steam power had been applied, the little mill pro-

Muley saw in the Tripp Sawmill at Greenfield Village. Picture taken about 1940. Note that the saw does not cut all the way through the log.

duced only about the same amount of lumber as one driven by water power. In 1836 and 1837 Mr. Williams built a second mill, called the Emerson Mill, at Saginaw.

Soon many little steam sawmills were springing up across the state along the northern shore of Lake Michigan and Lake Huron where pine logs could be taken from the pineries.

At Greenfield Village, in Dearborn, now stands the Tripp Sawmill which was built in Franklin township, Lenawee County, in 1835.

About three or four miles from the present city of Holland, a little village, called Superior, was platted on the shore of Lake Macatawa in 1835. Industry followed the founding. A tannery was built and a shipyard started. A sawmill was set up in 1836. Disaster threatened from the very first. The harbor was blocked with sand, and boats could not get in or out. The village was abandoned. When the Dutch arrived they bought what remained and built the first post office and hotel at Holland from the old buildings at Superior.

In 1836 a little mill was built at Portsmouth. This was the second mill in the Saginaw Valley.

Lumbermen soon found ideal places for sawmills on the western side of the state along the shore of Lake Michigan. One of the first sawmill towns to develop was Muskegon, which derived its name from a Chippewa word "Muskego," meaning marshes or river of marshes. In 1837 the first sawmill on Muskegon Lake was built. In 1841 this mill burned, and the machinery was later moved to Grand Rapids. By 1840 there were three mills cutting lumber at Muskegon, but all together they could cut only about 13,000 feet of lumber a day.

Like many other western Lake Michigan cities, Muskegon is located by a large lake at the mouth of a river. The far-reaching Muskegon River, with vast pineries scattered up its meandering valley for some two hundred miles to Houghton and Higgins lakes and with Muskegon Lake at its mouth, made Muskegon an ideal location for a busy sawmill town.

In the spring of 1839 the first attempt was made at running logs down the Muskegon River. The river drivers found that many old logs, stumps, and fallen tree tops had to be removed from the river bed to let the logs come down the river, but the drive did reach the mills. This little drive was but a beginning of the many that were to follow it, for it is said that before Muskegon's lumbering days were ended, the Muskegon River floated more pine logs to the sawmills than any other river in the world.

Another mill was built at Menominee in 1841 and still another in 1854. Escanaba had its first mill in 1841 and Ontonagon in 1852. All of these early mills cut timber from the nearby forest to supply the needs of a local market, but as early as 1838 Charles Mears bought a ship called the "Ranger" and began shipping lumber to Chicago. By 1849 larger mills had appeared which turned out quantity production. By 1854 there were sixty sawmills in the state. These mills were cutting about 108,000,000 board feet a year. As early as 1858 a bandsaw was first used at Bay City, but the attempt was unsuccessful as the right tension on the saw could not be maintained.

By this time sawmills had also improved in other ways. The driving machinery was usually located on the ground floor while the upper floor was reserved for the mill proper. A sloping incline called a "jack ladder" was used to bring logs up into the mill. At first logs were pulled up the incline on a carriage. Later a wheel called the "bull wheel," because it was at first powered by a bull, was placed at the top to drive an endless chain, called a "bull chain," that ran in a slot up the bottom of the jack ladder. Logs placed in this slot were grabbed by spiked teeth projecting upward from the bull chain and thus carried upward into the mill.

Even greater changes were soon to appear. A new circular saw came into use around 1850 and soon its shrill whine, as it gathered

Circular sawmill, Greenfield Village

speed for its next cut into a log, could be heard in many places throughout the state. This new saw brought as great a change in sawing methods as did the gate saw when it replaced hand sawing. The circular saw's invention is credited to Benjamin Cummins. He is said to have made the first circular saw at Bentonville, New York, in 1814 with the crude tools found in a local blacksmith's shop. Mr. Cummins died in 1843 and is now buried in a rural plot in Kalamazoo County.

At first the use of the circular saw was limited and there was much trouble with the teeth breaking off. A few years later the circular saw was greatly improved by the invention of individual teeth that could be easily replaced if damaged. Then the circular saw really began to bite into the timber of Michigan.

As the number of sawmills in Michigan increased, they demanded more and more logs. The timber around the mills was soon cut and men had to push farther and farther up the waterways in search of more and more timber.

A new type of speculator then began coming to Michigan. He was the lumberman. Soon whole tracts of land were being sold, not to settlers, but to those men who looked upon land not as a place to build homes but rather as a place from which to cut logs.

Beginning in the 1830's "timber cruisers," sent out by eastern firms, began coming west along the Erie Canal. They did not come here to clear the land, burn the trees, and make little farms. They came looking for the choice stands of pine that could be felled and cut into lumber. To the settler it was the land under the trees that was considered of value. To the lumbermen the land was of little, if any, value. It was the pine trees that stood on it which had value to them. These men knew what they were after because they came from a long line of lumbermen who had had two hundred years of training. When they came here they brought this knowledge of lumbering with them.

Timber cruisers usually did their work in the winter when the forests were more open from underbrush, mosquitoes and flies were gone, and swamps were frozen. Sometimes cruisers used dog teams to carry in their supplies, but usually they carried their few supplies on their backs. Leaving the settlements these men pushed into the forests where perhaps government surveyors were the only white men who had ever been there. Among the forest lands they searched for the best stands of white pine to be found close by the river banks.

Because pine logs floated, and as there were no roads or railroads, the rivers of Michigan became the first carriers of the logs. Logs were a heavy commodity, and as such they could not be easily hauled for any distance as long as men had to depend upon muscle power as the source of energy. Back east in Maine men had been floating pine downstream to the mills for many years. When these men came to Michigan they used the same methods here.

When a cruiser located a fine stand of pine near a river he then went about estimating its size. Five hundred paces equalled about eighty rods. Two thousand paces equalled about one mile. Here and there around the stand he would choose an acre of trees about the average of the stand. These trees he would count and scale. By doing this he could estimate the amount of lumber that the trees in the stand would cut.

He would then make pencil recordings in his little notebook. These recordings were of the size, quality, and location of the stand. Then if he were sure that this would be a good pinery he would look up a government survey stake and from there pace off its location and carefully record it in his notebook. Sometimes a cruiser would locate several tracts on one cruise trip. Then he or some member of the lumber company would go to the government land office and purchase the land if it had not already been sold. Cruisers were sometimes paid in cash for their work, but often they received title to part of the timber lands they had found. This method of payment made them interested in searching for the best stands.

Up to the time of the Civil War only crude little sawmills were to be found in this country. But small as they were, by 1860 they had cut nearly all the good timber in the East. First the good pine of Maine had been cut. Then as the supply of pine there grew smaller and smaller, the lumbermen pushed west into New York and Pennsylvania. Even here the supply of pine trees was not endless, and as early as 1830-1840 timber men were looking with interest at the fine pine timberlands in the Great Lakes area and buying large tracts from the government.

Each year more and more lumber was needed to build the rapidly growing cities back East and to build barns and houses for the settlers pushing westward out onto the treeless plains of the Middle West. Large quantities of timber were also needed for building plank roads, railroads, bridges, ships, and as braces in the mines.

When one spoke of lumber in those days one usually referred to pine lumber. Some lumber such as cherry, maple, oak, and walnut was used in making furniture, wagons, and buggies, but by far the largest amount of lumber used was pine lumber. Pine was used because it could be sawed more easily, was more easily planed by hand, and could be more easily worked into the shapes desired than could hardwoods.

In the United States there are thirty-four species of pine trees. Only three of these are native trees to Michigan. These three are the jack pine, the red or Norway pine, and the white pine. Of these three the white pine was by far the most valuable for making lumber. In general white pine trees reached to a height of about eighty feet, although in good soil they often grew to a height of one hundred to one hundred fifty feet. The bole, or trunk, of the white pine often measured from four to seven feet in diameter. The wood of the white pine is soft, straight-grained, light brown in color and easily worked. If protected from the weather, it is very durable.

The red pine, or Norway, was very common in northern Michigan, but it was not so well liked for timber to make lumber. Red pine trees are usually smaller than white pines, being only two to three feet in diameter at the bottom of the bole and fifty to seventy-five feet in height. In the lumbering days the red pine was usually spoken of as Norway pine. Norway pine seems to have taken its name from the little town of Norway in the state of Maine. Today these trees are usually called red pine because of the reddish color in their bark and in their inner heartwood.

The third native pine of Michigan is the jack pine or, as it is sometimes called, the scrub pine. Jack pines are small scrubby trees that grow only to a height of about twenty or thirty feet. They grow only on the poorest sandy soils. Jack pine trees were very common from Clare County northward, but they also appeared as far south as Grand Haven and Port Austin. These trees were not cut by the lumbermen.

From eastern Ontario westward across northern Michigan, northern Wisconsin, and northern Minnesota stood vast forests of pine trees which, up to 1860, had hardly been touched by an ax. Until the opening of the Erie Canal and the coming of the railroads these vast stands of pine were of little, if any, value as there was no way to get the lumber to the market once it had been cut. With the increased demands for lumber, the rise of better transportation, and the coming of the steam sawmill, lumbermen soon began to see the money that could be made by cutting the pine forests in the Great Lakes area.

Much of the finest of these spreading stands of white pine once stood in Michigan. By 1860 the hardwoods of the southern part of the state had been mostly cut and burned. Beginning at a line drawn from Muskegon east to Bay City and Saginaw the whole upper half of the Lower Peninsula and the eastern half of the Upper Peninsula were, until about a hundred years ago, a vast forest made up mostly of cone-bearing trees. Among the pine trees stood strips of hardwood trees such as beech, ash, and maple that were of little interest to the early lumbermen. They were hard to saw. In general the hardwoods would not float, and thus there was no way to get them to the mills.

Before the Civil War, Michigan's first lumber camps had already come into being. They were small and crude compared with the later camps that were built after the Civil War by the big lumber companies, but they were camps nevertheless. The men working in them had begun the rich harvest of Michigan's timber lands.

These early logging camps were built much like the frontier cabins of the settlers. They were made of logs and chinked with mud and chips. The building where the men slept was called the "bunkhouse." Many of the earlier bunkhouses did not have any windows.

In these earlier bunkhouses there was usually an open place in the center of the room where a fire could be made. It was really a sand box six or eight feet long by six or eight feet wide. Upon this sand a fire was built to warm the bunkhouse and cook the food. The smoke from the fire passed out through a large hole in the center of the roof. Sometimes a wooden chimney the same size as the hole carried the smoke above the roof. On this open fireplace, called a "caboose," the "shanty boys," as lumberjacks were then called, would place large logs five or six feet long. These logs were brought in from outside by three or four men. Two men would place a stick under one end of a log and carry the front end of it across the fire while the others carried the back end of the log. Thus they could place good-sized pieces of wood upon the fire.

This crude fireplace furnished the only means of heating the bunkhouse. It was often the only source of light during the long, dreary, winter evenings. The only other light in those days came from a candle or two placed at one end of the bunkhouse. Most of the heat from the fire went up the large open chimney. If the fire did not furnish much heat for the men, at least it can be said that it did provide plenty of smoke as each wintry gust of wind blew down the smoke hole. The early shanty men who spent long winter nights in the bunkhouse often had sore eyes because of this primitive condition.

On the inside of the bunkhouse along the walls were rows of upper and lower bunks. Sometimes shanty boys got into these bunks from the end. These bunks were called "muzzle loaders." Others called "side loaders" were gotten into from the side. These lumber camp bunks could hardly be what one would today call comfortable beds. They were usually boxes in which sawdust, pine needles, or cedar boughs had been placed for the men to lie upon. For bedding, the shanty boys used a few blankets which were often not washed from one fall to the next. The best that can be said for lumber camp bunkhouses in the early days is that they were dark, smoke-filled places in which the men spent the winter nights.

Men seldom washed their clothing, and body lice, called "graybacks," were very plentiful. Graybacks, flies, bedbugs, gnats, and mosquitoes were all part of the shanty boy's life.

Another log building served as a barn. There the oxen were stabled during the cold winter nights. Often another building housed the camp supplies of food, such as barrels of flour, salt-pork, corned beef, dried apples, beans, and potatoes. From these supplies the cook prepared the meals for his crew. Butter, cream, milk, and eggs were seldom used in cooking.

All trees were cut by using only axes. Once the trees were down,

Courtesy Gogebic Industrial Bureau

Modern underground iron ore mine located on U.S. 41 in Negaunee about one and one-half miles from the site of the discovery of iron ore in the Lake Superior District in 1844. Owned jointly by the Bethlehem Steel Company and The Cleveland-Cliffs Iron Company, it is one of the largest iron ore mines in the world. Its shaft reaches a depth of 3600 feet. (1961)

the whole trunk, or bole, was usually dragged by ox teams to the river. There on the river bank the trunk was chopped into logs.

In this way the early lumbermen began to cut Michigan's pine forests and to provide lumber for a growing nation.

Courtesy of the Cleveland-Cliffs Iron Co.

Open cut at Jackson Mine near where ore was first discovered in 1845. (Picture taken about 1860.)

Chapter XIII

EARLY BEGINNINGS IN THE UPPER PENINSULA

The Upper Peninsula of Michigan had hardly become a part of the state before it became the scene of one of the earliest mineral rushes in American history. Copper and Lake Superior had been thought of together since the earliest French missionaries and traders had visited the shores of Lake Superior. Just where the copper metal came from the French never discovered, although they searched for the source of the metal. Not even the friendly Indians, then living in the Upper Peninsula, knew from where the copper metal came. The only copper known to the French and to the Indians of that time was pieces of "float" copper that were found lying on the ground among the decaying leaves and glacial drift of the ages past. We today call such pieces of copper "float" copper because it had been carried away by the glaciers from the place where it was formed. Pieces of float copper have been found as far south as Illinois and Indiana.

The first copper mine, in what is now Michigan, was started by Alexander Henry in 1771, during the period when England still controlled the Great Lakes. Two years after the massacre at Michilimackinac, from which he was fortunate enough to have escaped, Mr. Henry had discovered a mass of pure copper in the bed of the Ontonagon River. This boulder had lain in the river bed a few miles up the river from Lake Superior. Mr. Henry had cut from the Ontonagon boulder a piece of copper that weighed about one hundred pounds. He had also discovered an outcrop of copper in the rock along the river bank.

In a small sailboat, Henry's miners and supplies were taken from Sault Ste. Marie to the mouth of the Ontonagon River. During the following winter the miners dug a hole some forty feet into a hill a little way up the river and did secure some pieces of pure copper. The hole that they had dug caved in with the coming of the spring rains and the melting snows. Supplies for the miners were sent the next spring, but the miners had put in one winter on the Ontonagon, and they had had enough of copper mining in Michigan's cold Upper Peninsula. Leaving their caved-in mine behind, they returned to Sault Ste. Marie on the supply boat. Thereupon Mr. Henry gave up the idea of mining copper and nearly seventy-five years passed before other men again tried to mine copper on the south shore of Lake Superior.

Not long after Mr. Henry's venture, the Great Lakes area passed from England to the new United States. In the formation of the northwest boundary of the new United States, there were three choices that England could have taken. The Ohio River could have been chosen as the boundary between the United States and Canada. A line could have been run due west from the eastern end of Lake Erie to the Mississippi River. The third choice was the present line drawn north and west through Lake Erie, Lake Huron, and through Lake Superior. Just why England agreed to the third plan that added so much territory to the new United States no one seems to know.

The following story is sometimes told in trying to explain what happened. When Benjamin Franklin was in Paris making the terms of peace with England after the Revolutionary War, he read some early records of the Lake Superior region which had been made by French explorers during the time that the French had controlled Lake Superior. These records told of mineral resources that might be found in the Lake Superior area. Mr. Franklin probably also knew about Mr. Henry's copper mine on the Ontonagon River. Franklin, therefore, it is said, drew the northern boundary of the colonies so that the line would pass through Lake Superior and give to the colonies much of this valuable mineral land. It is also said that when he did this he said the time would come when drawing that line would be regarded, by the people of the United States, as the greatest service he ever rendered to his country.

From Franklin's time to 1837 no one but fur traders seemed to be much interested in the Upper Peninsula. The area was far north of the westward routes that people were then using in going west to new farm lands. The American Fur Company had its trading post on Mackinac Island, and traders and trappers still used the Keweena Portage in going to and from the fur lands of the West. Lewis Cass passed along the portage way in 1820. Others like Henry R. Schoolcraft, the Indian agent at Sault Ste. Marie, used the portage as they journeyed along the south shore of Lake Superior. Four or five small sailboats were built to carry furs from the Grand Portage to Sault

Ste. Marie. But, though few people visited the area, stories of copper still interested some people. But what good was copper when it was so far from even the small market for it in that day? What is more, no one had really found much copper anyway. So no one but fur traders, missionaries, and government agents seemed to be interested in the land lying south of the huge cold lake that separates northern Michigan from Canada.

When Michigan received the Upper Peninsula in return for the disputed Toledo strip of land, most people then living in Michigan thought that the new state had received the bad end of a very poor bargain. They looked upon the Upper Peninsula as being a land of little value to the new state of Michigan. Michigan had given up some 470 square miles of its best farm lands to Ohio, but she had received in the Upper Peninsula some 15,600 square miles for the 470 she had given up. But what good, thought the people, who really knew little about the Upper Peninsula, were all these cold, worthless acres? People wanted farms and more farms, and the Upper Peninsula seemed to them a poor place to start farming. In truth, very little was known about the Upper Peninsula. Lewis Cass and Henry R. Schoolcraft had gone along the southern shore of Lake Superior in 1820. English, French, and American fur traders had followed the old trade route to the Grand Portage for over 150 years, but they knew little or nothing about what secrets lay hidden in the dense wilderness a few feet back from the wooded shore.

It remained for a young man named Dr. Douglass Houghton to really tell the people of Michigan about the good bargain they had received in having the Upper Peninsula added to the newly formed state. Soon after Michigan became a state in 1837, the state legislature provided money for a geological survey of the Upper Peninsula. The state legislature chose Dr. Douglass Houghton to do this work. Thus Dr. Douglass Houghton became Michigan's first state geologist and soon began making a geological survey of the Upper Peninsula. The area was not entirely new to Houghton, as he had gone with Lewis Cass and Henry R. Schoolcraft as their medical doctor when they made their trip in 1820. From the time he was appointed to find out about the geology of the Upper Peninsula until his death in 1845, Dr. Houghton did much to let the people of Michigan know about the mineral resources of the Upper Peninsula.

In 1841 Dr. Houghton made his first report. The report stated that copper and iron ore were both to be found in the Upper Peninsula, but as yet they had not been found in large enough quantities to pay for mining. Dr. Houghton had worded his report very carefully, for he feared that prospectors would rush into the area and at that time it still belonged to the Indians. This would have caused trouble with the Indians and would have created a wild and useless iron and copper mining rush as well.

In 1842 the United States Government made a treaty with the Chippewa Indians for the Upper Peninsula lands. In the treaty the Indians gave to the United States the Lake Superior lands east of Fond du Lac, Wisconsin.

In spite of Dr. Houghton's care in making his geological report, the words copper and iron seemed to be magic ones that stirred men's imaginations. Facts grew larger with each telling and quickly mixed with gossip and idle fancy. Whole mountains of copper were said to reflect the setting sun and turn Lake Superior to a brilliant copper color.

In the summer of 1843 another event occurred that helped to arouse people's interest in Michigan's Upper Peninsula and the copper that was thought to be there. On October 11 of that year a Mr. James Eldred unloaded from a boat at Detroit the famous Ontonagon boulder that Mr. Henry had discovered in 1765. Soon he was charging twenty-five cents for each person to see it. There seems to be much dispute as to just who raised the boulder from the Ontonagon River, hauled it to the mouth of the river, placed it on a boat, and portaged it around the rapids at Sault Ste. Marie. But there it was at Detroit—a huge block of pure copper from the Upper Peninsula.

For some reason the Federal Government seems to have purchased the boulder from Mr. Eldred. It was shipped to Washington, D.C., by way of the Erie Canal, the Hudson River, the Atlantic Ocean, and the Potomac River. At Washington the boulder was placed in the yard of the War Department. It then seems to have been forgotten for some time. In 1881 the boulder was moved to the Smithsonian Institute. There today rests what remains of the huge mass of copper that once lay in the Ontonagon River and interested so many passers-by. It is four feet six inches long, four feet wide, and seventeen inches thick.

Stories about copper spread from person to person. Copper was the magic word on many people's lips. But where were the mines to be found? Soon the first big mineral rush in the United States was on. People began going across the portage at Sault Ste. Marie and then passing on west to the mineral lands in the Keweenaw Peninsula which Dr. Houghton had told of in his report. The few boats that were then on Lake Superior were soon crowded with prospectors and their supplies. Many copper seekers could not get passage on the boats and were forced to continue their journey from Sault Ste. Marie with French *voyageurs* who took prospectors and their supplies to the Keweenaw Peninsula in canoes.

Few, if any, in this wild rush of speculators in 1843 were miners. One thing they had in common: they were all sure that their fortunes would be made just as soon as they reached the "copper lands." Teachers, doctors, pharmacists, and many others all braved stormy Lake Superior to reach the land where copper metal was said to be found, the copper that was soon going to make all of them rich. Just how this was going to be, they did not stop to think, for in those days there was really little use for copper. Some of it was used to make pots and pans, buttons, and ornaments. Most of it was used to put on the bottoms of ships. The copper bottoms helped to keep off the barnacles that formed on the ships' bottoms as they rested in the salt water of the oceans. But ocean ships were far away, and copper was a heavy metal to carry for any distance.

Filled with the idea that they would strike it rich, the prospectors, during the summer months, roamed across the Keweenaw Peninsula in search of copper deposits. Here and there among the decaying vegetation they found a piece of float copper lying on the ground. They walked over deposits of copper worth millions. They climbed into and out of old Indian copper pit mines, little dreaming as they did so what these holes were or what lay buried underneath the rotting leaves and trees that by then nearly filled the ancient mining pits. With shovels and picks they dug among the leaves. They chipped off pieces of hard rock. But where was the copper?

The Indians then living in the area were not miners and seemed to know nothing about the people who had dug copper from the ground long before they came. Neither they nor their fathers had been copper miners or knew where the metal could be found. There was nothing in their legends that told of copper mines.

Copper outcrops were few and hard to find. Nearly ninety-five per cent of the Keweenaw Peninsula lay buried under glacial till that the glaciers had left behind when the ice melted. What is more, nearly all the land was covered by dense forests of cedar, spruce, and tamarack. During the summer large black flies and huge mosquitoes made the lives of the prospectors very uncomfortable. But all that summer of 1843 and for several summers that followed, the search for copper went on. Men wandered through the forests and waded across the swamps. They dug a little here and picked into this rocky face and that. There must be copper here somewhere, for from time to time they picked up pieces of float copper that lay here and there upon the ground. But from where had these pieces of copper come?

Nearly all the prospectors left the area when fall came. One could not search for copper under the deep drifts of snow that settled on this forest land. Winters on the Keweenaw Peninsula are long and cold. Even the huge cold lake across which they had come grows colder until at last its shores are frozen fast. When ice closed the shipping season on Lake Superior, there was no way to get out of the Keweenaw Peninsula unless one walked on snowshoes two hundred miles overland to the south. Winter in the Upper Peninsula in those days meant being shut off for four or five months from all friends and relatives "down below." Each fall, during the following few years, most of the prospectors left the area. Often they took with them a piece or two of the copper metal they had found lying on the ground.

Three mining boom towns sprang up during these early years of prospecting: Copper Harbor, Eagle Harbor, and Ontonagon. Each

Courtesy Copper Country Vacationist League

Fort Wilkins—built in 1844 by the Federal Government to protect the whites from Indian attacks

summer, for the next few years, tents spread along the lake shore at each of these places. Saloons quickly followed, and the typical rowdy life of a frontier community was to be found the entire length of the Keweenaw Peninsula.

Pieces of copper were not the only reason for people becoming interested in the Upper Peninsula. Fort Wilkins, at the tip of the Keweenaw Peninsula, had been built in 1844 and was garrisoned by a small detachment of United States troops. The Federal Government, too, was interested in the area and was pushing ahead its land survey so that title to the land could be given to prospectors and settlers in order to do away with the need for mineral land permits.

Courtesy Oliver Iron Mining Co.

Monument marking the place where iron ore was first discovered*

In the year 1844 Mr. William Burt and his party of government surveyors were pushing their linear and geological survey near the present site of Negaunee. Burt's party of surveyors were doing two jobs at once. They not only were surveying the section lines, but also were making notes in their survey reports of the geological nature of the land as they went along. On September 19, 1844, Mr. Burt and his surveyors were working on the west line of township forty-seven north, range twenty-seven west when they began to have trouble with their survey work because of the strange behavior

*This monument is made of every kind of rock, ore, and mineral found in Iron County.

of their compass needle. It did not act properly. Instead of pointing north, the compass needle spun crazily in all directions.

Those in charge of the survey thought that minerals in the ground were the cause of the compass needle's strange actions. Leaving their work, the surveyors set out in search of the cause of their trouble. Before long the mystery was solved, for pieces of magnetic iron ore were discovered near the place where they had been working. Thus, by this mere chance, the first of the huge iron ore deposits of northern Michigan was discovered.

Shortly after Mr. Burt's find of iron ore, the first deposit of copper was located. In the fall of 1844 a soldier at Fort Wilkins led a party of prospectors to the first copper find just back of the fort. In December of that year the first copper mine in the Upper Peninsula was opened at Copper Harbor. But this mine, although it caused much excitement at the time, did not last long. It was only a small sample of what was to follow. Fifteen feet down, the copper pocket gave out entirely. Copper had at last been really mined on the Keweenaw Peninsula.

The year following the opening of the first copper mine at Copper Harbor the same company started digging at another place about twenty-five miles down the peninsula and south of Eagle Harbor. Here, at what later became the Cliff Mine, the first large deposit of native copper ever discovered in the world was found in 1845. Soon huge masses of bright, pure copper were coming from the ground. A real strike had at last been made, and the Cliff Mine became the first mine to pay dividends to its stockholders. In the years that followed, much copper was taken from this mine. Before the Cliff Mine closed down, it produced some forty million pounds of pure copper. Most of it, about two thirds in fact, was made up of huge masses of solid copper that lay buried in an old lava flow.

The years 1845 and 1846 were busy years of anxious prospecting and speculation. While hundreds of men wandered across the Keweenaw Peninsula looking for copper or iron deposits, Mr. Burt and Dr. Houghton went on with their survey work. Mr. Burt, although the first to really locate iron ore, was a surveyor at heart and never took advantage of his great discovery. Dr. Houghton, too, left prospecting to others and went on with his geological survey until he was drowned near Eagle River on October 13, 1845.

During these early years, hundreds of copper and iron mining companies were formed. One of these companies was formed by

COURTESY RALPH PRICE

Sailboats, such as these seen drying their sails in Round Lake at Charlevoix in the 1890's, once carried much of the commerce of the Lakes. This same dock is now used by lake cruisers.

This picture of Boyne City with its four sawmills about 1890 is typical of many of Michigan's lumber towns. Note the many piles of lumber drying by the lake.

COURTESY RALPH PRICE

Cut-over land near Mecosta. In spite of the years that have passed and the many forest fires that have burned over the area many pine stumps can still be seen in northern Michigan. Photo 1957.

A little sawmill in Boyne Falls in 1957. Many little mills like this one with its circular saw are now making lumber from Michigan's second growth trees.

Eagle Harbor on the Keweenaw Peninsula. This little harbor was once the site of one of the first mineral rushes in the United States. Photo 1957.

Here, at the old Jackson pit, iron mining began in Michigan. The present Negaunee shaft of the large Mather Mine can be seen in the background. Photo 1957.

This little building now stands over the shaft hole of the old Cliff Mine. From this first real copper mine came many hundred pounds of pure copper. Note the cliff behind the shaft hole. Photo 1957.

This pretty red lighthouse now stands at Eagle Harbor. It marks the entrance into the harbor as well as giving warning to freighters as they pass around the tip of the Keweenaw Peninsula. Photo 1957.

Philo M. Everett at Jackson, Michigan. It was known as the Jackson Mining Company. In July, 1845, Mr. Everett, with two other members of the new company, set out for the Upper Peninsula to look for copper. They went by train to Marshall, by stage coach from there to Grand Rapids, by wagon from there to Mackinaw City, by canoe to Mackinac Island, then by steamer to Sault Ste. Marie. At Sault Ste. Marie they bought a Mackinaw boat and had it hauled around the rapids. In this boat they coasted along the south shore of Lake Superior to the place where the city of Marquette now stands. Thus to go from Jackson to Marquette in the year 1845 took Mr. Everett and his friends twenty-one days of travel.

Mr. Everett and the other members of his company had come to the Upper Peninsula looking for copper but on their way up had become interested in the iron ore deposit that Mr. Burt had discovered the year before. At what is now Marquette the party was kindly received by an Indian who was living there. His name was Marji-Gesick. The following day this friendly Indian took Mr. Everett and his friends up the hill to the south of Marquette and showed them where iron ore lay hidden under the roots of a big pine tree. That day the Jackson Mining Company changed from a copper mining company to a successful iron mining company.

Mr. Everett took home some samples of the iron ore to show his partners in Jackson. The next year, 1846, members of the Jackson Mining Company again visited the area and again took home more samples of the iron ore. The company began mining iron ore in 1847 at the Jackson Mine, located near the Carp River and not far from the present city of Negaunee. Here on the Carp River a forge was built and the first iron smelted. Iron production, as well as copper production, had now begun in Michigan. Later, furnaces were erected near the mine. Smelting iron ore in those days was a difficult task. There was no coal supply, and charcoal had to be used for fuel. Large areas of hardwood forests were cut to make charcoal for fuel to run the furnaces that melted the iron ore. Yet the task once begun was carried on, and in 1850 the Jackson Mine made its first shipment of five tons of iron bars.

The second big strike in copper was found in the year 1847. In that year Mr. Samuel Knapp was prospecting for copper near where Rockland is now located. He was looking far to the south of the earlier finds, at the top of the Keweenaw Peninsula. He did not know it then, but he was coming into the copper range from its southern end. One day a line of slight depressions in the ground caught his eye. Were these holes pits of earlier Indian diggings? With a pick and shovel he cleaned out one of the pits. Along with decayed trees and the wind-blown and fallen debris that almost filled the pit, Mr. Knapp found many Indian hammers—in fact, many wagon loads of them—that had been used by the Indians long ago when they were toiling in the pit. Eighteen feet down Mr. Knapp came upon a mass of pure copper ten feet long, three feet wide, and two feet thick. There can be no doubt that the Indians had once tried to raise this huge mass of copper from where it lay in the pit, for the whole mass was still resting upon oak timbers just as the Indians had left it centuries before Mr. Knapp again opened the mine. Thus Mr. Knapp uncovered one of the old Indian mines and brought into being the Minesota Mine. The following year, 1848, the Minesota Mine sent ten tons of copper down the Ontonagon River to Ontonagon. In the years that followed, the Minesota Mine paid more profits to its stockholders than all the rest of the Ontonagon copper mines put together. At first the ore was sent down the Ontonagon River, but in 1859 a plank road was built from Rockland to Ontonagon. Another plank road was built to Greenland in 1874.

In 1849 the Cliff Mine paid the first dividend in copper history. The Minesota Mine paid $30,000 in dividends in 1852. Thus Michigan by 1852 had two good paying copper mines. Several other mines were started and a good many companies formed, but most of the mines were shallow and soon gave out. Others failed almost before they had begun. Both the Cliff and Minesota mines were mines in which copper was found in its pure state. It came in chunks or masses and was found in the old lava flows of the Killarney Mountains. Some of the pieces were small, but others weighed five or six hundred tons.

In 1848 copper deposits were discovered midway between the two ends of the range, and the Quincy Mine and Pewabic Mine were started near Hancock. For many years the Quincy Mine was one of the largest and best known copper mines in Michigan. Its number two shaft went down into the ground at an angle for some 9,400 feet, and was the deepest mine shaft to be found in North America. If this shaft were straight down, it would be a shaft some 6,400 feet in depth. The Quincy and Pewabic had hardly started to produce when mining began just south across Portage Lake at Houghton. Here, at Houghton, the Isle Royale Lode was discovered in 1852 and the

Huron in 1853. In 1854 John Slawson found an ancient Indian pit east of Eagle River. This discovery became the Central Mine.

Eagle Harbor, Copper Harbor, Eagle River, and Ontonagon all became copper ports from which copper bars were sent from the Keweenaw Peninsula. For some time the copper that came from the mines at Houghton and Hancock had to be taken to the mouth of the Portage River and there loaded onto boats.

The iron mining companies had a harder time getting started than did the copper companies. By July, 1846, over 104 iron mining companies had been formed. Samples of the iron ore which were sent to the smelters of that time proved to be too high grade for the furnaces of that day, for the smelters were then still using mostly bog iron ore. What is more, there was at that time no good way to ship iron ore to the iron centers south of Lake Erie. The mining companies therefore turned to making iron bars, or "blooms" as they were called, near the mines. These blooms were two feet long and four inches square. To heat their furnaces, charcoal was used. Near the mines there were dense stands of hardwood. The hardwoods were cut by French Canadians and the wood made into charcoal. The charcoal was then used in the furnaces to smelt the iron ore. Once the blooms had been made, they were hauled on sleighs in the wintertime to Marquette. Marquette, in 1849, was merely two log houses and about a half dozen Chippewa Indian wigwams. Blooming did not pay and the iron companies therefore began to look for a better way to ship their iron ore direct to the smelters south of Lake Erie.

The first shipment of iron ore down the lakes was made on July 7, 1852. It was six barrels filled with iron ore which was being sent to the furnaces "down below." This wasn't much of an ore shipment, but it marked the beginning for hundreds of thousands of tons of iron ore that were to follow during the next hundred years. Shipping iron ore in barrels was too expensive. Could it be carried as bulk freight? Soon some boats began to carry the red ore on their decks, but the boat owners did not like to dirty their boat decks with the red, dusty iron ore. Then, too, this was far from a satisfactory way to ship the ore, as it had to be portaged at Sault Ste. Marie. This added much to the cost of shipping. A new and better way of shipping iron ore had to be developed.

During the summer the mines at Ishpeming and Negaunee mined the red hard ore. When winter came, the ore was moved by sleigh to the little dock at Marquette. Horses and mules pulled the sleighs, and about one thousand tons of iron ore could thus be taken to Marquette in a winter season. It took many horses and mules to haul the iron ore to the dock. Hay was costing the mining companies about fifty dollars a ton, and money was then worth much more than it is today. There was no one raising hay in the Upper Peninsula, and hay was a bulky load to haul all the way around the portage at Sault Ste. Marie and across Lake Superior. Horses and sleighs seemed to be the only way to take iron ore from the mines to Marquette. Horses and mules were expensive at that time in the Upper Peninsula, and often they were killed when a sleigh load of ore got going too fast and overran the team.

Changes were soon to come in the manner of transporting iron ore. The mine owners saw great possibilities in mining iron ore if it could be more easily transported to the lake cities along the southern shore of Lake Erie. Soon they began to propose the building of a canal around the rapids in the St. Mary's River so that boats could go from Lake Superior to Lake Huron. Yet to build a canal so far away in the wilderness seemed to many people like wasting money. Still, the idea grew, and today the St. Mary's Falls Ship Canal, briefly called the "Soo," carries more traffic than any other canal in the world.

If you look at a map of the St. Mary's River, you will see that the St. Mary's River connects Lake Superior to Lake Huron. The length of the river is about sixty-three miles. The river's mouth is about twenty-two feet lower than its source, where it leaves Lake Superior. Most of this drop is made at one place about forty-nine miles up the river. There, in a distance a little over half a mile, the river drops about eighteen feet. This rapids is known as the Sault.

Because of this sudden lowering in the level of the surface of the St. Mary's River, boats could not go from Lake Huron into Lake Superior. During the days of the French and English occupations, the fur traders and Indians portaged around the Sault. This was hard work and caused much delay.

In 1797-1798 the Northwest Fur Company built on the Canadian side of the river the first canal and lock at the Sault. The canal and lock were to aid in getting canoes and other small boats of that day around the rapids. The lock was very small, only thirty-nine feet long and eight feet wide. Much of this early work was destroyed by American troops during the War of 1812.

As soon as Michigan became a state, people began to talk about making a canal at Sault Ste. Marie. In 1837 the state legislature made plans for building a canal, and granted $25,000 for the purpose. The following year $25,000 more was provided, and, when surveys had been made, a contractor was hired to build the canal. When the contractor reached the Sault, he found that the canal was to pass over land that then belonged to the United States Government. When he commenced work, he and his men were driven away by United States soldiers.

In 1840 the United States was asked to aid the state in building the canal. Iron ore and copper had as yet not been found in the Upper Peninsula, and most people could see little value in building a canal so far from where people lived. Henry Clay, who was in the United States Senate, strongly opposed Federal aid, and Congress could not see the spending of money on a canal which was then thought to be too far back in the woods to ever be used.

The developing iron and copper mines called people's attention to the need of a canal at the Sault. In 1852 Congress did awaken to the need of a canal at the Sault, and offered for sale three quarters of a million acres of government land to raise the funds.

Following this Federal grant, the State Canal, 5,674 feet long, was built in 1853-1855. The canal was provided with two locks, one leading into the other. At first it had been planned to make them just 250 feet in length. People laughed at Mr. Harvey when he said that the locks should be larger. But Mr. Harvey, who was put in charge of the work of building the canal, won the state legislature to his plan, and the locks were built as he had suggested. Each was 350 feet long and 70 feet wide. Their sides were lined with limestone blocks that were quarried on Drummond Island. These locks allowed the passage of boats which did not sink more than twelve feet into the water. Each lock had a lift of nine feet. At the time these locks were made, they were the largest in the country.

The building of the "Soo" canal was a large undertaking for that day. All of the canal had to be cut into the Cambrian formation that you read about in Chapter One. To cut away the rock with the tools of that time was a slow, hard task. Immigrants were secured to do much of the labor, and real labor it was, especially in the wintertime when the ground was frozen and the temperature remained below zero for days at a time. There were no railroads to bring in the needed supplies. Supplies had to be brought to the Sault by boats. During the winter the lakes were frozen, and then the boats stopped running. To send a letter to New York and receive a reply took about six weeks.

To help pay for the cost of building the canal and locks, tolls were charged on each ton of freight that passed through the locks. At first the rate was six and one-half cents per ton. Later it was gradually reduced to two and one-half cents per ton. Then later it was done away with, and boats were allowed to use the canal free.

The new canal was ready for use on June 18, 1855. The first boat up-bound was the "Illinois." The first down-bound boat was the "Baltimore." Two months later the little schooner "Columbia" passed through the locks carrying on her deck a shipment of iron ore. It was 120 tons of the red metal going from Marquette to Cleveland, Ohio. Four days after the "Columbia" passed through the locks, the schooner "George Washington" passed downward bound with 322 tons of iron ore on her deck. That first season 1,447 tons of iron ore passed through the locks of the new canal. A new day in shipping had come to the Great Lakes.

While the canal was being built, the mine owners began to improve the manner of getting iron ore from the mines to Marquette. In 1855, the year the canal opened, a plank road was built from the mines to Marquette. In that year only 1,447 tons of ore were hauled, but the next year, 1856, when the new plank road had been finished, the tonnage increased to 11,297 tons. Each team still made only one round trip a day, but as much as four tons of ore could now be hauled at one time. The plank road was not used for long because in 1857 the Iron Mountain Railroad Company opened its line from the mines to Marquette. Soon whole trains of ore cars filled with red ore were coming from the mines to the dock at Marquette. The days of horse-drawn sleighs for hauling iron ore were past. The mines had horses and mules for sale.

Soon after the opening of the "Soo" canal, the Civil War threw the states into a bloody conflict. In 1861 copper was selling for seventeen cents a pound, but in 1864 the price had gone up to fifty-five cents a pound. Copper and iron mines that otherwise would not have been self-supporting began to pay a profit. The Union armies demanded more and more iron and copper. Although copper was not then used for shell casings* as it is today, the Union army wanted copper to make copper canteens, brass buttons for the soldiers' uniforms, and bronze for the cannons of that day.

*Copper cartridges were beginning to be made by the end of the war.

By the time of the Civil War ~~several mines were~~ producing copper. The Cliff Mine had been worked since 1844. The Minesota had been producing since 1848, and the Quincy and Pewabic had been putting out ore since 1848. In all, over three thousand copper mining companies had been formed between 1845 and 1864. However, only thirty were mining copper ore by 1865.

Many of the copper mines were started on old Indian pits that had been abandoned by the natives centuries before. By the time the prospectors found the pits, they had become nearly filled with leaves and decayed trees which showed plainly that they had not been worked for at least three or four hundred years.

In 1860 the waterway leading into Portage Lake from Lake Superior was deepened so larger boats could come into Portage Lake from Lake Superior. This work was started in 1859 by several mining companies located near Houghton and Hancock so that supplies could more easily be gotten into the mines on Portage Lake. Before that time all supplies had to be unloaded at the mouth of the Portage River, hauled overland, and then again put on boats on Portage Lake and taken to Houghton and Hancock. In 1861, some 230 boats used the new channel and entered Portage Lake. The new waterway made Houghton and Hancock important shipping centers, and their importance increased when copper was discovered at Calumet in the area just north of Portage Lake.

The Calumet Lode was discovered in 1856 by Edwin J. Hulbert who at that time was one of the leading figures in the Huron Mine at Houghton. In 1855, while making a survey for a new road that was to run between Ontonagon and Copper Harbor, Mr. Hulbert located a copper deposit where Calumet now stands. This new mine, however, was not opened until 1864. It has since proven to be the richest of all of Michigan's copper mines. In the years that followed, the Calumet Mine was driven down to a depth of 9,600 feet. The Tamarack number five shaft went straight down into the rock for over a mile.

Michigan's copper mines are found in a long, narrow corridor of ore-bearing rock that stretches some one hundred miles south through the Keweenaw Peninsula from Copper Harbor to south of Ontonagon. The width of this copper-bearing rock varies from two to eight miles and extends down into the earth to an unknown depth. In some places the vein widens out as it goes deeper into the ground. In other places it gives out altogether. In general, the deeper the vein, the less copper-bearing rock is found in each ton.

All of Michigan's copper is known as mass or native copper. It is found in a pure state and is mixed with rock in one of three ways. In the Cliff, Minesota, Ahmeek, Quincy, and Isle Royale mines the copper is known as amygdaloid and is found in chunks or masses buried in the volcanic rock. These chunks vary from the size of pinheads to huge masses of pure copper weighing tons. These masses had to be cut into smaller chunks while still in the mine in order to get the whole mass of copper up the mine shafts. Huge masses of copper were hard for the miners to cut up and thus get out of the mine. One huge mass in the Minesota mine that weighed 572 tons took twenty men fifteen months to cut up and bring to the surface. Such mass copper is found in lava flows in the cones of old volcanoes that once were a part of the Killarney Mountains when they stretched across the Keweenaw Peninsula. Some four hundred extinct volcanoes are known to exist in the area.

The second type of copper-bearing rock is called conglomerate. This type is found in the Calumet Mine. Conglomerate is a sedimentary deposit and is made up of copper, sand, gravel, and pebbles all mixed together and packed into a very hard rock. The copper found in this type of formation often comes in strings, and is very hard to free from the hard rock with which it is mixed.

The third and most common type of copper deposit throughout the length of the copper range is found in the White Pine Mine. Here the copper is found in very small pieces in a sandstone layer. Often the pieces of copper in this third type of deposit are smaller than the sandstone particles that make up the rock in which the copper is found.

Silver was also found in many of the copper mines. This was especially true of the Minesota Mine. From that mine, kegs filled with the precious metal were shipped south. Most of the silver was usually deposited near the surface. Often these pieces of precious metal found their way into the miners' pockets. There seems to have developed an unwritten law that said copper was for the company but silver could be taken by the miner lucky enough to find it.

Mining copper was far harder and more costly than the early prospectors had imagined it would be. All of Michigan's copper was buried in hard rock. In those days all drilling had to be done by hard labor. One man held and turned the drill as it slowly cut into the lava flow or the sedimentary rock. Two other men with sledge hammers pounded the drill as it went down, sideways, or even up into the rock overhead. This type of drilling was very slow, hard work. When enough holes had been drilled, the holes were filled with black blasting powder. This was the only blasting force known at that time. When the powder was exploded, the rock containing the copper was shattered. In this manner shafts were sunk into the ground. As the shafts went downward, floors or levels branched out from the main shaft. These levels grew in size as the miners blasted farther and farther away from the main shaft.

All the fallen rock had to be shoveled or lifted by hand into little cars and then pushed to the shaft. Then the cars were hoisted to the surface. At first the copper and rock were raised by horsepower. A crude lifting device known as a "horse-whim" had a large round drum on which the cable was wound as one or more horses walked round and round, turning the drum beside them. As the cable was wound up, the cars of rock were raised to the top of the mine.

When the rock was out of the mine, the work of freeing the copper from the rock was still far from finished. The rock had to be further crushed before it would let go of the copper. During the early days of copper mining, the ore-bearing rock had to be crushed by hand. Strong men pounded the rock with heavy sledge hammers to crush it and thus free it from the copper masses. But in this crude manner of crushing the hard rock only a part of the copper was freed from the rock. Thus, much copper, perhaps one fourth of it, was thrown out with the discarded rock. Later very expensive crushing mills were developed, but even these huge mills still left as high as one fifth of the copper in the discarded rock which the miners called "tailings."

For a few years the rock was taken from the mines to the crushing mills on wagons. Because the roads were so poor, only a small amount of rock could be carried on any one load. As in the iron mines, this type of transportation was slow and expensive. When the copper had been freed from the rock, it was then melted into bars for shipment down the lakes. These heavy bars were taken from the mines to one of the copper ports on sleighs in the wintertime.

For several years the iron mines all were worked as open pit mines, but the copper mines began as shaft mines almost from the very start. Down, down, far into the stumps of the old Killarney Mountains went the copper miners as they pounded on their steel drills. Black powder blasted and shattered the rock until tunnels, drifts, and crosscuts grew far longer than the length of the streets of the little mining towns which sat near the top of the shafts. In thinking of these huge mines, you should imagine them as very large skyscrapers sunk far into the ground. So deep are they that sometimes they go into the ground seven or eight times as far as a skyscraper is tall.

The copper mines developed three rather definite mining areas. In the area south of Ontonagon many mines were developed. Some of them were the Nonesuch, White Pine, Minesota, Mass, Victoria, and the Adventure. In this area grew up the villages of Ontonagon, Bergland, Rockland, and Mass and several other smaller places.

The second district grew up around the old Keweena Portage. Here can be found the mines of Quincy, Atlantic, Superior, Baltic, Champion, Huron, and Isle Royale. These mines centered around the twin cities of Houghton and Hancock.

North of the Keweena Portage area many other mines developed along the copper range. In this third area can be found the Calumet, Allouez, Ahmeek, Seneca, Ojibway, Cliff, Phoenix, and Central mines, as well as several others. The communities of Calumet, Laurium, Eagle Harbor, Eagle River, and Copper Harbor grew up in this area.

Today many of these copper mines, which were busy places one hundred years ago, have been abandoned. The mines are filled with water. The houses where people once lived have burned down or have been torn down. Often only site markers tell the modern tourists where the villages and mines used to be.

The first group of men to work in the new copper and iron mines were Cornishmen. These men came from a long line of men who had worked as miners in the Duchy of Cornwall in England. They knew mining as well as a sailor knows the sea or a farmer knows his land, and they loved it just as much. As the years passed by and newer immigrants came to work in the mines, they were usually put to work under a Cornish mine captain.

During the Civil War years many Swedes, Finns, Danes, and Norwegians came to the United States. Many of these people found their way to the Upper Peninsula of Michigan to work in their newly adopted country. In many ways the Upper Peninsula reminded these immigrants of the lands from which they had come. It was a pine country filled with many pretty lakes. Even the winters were long and cold like the winters were in their native lands. Many Canadian French also came, but mining had no attraction for these men who had spent their lives in the forests. Why live in the dark, damp underground when one could work in the open woods amid the fresh air and sunshine? These French Canadians usually supplied the wood that was used to make charcoal for the iron mines. During the war years many of these newcomers left their jobs and joined the Northern army.

Each of these groups has left its mark on northern Michigan. Towns like Bergland, Rockland, and Greenland remind us today of the people who came here from Scandinavia to start life anew in the little houses not far from the shafts of copper and iron mines. Many Finnish farmers now living in the Upper Peninsula can tell you tales about the early days when their grandfathers or great-grandfathers came into the area when it was still a rough wilderness. One cannot visit these mining districts even today without becoming aware of the Cornish pasty that comes fresh from the baker's ovens every day. Mining was hard work, and a miner needed plenty of good, solid food for his noonday meal. This the Cornishman's wife fixed for him in his daily "pasty" which he took into the mine each morning. A pasty was made from vegetables and meat all folded nicely into a wrapper of pie dough. The whole was then baked to a golden brown in the family oven. At noon a miner placed his pasty on his shovel and held the shovel over a candle until the pasty was thoroughly heated. Thus he had a well-balanced, warm meal, though he was eating it deep underground in a mine.

Men working in the copper mines always faced hazards that often took their lives. Sometimes the black powder did not explode as it should have done. These unexploded packings of powder the miners called "sleepers." While the broken rock was being shoveled into the cars, these sleepers sometimes exploded and killed some of the miners. Falling rock was also a constant danger. To brace up the rock ceilings huge timbers like telephone poles were placed in the mines. These sometimes caught on fire. Such fires filled the mines with smoke and fumes. Sometimes these timbers burned for days before the fire could be put out. In the early mines, in the days before fans were developed, the air was often bad and the "wet damp" from blasting spread throughout the mines. Water seeping into the mines was a problem from the start, but pumps were soon used to bring the water out of the mines.

At first miners used only candles for light. These candles were fastened to the front of their hats. As you know, candles give very little light, so mines in those early days were very poorly lighted.

Because the winter days are short in the Upper Peninsula, the miners saw very little sunlight except in the summertime. A few years later candles were replaced by paraffin lamps that were worn on miners' hats just as the candles had been worn.

By the time of the Civil War, mining had become one of Michigan's major industries. Around each mine shaft houses were built of fresh-cut lumber, and new towns, several with Indian names, came into being. To these towns came Cornishmen, Swedes, Norwegians, Finns, and French Canadians. Stores were built, schools were begun, and churches were built for both Catholics and Protestants. Over the mine shafts, shaft houses were built, and refineries were set up in which the copper was freed from the crushed rock and melted into bright, pretty copper bars. Each summer, boats carried these shiny bars away from the copper ports.

But the mining towns a hundred years ago, in those days of poor transportation, were still very far from the other towns of Michigan "down below." During the summer when the boats came sailing westward across the cold, blue waters of Lake Superior, the mining people felt a little nearer to other people. But when ice formed on the lake and the black smoke of the steamers or the white sails of the sailboats could no longer be seen coming across the water, the people of the mining towns felt as if they were living far, far away from their friends and relatives.

Winter with its cold, snow, and ice blocked the water highway for nearly five months of the year. Between the mining towns and their closest neighbor, Green Bay, Wisconsin, lay two hundred miles or more of snow-covered forest land that could be crossed only by walking on snowshoes. Little in the way of food could be brought in through the snow-covered forests, for there was not even a road through the forest land. All food and supplies had to be brought in during the summer shipping season. Sometimes, when the last boats could not come because of ice and storms, the people in the early mining towns had few supplies to last them through the winter. Mail for the area had to be brought in from Green Bay by dog sleigh in the wintertime. This method was used at Ontonagon until 1864.

When spring came, the ice in Lake Superior turned to water, the green leaves again grew on the hardwood trees, the birds came back to their nesting grounds, and the boats again came westward from Sault Ste. Marie to carry away the copper and iron ore that had been mined during the winter.

Up to about 1875 there was only one iron mining region in the Lake Region, and all the iron ore was shipped from Marquette or Escanaba. This range, known as the Marquette Range, reached some thirty-five miles, from Ishpeming and Negaunee almost to L'Anse. Besides the Jackson Mine at Negaunee and the Cleveland Mine at Ishpeming, some fifty or so mines by 1878 spread across the range, giving rise to many iron mining towns such as Champion, Michigamme, and Republic.

Iron is a very heavy commodity, and a hundred years ago, in the early days of iron mining, there were none of the huge machines to handle the ore that there are today. The red, heavy ore had to be shoveled into cars in the mines. Then it had to be wheeled and dumped into sleighs or ore cars which carried the ore to Marquette.

At first the ore dock was small, and until loading docks were built, the ore had to be loaded into boats by hand labor. In the holds of the new iron-ore boats which were beginning to appear in the shipping trade, men called "trimmers" shoveled and pushed the ore around so that the boat would not list to one side. This was hot, dirty work on a warm summer day.

Loading an ore boat was hard enough, but going down into an ore boat on a hot day, when the sun was beating down upon the boat's metal sides, and shoveling out the heavy ore was a task almost beyond human endurance.

Later, as we shall see, powerful machines came into the mines to do much of the work, huge loading docks were built to load the boats, and huge bucket scoops were developed to do the hard work of unloading. Such machines as we have today to handle our vast shipments of iron ore were beyond the imagination of the men who worked in the iron mining industry in the earlier days that you have been reading about.

Upper left: Big wheels. Upper right: Decking ground. Lower left: A lumber camp. Lower right: "Banking grounds."

Chapter XIV

THE LUMBER STORY
(1860-1910)

With the westward push of the settlers across the nation, the changes in transportation and communication, the rise of local industries that demanded lumber, and the rapid growth of the nation's cities, several demands for more and more lumber came into being. The builders of boats needed beams, planking, and masts. The settlers pushing west, and then settling the Great Plains, needed boards to build their houses, barns, and sheds. Thousands of ties were needed for the new railroad tracks that were then spreading across the nation. Poles were later needed for the new telephone and electric lines. Lumber was also needed back East to build homes, stores, churches, and schools in the rapidly growing cities in an area in which most of the timber had already been destroyed. As these demands for lumber increased, so did the ring of the woodsmen's axes and the ringing, high-pitched whine of the saws in the lumber mills of Michigan.

In an earlier chapter it was shown how, after the pine had been cut in the smaller pineries along the St. Clair River, the lumbermen turned to the larger pineries lying in the Saginaw and Muskegon River valleys. A hundred years ago pine logs came floating down the Saginaw and Muskegon Rivers every spring. But as the demand for more and more lumber increased, lumbermen went farther and farther north and built steam-driven sawmills at the mouths of many of the smaller streams which flowed into the Great Lakes. Upstream along the banks of these rivers were stands of pine that could be easily floated to the little sawmills which had been built at the mouths of the rivers.

Lumber camps were built at dozens of places in the forest. More and more men came to Michigan to help in the timber harvest. Among the people coming to Michigan were many immigrants from Europe. Poles, Finns, Swedes, and Norwegians came to work in the forests. Many sons of the earlier settlers who had come to southern

Michigan some thirty or forty years before went to homestead land in northern Michigan and to work in the lumber camps and sawmills.

Up to about 1870, the timber supply for the sawmills had been cut near the sawmills, but as the nearby forests were quickly destroyed, lumbermen had to go farther and farther up the rivers to get logs for their mills.

Soon after the Civil War thousands of pine logs began coming down the Au Sable, the Rifle, the Black, the Jordan, the Boardman, the Manistee, the Pere Marquette, the Manistique, the Menominee, and many other smaller streams every spring to add their numbers to those already coming down the Saginaw and Muskegon rivers. It seems that any stream large enough to float a pine log, if it flowed through pine country, was used during this period of logging to carry pine logs to the busy sawmills.

It became the usual custom during those years of logging in Michigan for a man preparing to log his land to go with, or to send, a crew of men into the forest to the area where the winter's cutting was to be done. These men usually went into the woods in the early fall. The first thing they did when they reached the site of the lumber camp was to clear a road from the "cuttings" to a high bank on the nearest river. Over this road the logs, which the men would cut during the coming winter, would be hauled to the river bank. Then the men built the lumber camp itself. Soon after it was finished the logging crew arrived and began their winter's work in the woods.

By 1880, logging in Michigan had become big business as eastern capital came west with the lumbermen. More and more of the big lumber companies at that time began operating so many lumber camps that their camps were often referred to just by number.

In the lumber camps of that time there were usually several buildings. One of the buildings, called the "bunkhouse," was the building in which the men slept. Then there was usually another building used as the "cook shack" and dining room. Still another building was used as a barn for the horses. Other buildings were used for storing supplies and for the camp office and "van." The van was a small store where the men working in the camp could buy such items as socks, mittens, shirts, and tobacco.

The old "bunkhouse" of the earlier logging days had, by 1880, given way to a newer and better one. The bunkhouse in these later camps was usually a long, narrow building. Whereas in earlier days the bunkhouse had been built out of logs, most of the bunkhouses of this period were built out of lumber and then covered with tar-paper. Logs were becoming too valuable to be wasted in building camp buildings. What is more, a building made of boards and covered with tar-paper could be more easily heated than one made from logs. When a camp was no longer needed, the buildings were often torn down and the lumber used to build another camp at some other place in the forest. The old "caboose," in the center of the building, had by now been replaced by a large iron stove. Sometimes these stoves were as long as eight feet. A stovepipe ran upward from the stove and then divided and ran the entire length of the building where it entered a smokestack at each end of the bunkhouse. By running the stovepipe lengthwise of the bunkhouse, heat was spread over the entire room. The old wooden bunks were slowly replaced by beds, or bunks, made of iron. These beds usually ran along both sides of the bunkhouse. Usually they were double-deckers and had some type of wire springs. The bunks were usually double; that is, two men slept below and two above. In front of the bunks on each side of the bunkhouse were benches, called the "deacon seat," which ran the entire length of the room. These deacon seats were the only places, besides the edge of the beds, where a "shanty boy" could sit. A long wire, running on each side of the room between the stove pipe and the bunks, was used by the shanty boys as a clothesline on which to dry their wet clothing.

Loggers, up to about 1890, were known as shanty boys or shanty men. This term no doubt came west with the lumbermen and got its origin in the East where the loggers lived in buildings in the woods which were known as Maine shanties. After about 1890 timber cutters began to be called lumberjacks. Today such workers in the forests are called loggers.

The cook shack, or cook house as it was called, was another long building. It was usually divided by a board partition into two rooms. In the smaller room, called the kitchen, the cook and his "cookee" helpers prepared the meals on one or two large iron cook stoves, then called "wood ranges." The meals were served to the shanty boys in the larger room at the other end of the building. Long, heavy tables and benches were the usual dining room furniture. Kerosene lamps and lanterns furnished the only light.

The barn was usually large so as to care for the many teams of horses that worked in the woods. The barn, like the bunkhouse, was built of lumber, but whereas the bunkhouse had rough plank floors made from two-inch unplaned pine, there often was no floor in the barn. By 1880, horses had, with few exceptions, replaced the slower oxen that had been used in the woods in the earlier lumbering days. Logging horses were medium-sized horses weighing about fifteen hundred pounds. They were known as woods horses, and after a winter or two of lumbering they, like the shanty boys, became skilled in solving the problems of getting the logs from the forests. A man known as the "barn boss" had general charge of the barn and the horses. He was usually an old teamster who knew much about horses. The horses were kept well shod, well fed, and well groomed. Every teamster took pride in his team and often he would spend many hours in the barn currying them and seeing that his horses were well cared for. Sometimes, in the smaller camps, farmers who came to work in the woods during the winter brought their teams with them. Often their teams earned more money for the farmer than he could earn for himself. Most of the larger camps had a blacksmith shop. In this building the blacksmith shod the horses, repaired the logging chains and built the huge bobsleighs and fastened on their large iron runners.

After a hearty breakfast the shanty boys picked up their axes, swung their saws over their shoulders, and started walking down the road behind the bobsleighs, teams, and teamsters to the "cutting ground." On the cutting ground new changes had also taken place since the earlier days in lumbering. Whereas before the Civil War trees were felled by chopping them, the shanty boys of this period now began using cross-cut saws. These new saws cut much faster and also saved much good timber. A "feller" would determine the direction a tree should be felled, then with his ax he would chop into that side of the tree. When he had finished chopping, two men called "sawyers," using a six-foot cross-cut saw, started to saw the tree from the opposite side. As the saw neared the chopped place, the huge pine tree started to fall toward the ground. As the large crown of the falling tree began its long arc earthward, the sawyers cried out "TIMBER-R-R-R" to warn other nearby workmen that the tree was coming down. Then the sawyers quickly stepped away from the falling tree so that if the butt of the tree should bounce they would not be hurt. This method of felling trees with cross-cut saws saved two or three more feet of the valuable trunk of the tree in the lower and larger part near the ground. Later, as lumber became more and more valuable, sawyers began to saw the trunks of the trees closer to the ground so the stumps would have as little good wood left as possible.

When the huge pine was down, other men, called "limbers" or "axemen," came up to the fallen tree and began chopping off the branches. When the huge trunk, or bole, lay stripped of its branches, other men called "buckers" began to saw the bole of the tree into saw-logs of 12, 14, 16, 18, or 20 feet in length. Buckers also used the new cross-cut saw, and two men working together could usually "buck" about one hundred saw-logs in a day. Just when it became the practice to cut the tree trunk into logs in the woods we do not know, but whole trunks were now seldom taken to the "landings" in one long piece as they had been in the earlier days of logging.

Oxen and horses were used to draw the logs from the woods. (Picture taken about 1910.)

The distance which the timber now had to be hauled was too far to log in that way. This new custom of cutting the tree trunks into logs while the tree still lay in the forest was called the "Canadian way."

After a tree had been cut into saw-logs, a teamster, following a path that had been cut by men called "swampers," brought his team of horses up to the newly cut logs. Behind the team, on the ground, dragged a pair of "skidding tongs" that were really a pair of large pincers having a barb like a fish hook has at each end. These tongs were then fastened into the small end of a log. Then the log was dragged, or "snaked," from the woods to a nearby spot known as a "cross-haul." At the cross-haul the logs were loaded onto bobsleighs.

By this time the lumbering sleigh, or "bobsleigh," had been developed into the major vehicle for carrying saw-logs from the forests to the landings beside the rivers. A bobsleigh was made with two pairs of large runners. The runners were six or eight inches wide and about six or eight feet long. They were fastened together by cross chains so that the back runners would follow in the path of the front runners. Above each pair of runners was fastened, by means of a "kingbolt," a large wooden cross beam known as a "bunk." The kingbolt would let the runners turn freely under the bunk. Bunks were usually about nine feet or ten feet wide, although some bunks were as wide as fifteen or sixteen feet.

Onto these bunks the logs were rolled at the cross-haul. At first the logs were rolled onto the bobsleigh up inclined skids by a team of horses pulling a chain which ran at a right angle to the bobsleigh. Thus the loading place was called a cross-haul because the team pulled at a right angle to the road. Later, lifting devices known as "jammers" raised the logs onto bobsleighs or railroad cars. When the logs were loaded and securely fastened by a "binding chain" or "toggle chain," as it was called, the teamster started his horses on the road to the banking ground, or landing, beside the river.

During most of the logging period in Michigan's history, logging roads and rivers were the important lanes of log transportation. Roads were built from the cuttings to the riverbank. Over these roads, during the winter days, the logs were hauled to the river's edge. In winters of good snowfall logging roads were quite easily kept in good hauling condition. However, some winters the snowfall was light, and then snow had to be hauled and dumped onto the road. This the shanty boys jokingly called a "Swedish snowstorm." This was costly for the logging companies, in a day when the snow all had to be shoveled by hand, but there was no other way to get the huge pine logs moved from the cuttings to the river bank. To make the roads firmer and more slippery they were sometimes iced during a cold winter night. Many camps had what was known as an "icer." The icer was a sleigh with a watertank on it. While the rest of the men slept, the icing crew filled the water tank at a pump or stream. A small fire under the tank kept the water from freezing. Then as the horses pulled the icer over the road, the water was sprinkled along the sled tracks. When it froze it made a good hard surface for the large bobsleighs. A team of horses could pull a huge load on these well-iced roads. It cost the logging companies much money to cut, grade, and keep up these logging roads, but they were one of the necessary expenses of running a lumber camp.

In every camp one or more men, called "road monkeys," cared for the roads. Sleighs must move easily but not too fast. If they did they overran the horses and often killed them. If the road became too slippery, the road monkey sprinkled sand on it to slow down the huge loads of logs as they came down the hills from the forest. All horses working in the woods were kept "sharp shod." That is, they were shod with shoes that had sharp points, or spikes, on them. The sharp points kept the horses from slipping and also helped the horses' feet to catch into the ice so that they could move the huge loads of logs.

A shanty boy's work day was a long one. Usually he worked at least twelve hours in the cold and snow in the woods. At noon the cook brought the noonday meal to the place where the men were working. This noonday meal, or dinner served in the woods, was called "flaggin's." Taking his plate of hot food from the lunch wagon, the shanty boy would find a log or stump on which to sit and there in the forest eat his warm noonday meal. While the men were eating their food, the horses ate their noonday meal of oats from nosebags. Then when the meal was over, the men and horses went back to their work in the woods.

When the long day's work was done and the darkness fell over the snow-covered forests, the weary men and teams left the cuttings and took the road to camp. One by one as the men reached camp they filed into the bunkhouse. The teamsters drove their tired teams into the barn. Next, often by lantern light, amid the sound of crunching oats and hay, the teamsters slid the harnesses from the backs of the horses and hung them on the wooden pegs behind the stalls. Then they too went into the bunkhouse.

Wet clothing was changed for dry. Hands and faces were washed. Pipes were lit. Gradually the deacon seat was filled with men eager for their supper after a hard day's work in the fresh, cold air. Then came the call for supper. Sometimes the cook beat on an old dishpan; sometimes he struck a triangle bar with an iron bar. Some cooks blew a horn, but whatever the source of the noise it meant the same to all tired, hungry shanty boys: "Come and get it." The cook was ready and so were they. Quietly they filed out of the bunkhouse and into the cook shanty.

Lumber companies of this period saw to it that the men were well fed. The cook was one of the most important and best paid men in a lumber camp. Failure to have a good cook meant discontent among the men, and often they went to work for other lumber companies. Most of the cooks were men, but sometimes women did the cooking. All the meals, even breakfast, were hearty ones for the shanty boys. Beans, ham, thick bacon, dried-apple pie and raisin pie, fried potatoes, hash, prunes, and buckwheat pancakes all found their way to the breakfast table. Even the tables had changed by this time. On most of the camp tables there now began to appear the new oilcloth that was then being manufactured. Some of the lumber companies even began to give their men coffee and tea. Canned goods, which were then beginning to appear on the market, also found their way onto the lumber camp tables.

While eating their meals shanty boys never talked to each other, except to ask to have something passed to them. That was usually not necessary, for the cookees saw to it that there was plenty within easy reach of every man. The evening meal was called supper. Though it was a hearty meal and though each man ate much, the time spent in the cook shack was usually not very long. Shanty boys ate quietly and quickly.

After supper the men went back to the bunkhouse. There the red-hot stove kept the men warm and comfortable. As the cold winter night settled down upon the camp, the kerosene lamps and lanterns that had replaced the earlier candles and light from the fire in the "caboose" gave a feeble light that cast long, dim shadows about the room. Small groups of men sat around on the deacon seats, smoked, and swapped stories. A few of the men played cards with ragged, dirty, worn cards. The thick, heavy tobacco smoke from their pipes soon filled the bunkhouse. This was mixed with fumes from the drying socks, clothing, and the fumes from kerosene lamps. There was usually no fresh air in the bunkhouse, and before long it had an odor which was all its own. For some unknown reason shanty boys took their fresh air only in the daytime. As bedtime neared, teamsters sauntered out to the barn to make one last check on their horses.

Some men went to bed early, and by nine it was "lights out" for all.

The day's work was finished. Heavy snores filled the bunkhouse as the tired men rested from their work. As they slept, their clothing slowly dried by the dying fire.

The wood fire in the bunkhouse stove died down to a bed of red coals, then turned to a pile of warm, soft, gray ash. The air in the bunkhouse slowly took on a wintry chill. The sleeping men pulled their blankets closer around them. Then, as the cooling chill of the night settled on the camp, the boards of the bunkhouse, like the logs in the settler's cabin, snapped with a loud crack like the shot of a rifle. Outside in the moonlight from across the hills could now and again be heard the howl of timber wolves.

Sometimes during the night a wintry storm would roar and cover the camp and roads with a new layer of downy whiteness. The snow, driven in gusty whirls, was piled against the bunkhouse and the other buildings, around stumps, and against fallen logs or trees. When morning came, new sights and strange shapes greeted the men. Strange mounds of white snow appeared where sleighs, stumps, barrels, or bushes had stood the night before.

The first one up at camp in the morning was the "chore boy." He was usually not a boy at all but an old shanty boy who could no longer stand the hard work in the woods. Usually he was up by four in the morning. Building fires in the cook shack and the bunkhouse was his first task. Then he called the cook, the cookees, and the teamsters. While the rest of the shanty boys still slept, the cook and the cookees started getting breakfast. Meanwhile the teamsters went to the barn to feed their horses. The fire in the stove in the cook shack melted the ice in the water pails. With some of this water to prime the pump, one of the men, properly clad against the cold, went out to get fresh water. Sometimes there was no pump and water had to be carried from a spring or a brook. Often the man sent for the water had to cut a hole in the ice before he could get any water. But the water was brought and soon coffee was being made on the huge wood range. The pleasant smell of coffee, frying bacon, and pancakes soon filled the cook shack.

About four-thirty in the morning one of the cookees, called the "Gabriel blower," blew the "Gabriel," a long tin horn. This aroused the sleeping men and then someone called out, "Get up, you lazy lumberjacks; it's daylight in the swamp." Aroused from their deep sleep the men would roll from their bunks. Pairs of legs, clad in long, bright-red underwear, would swing down from the edges of the bunk beds. Rough, calloused hands rubbed eyes yet sleepy from the night and pushed back mussed-up hair. From the wire strung along between the stove pipe and the bunks each shanty boy pulled his heavy wool socks, which by then were dry. Quickly, over his long underwear, he put on one or two pair of heavy wool socks, heavy woolen pants, a pair of heavy shoes, and one or two heavy woolen shirts. Pants were held up by wide bright-colored suspenders. Most shirts were bright plaids.

At one end of the bunkhouse was a bench that ran across the room. Upon this bench there were usually several tin wash basins. To these wash basins the men went to wash before breakfast. Dipping the basins into one of the water barrels, which had been filled by the chore boy, the shanty boys washed for breakfast. One by one they used the basins and then threw the wash water out the bunkhouse door. There the water gradually froze into a pile of ice which often did not disappear until the coming of spring. All the men, as a usual thing, used towels that were furnished by the company. No one thought of such a thing as sanitation or very much about cleanliness. Why should a man refuse to use a towel? Was he any better than the fifteen or so men who had used it ahead of him?

About five o'clock came the call for breakfast. Soon the men were helping themselves to huge chunks of sausage and large thick pancakes and plenty of blackstrap molasses. All their food was eaten quickly and washed down with gulps of strong coffee. Within a few minutes all had been fed and quietly, one by one, they left the cook shack. The teamsters went to the stable and finished harnessing their horses. Soon they were on their way to the cutting grounds for another day's work.

Cold was no excuse for not working. With good woolen socks on their feet, with warm mittens on their hands, and often with a short-stemmed pipe, called a "nose warmer" and smelling ages old, the shanty boys did another day's work in the woods. Often when they had reached the cutting grounds where the winds could not hit them, they became so warm from working that they had to take off part of their heavy clothing.

On Sundays no work was done. The meals were served at the usual hours, but the rest of the time the men were free to do as they wished. Sunday was known as "boil up day" because many of the men used part of the day to do their washing. Boiling their clothes not only freed the dirt from the clothing but also killed the lice and bedbugs in them. Only a few of the men could write. Sometimes these men wrote home to their families or to the families of other men who could not write. These letters went to town with the "tote teamster" the following week when he went to town for supplies. Sunday was a good day to play jokes on "greenhorns" who had just come into camp. Some men played cards in the bunkhouse. Others spent hours sharpening their axes on the grindstone. This was a slow, tiring job, but a sharp ax was a shanty boy's best tool. For hours they turned the slow-cutting grindstone as the axes were sharpened for the coming week. Sometimes a man passed the idle hours playing on his violin or mouth organ. A few of the men read papers and magazines which were often weeks or months old. Some rested in their bunks. Others sat outside, if the day was warm enough, and whittled aimlessly on pieces of clean fresh pine.

Usually the lumbermen cut only the timber that was on the land the company had purchased. However, some companies lumbered what were called "round forties." They would purchase a piece of land and then cut all the area around it, thus stealing government or privately owned timber. Nothing much was ever done about this practice during the lumbering days, but in 1903, after most of the timber was gone, the state legislature finally passed an act making it illegal to cut timber on state-owned land.

Every day, all winter long, teams of horses, or oxen, were busy hauling logs from the cuttings to the landing on the river bank. By early spring huge piles of brown pine logs lay "decked" along the banks of many of Michigan's rivers. The places where the logs were piled, or decked, were called "landings," "decking grounds," or "rollways." The rollways were usually on a high bank along the deep side of a stream. Even today these old rollways can often be located by the scars that the logs left on the river bank as they were rolled into the water.

Carefully the woodsmen watched the river. Too little water in the upper branches meant that the logs would ground on the river bottom. Too much water meant the flooding of the stream, and then valuable saw logs would be carried from the main course of the river and pushed into swamplands or marshes where they would be left by the river. To get these "stranded" logs back into the stream often took much time and hard work.

At last, when the spring rains and the melting snows had raised the river high enough, the river drive began. The decks of logs were rolled over the bank and into the river. "Breaking the rollways," as this was called, was dangerous work, for the rolling logs now and then hit a shanty boy and killed or injured him. With a rumble and a roar the logs went rolling over the bank and splashed into the river. Water splashed high into the air as the first rolling logs hit the running river. Up and down the logs bobbed and churned as others rolled in on top of them. Slowly they began to move downstream with the running water. If the river was high and running free, the first logs soon began to disappear around the first bend of the river. Thus the logs began the second part of their journey from forest to sawmill.

Galliger's Banks, Manistee River west of Frederic. This rollway was used about 1880. (Photo 1915)

In rain, snow, sleet, and spring sunshine, the river drivers, called "river jacks," "river hogs," "river pigs," or "white-water men," worked at the task of getting the winter's cut of logs into the river. Logs piled farther back from the river bank had to be rolled by a peavey to the water's edge. This "tailing down" was hard work but required no great skill. In a few days' time all the winter's cut had been rolled into the stream. The winter's work in the woods was finished. Most of the men packed their belongings in their "turkey" and started for town or home. Only a few river drivers remained behind to bring the logs down the river. When the men reached the nearest town, some of them spent all their winter's hard-earned money in one wild "spree" that lasted only a few days. Others carefully guarded their earnings and took the first train or boat and went back to their families and to a summer's work on their farms.

Sometimes so many logs floated on the water that the surface of the river looked brown. The river drivers could walk about on the bobbing pine logs wherever they pleased. Not all shanty boys could be white-water men. River drivers had to have a good sense of balance, a quick step, and a good eye to judge logs and sudden movements of the river.

Many of the early river drivers were French Canadians and forest workers who had come to Michigan from Pennsylvania or Maine. They had a costume as gay and typical as any in American history. They dressed in red, blue, or yellow plaid mackinaws. Their trousers were also of heavy woolen material like their mackinaws. Usually they wore two or three pair of socks which came up above their shoepacks. Sometimes their trousers were "stagged off" short with an ax in order to keep from catching their "spikes" in them. At other times their trousers were tucked into the tops of their socks. Around their belts they often wore sashes made of very bright colored yarns. Their "mits" were often tucked in behind their sashes. Tobacco pouches hung from strings around their necks.

The river drivers, carrying their peaveys with them, stepped from the river's edge onto the bobbing logs and began their ride from the camp to the town at the river's mouth. Sharp "calks" on the bottom of their shoes jabbed into the bark of the logs and kept their feet from slipping on the wet and slippery logs as they turned and slid in the cold running water. Riding the logs was fun as well as hard work for the river drivers. Most of the time the logs usually floated along with the current, but at other times they were caught by stumps, dead logs, or old trees which were lying in the bed of the stream. Stepping from log to log, or riding the one that they were on, the river drivers kept the logs floating downstream toward the sawmills.

But all the logs did not go easily downstream. Some logs called "sackers" drifted, or were pushed, into swampy places where the river had flooded the lowlands. Others grounded on sand bars in the bed of the stream. Each of these logs had to be worked back into the running stream. This was hard, wet, cold work for the "sacking crew" or "rear enders" who came along behind the drive to clear up the stray logs. They had to splash about in the mud and cold water as they heaved and pulled on their peaveys to get the stranded logs back into the river.

Behind the sackers came the "wanagan." The wanagan was usually a raft on which had been built a small shed to carry the "chuck" and extra supplies such as tools and clothing that were needed by the men working on the drive. When night came, the river men walked back to the wanagan ready for a "real feed" before they rolled up in their blankets to spend the night on the bank along the river. Somehow, in spite of moving, rain, snow, or other misfortunes that overtook the wanagan, the cook always managed to have good meals ready for the tired, hungry river drivers. After they had eaten, the river drivers lay down to a carefree rest, for was it not true, as they believed, that logs always ran free at night, especially in the full of the moon?

When morning came again the river drivers were up early. After breakfast in the wanagan they began walking along the path beside the river or stepping out onto the logs to keep them on their way down to the sawmill. Sometimes the river men sat idly by on the river's bank watching the large, brown logs drift quietly by. But always they were watching to see that the logs did not start a "jam."

Beside the river ran a path through the brush. Usually it was an old animal path that the lumbermen had taken over. Along these paths they walked back and forth as the brown logs ran free with the moving current. From the path they could nearly always see the moving surface of the river. Sometimes this path ran along firm sandy ground beneath pine trees. At other times it dropped to the low marshy ground along the river's edge. Up hill and down, across sandy plains and through soggy bunch grass, ran the path beside the river that was now torn free and soft by calks on heavy shoes. Along these paths, among trees and bushes still leafless and bare in the early spring, walked the rivermen as they watched the logs drift downstream toward the sawmills. The last such river drive was on the Menominee River in 1910.

In a week or two after leaving camp the river drivers brought their logs into the booms at the river's mouth where there were sawmills waiting to cut the logs into lumber. On the faster-floating streams like the Au Sable and the Manistee the logs ran quite free once they had reached deep water. On these streams the logs could be floated all the way to the river's mouth. Often a river driver, peavey in hand, came riding into town standing on one of the brown logs that he had cut in the forest during the last winter.

Each logging company was eager to get its logs to the sawmills while the water in the stream was still high enough to float the logs. Therefore, most of the rollways were broken about the same time and the saw logs from several camps were often mixed together in the running water. Sometimes lumber companies got into arguments over driving rights on the streams, and many laws regarding river rights were passed by the state legislature.

In order to do away with the problems that arose when several lumber companies drove the same stream at the same time, "booming and driving companies" were sometimes formed. There were several of these booming and driving companies in Michigan. One of these companies was formed to drive the Tittabawassee River. Another one was formed to drive the Muskegon River. The Menominee River Boom Company was started in 1868, and by 1919 it had handled over ten billion board feet of logs. These booming companies were sometimes formed by the lumbermen whose men were driving the same river. At other times special driving companies were organized by other men. These booming companies drove the logs for the logging companies for a set rate of so much money for every thousand feet of timber brought into the sorting booms at the river's mouth.

Before the time of the spring drive the booming company would get the river ready for the drive. Dams were built to hold back flood water. Stumps and dead logs called "sweepers" were dragged from the river, and "glance booms" were made so that the logs would have less chance of being stranded. A crew of expert river men would be ready to work for the booming company. It would be the job of these drivers, working for the booming company, to bring all the logs down the river. When spring came, each lumber company rolled its logs into the stream, and the booming company then took up the task of driving the logs from the rollways to the sorting booms at the river's mouth.

These booming companies sometimes also carried on rafting operations. At the mouth of the Tittabawassee River, logs were sorted according to company brands. These logs were then formed into rafts, or held in "bag booms," and then towed down the Saginaw River by tugs to the mill ponds at Bay City and Saginaw. At Muskegon and other places booming and driving companies sorted the logs and rafted them to the various sawmills where they were to be sawed into lumber. As the logs grew scarce, some log rafts were even brought down from the Upper Peninsula and from Canada. Tugs pulled such huge masses of logs, caught in "bag booms," across the Great Lakes.

As the number of lumbering companies increased, it became necessary for each company to mark each of its logs so that its logs could be sorted from the others at the end of the drive. At first the lumber companies marked their logs by cutting their mark into the bark of each log with an ax. This method required great skill on the part of the axman so that there would be no variation in the mark used. Because axmen were not always accurate in cutting the mark and because the bark sometimes fell from the log, newer and better ways of marking logs were soon developed. The "stamp hammer" came into common use during this period. The stamp hammer was a heavy hammer, having raised on the head of it the brand of the lumber company. By hitting the end of a log with the stamp hammer the brand, or "logmark," of the lumber company was dented into the end of the log. Soon hundreds of logmarks were registered by the lumber companies. Sometimes a lumber company used the initials of the company owner. At other times pictures of animals or birds were used. Horseshoes, buildings, etc., were all used to brand the logs that came down Michigan's rivers. Each county kept in its files a record of the logmarks used in the county. Because of this we know that over three thousand five hundred logmarks were used here in Michigan by the lumber companies to mark their logs as they came down the rivers. By thus marking the logs, the "pike-pole men" working on the sorting booms at the river's mouth were able to pick out the logs that belonged to each of the logging companies that were driving the stream.

As the logs entered the sorting booms at the river's mouth, they passed along a narrow waterway where men with long pike-poles pushed the logs into the pockets of the various lumber companies. When a number of these logs had been gathered into a pocket, they were formed into a raft or enclosed in a bag boom. A boom was made by fastening several logs together with short iron chains called "boom dogs." These chains were short and had an iron pin fastened to each end. These pins were driven into the end of two logs and thus the logs were fastened together with the chain. Several of these logs fastened together formed a boom. A "bag boom" was made by bringing the two ends of the boom together and thus enclosing within it the logs that the booming company wished to deliver to the mills.

In driving logs, every lumber company lost many of them. Some logs, known as "dead heads," became filled with water and sank to the bottom of the streams. Sometimes logmarks were very similar, and timber thieves would place their logmark over the old one and thus change the ownership of a log while it was coming down the river. Other timber thieves would sometimes steal logs from the river or booms and saw off a short cut on each end. This would remove the owner's original brand. They would then place their mark on the logs and send them on their way down the river. Such stealing of logs, however, was usually difficult to do because of the many rivermen going up and down the river watching the drive.

Nearly all the cities and villages now located in the upper part of the Lower Peninsula and the eastern half of the Upper Peninsula had their beginning because of the lumber industry. Some of these are known as inland towns while the others are known as port towns. The port towns sprang up first. Among the port towns might be listed Alpena, Tawas City, Oscoda, Cheboygan, Boyne City, East Jordan, Frankfort, Menominee, Escanaba, Manistique, Ontonagon, and Munising. These towns grew up around the sawmills that had been built at a river's mouth where saw logs could be had for the sawmills.

Sawmill near East Jordan (1954)

The life of these towns depended upon the spring log drive and upon the fact that before them spread one of the Great Lakes over which boats could come to carry the newly cut lumber to market.

The river mouths, where these early sawmill towns were located, made very good harbors if the sand bars were not too high to keep the boats from entering. This was especially true on the west side of the state where the drifting sand dunes often made a large lake at the mouth of each river. These lakes made good harbors for the lumber boats and also provided quiet waters for booming grounds where logs could be sorted and stored until they were needed in the sawmills.

At first these port sawmill towns were rough, rowdy places. But as time passed there grew up around the sawmills large villages with houses, churches, hotels, saloons, and schools all built of the newly cut lumber. Women brought home life to the sawmill towns. Churches were started. Schools were built and children went to school. Sidewalks, made from planks, ran along the village streets in front of the houses. Bright, yellow sawdust was sprinkled along the streets to keep the lumber wagons, with their wide, flat, iron tires, from sinking into the sand. In the summertime this sawdust also kept the dust of the street from blowing into the houses. White picket fences were built around many homes and gardens.

As the cutting continued in the pineries upriver, many of the sawmill towns grew in size and took on a more dignified appearance. As the forest grew smaller, the number of wealthy lumbermen and their fortunes grew in size. These newly rich, many of whom had worn the calked boots of a shanty boy only a few years before, built large frame houses on spacious lots along the city streets of many of the growing sawmill towns. Today these huge old houses, built when good lumber was thirteen or fourteen dollars a thousand board feet, stand with their cupolas, fancy cornices, and spacious porches to remind us of the "Gay Nineties." They tell of an era when pine was king and gentlemen and ladies rode in surreys pulled by prancing bobtailed horses with heads held high by taut check reins.

At these port towns, to which the streams brought their annual spring supply of logs, the logs were cut into lumber. Each morning the whistles of the sawmills announced the beginning of another day's work in the sawmills. Then the shining, buzzing, noisy saws again took up their daily task of cutting logs into bright yellow lumber. The fresh-cut lumber was carefully stacked in lumber piles along the harbor where it could easily be loaded onto the boats that would carry it to market. During the long, warm summer days the hot sun shone down upon the fresh-cut, drying lumber. The soft, warm wind from the forest land carried the pleasing pine smell of the newly sawed timber out over the blue waters of the nearby lake or inland across the countryside. At night or on cloudy days sailboat captains said they could tell by the pleasant pine odor which came to them that they were nearing a lumber port.

At first the sawmills ran only in the summertime, and many of the shanty boys, after they had spent their winter's wages, worked in them during the summer. But by the end of the last century sawmills were running all the year around. When better lights were developed, some of the mills ran both day and night. A day's work in these early mills was ten to twelve hours. The mills ran six days a week, so a sawmill worker around 1880 worked a sixty-hour week or more.

With the increase in camps and sawmills Michigan rapidly became a leading lumber-producing state. For a few short years it was the largest lumber producer in the United States. From its many noisy mills came lath, shingles, pickets, lumber, barrel and keg staves, barrel and keg hoops, and barrel and keg heads. Smaller trees, not large enough for lumber, were cut to make thousands of railroad ties to firmly hold the new steel rails that were then spreading across the growing nation, and to make fence posts to enclose the ever-increasing farm lands of the western plains.

At first the lumber came slowly from the little sawmills, but the rate of cutting steadily increased. In an earlier chapter it was shown how the gate saw was replaced by the muley and how the muley gave way to the circular saw. After 1876 the band saw gained first place

An early circular saw. Note the hammer marks left by the saw filer where he hammered the saw to make it run true.

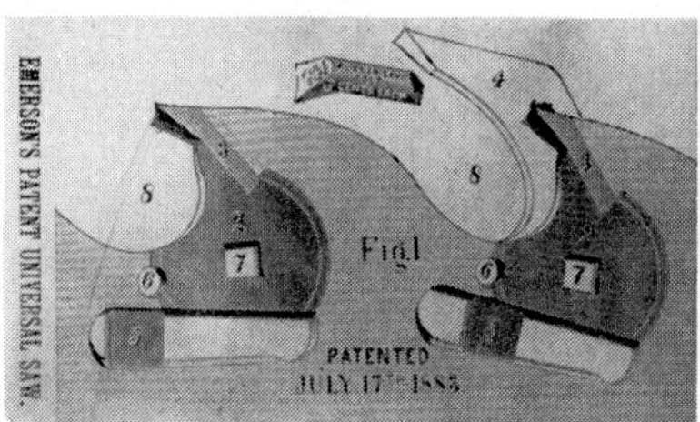

Teeth on a circular saw. From Sawyer's Own Handbook, Emerson Smith and Company, 1883-1884.

over other saws then in use because of its thinner "kerf." The band saw not only was able to cut a log up quickly, but because it was thinner, it cut a smaller kerf, or gash in the wood, and thus the sawmill owners were able to get more lumber from each log since the thinner blade of the band saw saved as much as twenty per cent of the log.

Another type of saw commonly used in the sawmills during this period was called the "gang saw" or "hog." The gang saw was a series of upright saws all standing parallel with each other and spaced as wide apart as the lumber was to be cut. The blades had an up-and-down motion like the older muley and gate saws. Whole logs could be pushed through a gang saw at one time and thus cut into a series of slabs. However, the usual method was to "cant" the log first. To do this a log was passed by a band saw four times. Each time one of the edges of the log was taken off. Thus a huge squared beam was made. This was called a cant. When this squared beam, or cant, was pushed through a gang saw, the lumber that came from it was thus cut and "edged" at the same time, and this saved several extra operations and cut down the cost of making lumber.

To make lumber, a slab not only had to be cut from a log but the two edges of the slab had to be removed so that the board would be the same width for its entire length. This was called "edging." As the slabs fell from the band saws and circular saws, they were taken to smaller saws, called "edgers," which were set to cut the boards their desired width. By pushing the slabs between these edging saws the width of the board was made uniform.

In the early sawmills the slabs coming from the saws were carried away by men known as "offbearers." But as the saws were speeded up, this task became too hard for men, and live rollers were put into the mills to carry the lumber away from the saws. Sometimes endless belts were used. Better saw carriages, with steam "niggers" for holding and turning the logs on the carriage, and other mechanical devices helped to make the sawmills more efficient as well as to increase the rate of cutting. Planers were developed to change the rough lumber into finished boards ready for use.

From the saws, edgers, and planers there now came an ever-increasing amount of scrap material, sawdust, bark, edgings, planer chips, and slabs of all sizes. Smaller saws called "slash saws" cut the larger scrap pieces into lath or pickets and thus part of the waste was saved.

However, there was still a large amount of waste. Large piles of bright-yellow, sweet-smelling sawdust grew up beside the sawmills. At other places the refuse was dumped into a nearby lake. For years many of Michigan's lakes had in them water-soaked logs which had sunk to the bottom and were never raised for the mills, chunks of logs, and sawdust. During the past fifty years many of these old logs have been raised from Michigan's lakes and rivers and sawed into lumber. By now most of the old sawdust that once filled these lakes with decaying material has rotted away. At other mills a series of blowers, belts, and chutes carried the waste material to the boiler room where it was burned to make steam to run the sawmill. Sometimes there was far more of this waste than could be used by the mill, and the excess was then burned in large refuse burners to get rid of it. When salt was discovered at Saginaw and on the west side of the state at Manistee, some of the sawmills used their waste to evaporate the water from the salt brine. Thus the waste from the sawmills became useful in helping to develop Michigan's early salt industry.

Men called "filers" were hired by the sawmill owners to take care of the saws in the mill. These men made their work a secret skill. Usually they worked in a small room all by themselves, and the secrets of their trade they kept carefully guarded. By hammering, filing, and grinding they kept the saws sharp and running true. Later, machines were developed to grind the saws and fit them for cutting.

Nearly all sawmills by 1880 were driven by steam engines. As the steam engines increased in power and size, so did the size of the sawmills and the speed of the saws increase. All the power to run a sawmill came over one large belt from the boiler room. This belt turned an overhead shaft or shafts, and all saws and other machinery took their power by means of smaller belts from the main shaft. Various-sized pulleys gave each machine the desired power or speed. It took many miles of belts to keep Michigan's sawmills running. In the larger sawmills craftsmen known as "belt lacers" kept the belts in running order.

In the Saginaw area there were fourteen sawmills in operation in 1857 and this number grew to thirty-six in 1872. Between 1873 and 1879 there were 105 sawmills in the Saginaw Valley alone. Seventy-nine of these were between Saginaw and the mouth of the river. These mills were then cutting about four million feet of lumber a day. Thus in 1880 Saginaw alone was cutting about one billion feet of lumber a year. At their peak 112 sawmills were spread along the Saginaw River bank for twenty miles. To carry away the newly cut lumber, schooners, called "lumber hookers," sailed into Saginaw Bay and were then towed by tugs up the Saginaw River. So many lumber boats came to carry away the lumber from the busy sawmills that the bridges over the Saginaw River at Bay City often had to be opened as many as fifty times in a single day to let the boats pass.

For many years Muskegon was a typical rough, frontier lumber town. By 1859 there were six mills at Muskegon. In 1874 a fire burned seventy business places and some two hundred houses. Yet the brown pine logs still came floating down the Muskegon River every spring and before long a new and bigger Muskegon was built. By 1887 there were forty-seven sawmills lining Muskegon Lake, and a maze of booms, where the logs were sorted for the sawmills,

Photo by Ernie Grayson

The last sawmill on the Saginaw River (1949)

spread out across the water in Muskegon Lake. In that year the sawmills of Muskegon cut 665,450,000 board feet of lumber and made more than 520,000,000 shingles. More lumber is said to have been cut in Muskegon than any other single point in the state. Because of this record, Muskegon was known during the lumbering days as the "Sawdust City" and the "Lumber Queen of the World."

The harbor at Muskegon was filled with schooners and "hookers" loading the fresh-cut lumber for the Chicago market. Some of the lumber stayed there and helped to build the rapidly growing city of Chicago, but most of it was sent on to the West to build villages, cities, farmhouses, and barns in the rapidly growing Midwest where hundreds of settlers were taking up land along the expanding railroads.

Into the busy smaller port harbors spread along the shores of the Great Lakes came hundreds of white-winged schooners, especially designed for the lumber-carrying trade, during the warm weather shipping season. They slipped silently into port to carry the clean, knotless, dry lumber to the busy lumber markets at Tonawanda, New York, in the East, and Chicago, Illinois, in the West. Into their empty holds and upon their decks the light, clean, sweet-smelling pine lumber was piled. Then with sails spread wide to catch the offshore wind the schooners stood out across the lake, until even their top sails disappeared beyond the distant horizon. Another boat load of Michigan's choicc pine lumber had gone to market.

As the steadily increasing cutting of the uplands bit farther and farther into the forests, the haul to the river bank became longer and longer. Soon the busy sawmill days of the port cities had passed. Some remained shipping centers where lumber, cut in the inland towns, was transferred from trains to ships, but to others the lumber ships came no more. Far out on the horizon could be seen their trailing smoke as they steamed to other lake ports in the Upper Peninsula where the sawmills were following the cutters in the woods. By 1890 Menominee claimed to be the largest lumber port in the world.

During the second half of the last century, railroads pushed into the upper part of the Lower Peninsula and into more of the Upper Peninsula. There were still great tracts of land that could not be lumbered by the older methods but could be cut if the railroads were used to bring the timber from the pineries to the rivers or the sawmills. A railroad was built from Bay City to Mackinaw City by way of Alpena and was called the Detroit and Mackinaw Railroad. Another line was pushed up from Bay City through the central part of the state to Mackinaw City. This line, once called the Jackson, Lansing, and Saginaw Railroad, is now part of the New York Central lines. By about 1876 this line reached as far north as Gaylord. Another line, then called the Grand Rapids and Indiana, was pushed north from Grand Rapids to Mackinaw City. This line is now part of the Pennsylvania system. Branch lines ran from these main railroads to the small inland sawmill towns and to the many lumber camps.

Both the federal government and the state government aided the building of Michigan's railroads by granting timber lands to the railroad companies. When a new railroad was planned, the route was laid out and then the state or Federal Government often gave the railroad company land on each side of the track. As the most valuable lands were the pine lands, the early railroads often ran their tracks so that they would get as much of the best pine land as possible. Although this seemed a wise move at the time, it later proved to be very unwise. The areas covered by pine forests did not make good farm land and thus today Michigan's railroads sometimes run through the poorest farming areas in many places. Sometimes the railroads were granted land in every section touched by the line. This often caused strange wanderings of the railroad so that as many sections of land would be touched as possible.

Train near Hillman (about 1910)

These new railroads brought into being the inland lumber towns. By the time that lumbering reached its height, steam-driven machinery made it possible to locate a sawmill at any convenient place. As the timber cutting spread farther and farther away from the rivers, new inland sawmill towns came into being on rivers where railroads crossed, and on lakes where booming could be easily carried on.

Along the railroads the inland lumber towns sprang up. Among these towns might be listed Big Rapids, Cadillac, Kalkaska, Mancelona, Alba, Roscommon, Grayling, Topinabee, Vanderbilt, Wolverine, Atlanta, Seney, and many others. These little towns, of which there were many, came into being quickly and sometimes lasted only a short time. Some were deserted as cutting spread to new areas. Some of these sawmill towns were small. Others grew to be good-sized communities and then with the passing of the lumber days they disappeared altogether. Some few remained as thriving communities because of their ability to turn to other ways of making a living.

The coming of the railroads brought many changes in logging methods. Hundreds of miles of private railroads were built into the timber lands by the logging companies. At loading points, the logs from the forest were loaded onto flat cars by hoisting devices called "jammers." Most jammers were worked by a team of horses, but as the last century came to a close, some of the jammers were worked by steam and were called steam loaders. When an area had been

Sawmill at Lewiston (1905)

cut, the branch lines of the private companies were extended to new cuttings or they were taken up and laid down in other forest areas belonging to the company.

Sometimes the new railroads carried the logs to the old rollways on the river bank. There the logs were dumped into the river and driven to the mills. But as railroad transportation improved, the river drives grew fewer and fewer. Finally the puffing engines were bringing the logs all the way to even the older sawmill towns.

By 1900, with the coming of the railroads and other changes in lumbering, lumbering became a year-round industry. In the wintertime the logs were still hauled from the woods to the railroad tracks on sleighs, but in the summertime they were now hauled from the woods on "big wheels." These big wheels were so large that their axles could clear a small pile of logs. When the wheels had been driven over the logs, a chain was passed under one end of the pile. The tongue on the wheels acted as a long lever, and when pulled down by the team it raised one end of the pile of logs from the ground. When the logs had been raised, a chain held them in place. The other end of the logs trailed behind on the ground as the horses pulled the big wheels and the logs to the decking ground beside a railroad track.

The railroads brought many changes in logging methods. Pine was becoming scarce, but the new railroads could haul the hardwoods that could not be driven down the streams. As the pine grew scarce, long trains of flatcars, some over one hundred cars in length, brought the hardwoods from the forests to the sawmills until about 1918. Railroads, too, made it possible to cut forest areas that were too far from the streams to be profitably hauled by team to a river bank. Because of the coming of the railroads, many mills in the Saginaw Valley continued to run for some years cutting timber brought to them from the north by rail, but one by one the noisy mills stopped running and the huge piles of lumber, once stacked like canyon walls along the river bank, grew smaller and smaller. Once the river had been filled with schooners loading the fragrant, clean lumber, but now the boats came less and less often. There remains today not one of that noisy, screaming chorus of sawmills that once lined the busy river front.

The area around Cadillac was once covered by mixed stands of hardwood and coniferous forests. Cadillac's real development followed the building of the Grand Rapids and Indiana Railroad. Soon Cadillac became an important inland lumber town. Its location on the easterly shore of Lake Cadillac had the advantage of westerly winds helping to keep the logs in the booms. For many years Cadillac was a busy center of pine sawing, and millions of board feet of pine lumber were shipped away on the flatcars that had brought the logs in from the forest.

Once many miles of logging railroads spread into the adjoining area and reached as far away as Emmet County. Over these lines, trains loaded with logs to feed the whining saws came puffing into the city. In 1872 four large sawmills were cutting 4,000,000 board feet of lumber a day. By 1907 the white pine and Norway pine upon which the sawmills of Cadillac had depended were nearly all gone. As the pineries gave out, Cadillac turned to making lumber from hardwood and then to the manufacture of hardwood products. Maple flooring began to be made during the years just before 1900. Cadillac became the first manufacturing center of maple, beech, and birch flooring. Soon its mills were literally "flooring a nation," for it was found that Michigan's hardwoods were well adapted to this use.

From about 1875 on, some of the lumber from Michigan's hardwoods was used in industries manufacturing agricultural implements such as binder and reaper parts, plow handles, and wagons and wagon boxes. Furniture, buggies, interior finishes, and veneer also were made from hardwoods. But even these manufactured products declined as the wood supply became exhausted and industry turned more and more to the use of steel.

By 1900 most of Michigan's timber had been cut. After the lumberjacks had passed, they left behind drying branches, rotting bark, and many stumps. Then came huge forest fires whose flaming tongues of red grew bright as they went burning across the "slashings" that had been left behind by the lumbermen. At night the horizon glowed with the yellow-red of the forest fire, and by day the sun was turned to an orange color by the dense clouds of wood smoke and soot that filled the air. Year after year such fires swept across large areas of the state. Behind remained smoking stumps, smoldering logs, and fire-scarred, black ground. These were all that remained to remind one that a stately forest had stood there before it met its greatest enemy, man. Sometimes these fires burned farm buildings, lumber camps, and even some sawmill towns. So large and hot were some of these fires that people could not flee from them and were burned to death. So hot were these forest fires that not only did they burn the wood upon the surface of the ground but also the best soil, called humus. So completely did the forest fires destroy much of the soil that it will be many, many years before some areas again will have good soil deep enough to grow trees of any size.

After the forest fires had passed, another force set to work to further destroy the cut-over lands: erosion. The forests had kept the soil in place and checked the run-off water that fell upon the land. But now that the forests were gone and the soil had been burned to a black-gray powder, much of the soil began to blow away. The rains too helped to destroy the land. The quick heavy rains of summer fell upon the wasted land and carried some of the soil away. Hills gullied. Plains were washed and blown bare. The barren sand beneath the good top soil was swept clean.

But forest fires, if they did not burn standing timber, were of little interest to Michigan's "lumber kings." They thought only of the dollars that could be made from cutting Michigan's trees. To them it was a policy of "cut out and get out." When Michigan's forests were destroyed, they moved farther west into the forests of Wisconsin and Minnesota. They took the large trees and destroyed many of the smaller ones and put nothing in their places. Lumbering one hundred years ago was far different from our modern ideas of tree farming.

In 1870, Michigan cut a little over two billion board feet of lumber. In 1880 the cut was 4,172,572,000 board feet. The highest cut was in 1890 when Michigan produced 4,245,717,000 board feet of lumber. But trees could not last forever, and in 1899 the cut had dropped to 3,012,057,000 board feet. By 1890 most of Michigan's timber had been cut. The frontier came to an end here in Michigan at about the same time it did in the West.

Lumberman's Memorial on the Au Sable River West of Oscoda

In what had been busy sawmill towns, the sawmills ran less and less until they stopped running altogether. What once had been bright-yellow piles of sawdust soon turned to gray-black, rotting, wood fiber. In some towns the sawmills burned down and were not rebuilt. In other towns they were wrecked for their lumber and machinery. The machinery was sent away to new sawmills where forests were closer. When the mills stopped running there was no longer any work for the families living in the little sawmill towns. They too left and followed the sawmills into new areas. Morning came to the deserted sawmill towns, but no longer did the mill's morning whistle call men to their day's work. The trains of logs came no more. The railroad rails were taken away to make new lines where timber still grew. Weeds and young trees sprang up between the abandoned, rotting ties. Sawdust-covered streets, where once straining horses had hauled wagons loaded with lumber, grew up to fresh grass. Board sidewalks, on which a busy people had once gone to church, to visit a neighbor, or to a day's work, now lay rotting and half hidden in the tall grass and weeds that had sprung up between the boards over which the shanty boys and sawmill people had once trod. Houses stood deserted. Broken windows were not repaired. Doors swung on creeking hinges and the winds from the cut-over and burned-over lands passed unhindered through the buildings which had once been homes where families had lived. Many of the houses were later wrecked for their lumber and the lumber was sent to help build the growing cities of Flint and Detroit. Michigan's "lumber ghost towns" had come into being. The list of such places is a long one. Today many are still small communities, but in other places, like Eldorado, Seney, Deward, and Waters, few, if any, people now live.

Once the lumbermen had cut the trees from the land they had little or no use for the land. Often they let it go back to the state rather than pay the taxes. Sometimes they sold part of it to people who wished to settle on it and make farms. Many people, especially immigrants from Europe that came to work in the camps, bought farm lands in the lumbered areas. In a few spots successful farming on the better land was later developed, but in much of the area the soil was found to be too poor for farming. Much of it was too sandy and lacked minerals. Other areas had been so badly burned by the forest fires which swept across the cut-over lands that there was no longer soil deep enough for farming. Then, too, like all forest lands the soil had much acid in it.

For a few years men and women sometimes struggled along on these little farms. As long as the men could get work in the camps in the winter to help increase the family income they stayed on the land. However, when they had to depend upon the income from the farm alone, they found that it was not enough and the land then had to be abandoned. Hundreds of these deserted farms can be found in northern Michigan today.

Today the land that once grew the spreading forests, that drew the lumberman to Michigan a hundred years ago, is a different place. Although in some places there are farm lands, most of it is not suited to agriculture. Forests, cared for by private owners and the State Department of Conservation, are again growing in the badly burned-over and cut-over areas. Trees, once vanquished by the woodsman's ax, are again taking possession of their ancient lands, and the fragrant odor of the pines is again being carried by the northern winds that blow across the forest lands. We have come to learn that trees are a crop and should be harvested just like any other crop when they are ripe. Mature trees should be cut and the others left to grow until they too are ready for harvesting.

Although Michigan's lumber industry destroyed her forests and ended the fur trade, it aided Michigan's growth in many ways. As the lumber was shipped out, supplies were shipped in to care for the men in the mills and in the camps. It brought people to Michigan. In those days of poor transportation, it gave many farmers, especially those living near the lumber camps, a market for their products. Farmers sold to the camps berries, hogs, veal, potatoes, and vegetables and took money or supplies such as flour, sugar, and salt. Many of Michigan's early farmers found work in the lumber camps in the wintertime and thus they were better able to support their families and to pay for their farms. It laid the ground work for some of Michigan's industries, for the lumbermen needed manufactured products. It brought money into the area in exchange for the timber that was shipped out. The lumber industry brought many of Michigan's towns into being. It helped in the building of the railroads. It aided the beginning of the salt, petroleum, and pulp mill industries. It aided the building of some of Michigan's roads. Many of Michigan's fortunes, later used to develop some of her other industries, were started in the lumber industry, for many were the men who made themselves millionaires by cutting and selling Michigan's forest trees.

Chapter XV

THE GREAT LAKES CARRIERS AND THEIR CARGOES

After the Civil War, the northern part of the United States entered a period of very rapid industrial growth. Steam engines had, by then, been developed in size and power and were being used in ships, railroad engines, and the new factories and sawmills which were springing up across the country. Our vast natural resources of coal, iron ore, copper, and other minerals had hardly been touched. In fact, many mineral deposits had not yet even been discovered. High tariffs on foreign goods protected the new and growing industries. Large cities were growing rapidly around the increasing number of steam-powered factories. Railroads were pushing west across the Great Plains and through the mountains to the Pacific Ocean. The vast plains west of the Mississippi River were being rapidly turned into farm lands as settlers pushed on to them to take up homesteads along the new and spreading railroads.

Michigan played a leading part in this industrial boom that followed the Civil War, for here in Michigan at that time were located copper mines, iron mines, and spreading forests from which lumber could be made. Here, too, shortly before the Civil War, Mr. Kelly worked on some of his early experiments in making steel. The lumber story, the copper story, or the story of the rise of steel-making in the United States cannot be told without telling about Michigan's mines, ports, boats, and shipping lanes on the Great Lakes.

In 1860 there were 138 sidewheelers, 197 propellers, and 1,122 sailboats carrying the commerce of the Great Lakes. Although the number of steamboats was growing, the sailboats had not yet reached their largest number. By 1860, 120,000 tons of iron ore from Marquette had passed through the "Soo" on its way to the blast furnaces south of Lake Erie. The Civil War created demands for both copper and iron and many early mines made profits because of the high war prices. By the time the Civil War ended, the "Soo" canal had been in operation for ten years.

In those days almost everything was still made from wood. Wood was used to make roads, houses, barns, sidewalks, wagons and buggies, and even machinery parts. Most of the boats then used in Great Lakes shipping, both sailboats and steamboats, were boats whose hulls were made of wood. From Michigan's forests, and from the forests of Wisconsin and Minnesota, came the heavy oak timbers which sailors of that day wanted to fashion into the staunch wooden hulls of the Great Lakes boats.

During the period from 1860 to 1890 the building of lake boats formed a major occupation in many of the lake port towns. Bay Port, Oscoda, Alpena, Cheboygan, Manistee, and Muskegon were all lake ports in the northern part of the Lower Peninsula where boats were built. At Saugatuck, on the Kalamazoo River, at Bangor, inland from South Haven in the Grand Valley, at South Haven, and at Benton Harbor boats were built in the southern part of the state. Tugs, schooners, propellers, and sidewheelers all took their places in the growing lake trade and helped to carry the copper, lumber, iron ore, grain, and passenger commerce of their day. In general the boats of that day were very small by modern standards. However, they could be sailed into and out of the shallow mouths of the rivers, especially those along Lake Michigan where sand bars often blocked the rivers' mouths.

Bay City and Saginaw were also important shipbuilding centers during the years between 1860 and 1870, for in the Saginaw River Valley grew both the needed white oak for hulls and pine for masts. At Bay City, shipbuilding continued past the end of the nineteenth century and into the present era of the modern huge steel freighters, but Saginaw saw her last boat built in the year 1889.

To meet the new and growing demands for faster shipping and larger cargoes, a new type of freight steam barge began to be built in the early 1860's. These barges, which at first had rather strange shapes, were a new challenge to the older staunch schooners because they could move on regular schedules, whereas the older schooners had to depend upon the changing winds. What is more, the new steam barges found no trouble in going up the Detroit and St. Clair rivers or in and out of the narrow channels leading into some of the harbors.

Many of the smaller boats from 1850 to 1870 were known as package freighters. They were given this general name because they carried freight in packages, boxes, crates, barrels, kegs, or hogsheads.

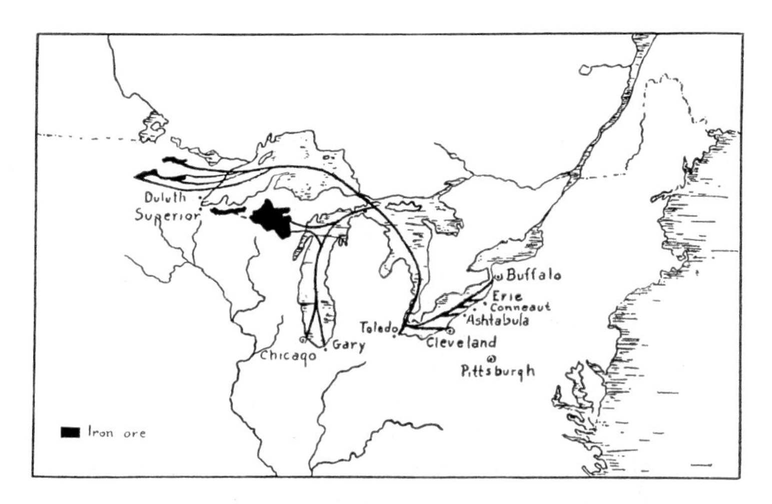

None of their cargo was bulk cargo. These package freighters were the railroads and trucks of their day, for they supplied freight service to many small communities along the lake shore that had no other way to receive goods from the outside world. It was these package freighters which kept many little communities of that day alive.

As commerce increased on the Great Lakes, larger boats were built. Many of these larger boats found difficulty in getting into the harbors where sand bars blocked the entrance. If boats were built too shallow they often slipped sideways while sailing on the lakes. But boats of deeper draft could not get into many of the harbors. For this reason some of these early craft were built with centerboards that sailors could drop down while on the lakes and raise when they entered a harbor. But the centerboard took up valuable cargo space in the very center of the hold.

To aid lake shipping many of the entrance ways leading into harbors were later dredged so that the newer and larger boats could get in and out. As early as 1872, the channel through the St. Clair Flats, where the St. Clair River empties into Lake St. Clair, was deepened so that the larger boats could pass up and down the channel. Some buoys were also set up so that sailors could more easily follow the winding channel in the river.

In 1871, the United States Government and the Canadian Government signed a treaty that gave both countries the use of the entire Great Lakes-St. Lawrence System. That is, boats of either nation could use the waterways of the other. Today a freighter going from

Lake Erie to Lake Superior passes through waters belonging to both countries.

As early as 1859, some people were making plans for building a canal across the Keweenaw Peninsula along the old portage route past Houghton and Hancock. Such a canal would not only shorten the distance from Keweenaw Bay to the west side of the peninsula by some eighty miles but would also do away with the dangers, during a storm on Lake Superior, of sailing around the rocky peninsula.

In 1865, Congress granted 400,000 acres of land to the state of Michigan to aid in paying for the cost of building the Portage Lake Ship Canal. In that same year work on the new canal was begun. Eight years later, in 1873, the new canal, thirteen feet deep and one hundred feet wide, was opened for lake traffic along the old Portage route. No longer would boats have to take the long and dangerous route around the Keweenaw Peninsula. At first tolls were charged for the use of the canal, but in 1891 the Federal Government paid the canal owners for their rights in the canal and the waterway then became Federal property, free to any boat that wished to use it.

Later the canal was widened and deepened so as to care for the larger boats appearing on the lakes. Today this waterway is maintained by the Federal Government. A Coast Guard station now stands at the western entrance to the canal. Each year many ore carriers pass through the Portage Lake Ship Canal on their way to or from the western end of Lake Superior and the lower lake ports. The canal is a harbor of refuge for ore boats and small pleasure craft when heavy storms sweep across Lake Superior. Ore carriers, by using this canal today, can often make better time than by going in the open lake around the Keweenaw Peninsula.

The period from 1850 to 1900 was a colorful era in the story of Great Lakes shipping. The little boats of that day—sloops, barques, brigs, brigantines, schooners, and barquentines—were usually privately built and owned. Their grayish-white, billowing sails made a pretty contrast against the white-caps on the deep-blue color of the water and the lighter blue of the summer sky.

Many of the sailing boats of this period that were engaged in the Great Lakes lumber trade had only two masts. These two-masted schooners became the most popular type of sailboat. Their construction was best for the lumber-carrying trade because there was more room in their hold to pile the lumber. These, as well as all the other sailing craft and steam lumber boats then carrying lumber from

Courtesy Defoe Shipbuilding Company

The USS Wilson, DDG 7. This is a Guided Missile Destroyer. It is 437 feet in length. (1961)

Self-unloader vessels of the Bradley Transportation Line of Michigan Limestone, a division of United States Steel Corporation, take on their cargoes of high quality limestone at the Port of Calcite, Rogers City, Michigan, for delivery to steel, cement or chemical industries around the Great Lakes. (1961)

Courtesy Michigan Limestone Division, United States Steel Corporation

Courtesy Chesapeake and Ohio Railway

Loading operations aboard the S. S. Spartan, Chesapeake and Ohio Railway trainferry, at Milwaukee, Wis. (1961)

Passenger vacation cruise ship North American. (1961)

Courtesy Chicago, Duluth & Georgian Bay Transit Company

Courtesy New York Central System

A Modern Passenger Train. (1961)

A tri-level car on Chesapeake and Ohio Railway train. (1961)

Courtesy Chesapeake and Ohio Railroad

Courtesy New York Central System

These cars are used to haul truck trailers. (1961)

Aerial view of Chesapeake and Ohio Railway trainferries, S. S. Badger and S. S. Spartan, en route to Ludington, Mich., across Lake Michigan. (1961)

Courtesy Chesapeake and Ohio Railroad

the sawmill port towns to the market, were known as "lumber hookers."

By 1870 there were fifteen hundred sailboats sailing the Great Lakes. The largest number of sailboats on the Great Lakes was reached in the year 1873. After that date the number of sailboats grew steadily smaller and smaller as larger and larger steamboats took their places in the carrying trade. By 1880 the number of sailboats had dropped to about fourteen hundred. By 1890 the number had dropped to a little over twelve hundred, and by 1900 there were only about eight hundred sailboats left.

As the lumbermen cut deeper and deeper into the northern forests, the piles of drying lumber grew beside the sawmills at the port towns. It was the new steam barges and the early sailing boats which, during Michigan's lumbering days, carried much of this lumber from the little port towns to the cities of Cleveland, Tonawanda, and Buffalo in the East and to Chicago in the West. On these old sailing boats and barges went billions of board feet of the finest pine lumber as well as shingles, laths, fence posts, railroad ties, and telephone poles. The lumber-carrying trade was a major part of the carrying trade on the lakes between 1860 and 1890.

But sailing vessels on the Great Lakes, as on the high seas, had many disadvantages that in the end resulted in their being replaced by steel steam-driven boats. Sailing boats were always slow and uncertain. Their sailings depended on the winds, and during a limited season of navigation, as on the Great Lakes, shipping time became a valuable factor in transportation. Then, too, narrow channels, such as the Detroit, St. Clair, and St. Mary's rivers and those leading into some harbors, were hard for these little sailboats to master, especially when they had to sail against the current of a river. Sometimes, in the early days, the sailboats were towed through such channels by sailors, horses, or oxen. With the coming of steam tugs, they were pulled through by steam power. The decks of the sailboats, too, were partly covered with masts and rigging that made it impossible to easily pile the lumber or to install the newer, faster, and cheaper loading machinery that was then being placed on the steamboats whose decks were clear of rigging.

Another thing that hastened the end of the sailboat era was the change in the type of freight then beginning to be shipped on the Great Lakes. Small bundles of furs, boxes, and barrels were giving way to larger and bulkier cargoes. Huge holds filled with coal, iron ore, wheat, or lumber became the standard type of cargo as the last century came to its close.

To increase their speed, to cut labor costs, and to adapt their sailboats to the changing age of steam power that was coming to the Great Lakes, some owners, as early as 1860, began to have their schooners towed. During the last half of the last century steam barges ofttimes towed as many as five or six of the older sailing craft behind them in a long string. Such a string, often called a "sow and her pigs" by the sailors of that day, was a common sight on the Detroit and St. Clair rivers in the 1870's and 1880's.

From Lake Erie, boats coming up the Detroit River had to pass through a narrow channel at the mouth of the Detroit River then known to sailors as "Hell Gate." Though the Detroit River is broad at its mouth, it is very shallow because the river flows over the rim of the Devonian Saucer as it enters Lake Erie. "Hell Gate" was a narrow and slightly deeper channel leading from Lake Erie into the Detroit River. Once through the narrow channel the little steam-barges towed their strings of sailboats, with sails furled, up the Detroit River, on across Lake St. Clair, up the St. Clair River, and out into Lake Huron. If the tows still had sails the sailors then spread them and the little sailboats continued on their way up the lakes to a lumber port. The others were towed on to some port where they too were filled with lumber.

As many of the sailboats became old and rotten, they were discarded or burned. On some of the better ones the masts were taken down. Only a few years before, they had been sailing proudly under their own power with the grace and beauty known only to sailboats. Now they became lifeless hulks to be towed here and there about the Great Lakes in the wake of the sudsy foam of a steamboat. If these former sailboats still had masts and sails, the sails were only used when the wind was blowing in the right direction or when a barge broke its tow line and became separated from its mother tug or steam-propelled barge.

By 1870, lake shippers were beginning to see that the future cargoes of the Great Lakes were not to be package freight, passengers, or lumber but iron ore. At that time nearly all the boats built, both sail and steam, were still made of oak hulls and none of them were really designed for the iron ore trade. Sailboats could only carry three or four hundred tons of the dusty red ore and their construction was poor for that trade. Large chunks of iron ore coming from the chutes in the ore docks sometimes punched holes in their wooden bottoms. They were difficult also, because of their masts, to load and trim. Better boats and better waterways had to be made so that the iron ore could be carried down in greater volume to meet the ever-growing demands for more and more of it. But the days of the real ore carriers were yet some twenty years away.

By 1880, the era of the sailboats was passing away. Better harbors and deeper channels, built at government expense, brought into being larger and larger steamships and more and more screw propellers.

The last of the locally built wooden sailboats on the Great Lakes, "Our Son," sank in a storm on Lake Michigan in the fall of 1930. Along the shores of the Great Lakes and in some of the river harbors, stuck fast in the muddy bottom, still lie some of these old rotting sailboats of a day when sails were common sights on the lakes. Some of them, though very rotten, still bear the names which they once carried when they, too, sailed from port to port carrying part of the lake commerce of their day.

For some time the "J. T. Wing," one of the last of the Great Lakes windjammers, lay rotting at a dock at Marysville on the St. Clair River. In 1949 she was refitted and served as a marine museum at Belle Isle in the Detroit River. But dry rot continued to weaken her timbers and she became unsafe for public use. She was burned at 12:30 p.m., November 3rd, 1956.*

The sailboats slowly passed from the lakes as the lumber-carrying trade declined. But newer and larger steel boats took their places on the lakes to carry the increasing cargoes of iron ore that were then coming down the lakes to make steel. The age of wood and iron had passed. Our nation had entered into the age of steel.

In 1856, Henry Bessemer, in England, discovered that if large amounts of air were blown through molten iron ore, the carbon and other impurities would be removed from the ore. Once removed, the proper amount of carbon could again be added to the molten ore to make steel of any desired quality. At about the same time that Mr. Bessemer, in England, was experimenting with this method of making steel, Mr. William Kelly was making similar experiments in Kentucky and at Captain Ward's Eureka Iron and Steel Company which then stood on the present site of Wyandotte in Michigan.

By 1880, a few eastern steel plants were using the new Bessemer process for making steel, and steel was beginning to come from their

*See page 194.

blast furnaces in ever-increasing amounts. In 1875 steel production in the United States was 375,000 tons. By 1879 it had increased to 929,000 tons. The Bessemer process was a great step forward in the steel industry. It meant that larger and larger quantities of cheap steel could be made for railroad rails, railroad engines, steel plates for ships, machines, bridges, and a thousand other things now common in America.

As transportation on the lakes was still very poor, several of the iron companies at first tried to smelt the iron ore near the mines and to make it into pig iron there. If the iron ore could be made into pig iron near the mines it would greatly reduce the amount of cargo that would have to be shipped down the lakes. What is more, it would be easier to handle the iron bars than the red, dusty iron ore that dirtied the decks of the boats and often caused captains and sailors to lose their tempers. Furnaces to smelt the iron ore were built at several places and crews of men were sent into the hardwood forests to cut hardwood to make charcoal. The year 1896 marks the high peak of charcoal production in the United States, and in that year Michigan produced one third of the total. Some of these charcoal furnaces operated as late as 1922 when the supply of hardwood for charcoal became exhausted.

As the years passed, the center of the iron and steel industry developed along the upper Ohio River Valley and in the East where extensive soft-coal fields easily supplied abundant coal that could be made into good coke. During the years between 1850 and 1900, the steel industry chose to take the iron ore to the coal fields rather than the coal to the iron mines. Fortunately for the steel industry the Great Lakes provided a broad highway over which huge bulk shipments of iron ore could easily be carried to the lake ports in northern Ohio. There are two reasons why the iron ore is taken to the coal. First, iron ore is less bulky for its weight than is coal. Therefore, it takes less shipping space on a carrier. The second reason is that it takes about one and one-half ton of coal, in the form of coke, and one-third ton of limestone to refine one ton of iron ore into pig iron. Therefore, you can easily see that if the coal were taken to the iron mines, a ton and one-half of coal would have to be carried where only one ton of iron ore is now carried. What is more, when the iron ore is smelted in the Ohio-Pennsylvania area it is already near the center of population and the market.

For a few years after the discovery of iron ore in Michigan the

Marquette range was the only range producing iron ore, and Marquette was the only place from which iron ore was shipped on the Great Lakes. But later a new iron port was opened on the south side of the Upper Peninsula, at Escanaba, and iron ore from the Marquette range began being shipped to Escanaba by train as early as 1864. This railroad was in a way a war measure, for if anything happened to the "Soo" locks the ore could still be taken by train to Escanaba on Lake Michigan.

Fortunately for the steel industry other sources of iron ore besides the Marquette range were soon discovered northwest of Escanaba. Iron had been known to exist in that area since 1870. Within a few years deposits worth mining were located. This second range became known as the Menominee range. The Menominee range runs south and west of Marquette County into Iron and Dickinson counties. The iron from this district was first taken to Escanaba on sleighs but in 1877 a railroad was built from Escanaba into the Menominee range. After that date railroad cars, filled with the "red gold," were carrying iron ore to Escanaba from the mines in the Menominee range as well as from the Marquette range.

Several mining centers developed in the Menominee range. The Vulcan Mine was opened in 1874, the Norway in 1877, the Iron Mountain district in 1878, and the Iron River and Stambaugh areas in 1882. Escanaba became a busy lake port sending to market fish, lumber, and iron ore. For some years it was known as "The Iron Port of the World."

As the steel industry grew, so did men's ideas about the boats on the Great Lakes. Oak for hulls was almost gone. A new building material was needed. Iron boats had been built as early as 1861. In that year the "Merchant" was built of iron for service on the Great Lakes. The coming of iron boats was a great advance in lake shipping. The older wooden hulls had been rather small so that the timbers could withstand the gales and wear of service. The new iron hulls gave promise of larger boats and still larger cargoes. Why not make new and even larger boats from the steel that was now coming from the blast furnaces or, as it were, from the very red ore that they were then carrying down the lakes?

In 1882 the first commercial steel ore carrier, the "Okomo," began service on the Great Lakes. So vast was this shipping of iron ore to become that only here on the Great Lakes and nowhere else in the world could a boat, over many, many years of service, wear itself out carrying just one type of cargo. By 1888, ore carriers were docking at Marquette and Escanaba that were able to carry in their larger holds between 2,500 and 3,000 tons of the heavy red ore.

By 1878 there were fifty-five mines producing ore on the Marquette range. In 1886 there were sixty iron mines in operation in Michigan. During the years between 1886 and 1900, Michigan ranked first as an iron ore producer in the United States.

During the years after the Civil War Michigan supplied not only iron ore from the Marquette range but also much copper from the Keweenaw Peninsula. These were busy days in the copper country. In 1872 the first bridge was built across Portage Lake between Houghton and Hancock. The Portage Lake Ship Canal was completed in 1873. In 1879 a road was completed between Ontonagon and Copper Harbor. In 1883 a railroad reached Houghton. Between 1847 and 1883 Michigan alone produced over half of all the copper produced in the United States. Until 1887, Michigan ranked in first place as a copper producer, and once again, in 1891, it ranked first.

Some of the early copper mines had proved to be shallow and had soon been abandoned. Other new ones were opened. Up to this time all the drilling had to be done by hand. The ore and rock had been shoveled into cars by the miners who still worked by candlelight far under ground in the dark and dampness. Mules were still used in the copper mines as late as 1880 to haul the little cars, filled with ore, to the shaft. But new changes came into the copper mines as well as into the iron mines during this period. Air drills began to be used in 1871. Electric pumps appeared in 1892. Acetylene lamps, giving a bright white light, replaced the candles on the miners' caps. These new lamps not only reduced the danger of fire but also gave the miners a much better light to work by. Mechanical crushers replaced the hand-pounding that had been used to free the copper from the rock. A canal was dredged between Portage Lake and Torch Lake so that the largest boats of that day could pass into Torch Lake.

The new discovery of electricity created a demand for more and more copper wire. By 1905 the Calumet and Hecla Mine alone had produced 95 million pounds of copper ore.* Down, down went the copper miners far into the earth. From far below the ground came the ore-bearing rock that was crushed in the large new crushing plants that had been built. Torch Bay was jokingly called the "Red Sea"

*Total copper production in Michigan from 1845 to 1958—10,479,780,811 pounds.

because of the red color of the water caused by the red oxides that came from the copper stampings which had been dumped into Torch Bay by the big copper stamping mills on the west shore.

Calumet, Laurium, Houghton, Hancock, Mass, and Rockland were all known for the bright shiny copper ore that came from their copper mines. In those days when one spoke of copper one thought of the Upper Peninsula of Michigan.

This constant mining for copper honeycombed vast areas under the mining towns with drifts, shafts, and tunnels. By 1896 the Red Jacket shaft of the Calumet and Hecla Mine was 4,900 feet deep. Hancock is located over a mine that is five thousand feet deep. Unlike iron ore, most of the copper was smelted near the area where it was mined. To do this, much wood was used at first, but later the large ore freighters returning from Lake Erie brought shipments of coal to be used in the smelters.

Courtesy Copper Country Vacationist League

Under ground in a copper mine

By 1900 the copper mines were running into trouble. In 1887 new shallow surface mines in the West were beginning to produce copper at ten cents a pound. By this time the shallow copper mines in the Upper Peninsula had been abandoned and the workers in the other mines were digging far below their very homes. In these mines sometimes as much as six miles and more of cable were wound on an elevator drum each time a skip was raised from the bottom of a mine. To hoist the rock and crush it to free the copper began to cost the mining companies more than the value of the copper that was mined. To keep the deep mines dry also required huge pumps that worked day and night. Some of these pumps pumped enough water to supply a large city. One by one the mines closed down. The huge pumps were stopped and the mines were allowed to slowly fill with water. The copper ore bars coming down the lakes steadily grew fewer in number. The miners, now out of work, left the mines to find other employment. Many came south to Detroit and the other growing cities in the southern part of the state and found work in the new automobile factories and other industrial plants.

Courtesy Oliver Iron Mining Co.

Iron miners

The third Michigan iron range, known as the Gogebic range, was discovered in 1884. This range, which began to be developed in 1885, runs through the extreme western end of the Upper Peninsula and into Wisconsin. In this area the mining centers of Ironwood, Bessemer, and Wakefield developed. At first the ore from this range was sent to Escanaba, but when the Chicago and Northwestern Railroad extended its lines from Ashland, Wisconsin, the iron ore from this range began to be shipped from that port on Lake Superior.

Many of the earlier mines on the Marquette range were soon worked out and abandoned. Champion, Michigamee, and Republic declined when their mines closed down. Up to 1880, most of the iron mining had been open-pit mining in which the ore was dug from huge holes in the ground, but by that year deep shaft mining was well on its way to becoming the usual way to mine iron ore in Michigan. The diamond drill had come into use about 1870 and this drill made it easier for the miners to cut down into the rock.

Shaft mining was more expensive, but as the surface deposits gave out miners were forced to dig deeper and deeper to get the iron ore from the pockets where nature had deposited it long before. The coming of electricity made it possible to light the deep shaft mines better and more safely. Electric power also brought into being better hoisting equipment to lift the iron ore from the mines. Huge steam plants were set up to pump the water from the mines.

The presence of iron ore in northeastern Minnesota had been known as early as 1875. In 1890 a rich deposit of high-grade hematite iron ore was discovered on the Mesabi Range. This was by far the best discovery of iron ore up to that time. But the deposit was located far inland and it would have been a long railroad haul to bring it to a dock on Lake Superior. Then, too, it would take more hours sailing time for a carrier. So high was this iron ore in quality that it took fifteen years for steel men to learn how to use the high quality ore found on the Mesabi Range. But once the Minnesota mines got into production they soon surpassed the Michigan mines in volume production.

The part of Michigan, Wisconsin, and Minnesota bordering on western Lake Superior has been the largest iron ore producing section in the world. About seven eighths of all the iron ore now produced in the United States comes from this area.* Fortunately for us, these vast mineral deposits of iron ore lie close to Lake Superior and Lake Michigan and can therefore be easily shipped on the greatest inland waterway in the world.

As the cargoes of iron ore increased in size and volume, men began building special boats designed for the iron ore carrying trade. One of the first of these special boats was known as the "whaleback." A whaleback looked like a huge cigar upon which, at one end, was placed a pilot house and, at the other end, a cabin. The prow, or front, usually rose above the water like the pointed end of a cigar except that instead of coming to a point, a whaleback had a round, flat plate for a nose. Her deck, which was almost round on the top, let the waves of the lake pass freely over her. The sailors of that time called these boats "pigs" because of the way the whalebacks rooted through the waves.

In 1888 the first whaleback appeared on the Great Lakes. This boat was only 187 feet long, twenty-five feet wide, and eighteen feet,

*Michigan produced 13,123,000 long tons, gross weight, of usable iron ore in 1957.

three inches deep. Between 1888 and 1898 some forty of these newly designed ore carriers appeared on the Great Lakes.

The whalebacks built at Duluth, Minnesota, and Superior, Wisconsin, were given numbers such as 101 and 102 in place of names. It was the "102" which carried the first cargo of Mesabi iron ore to Cleveland, Ohio. This first cargo of iron ore from the Mesabi of 2,073 tons was loaded at Superior, Wisconsin, on November 11, 1892.

In 1892 one of these whalebacks was made into a passenger boat named the "Christopher Columbus." It was used during the World's Fair at Chicago in 1893 to carry people from Chicago to Jackson Park, which was six miles away. Later this whaleback was used on the passenger run from Chicago to Milwaukee. In 1936 the "Christopher Columbus" was dismantled at Manitowoc, Wisconsin.

Courtesy of the Henry Ford Museum, Dearborn, Mich.

The "Christopher Columbus"

The whalebacks did not prove to be as satisfactory ore carriers as their designers had expected. They were too small, carried too small a cargo, and were too hard to unload. They were good for their day, but as time passed they were replaced by larger and better boats. Some were used for a time as tows, but they have almost disappeared from service on the Great Lakes. Two of these old whalebacks are still in service on the lakes, the "Meteor," built in 1896, and the "Comet," built in 1913. They are now used as tankers to carry gasoline and fuel oil.

As the number and size of the boats increased, the State Locks at the "Soo" became too small. Then too, some people thought that there should be no toll for boats using the locks. Up to 1877, any boat passing through the locks had to pay four cents a ton for every

Courtesy "Steelways," published by American Iron and Steel Inst.

Whalebacks locking through the "Soo" Canal

ton of cargo. In 1877 the toll was reduced to three cents a ton for all boats except those belonging to the United States Government or boats that were carrying army supplies or Federal troops. In 1881 the State Canal was taken over by the United States Government. Since that time it has been free to any ship of any nation desiring to use it.

In 1876 work on a second lock at the "Soo" was begun. Whereas the State Canal had had two locks, this new one was to have only one lock which would raise and lower a boat in one operation. This new lock, called the Weitzel Lock, was to be 515 feet long, eighty feet wide, and seventeen feet deep. This seemed at the time large enough for any boats that would ever be built on the lakes. This new Weitzel Lock was opened on September 1, 1881. But the Weitzel Lock had hardly been finished before lakemen found that new and larger locks were needed at the "Soo."

In 1886, Congress set aside funds for a new lock which was to be called the Poe Lock. This new lock was to be built on the site of the old State Canal that had been completed thirty-one years before. The old State Canal locks were removed and the new lock, built on the site of the former State Canal, was opened in 1896. This new lock was eight hundred feet long and one hundred feet wide.

In 1895 a Canadian lock was opened on the Canadian side of the St. Mary's River. This new lock was nine hundred feet long.

But as shipping increased, more locks and larger ones were needed at the "Soo." In 1908 work was begun on a new lock. This third lock at the "Soo" was called the Davis Lock. It was opened in 1914, the same year that the Panama Canal was opened. This new lock was 1,350 feet long. Just as it was finished, World War I began. Steel in ever larger amounts was demanded, and all three locks at the "Soo" were soon busy raising and lowering the ore carriers as they hurried along the lakes with their cargoes.

In 1913 a fourth lock was begun. It was built beside the new Davis Lock and was called the Sabine Lock. This new lock was opened in 1919.

By the close of the last century the shipping of iron ore from northern Minnesota and Michigan had become big business. Men not only began thinking about how larger and better boats could be built but also how they could be better loaded and unloaded. At the Lake Erie ports men were still shoveling the dusty, red ore from the holds of the large freighters. To aid them, horses and mules were now used. Tubs or barrels were now lowered into the ore carriers. Then when they had been filled by the sweating men who were shoveling the ore in the carrier's hold, mules or horses pulled on ropes that ran through a crude pulley hoist arrangement that raised the barrels or tubs to the deck of the boat. Men using wheelbarrows then wheeled the red ore from the boat to the dock.

In 1899 a new type of steam-powered unloader, invented by George Hulett, was first used at Conneaut, Ohio. It was a huge clam shell that could raise ten tons of iron ore at once from the hold of a carrier. Above the large clam scoop was a cab from which the operator controlled the movement of the scoop. Once a scoop full of ore had been raised from the hold of the carrier it could be rolled sideways along the dock. In eight hours this new machine unloaded as much iron ore as a hundred men could unload in a week. No longer would men have to shovel the red ore from the freighters and, what is more, the ore carriers could be much more quickly unloaded. Because of it, carriers could spend less time unloading and more time on the water bringing down iron ore.

The rise of the auto industry and World War I created even larger demands on the lake commerce. Luckily for America, iron ore could be had in the Upper Peninsula and in Minnesota. World War II

Courtesy "Steelways," published by American Iron and Steel Inst.
A modern unloader

created even greater demands for our iron ore supply. The red ore came flowing down the lakes as the large carriers hurried to beat their own records.

By 1916, Michigan's resources began to show the effects of extensive digging and outside competition. By 1913, Michigan had fallen to third place among the states as a copper producer. In 1916, the Marquette range reached its peak production by producing 4,792,987 tons of iron ore. Since that date many of Michigan's iron mines and copper mines have closed.

Copper mining as an industry in Michigan has been on the decline for many years. The known copper deposits are far from being exhausted, but the cost of mining it has caused most of the mines to cease operation. Falling shafts, water-filled mines, rusting machinery, deserted homes, and towns declining in population mark the abandoned copper and iron mining communities in Michigan. Gradually the mine timbers are rotting and the earth is falling in. Where once was activity, desertion and decay now hold sway.

Our nation now uses many tons of steel each day, but only about one tenth of the iron ore comes from Michigan. Most of the iron ore now comes from Minnesota. Three fourths of all the steel now made in the United States is made from ore and limestone that is shipped as bulk cargo on the Great Lakes boats. For this reason shipping on the Great Lakes is sometimes thought of as the lifeline of our nation. Because of it each of us enjoys a higher standard of living. Because of it our country is better able to preserve our liberties.

On our Great Lakes today there are nearly three hundred ore boats. During the winter they are carefully overhauled and made ready for active service during the coming summer. When spring comes, the nine icebreakers which are run by the Coast Guard begin opening the channels and harbors so that another busy shipping season can begin. The 6,000-ton "Mackinaw" is the largest of the icebreakers. It is 290 feet long and strong enough to force its way through any ice found on the Great Lakes. Each spring it opens the St. Mary's waterway through the "Soo" to Lake Superior and then keeps the channel open so that ore boats will not be stopped by new or wind-blown ice. Icebreakers are stationed from Duluth, Minnesota, to Toledo, Ohio, and are under the control of the United States Coast Guard. So powerful are these icebreakers that they can force their way steadily along even through ice twelve or fourteen inches thick. After the ice has been crushed and navigation begins, the icebreakers act as buoy tenders and begin placing the buoys back on their regular stations so sailors can be guided across the lakes and through the narrow winding channels during daylight, darkness, or storm.

Navigation continues all through the spring, summer, and fall. In December the lakes freeze, and all boats but railroad car ferries are docked for the coming shipping season.

As soon as the shipping season opens, the lake boats leave their winter harbors and start up the lakes to begin another busy shipping season carrying iron ore, oil, grain, coal, and limestone. Escanaba, because of its more southerly location on Lake Michigan, is usually the first iron port to load a cargo of iron ore each spring.

At the turn of the century much package freight was still being carried on lake boats, especially the passenger boats, and steamship lines had warehouses where the freight was collected and from which it was distributed. Since 1942 there has been no package freight carried on the American side of the Great Lakes.* All the cargo is bulk cargo, and the present fleet of lake boats is designed for such cargo.

During the busy shipping season the carriers run day and night, seven days a week. By changing crews every few hours the strong steel boats are kept steadily on the move. Lake boats do not corrode or rust like ships on salt water do; therefore many old boats are still in the active carrying service today. But each year finds new boats added to the number of carriers, and each year thus finds the total carrying capacity increased.

The bulk movement of iron ore, coal, wheat, and limestone during the past seventy-five years has brought into being huge steel freighters whose holds are large enough to carry thousands of tons of cargo. What is more, the lake boats have developed a type of construction that is all their own. Because of the winding channels and their shallow depth, the canals, and the sudden storms that blow across the lakes during the summer, the lake boats are built differently from ships used on the ocean. Ocean freighters must carry large supplies of fuel for the long distances they travel while on a voyage. They must also carry large supplies of food and fresh water. Therefore they can carry less cargo. The lake boats are never far from some port where fuel and water can be had, and therefore most of their huge hold can be used to carry cargo.

Many of the most modern ore boats are built much alike. Their pattern and speed is one that has been found to be best adapted to the "Soo" locks, the narrow winding channels of the rivers, and the wave action of the Great Lakes. In general they are about 600 to 650 feet in length, seventy feet wide, and thirty-six feet deep. They have a twenty-five-foot draft. That is, they sink into the water not more than twenty-five feet when loaded. This is the greatest depth in many of the channels, and many of the ore carriers are nearly

*"Fishyback"—truck-trailers carried on the deck of lake freighters—began in August, 1959, between Duluth, Minnesota, and Detroit, Michigan, and Cleveland, Ohio.

touching bottom as they pass along them. The average ore carrier carries a little over 11,000 gross tons. Some of the newer and larger ore boats have a capacity of 19,600 long tons. Up until a few years ago all the boats burned coal and were hand fired. Today some of the newer ore boats have oil burners to heat the water to make steam. In a normal shipping season an average carrier travels about 50,000 miles and brings down the lakes around 400,000 tons of iron ore.

If you were to go on board one of the large lake freighters you would find in the back, or stern, of the boat the machinery that makes her move. In the rear of the boat is the engine room. Ahead of it is the boiler where steam is made to turn the propeller shaft. Still farther ahead is the place where coal or oil is carried for fuel. At the back of the boat is a propeller which usually has three blades. When the propeller is turned the boat is driven forward or pulled backward. A huge rudder in the stern guides the carrier on her way. Above the engine room is the cook's galley and quarters for the cook, his two helpers, the engineer, the oiler, and the firemen. In the cook's galley good meals are provided for all of the crew. Near the back of the carrier are hung lifeboats that can be used if the crew has to abandon ship.

Ahead of you stretches the long, slim hull of the ore boat in which the bulk cargo is carried. The top of the deck is flat. On it you will see the large flat doors, called hatches, which lie flat with the surface of the deck. These doors are opened when the carrier is loading or unloading. On the new "George M. Humphrey" the hatch covers weigh twelve tons each and have to be lifted by a special electro-hydraulic crane which rides across them on rails. During the voyage the hatches are fastened down so that the waves of a storm can sweep over them and do no damage to the cargo in the hold. On the older ore carriers sailors had to walk on the open deck in going from one end of the boat to the other but in some of the newer ore carriers a catwalk passes along inside the hold and this allows a sailor to go from one end of the boat to the other without going along the open deck where sailors are sometimes washed into the water during a storm. The huge hull of the ore carrier is built with cargo in mind. The heavy shell must make space for the cargo and at the same time must be able to stand the pounding of the tons of ore dropped down upon its bottom. It must also be rigidly built so that during a storm the boat will not break in two and sink with the loss of the cargo and crew. In the construction of these boats there is a shell

COURTESY "STEELWAYS"

This picture shows men working on the Poe Lock at Sault Ste. Marie in 1894. Construction work was much different then from what it is today.

The "Soo" Canal from the air. The lock at the bottom of the picture is the MacArthur Lock, second the Poe, third the Davis, and fourth the Sabine. Note the rapids at the top of the picture. Photo 1956.

COURTESY "STEELWAYS"

A modern freighter being locked through the "Soo" Locks. This boat is bringing iron ore down from Lake Superior. Photo 1947.

Abandoned lake boat "Chieftain" in the Saginaw River just south of the Cass Avenue bridge in Bay City. Photo July 24, 1949.

COURTESY ERNIE GRAYSON

Building the George M. Humphrey. Note the air pocket in the bottom and sides that makes an ore carrier float its heavy cargo.

COURTESY M. A. HANNA CO.

Mess cooks at work aboard the Republic Steel Carrier, "Tom M. Girdler." Meals have to be served around the clock to care for the hungry crew.

COURTESY REPUBLIC STEEL CORP.

COURTESY REPUBLIC STEEL CORP.

The First Mate keeps a sharp eye on the load distribution when a modern ore carrier is loaded. All the iron ore is now graded and standardized before it is loaded into an ore carrier.

The "Tom M. Girdler" of the Repubic Steel Corporation steaming south across Lake Huron with a load of iron ore. Note the threatening sky and wave breaking over the deck.

COURTESY REPUBLIC STEEL CORP.

Courtesy Republic Steel Corp.

Left: Looking through a porthole down the deck of the Republic Steel Corporation carrier, "Tom M. Girdler," preparing to take aboard ore at Escanaba, Michigan. Right: Instructions from the bridge are received in the engine room of the "Tom M. Girdler" on the engine room telegraph by the chief engineer.

within a shell. The air chamber between the outer and inner shells causes the steel boat to float and to carry the heavy cargo.

The pilot house is located high above the deck on the front end, or bow, of the boat. It is on the second or top deck. It is usually a small room with glass windows all around so that the men in charge of the boat can see in all directions. In this room is found the large wheel that steers the boat by turning the huge rudder in the stern. That is how an ore carrier is guided across the lakes and through the channels from one lake port to another. On the ocean the man who steers a ship is called a "helmsman" but on the Great Lakes he is called a "wheelsman." Vessels on the ocean are called ships but the word "ship" is seldom used for the vessels on the lakes. They are called boats. The wheelsman must know the weather signals, the channel markers, and how to bring the boat safely into port in fair weather, foggy weather, stormy weather, during the daylight, or during the darkness of the night.

Under the pilot house are the captain's quarters. Here also are found the quarters for the first and second mates and part of the crew. Some ore carriers have rooms here also which can be used by the owners of the line and their guests. Under the officers' quarters, deep in the front of the boat, are rooms in which needed supplies and provisions are stored. On the new freighters the sailors' quarters are fireproof, steam heated, and furnished with private baths.

Some boats are now provided with radiophones. These radiophones permit the sailors on one boat to talk to the sailors on another boat. They can also talk to people on land. By using radiophones, company officials can give orders to, or receive messages from, captains while they are still far from land. Some lake boats also have radio direction finders. Some are also equipped with radar. Radar warns the crew of the presence of nearby boats or land. By using their radar equipment ore carriers can come into the "Soo" locks or any port, even in darkness or foggy weather.

The ore carriers are all loaded at one of the six ore docks. Ore docks are now located at Escanaba and Marquette in Michigan; Ashland and Superior in Wisconsin; and Duluth and Two Harbors in Minnesota. The present ore docks are really huge bins into which the iron ore is dumped from ore cars that are pushed along the top of the docks. When an ore carrier comes alongside to load a cargo of iron ore, huge chutes are lowered into the hatches. Then the iron ore is allowed to go rumbling down the chutes into the hold of the ore carrier. Limestone is loaded at one of the limestone ports in the same way. To load 15,000 tons of iron ore into an ore carrier takes about two or three hours, but it has been done in sixteen and one-half minutes. To carry this same load by railroad would take four trains having about one hundred cars each.

When their holds have been filled with wheat, iron ore, or limestone, the carriers set out across the lakes. The average ore carrier takes six and one-half days to make the round trip from one of the points along Lake Erie to Duluth, Minnesota, and back. Some of the newer ore boats are even faster. About one seventh of the iron ore goes down Lake Michigan to Gary, Indiana, and South Chicago. Some of it goes to ports along the Detroit River, but by far the larger amount goes to the iron ore receiving ports on the south shore of Lake Erie.

In order to keep an ore carrier from losing any time during the busy shipping season, provisions for each boat are usually supplied at Sault Ste. Marie. The Pittsburgh Steamship Division of the United States Steel Corporation has sixty-four ore carriers engaged in bringing down ore from Lake Superior to the receiving ports along the south shore of Lake Erie. This fleet of ore carriers is the largest inland fleet in the world. To provision this fleet the company keeps a supply store at Sault Ste. Marie. Ore carriers and other boats not belonging to the Pittsburgh fleet can also purchase supplies from the same supply store. Nearly everything is carried in stock that the men and boats might want or need—groceries, fresh meats, fresh vegetables, shaving supplies, dry goods, radios, and even chains and anchors large enough to hold an ore carrier should it need a new one. If supplies are needed quickly the needs are radioed ahead, but usually a shopping list is left when a boat passes Sault Ste. Marie on its way up the lakes. The supplies that have been ordered are then made ready while the ore carrier goes on to get her load of ore, and are picked up by the freighter as it passes Sault Ste. Marie on its way down the lakes.

Ore carriers do not carry unloading equipment but are unloaded by huge Hulett unloaders that are located at the receiving ports. Today there are over sixty of these Hulett unloaders in the receiving ports on the Great Lakes. A few years ago these huge unloaders were powered by steam but today they are all electrically operated. These unloaders are huge machines having a clam-like jaw that is capable of carrying seventeen to twenty tons of iron ore at one bite. These huge jaws, over which a man rides in a small control room, are lowered through an open hatch into the hold of a carrier. There they bite into the ore piled in the carrier's hold. Then the huge jaws, filled with iron ore, are lifted out and carried away from the boat on an overhead track. The ore is then dumped into huge stock piles. Five Hulett unloaders can unload 14,000 gross tons of iron ore in less than three hours.

Many of the ore carriers return up the lakes with no cargo, but others carry coal to ports on the Upper Lakes. During the past few years some fifty million tons of soft coal have left Lake Erie ports, each year, for ports on the Upper Lakes. In 1952, 572 million bushels of grain were shipped on the Great Lakes.

Some of the freighters on the Great Lakes are coal and limestone carriers. Because some of them are smaller boats, they can go into the smaller ports and leave shipments of coal. These boats carry their own unloading equipment and are called self-unloaders. Ore carriers are not self-unloaders because the lumps of heavy iron ore are often too large and heavy to be handled by a self-unloader. On the decks of the self-unloaders there is a huge crane, or boom device, that swings far out from the side of the boat. Endless belts carry the coal or limestone from the hold out along the boom and dump the cargo in a pile on the shore. There are some forty self-unloaders now sailing the Great Lakes. There are also some oil tankers operating on the Great Lakes.

After the days of the "Walk-in-the-Water," passenger boats ran on the Great Lakes for over one hundred years. The early passenger boats were discussed in an earlier chapter. From the Civil War period to 1900 many passenger boats were running on regular schedules between ports on the Great Lakes. The earlier ones, like the freighters of their day, were built of wood. At first these early steamers lacked the graceful lines of the later passenger boats. Almost all of them were boats which had a large paddle wheel on each side. Many of the earlier ones were also rigged with sails. This was then required by the insurance companies of that day, for they did not trust the new steam engines to safely bring the passenger boats back into port.

The names of many of the passenger steamers were well known by the people then acquainted with the lakes. Some of the best known of the passenger boats were the "India," "China," and "Japan." Each summer season thousands of people used these boats for transportation to new areas or took trips on them for a vacation.

The heaviest traffic on these boats ran between Buffalo, New York; Cleveland, Ohio; and Detroit, Michigan; but many smaller steamers ran between such ports as Detroit and Alpena, Duluth, Mackinac Island, St. Ignace, Milwaukee, and Chicago. These boats carried not only passengers but mail and package freight as well.

These larger passenger boats were like large floating hotels, for

Courtesy Detroit and Cleveland Navigation Co.

A Great Lakes passenger liner (1937)

they had not only rooms in which the passengers slept but also large dining rooms in which tastily prepared food was served to the passengers. There were usually one or more large ballrooms for dancing and entertainment.

With the coming of better railroad accommodations, better roads, and the automobile, fewer and fewer people traveled by lake steamer. By 1950, passenger boats on the Great Lakes were nearly a thing of the past. The last three old passenger boats were burned on Lake St. Clair on December 10th, 1956. Today two passenger boats on the Great Lakes, the "North American" and the "South American," run on vacation cruises each summer. The "Milwaukee Clipper" runs from Muskegon to Milwaukee, Wisconsin, carrying autos and tourists across Lake Michigan in the summertime, while the "Aquarama" runs between Detroit and Cleveland.

By 1900, a different type of passenger boat was taking people during the summer season from Detroit on short one-day trips to points of interest on the nearby lakes and rivers. Sometimes these pleasure boats took people to parks where the people found relief from the crowded cities. In the morning these steamers were waiting at their docks to welcome the eager crowd of people who were arriving, loaded with picnic baskets, ready for a day of pleasure and leisure.

From Detroit these pleasure craft ran up to Port Huron; to Tashmoo Park on Harsen's Island; to "Bob-lo" at the mouth of the Detroit River across from old Fort Malden; to Sugar Island at the mouth of the river; to Put-in-Bay in Lake Erie; and to Chatham, Ontario. In the evening they brought the weary pleasure-seekers back. With empty baskets on their arms, and wearing clothing soiled by the picnic activities of the day, the tired passengers crowded across the gang plank to the land and then hurried up Woodward Avenue on their way home.

Today most of these boats run no more, but to those who rode on them during the period from 1900 to 1935 such names as "Tashmoo," "Put-in-Bay," and "Columbia" are familiar reminders of happy days on the Detroit River.

The icebreakers are interesting boats to read about. When the lakes and rivers freeze, traffic must stop unless the ice is broken open so that boats can move. Sometimes, in order to keep the water open to navigation, icebreakers are used. They are also used to free freighters that have been caught in the ice. Icebreakers are special boats that have been built for this purpose. The "Mackinaw" is the largest icebreaker. She has three propellers. One is in the bow and the other two are in the stern. A large icebreaker sucks the water from under the ice just ahead of it. Then the huge prow of the icebreaker is shoved upon the ice and it breaks the ice with its great weight. Thus a passage is broken open and other boats can follow.

There are only a few tugs left on the Great Lakes. But if you had visited one of the busy lake ports fifty years ago you would have seen many of these busy little boats. They were built just big enough to carry a large, powerful steam engine and a small amount of fuel but no cargo. Their job was to push and pull the sailboats, freighters, and passenger boats when they could not operate under their own power. If one of the larger boats got stuck in shallow water the tugs pulled her off and into deeper water. These busy little fellows, though not large in size, once played an important part in lake commerce just as they do in ocean commerce today. However, with the passing of the sailboats, the improving of the harbors and channels, and the use of only the larger major ports, there is no longer much need for tugs in Great Lakes shipping.

At Detroit a small boat, known as a mail boat, meets the freighters and gives them mail and takes the letters that the sailors have written. You would enjoy watching this busy little craft at work as it hurries up beside each passing freighter. Men on the mail boat catch the mail bag that is thrown down to it. They also fasten another mail bag to a rope by which it can be pulled on board the moving freighter.

In some ports, such as Detroit, you will see fire boats. These boats are used to fight fire just as any fire engine. When a fire breaks out on a boat, or in a building near the water front, these boats hurry to the fire. On the decks of these craft are long nozzles through which great streams of water can be forced to put out the fire.

For many years boats known as ferries carried people and vehicles across the Great Lakes and their connecting waters. Little ferries ran for many years between Detroit and Windsor, Ontario; between Port Huron and Sarnia, Ontario; between Sault Ste. Marie, Michigan, and Sault Ste. Marie, Ontario; between Mackinaw City and St. Ignace; and between Mackinaw City, St. Ignace, and Mackinac Island. Auto ferries no longer run between Detroit and Windsor. Auto traffic uses the tunnel under the river or the Ambassador Bridge. Railroad-car ferries still cross the Detroit River although there is also a railroad tunnel under the river. Since the building of the Blue Water Bridge

Courtesy Chesapeake and Ohio Railway

Chesapeake and Ohio Railway's trainferry, S. S. Badger, crossing Lake Michigan. (1961)

at Port Huron, auto ferries no longer run between Port Huron and Sarnia, Ontario. Railroad cars here use the tunnel under the river. Auto ferries still cross the St. Clair River at five different points to carry autos and passengers between the American and the Canadian sides of the river. Auto ferries still run between Sault Ste. Marie, Michigan, and Sault Ste. Marie, Ontario. Railroad car ferries still run across the Straits of Mackinac but the automobile ferries stopped running in November, 1957, when the new Mackinac Bridge was opened for auto traffic. This new bridge now provides a four-lane highway between the Lower and Upper Peninsulas.

To haul railroad cars around the Great Lakes often causes much delay as well as added expense to the shippers. To carry railroad cars, special car ferries have been built. These ferries have a wide, flat deck so that railroad cars can be pushed onto the railroad rails that are fastened to their decks. All the machinery in these ferries is placed beneath the main deck in the hull of the ferry. This leaves the deck flat and clear. These boats tie up at a dock so that the rails on their deck match rails leading from the railroad. Usually the deck carries four or five sets of tracks upon which strings of cars are pushed onto the ferry by a railroad engine. Other engines pull them off at the other side of the lake or river. These ferry boats are used to carry railroad cars across the Detroit River, the Straits of Mackinac, and Lake Michigan.

The ferries used on the Great Lakes to ferry railroad cars from one shore to the other are more deeply hulled vessels than those used on the rivers. As the winter ice, which has to be broken, is often thick they have much power and very strong hulls. A Great Lakes car ferry must be well built for when cold winter weather comes the Great Lakes often freeze as far out as thirty miles from shore. When the ice breaks in the spring the strong winds that blow across the lakes often pile the drift ice into huge ridges along the shore. These ridges have to be crushed by the car ferry as it drives into or out from port with its load of railroad cars, autos, and passengers.

To make all these boats and to keep them in repair requires many shipyards. At first these shipyards were large carpenter shops where boats were built of lumber. However, today, because boats are made of steel, the shipyards have greatly changed. If you were to visit a shipyard today you would see the men using huge cranes to handle the heavy steel plates with which the boats are built. Then, too, you would hear the rivet hammers as they rivet the large plates into place before they are welded together.

In the early days there were few provisions for the safety of the passengers or the sailors. During the darkness of a storm, boats were sometimes driven against rocks or upon the shore. Going through the narrow channels was always a dangerous and trying task. When a vessel had to pass through these places a special pilot, who was familiar with the dangers, was often hired to guide the boat.

All this has greatly changed during the past one hundred years. Today all boats must be provided with life preservers and lifeboats. The coming of the radio, radio-telephone, and radar has helped to produce greater safety for those who travel on the Great Lakes. When a boat is in distress, a radio message can be sent to ask for help from nearby boats or from a lifesaving station. Warnings of approaching storms can also be sent to boats far out on the lakes.

The United States Government has done much to improve shipping on the Great Lakes. Each spring the channels of the rivers are carefully marked with buoys of various kinds which tell the sailors where the channels are and how deep the water is. There are many kinds of buoys used: nun buoys, can buoys, spar buoys, whistling buoys, bell buoys, and light buoys. Each one has its special meaning to the men sailing the lakes. These signals are so made that a wheelsman can follow his course by them during the daytime, at night, or during the blinding darkness of a storm.

Other safety measures are also provided. Along the coast at dangerous places are lighthouses. Each of these houses has a large light that shines far out across the water of the lake. Not all of them have the same kind of light. Some are red, others are green, but the usual color is white. Some lights burn all the time while others flash their light at regular intervals. A good sailor can tell just where his course is by the way the lighthouses are painted or by their lights.

To help guide lake boats little vessels, known as light ships, are sometimes used. One such light ship, known as the Huron, is stationed at the south end of Lake Huron, near Port Huron, to help guide boats coming south across Lake Huron into the narrow channel of the St. Clair River. Each shipping season this little light ship is manned by men in the United States Coast Guard. Usually light ships have no power of their own and remain anchored in one place all during the shipping season. All the machinery is automatic but is constantly checked by the men on duty. A radio beam is flashed constantly. Bells, fog horns, whistles and lights are also used. When night comes the light is turned on and its beams begin to flash across the lake through the darkness. When a fog comes the fog horns begin to blow.

The National Government has also spent millions of dollars to make breakwaters and deepen the dangerous and shallow channels so that larger boats can be used and shipping will be more safe. The Livingstone Channel near Grosse Isle has been deepened to twenty-seven feet so that larger boats and ocean freighters can go from Lake Erie up the Detroit River. The National Government also maintains Coast Guard stations at dangerous points along the shore of the lakes. The life guards at these stations are provided with all the necessary equipment to rescue people from sinking boats.

In 1942, work was begun on a new and larger lock at the "Soo" to replace the Weitzel Lock. This new lock, named the MacArthur Lock, was completed in 1943 at a cost of fourteen million dollars. This new and larger lock is eight hundred feet long, eighty feet wide, and thirty feet deep. It can be filled with water in ten minutes and emptied in eight.

Before 1845, a single horse-drawn dray hauled all the freight that passed between Lake Huron and Lake Superior. Today the "Soo" canal is the busiest canal in the world from the point of freight tonnage passing through it. The Panama Canal has larger locks and cost more money to build, but it carries only about half of the freight tonnage that annually passes through the "Soo." This vast freight tonnage is caused by the large quantities of bulk cargo in the form of iron ore, wheat, and coal which are shipped through it each year.

At the present time there are four American locks at the "Soo." From the American side going out toward the rapids they are the MacArthur Lock, opened in 1943; the Poe Lock, opened in 1896; the Davis Lock, opened in 1914; and the Sabine Lock, opened in 1919. There is one Canadian lock, opened in 1895, on the Canadian side of the St. Mary's River. Beginning this year, 1960, a new lock 1,000 feet long, 100 feet wide and 32 feet deep, with a lift of 27 feet, will be built to replace the present Poe Lock. It is to be completed by 1964.

In 1954 the Congress of the United States passed an act that joined the United States with Canada in the construction of a larger and deeper St. Lawrence Waterway so that larger ships from foreign countries could enter the Great Lakes. The new St. Lawrence Waterway was officially opened on April 25, 1959. During the fall and winter of 1957-58 the Livingstone Channel was deepened to twenty-seven feet. Other channels have been, or are now, being deepened to the same depth. Now foreign ships can pass up from the Atlantic over this new 2,000 mile waterway to Chicago, or to ports on Lake Superior that lie 602 feet above sea level. Today eighty percent of the world's ships can enter this new seaway.

This new seaway will do much in the near future to change the routes of much of the nation's commerce. Large bulk freighters can load wheat at Duluth, or Canadian ports on Lake Superior, and can then sail directly to Europe thus avoiding trans-shipment costs. Other bulk cargoes will be wood pulp, petroleum, coal, coke, and iron ore. Big lake boats can carry grain to Sept Isles below Quebec and return to the lakes loaded with Canadian iron ore from Burnt Creek, Labrador. Because foreign ships can sail directly into the Lake Region it will be easier to bring in the many alloys used in making the various kinds of steel we need today. Foreign manufactured goods, also, can be sent direct to Detroit, Chicago, Duluth or any lake port with facilities for loading and unloading. American exports such as meat from Chicago and autos and trucks from Detroit and Cleveland can now be shipped direct to foreign ports. Many Great Lakes ports are now increasing the depth of their harbors and building new port facilities so that they, too, can take a part in this new world commerce that has come to Great Lakes area. Ocean-going passenger-cargo ships now carry vacationers on summer cruises all the way from Quebec to Chicago, Illinois, and Duluth, Minnesota. This new waterway, together with Michigan's many natural resources, will soon cause many industrial changes to take place here in Michigan.

Chapter XVI

MORE INDUSTRIES DEVELOP IN MICHIGAN

Up to about the time of the Civil War, Michigan was mostly an agricultural state. The farms of that time were nearly all in the southern part of the Lower Peninsula. Little sawmills were producing a small amount of lumber. Local gristmills were still grinding grain to be used by the people in the nearby area. Local cobblers made shoes for people, local tanneries provided leather for the cobblers, clothing was still made at home or by a local tailor, carpenters built houses, cabinetmakers made small articles of furniture, and village blacksmiths did the small amount of ironwork that was needed in each community. Every farmer was a "jack-of-all-trades" and with his ax and a few other crude tools made many of the things that were used around his farm and home. Farm women still made candles and soap. They also spun yarn and wove the cloth needed by the family. Ship building was done at many of the lake ports. Iron and copper had just been discovered in the Upper Peninsula, and mining there had just begun.

Commercial fishing has always been, until recently, one of Michigan's major industries. The Great Lakes' waters supplied large quantities of several kinds of fish: bass, perch, pickerel, pike, white fish, and lake trout. Of the many kinds of fish, the whitefish has proven to be the most marketable. Fish provided one of the major sources of food for the Indians and French trappers. The early settlers coming into this area also used fish to help build up their food supply. Many small communities along the shores of the lakes once depended wholly or in part on their catches of fish for their economic life.

Commercial fishermen were operating on the Upper Lakes soon after 1800, and by as early as 1830 they had begun using gill nets. Some fish were sold as fresh fish, others were smoked, but many were salted for the market, especially after the development of the salt industry in Michigan. Commercial fishermen have marketed over twenty kinds of fresh-water fish. In 1899 the catch of fresh-water fish was 113 million pounds. Since 1910, however, commercial fishing has been on the decline. By 1928 the catch had dropped to 63 million pounds. By 1957 the catch had dropped still lower to only 21½ million pounds. The catch in 1958 showed a small increase to 25 million pounds. The future of Great Lakes fishing seems to be one of little hope because of the blood-sucking eel called the sea lamprey that has come into the Upper Lakes from Lake Ontario.

This enemy of fish life in the Great Lakes was first noticed at Merlin, Ontario, in western Lake Erie in 1921. The native home of the sea lamprey is the salt water of the Atlantic Ocean. The adult life of the sea lamprey is spent in the ocean waters. When the adult lampreys are ready to spawn, they go up the streams that flow into the Atlantic. After they spawn, they seem always to die. A dwarf form of the sea lamprey has been known to inhabit the fresh waters of Lake Ontario for many years. Just how the sea lamprey got into Lake Erie is not known, but it is known that they hang onto the bottoms of lake boats and may have come through the Welland Canal from Lake Ontario in this fashion.

In 1927 sea lampreys were found in the waters of western Lake Erie. By 1930 they had entered the waters of the St. Clair River. By 1936 they were found in the waters off Milwaukee, Wisconsin, and at Elk Rapids in Michigan. By 1946 sea lampreys were reported spawning in sixty-eight of Michigan's streams flowing into the Great Lakes. In 1947 they had reached the far-off waters of Isle Royale in Lake Superior.

The adult sea lamprey reaches a length of fourteen to thirty inches. It has a long snake-like body. It is smooth and scaleless, with fins at the top and tail. It has seven gill openings on each side just back of the head. On the top of the head is a single nostril. The mouth has no jaws but is rather a round sucking disc with sharp needle-like teeth around the circle. The tongue is like a rasp and is used for puncturing the skin of the fish it has attacked.

The smooth, scaleless lake trout was the special prey of the sea lamprey. In 1935 the commercial catch in Lake Erie was 1,399,901 pounds. By 1945, it had dropped to a mere 172,937 pounds. When the supply of lake trout had diminished, the sea lampreys began attacking bass, whitefish, and even the large scaly carp. The attack of the sea lamprey has greatly reduced not only commercial fishing but recreational fishing as well. Many lakes once visited by fishermen because the lakes provided good catches of trout and bass now have only a small percentage of the number of fish they once had.

The sea lampreys move up the streams to spawn each spring. Their largest runs take place during late May and early June, usually during the night. The males go up the streams first and begin to make the nests. Later the females come and help the males. Nests are made in sand, gravel, and small rocks in shallow water in the streams where the water runs less fast. The adult lampreys carry the stones in their mouths and put them on the down side of the stream. Thus a nest twelve to thirty inches across is made. In this nest the eggs are laid. One lamprey will lay between seventy-five thousand and two hundred fifty thousand eggs. After spawning, the adult lampreys die. The eggs hatch in from one to three weeks. The little lampreys then burrow into the sand bed of the stream and there live for the next three to five years. They live on the little organisms that the stream brings down to them. Then they go through a rapid change and appear as little lampreys that set out downstream to attack fish in the Great Lakes. Both state and Federal conservation departments have tried to find a way to save the fishing industry. Today a chemical is put into streams. As it goes downstream with the water it kills most of the lampreys in the stream.

Another of Michigan's oldest industries is the making of brick. In the Dearborn area, the heavy clays were found suitable for brickmaking. Bricks for the Detroit Arsenal, located in present-day Dearborn, were made in the Dearborn area as early as 1833. Later the bricks made from local brickyards were used to build some of the large homes that were built in Detroit before 1900. Many of the farmhouses that are still standing from this period in Wayne County and the adjoining counties, were made from bricks made in local brickyards. Brickmaking in Michigan has now nearly become an industry of the past. Most of the old pits have been filled in, and some are even covered with city lots and homes. In 1900 there were nearly two hundred brick and tile manufacturing plants in the state, but since that time the number has steadily decreased.

During the past century there have been many advances made in conquering diseases. In this forward march of medicine Michigan has played an important part. Up to about 1850 people usually did not know what was in the medicine they were taking. Many medicines that were sold on the market were pure frauds and did the buyer little, if any, good.

Perhaps the first drug company in Michigan was the Michigan Drug Company which was started in 1819 at Detroit. In 1843

Eberbach and Sons formed a drug business at Ann Arbor. Another early company was Farrand, Williams and Clark, which was founded at Detroit in 1845. Hozentine and Perkins started in the drug business in Grand Rapids in 1852. Another pioneer in the drug field was Frederick Stearns. Mr. Stearns owned a drugstore in Detroit. In 1855 he started a little laboratory in which he prepared his first medical preparations. Another early Detroit firm was that of Parke, Davis and Company. This company was started by Dr. Samuel P. Duffield who at that time owned a drugstore. In 1862 Dr. Duffield began to manufacture a few medical supplies such as ether and nitre. Mr. Harvey C. Parke joined with Dr. Duffield in 1866, but in 1871 Dr. Duffield retired from the company. Mr. Davis joined with Mr. Parke in 1875 and thus formed the present company of Parke, Davis and Company.

In 1880 Dr. W. E. Upjohn was one of the leading physicians in Kalamazoo. Dr. Upjohn became interested in a new method of manufacturing pills. The new pills not only were given a coating on the outside but were so made that they would easily dissolve so that the medicine taken could easily work on the system. From this beginning has come the Upjohn Laboratories in Kalamazoo. In 1899 Nelson, Baker and Company started to manufacture drugs in Detroit. The Du Pree Chemical Company has been a leading drug producer in Holland. The Dow Chemical Company, although a large manufacturer of industrial chemicals, is also a producer of some medicines, such as aspirin.

Before 1900 one of the problems of a doctor was to know just how strong medicines were. Drugs were not then prepared with the care that they are today. Sometimes the drugs were too strong and thus injured the patient. At other times medicines were too weak to have the desired results. Modern drug companies have developed medicines of standard quality and strength. Now when a doctor uses these preparations he knows just how much of any drug he is giving his patient. When doctors found that they could rely upon the carefully prepared preparations that were being put on the market by these companies, they began to use more and more of them.

These pioneers in the field of medicines have not been content merely to standardize such drugs as are already known. The world has been searched for vegetables and herbs that would yield new preparations that would lessen the suffering of mankind. Exploring expeditions to distant lands were formed and paid for by the drug companies. As a result of this pioneering work in the field of medicines, these companies have developed many new preparations.

The little laboratories of a century ago have given way to large biological farms and huge laboratories in which hundreds of men and women work to make the many kinds of medicines and preparations that are used by doctors today. To these laboratories come boxes and bales of roots, herbs, and bark. These raw materials are carefully sorted and prepared for the market. Huge machines make capsules and pills of many descriptions. Each pill or capsule must be of a certain size and strength or else it is discarded by the machine. All is quiet, orderly, and clean. Each day the drug industry goes on preparing medicines that are already known, while scientists and doctors are continually doing more research work to develop new medicines for the benefit of mankind. Michigan's large drug companies are known throughout the nation for their leading preparations.

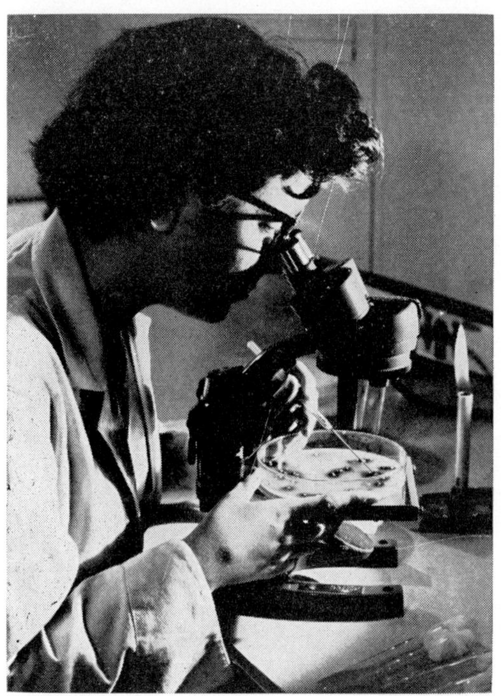

Courtesy Parke, Davis and Company

Ann Arbor, Mich.—A Parke, Davis & Company technician examines bacterial colonies. The information obtained may be used in development of new antibacterial drugs or vaccines. (1961)

Soon after the discovery of iron ore, as has been told in an earlier chapter, blast furnaces were built near the mines to melt the iron ore into pig iron. Other furnaces were also built at places located far from the mines. In 1853 Captain E. B. Ward, with some other men, organized the Eureka Iron and Steel Company. This new company bought land in Wyandotte and there built a blast furnace and rolling mill. In 1864 this plant installed one of the first Bessemer furnaces in the United States, and it was at this plant that the first Bessemer steel was made in America. Here also the first rolled T railroad rails were made. In 1874 the Eureka Iron and Steel Company was one of the largest industries in the Detroit area. Three years after Captain Ward started his plant in Wyandotte, Mr. G. B. Russell built a blast furnace and iron works in Hamtramck. This furnace and

Courtesy of the Detroit-Michigan Stove Co.

A page from an old stove catalog

iron works was known as the Hamtramck Iron Works and remained standing until 1905. The chief use made of iron ore in those days, here in Michigan, was in making stoves and supplying the iron needs of blacksmith shops for making horseshoes and household articles.

Today one of the leading industries in Michigan is the making of various kinds of heating units. This large industry developed from the early stove industry which was started here in Michigan, in 1864, by James and Jeremiah Dwyer. These two brothers began making stoves in a little foundry at the foot of Mt. Elliott Avenue in Detroit. The first stoves were made and sold by the two brothers themselves. Little did they know that within seventeen years Detroit would become the leading stove manufacturing city of the nation.

The Dwyer brothers believed that stoves, besides being able to give heat, should also have other qualities, such as beauty and usefulness. Moreover, they felt that stoves should be built to last a lifetime with only minor replacements, such as grates, lids, and other small parts that might break or burn out.

The Dwyer brothers were joined by other men, and the Detroit Stove Works was founded. Other stove companies that were later formed were the Peninsular Stove Company, the Art Stove Company, and the Detroit Vapor Stove Company. By 1881 the Detroit Stove Works and the Michigan Stove Works were each employing nearly one thousand men. Moreover, Detroit was then recognized as the leading stove-manufacturing center of the nation. The rapidly growing West provided a good market for stoves. Then, too, the beauty and serviceability of the new stoves became known in other nations, and soon the companies were exporting their products to foreign lands.

One should remember that half a century before Detroit became known as the automobile center it was known far and wide for its stove industry. The first stoves were made of cast iron and seem to us today to have been crude affairs. Since that time many kinds have been made—cook stoves, hard coal heaters, soft coal stoves, wood ranges, gas stoves, and even stoves that burned whale blubber for Eskimos. As the years have passed, stoves have given way to newer heating units. Today many companies scattered over the southern part of the state make heating units or parts such as oil burners, gas burners, stokers, fans, furnaces, boilers, safety valves, thermostats, and air conditioners. The output of their factories helps to keep Michigan in her place as one of the leading producers of heating units.

Another of Michigan's first industries was a Stained Glass Works which was started at Detroit in 1861 by a German immigrant youth. From this glass works came colored glass that was used in the growing number of wealthy homes that were then being built in Detroit before 1900. Some of this stained glass was also used in Great Lakes passenger steamers that were built during this same period. Much of it has been used all over the country for making church windows. The beautifully decorated windows of many of Michigan's churches have been made by this glass company which is still in operation.

With the coming of the railroads there grew a demand for more and more locomotives and railroad cars. As Detroit in those days was the hub of transportation in this area, it was only natural that the building of railroad cars began in Detroit in 1853. Locomotives, passenger cars, boxcars, and even flatcars for the growing logging industry were all made at Detroit. Later, interurban cars were also built. The Michigan Car Company was organized in 1864. The Peninsular Car Company was formed in 1885. In 1868 the Detroit Car and Manufacturing Company was organized. This company was bought in 1871 by George M. Pullman, now known for his Pullman cars, and in 1879 Mr. Pullman transferred its shops to Chicago. The railroad-car-building industry used iron and steel and also the local supplies of wood. At the turn of the century this industry employed around nine thousand men. The railroad shops were later moved to Port Huron, Battle Creek, Marshall, and Jackson.

In 1874 Berry Brothers began making paints and varnishes at Detroit. Since that early date other paint manufacturers have begun making paints and varnishes. Today Michigan is a leading center of the paint and varnish industry.

Ferry-Morse Seed Company, Michigan's well-known distributor of seeds, was started in 1856 by Dexter M. Ferry.* The idea of raising and selling choice seeds was just then appearing in the East. Up to this time people did not buy seeds to plant. Each person gathered his own seeds each fall and carefully saved them for the coming spring planting by wrapping the seeds in brown paper. Sometimes neighbors exchanged seeds and thus better varieties of plants slowly spread across the state. Mr. Ferry's idea was to select and raise choice plants and from these plants to carefully gather the seeds. At first, seeds were sent out in little, unattractive brown-paper en-

*Ferry-Morse Seed Co. moved to Fulton, Ky., in March, 1959, after being in Detroit 103 years.

velopes or in little bags tied with strings. The name of the kind of seed was printed on each package. After the Civil War a picture of the plants that could be grown from the seed was placed on each package by means of wood cuts. Later, pictures, bright with colors, showed the buyer the kind and color of plant he could expect from the seeds in a package. At first all these packages of seeds had to be carefully hand packed by girls, but today packing machines fill and seal the envelopes and packages. From 1879 to today this early seed company has done much to improve the quality of plants grown within the state. When the brightly printed packages of seeds arrive in the stores throughout our state, we know for sure that spring has at last arrived.

The making of tobacco products is another of Michigan's early industries. At Detroit, cigars, chewing tobacco, and snuff were manufactured. Clothing factories began to develop after 1880. A copper smelter was for some time located at a dock in Springwells, just below Detroit. In 1860, copper smelting was one of Detroit's main industries, but this industry was moved to Lake Linden, in the Upper Peninsula, soon after that date so it would be nearer to the copper mines. A brass foundry was started as early as 1833. Today, with the coming of the automobile industry, several brass working plants are now located in Detroit. The making of bicycles was one of Michigan's major industries just before the coming of the automobile at the turn of the century. In 1888 the Buhl Manufacturing Company at Detroit began making tin-dipped dairy milkware such as tin pails, milk cans, milk pans, and milk strainers. Bissell carpet sweepers and typewriters were manufactured at Grand Rapids.

An industry of a more general nature that developed here in Michigan about the time of the Civil War was the furniture industry. Only a few of the early settlers who came to Michigan brought furniture with them. Many of these early settlers were young people just getting started in married life. Others were so poor they could not afford to buy furniture. All, rich or poor, knew how hard it was, with the poor roads and bumpy wagons of that time, to bring bulky pieces of furniture to the new settlements. Usually when a family planned to move to Michigan they sold their farm and almost all their belongings in order to get money enough to buy the land for their new farm. Some families had a "choice piece" of furniture, as they called it, that had been made by one of their relatives or had been in the family for several years. These pieces of furniture the settlers sometimes brought with them. Such pieces of furniture are now highly valued by descendants of the early settlers.

Once they were settled in their little cabins, crude furniture was often made by the settlers themselves. Some of the settlers had been craftsmen in Europe or in New England. These craftsmen were called "cabinetmakers." They were usually carpenters and joiners who owned a kit of tools. The census of 1850 lists 704 men in Michigan who classed themselves as cabinetmakers. From the lumber of that day these men began making pieces of furniture such as chairs, tables, kitchen tables, and beds. They also made the coffins needed by the community and sometimes acted as the undertakers. As the settlers prospered and wanted better furniture for their homes, they often traded grain, flour, pigs, chickens, or beef to the cabinetmakers in exchange for such pieces of furniture as they wanted.

To make strong, lasting furniture required good wood that was well cured. To properly season wood so that it would be thoroughly dry at the center took about four years. Few craftsmen could afford to purchase a wood supply four years in advance or even provide a place in which to store it. Many of the pieces of furniture that were made by these early craftsmen continued to dry out after they had been made and thus fell apart. Sometimes, so we are told, the pieces of a chair would be brought back in a bag to the cabinetmaker who had made it. Later, as the industry grew, better methods of curing lumber in dry kilns were developed.

The really good pieces of furniture at that time were made at other places such as Boston or Cincinnati. If they were to be sent to Michigan, such pieces had to be carefully wrapped, crated, and handled with much care. Only the more wealthy people could afford good pieces of furniture. Most people used the locally made furniture which was then made at many different places in southern Michigan. But as the years passed, one Michigan city developed as the leading furniture center and that city was Grand Rapids.

The furniture industry began at Grand Rapids in 1836 when Mr. William Holdane set up a cabinet shop there and began making handmade furniture for sale. Other cabinetmakers also came to Grand Rapids. At first these cabinetmakers worked by hand and made chairs, bedsteads, bureaus, and such other pieces of furniture as would easily sell in the region at that time. In 1848 a circular saw was brought to Grand Rapids and soon other power machinery was used. A small steam engine was set up by Mr. Holdane in 1863 to

Courtesy Kelvinator Division, American Motors Corporation

Carousel operation, where refrigeration systems are evacuated and hermetically-sealed compressors are charged with oil and refrigerate gas. Grand Rapids. (1961)

furnish power for his little shop. From this simple beginning at Grand Rapids the furniture industry developed until the products of her factories became known throughout the world for workmanship, quality, and design.

After the Civil War several other furniture factories developed in Michigan, and this state began to be known for her quality furniture. By 1870, Michigan's furniture ranked in quality with any furniture made in the nation. Three manufacturers from Grand Rapids placed exhibits of their furniture in the Centennial Exposition at Philadelphia in 1876. Their designs and workmanship did much to increase the name of Grand Rapids as one of the foremost leaders in furniture making. To the furniture industry, style and workmanship are the measure of success. Mass production of good furniture has never been a goal of the furniture makers.

About this time, 1870 to 1880, furniture makers began making whole suites of furniture rather than only single pieces. Bedroom suites and dining room suites appeared on the furniture market. Each of the pieces of each set was made of the same design and of the same quality of wood.

For some time lumber produced in the state furnished the supply of raw material from which furniture was made. At first the clear, soft, easily worked pine was the common wood used for making furniture for the settlers. Later, as the settlers prospered, hardwoods were used. Oak, black walnut, and maple were all used to make quality furniture. But since the local supply of timber began to disappear and since the demand for more costly furniture increased, lumber has been brought from many foreign lands, such as Cuba, British Honduras, and even Africa. Brazil supplies rosewood. From France comes rare walnut. From Ceylon comes satinwood. All these rare woods are used in making the fine quality of furniture produced in Michigan. Because these woods are very expensive, they are usually made into veneer; that is, the material is cut into large thin sheets of wood and these pieces of wood are then glued over wood of a cheaper quality. Thus there is a great saving in cost. Moreover, the finished product does not warp so easily, and it looks more beautiful than if it were made of solid wood.

In 1890 there were 178 furniture factories in Michigan. Furniture is now being made, or has been manufactured, at Allegan, Ann Arbor, Big Rapids, Buchanan, Charlotte, Detroit, Grand Ledge, Holland, Manistee, Menominee, Monroe, Muskegon, Newago, Niles, Northville, Owosso, Saginaw, St. Johns, and Sturgis.

About 1890 the furniture factories in Grand Rapids began making office furniture. From that city came desks, filing cabinets, and bookcases. Soon many other companies in the state were also making similar pieces of office furniture. About this time also they began to produce large quantities of school furniture to meet the needs of the growing numbers of young people who were then going to school.

After 1900 many of these furniture factories built wooden iceboxes to meet the demands for home refrigeration. During the past thirty years many of the furniture factories have turned to metal as a material rather than wood. Today several companies make metal desks, filing cabinets, chairs, typewriter stands, and other pieces of office furniture. Iceboxes are no longer made, but new all-metal boxes covered with white enamel serve as refrigerating units.

In addition to the furniture industry, many of the earlier factories in Michigan used wood as a material for much of their products. Several companies made organs. Many others made doors, sash, tool handles, blinds, matches, boxes, barrels, barrel heads, and toothpicks. Fanning mills, for separating chaff from grain, were made at

Plymouth and near St. Charles. Corn planters were made at Grand Haven. Plows were made at Albion and forks and hoes were made at Jackson. Farm equipment, such as threshing machines and threshing engines, was once made at Birmingham, Battle Creek, and Port Huron. Wagons and carriages were made at Pontiac, Lansing, and Flint. At first, two-wheeled carts were made from the fine hardwoods found in the nearby forests. This industry developed into the making of wagons and carriages and gave Flint the name of the "Vehicle City." During the peak years of manufacturing the carriage makers at Flint were making nearly one hundred thousand wagons and carriages annually. One of these successful carriage makers at Flint was Mr. William C. Durant. When automobiles began to be made, the skills of the carriage makers were turned to making automobiles.

The making of paper and paper products has long been a major industry in Michigan. At first most paper was made from rags, but as the years passed more and more paper began to be produced from wood pulp. In 1850 there were ten plants in Michigan making paper or paper products. In 1905 there were thirty-one paper mills in the state. At that time Michigan ranked fifth in tonnage produced and seventh in the number of paper mills. Paper is now being produced or has been produced at some time in Kalamazoo, Manistee, Monroe, Munising, Otsego, Parchment, Plainwell, and Port Huron. The leading paper centers in the state today are Kalamazoo and Monroe.

One of Michigan's oldest industries is the production of salt. In Chapter One you learned how Michigan's salt deposits were formed. These salt beds, as you have learned, became covered with the fossil remains of little sea animals which lived in the ancient seas. The limestone layers left by these little animals formed a hard rock layer now called "dolomite." Dolomite is a very hard sedimentary rock, one through which water cannot seep. Because of this dolomite covering, the salt layers that were laid down in the ancient seas have been protected from the waters that would have dissolved them and carried them away. Most of Michigan's salt deposits are in the brine stage, but there is one place in Michigan where salt is actually mined.

Although the presence of salt was known to the early settlers, it was not produced in commercial quantities until about 1860. Perhaps the first company to produce salt was the East Saginaw Salt Company. In 1860 the state offered a bounty of ten cents a bushel to aid in

Courtesy Wyandotte Chemicals Corporation, Wyandotte, Michigan

Oxide Products Plant—North Plant of the Wyandotte Chemicals Corporation. Wyandotte, Michigan. (1961)

This view shows one of the early steps in production of Saran Wrap in the Dow Chemical Company's plastics department plant at Midland, Michigan. After molten saran polymer is extruded from circular dies, it is cooled quickly and transformed by special equipment into large "bubbles," as shown. Thus enlarged, the film passes through a series of rollers which deflate the "bubbles" and prepare the film for eventual winding on household and commercial rolls. Saran Wrap is made from vinyl-vinylidene chloride, a Dow basic plastic. (1961)

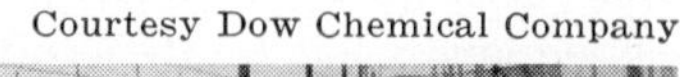
Courtesy Dow Chemical Company

the developing of the salt industry, and four thousand barrels of salt were produced that year. Nine years later, in order to improve the quality of the salt sent from Michigan a state inspector of salt was appointed. By 1886 there were 297 salt wells in Michigan.

Salt and sawmills went together in the early days of the salt industry. The sawmills in the Saginaw Valley had much scrap that they had to burn in order to dispose of it. This scrap was used to make steam to run the mills, but there was much more than was needed. This was burned to evaporate the water from the brines that were taken from the ground. Between 1860 and 1885 the Saginaw Valley was the main producing area. When the lumber industry declined, the salt production in the Saginaw Valley also declined. Later the salt industry spread to Manistee, Ludington, Algonac, and Marine City.

Once started, the industry grew rapidly. In 1880, 2,485,000 barrels of salt were produced. Since that time Michigan has been one of the leading salt producers of the nation. During the period from 1880 to 1890 Michigan produced nearly half of the total amount of salt produced in the United States. In 1907 Michigan produced over ten million barrels of salt.

In 1879 an experimental salt well was started at Manistee. A salt deposit was discovered in 1882. It lay at a depth of two thousand feet. Because of this, Manistee has been one of Michigan's leading salt producers. In 1887, salt was found under Wyandotte at a depth of 2,640 feet. Up to 1890 American glass manufacturers had to depend upon foreign sources for soda ash to use in making glass. In 1891, Capt. J. B. Ford, a Pittsburgh plate glass manufacturer, came to Michigan looking for salt deposits in order to supply his factory with American-made soda ash. He became interested in the drilling that had been made at Wyandotte on the property of the old Eureka Iron and Steel Company. Capt. J. B. Ford spent nearly a million dollars learning how to change this salt into soda ash. This early company began the alkali industry now located in the Wyandotte area. The J. B. Ford Company was for many years the world's largest manufacturer of specialized cleaning materials and heavy chemicals. Other companies developed in the area. Some of these earlier companies are now combined into the Wyandotte Chemicals Corporation. The salt of the region, together with limestone shipped from the Alpena area, provides the resources used in the principal industry, which is the changing of salt into its by-products, such as soda ash, chlorine gas, caustic soda, soda bicarbonate, and baking soda. Lye is also produced. In the plants at Wyandotte the salt brine and limestone are processed to form a group of basic alkalies. These alkalies are then carefully blended, under heat and pressure, and other materials are added to make a long list of products.

In 1878 a salt brine was discovered in the Midland area. As the state at that time paid a bounty on salt produced in the state, the early lumber mills at Midland turned to salt production as a side line. But by 1890 the lumber industry had passed on to the north and it seemed that Midland's days of prosperity, like those of so many other lumber towns, were fast passing. The unusual nature of the salt brine, however, had been noted by Dr. Herbert Henry Dow. In that year Dr. Dow came to Midland to further develop the brine resources and especially to try new ways of extracting from the brine certain impurities—bromine and calcium. If these impurities could be removed, Michigan's salt quality would be greatly improved, and bromine, which was then sent from Europe, could be made in the United States. After many trials and hardships the Dow Chemical Company was founded in 1897.

From this early beginning, new processes have been developed, and the Dow Chemical Company now produces over six hundred chemicals from the salt brine underlying the area. Of these a few might be named: aspirin, calcium, bromine, camphor, epsom salts, iodine, and sodium bromide. The Dow Chemical Company is one of the largest chemical companies in the United States. It is the largest producer of chlorine. The brine from which these chemicals are taken lies in a field of about three hundred square miles extending roughly from Midland to Mt. Pleasant. There are about 130 wells producing brine in this area. Tank cars carry the bulk chemicals throughout the nation.

There are three leading salt-producing areas in Michigan. These areas are along the Detroit and St. Clair rivers, near Ludington and Manistee, and in the Saginaw Valley. Some salt is known to exist in the Upper Peninsula, but the industry has not yet developed there.

Salt is secured from beneath the dolomite rock by three different methods. In some places, as in the Saginaw Valley, the salt is found in the form of brine. Wells are sunk through the dolomite and the brine is then pumped to the surface. The water is then evaporated and thus only the salt is left. In other places wells are sunk through the dolomite to the salt beds. Water is then forced down a pipe and into

Courtesy International Salt Company, Inc.

Main haulway in the International Salt Company's Detroit Mine. Huge electrically-powered bottom-dumping trucks carry 20-ton loads of Sterling Rock from the mine face to the primary crusher several thousand yards away. Note the alternate layers of salt (halite-white color-NaCl) and anhydrite—(dark color-CaSo4.) (1961)

the salt deposit. The water turns the salt into a brine and this brine is pumped to the surface and evaporated.

Michigan has one salt mine. It is located in Detroit not far from the Ford Rouge Plant in Dearborn. This mine produces salt from the Silurian formation. As early as 1895 salt was produced from this formation. In 1906 the Detroit Rock Salt Company started digging a shaft downward to the salt layers. After much difficulty and delay the shaft was completed, and the company began the production of rock salt in 1910. In 1913 this mine became one of the mines of the International Salt Company of Scranton, Pennsylvania. It is now known as International's Detroit Mine.

The mine covers some three hundred acres and spreads under the southwestern part of the Detroit area. There are two shafts that reach down 1,137 feet to the salt layers. One shaft is a twin tube, like the two barrels of a double-barrel shotgun. Each of these tubes is forty-two inches in diameter. Double-decked skips in each tube carry men and materials to and from the mine. One pair of skips rises as the other lowers. The other larger pair of shafts is used for skips to hoist the salt from the mine. Each skip carries about ten tons of salt each trip. One rises as the other one lowers. Men working in the mine also ride these skips in going to and from work. Air is forced into the mine at the rate of eighty thousand cubic feet per minute.

The salt layer is about twenty-six feet in thickness. It is made up of alternate layers of salt and anhydrite. If you look closely at the picture on page 307 you can see the alternate layers of salt and anhydrite. In order to keep the overhead rock layers from settling, the "room and pillar" system of mining is used. This forms a large checkerboard pattern. Rooms fifty to sixty feet wide are cut away while large pillars of the same size are left to support the overhead rock. You can see these rooms and pillars in the picture on page 307.

On the working face of the mine the miners undercut the room face with a large saw like a chain saw. This saw cuts back into the salt layer about ten feet and takes out a six-inch kerf that allows the salt to settle when it is blasted. Then another large machine, with many drills on its face, is moved up to the working face. Holes are then drilled into the face. Into these holes the miners place charges of dynamite. About midnight, when only a few men are left in the mine, these charges of dynamite are set off by electricity. One after another, they are exploded and the salt drops into a pile in the room.

On the next day electric scoop shovels pick up the blasted salt and drop it into huge trucks that can carry from fifteen to twenty tons. These electric trucks then carry the salt and anhydrite to the first crusher. From the crusher to the mine shaft runs an endless belt which is over one and one-fourth miles long. This belt carries the salt along from crusher to crusher and then to the hoisting shaft.

From the hoisting skips the salt is dumped into the tipple, where the salt is further crushed, cleaned, and classified. Rock salt is used for farmers' stock, for making chemicals, for preserving meats and foods, for curing hides, for bleaching and dyeing textiles, and for making water softeners, plastics, and synthetic rubber. Much of it is used each winter to keep our city streets and state highways free from ice. Salt from this mine is shipped away by rail, by truck, and by boats that dock on the River Rouge near the salt mine.

A deposit of bituminous coal lies under all the central part of the Lower Peninsula. This deposit of coal was formed during the Pennsylvanian period. Some coal was mined at Jackson as early as 1835. Coal was mined near Grand Ledge in 1838 and 1839. At one time coal was mined near Williamston. But there was little use for coal in a land that provided good firewood from wood lots and sawmills. But as the supply of wood grew smaller, Michigan's industries turned more and more to coal as a fuel.

Courtesy Robert Gage Co.

A Michigan coal mine

Around 1900, coal was mined at Saginaw, Bay City, and St. Charles and in Genesee, Tuscola, and Huron counties. At that time there were over thirty mines producing coal in Michigan. Nineteen hundred seven was Michigan's peak year in coal production. In that year a little over two million tons were mined. By 1920 there were only eighteen mines producing coal, and their production had dropped to about one and one-half million tons. By 1931 there were only six major mines still producing coal. Michigan's coal mines ceased operation in 1946. Today only local noncommercial mines are used.

Although Michigan has a large coal basin underlying much of the central part of the Lower Peninsula* and although Michigan uses a large amount of coal, all of the coal used in this state today is shipped here from other areas. Michigan's coal basin reaches from Jackson to Saginaw, and it is thought to contain about eight billion tons of coal. In general, the veins are thin except near Saginaw. The coal that was mined here was very soft and easily broken. It also had a high content of acid. It could not be made into coke and was therefore found useless in the iron and steel industries. Then, too, Michigan's coal miners faced many other problems. Unlike the coal veins found in many other places, the coal of Michigan is covered by glacial till instead of flat sedimentary rock that forms a protective

*See figure page 14.

ceiling. The loose sand and gravel of the glacial till slips and slides easily and must be heavily timbered to protect the miners. This is very expensive and coal from the mines cannot compete in price with coal mined in strip mines in other areas and shipped into Michigan by train or boat.

Slate is found near Huron Bay on Lake Superior. During the period from 1870 to 1890 some effort was made to secure and market this resource. The efforts, however, were not very successful for, although the slate was found to be of excellent quality, it was also discovered that nature had badly shattered the slate formations, thus making much of it useless.

Along the south shore of Lake Superior is found a sandstone that is called "brownstone." Several small quarries that produced this stone were once worked along Keweenaw Bay. From an old quarry at Marquette, opened shortly after the Civil War, came "brownstone" that was used in making buildings in Detroit and Chicago. This stone was also used in some of the early buildings at the Michigan College of Mines at Houghton. This stone is no longer used for building purposes because it turns a yellowish brown color when exposed to the weather. In the Southern Peninsula one of the underlying saucers is called Marshall sandstone. This sandstone was quarried at Marshall as early as 1840. It was also later quarried at Napoleon, in Jackson County, and at Grindstone City at the top of the Thumb. Sandstone from these early quarries was used for making grindstones. At Grindstone City can now be seen the old quarries from which the Marshall sandstone was once taken to make grindstones. With the coming of carborundum the grindstone industry has ceased to be. Grindstone City was once a busy center of this little industry but little remains there today to be seen of this early industry.

Michigan is fortunate in having vast deposits of marl, clay, shale, and limestone that can be used in making cement. These deposits are well scattered over the state so that cement can be made in many places. Cement was first manufactured in Michigan at Kalamazoo in the early seventies. Although the first attempt was a failure, cement plants made rapid progress after 1895. In 1900 there were six cement plants, and the production for that year was four thousand barrels. As cement is a very heavy product, it costs much money to ship it very far. Therefore, there are now ten cement plants scattered over the state. Each plant cares for the needs of its surrounding area. Large plants are located at Alpena and Petoskey. Lake shipping from these two ports provides a cheap method of transportation for this heavy commodity.

Because of Michigan's underlying limestone layers, limestone has for years formed the basis of one of her industries. The industries using limestone as a commodity have developed around the edges of the saucer rims where the limestone layers outcrop and can be easily worked. Fortunately for the limestone industry these outcrops appear near the Great Lakes, and cheap transportation by water can be had for the limestone products.

Because of the high quality and purity of Michigan's limestone it has been found to be a very good limestone to use as a furnace flux in the smelting of iron ore. An early quarry at Sibley, now part of the city of Trenton, provided limestone for the alkali industry at Wyandotte. This limestone was also used in the making of iron and steel. This early quarry is no longer worked. Limestone for the present day alkali industries is shipped by boat from the Alpena area. Limestone is also used for railroad ballast to form a firm bed for the rails, for sweetening agricultural land, for making granulated sugar in sugar beet plants, and in the manufacturing process of many other things, such as paper, glass, leather, soaps, and paints.

At Calcite, located just east of Rogers City, a high-grade limestone has been quarried since 1912. Each summer Michigan Limestone, a Division of United States Steel Corporation, ships vast quantities of crushed limestone from this port. The quarries are operated as strip mines. During the winter the glacial till overlaying the rock is removed. During the summer shipping season the limestone is blasted from its place in the sedimentary layer. The rock is then hauled to crushers where it is broken into the needed sizes. Ninety-eight per cent of the limestone quarried here is shipped by boats to smelters and manufacturers. This high-grade calcium limestone is used in blast furnaces in purifying iron ore into pig iron. About eight hundred to one thousand pounds of limestone are required for each ton of iron ore smelted. This limestone is also used to make steel in open hearth furnaces. Much of this limestone formation is locally used in the manufacture of cement. A new port from which limestone has been shipped since 1955 is Stoneport on the Presque Isle Peninsula between Alpena and Rogers City.

East of Manistique on the shore of Lake Michigan is Port Inland, from which limestone is shipped. Port Inland ranks second among the Great Lakes ports in the volume of limestone shipped. It is a privately owned port of the Inland Lime and Stone Company. It was opened in 1930. The limestone is hauled by rail to the port from the company quarries which are located about seven and one-half miles inland from the port.

On Drummond Island is located the world's largest dolomite quarry. Much dolomite was taken from this quarry to be used in making the footings for the Mackinac Bridge. A new port to ship high purity dolomite was opened in 1955 just three miles east of Cedarville at Port Dolomite on McKay Bay. This dolomite is used for fluxing by the iron and steel industry.

Gypsum is a formation similar to salt. In 1827 gypsum deposits were discovered along Plaster Creek in Kent County. A mill there began grinding gypsum as early as 1842. The crushed gypsum was used by the farmers to put on their land. Later, deposits were found at Alabaster and National City. From 1901 to 1907 Michigan led the states in the production of gypsum. The United States Gypsum Company operates quarries at Alabaster and also a port from which the limestone is shipped by boat. The National Gypsum Company has a quarry at National City. Three other companies have gypsum mines at Grand Rapids. Gypsum is used for making plaster, plasterboard, and insulating materials.

Battle Creek has been known as a health and cereal food center for many years. As early as 1866 the Western Health Reform Institute was formed here. In 1875 Dr. John H. Kellogg started the Battle Creek Sanitarium. Dr. Kellogg became interested in health foods. In 1895 the Postum Company was organized and began producing "Postum," a cereal coffee, and "Grape Nuts." At one time thirty-two companies in Battle Creek were producing health foods. Today two companies, the Kellogg Company, founded by Dr. Kellogg's younger brother, W. H. Kellogg, and the Post Cereals Division of the General Foods Corporation, produce breakfast foods.

The first telephone in Michigan was put in service in 1877. It was a small line running two miles between the office of the Frederick K. Stearns Drug Company and its laboratory. People were invited in to talk over the new phone. Many were sure that the new gadget was only a trick. But public attention was drawn to the spreading telephone lines of the time, and in 1883 the Michigan Bell Telephone Company was founded. Before many years had passed, people living in many parts of the state were able to talk to each other.

Michigan's water power became an important factor only after

Fish boats at the lower end of the Garden Peninsula. Once many boats like these brought in large catches of fish but during the last few years the fishing industry has greatly declined. Photo 1956.

Fish nets hung to dry on the lower end of the Garden Peninsula. Many nets like these were once used to catch Great Lakes fish. Photo 1956.

Brick making was once one of Michigan's major industries. This brick plant still makes brick in Dearborn. Photo 1955.

One of the old open pit coal mines at Williamston. Although Michigan still has much coal none has been mined commercially since 1947. Photo 1955.

COURTESY HENRY FORD MUSEUM

This picture, taken about 1915, shows what many of Michigan's roads were like at that time. There were a few miles of pavement and gravel roads but many country roads were like this one.

This train is like the one from which Thomas Edison was put off with his experimental equipment. Note the wooden coaches and the wood for burning in the engine to make steam.

COURTESY HENRY FORD MUSEUM

COURTESY MISS DENISE SCANLON

This picture taken in 1910 shows the new railroad tunnel under the Detroit River at Detroit. This tunnel made it possible to run trains between Detroit and Windsor, Ontario.

Large steam engines like this one were common in Michigan up to 1955. These large engines were the work horses of the railroads.

electricity began to be developed and larger dams were built across the streams. What is now the Consumers Power Company was started in 1886 by two brothers, W. A. Foote and J. B. Foote. They left their milling business in Adrian and went to Jackson to establish a city lighting system. They were joined by Samuel Jarvis, and the firm of Foote and Jarvis was started. Later these men started lighting systems in Albion, Battle Creek, and Kalamazoo. They had many problems but they also had one great idea. Because of their vision many homes are now lighted by electricity and thousands of people enjoy the benefits of electrical appliances.

In Grand Rapids, William T. Powers and his partners were also helping in developing electricity in Michigan. They installed on the west side of the Grand River the first hydroelectric plant in the United States. Foote's company began to work in the Muskegon River Valley on the problem of transmitting an electric current over long distances. In 1904 the Grand Rapids-Muskegon Power Company was organized and the Croton Dam was soon built by the company. In 1910 several small companies were combined into one single company named the Consumers Power Company. This company became a single system in 1915. At that time it had well over one hundred thousand gas and light customers. Since that time this company has done much to develop Michigan's water power and promote the transmission of electrical power.

At first poles were used to carry the transmission lines from the dams to the cities, but soon these were replaced by steel tower transmission lines. These steel tower lines were first developed here in Michigan. In 1906 a voltage of 70,000, a new record for the country, was carried over the company's lines. This record was broken in 1907 by increasing the voltage to 110,000, and again it was broken in 1911 by an increase to 140,000 volts.

Gradually this system has been expanded until today Consumers Power Company has thirty-seven dams located on the Au Sable, Kalamazoo, Thornapple, Tobacco, Muskegon, Grand, and Manistee rivers. These dams catch the water of the rivers and store it in huge basins between hills. As power is wanted, water is allowed to flow through huge turbines in the powerhouses at the bases of the dams. The turbines turn large generators that produce electricity. From there, electricity is carried by high-power transmission lines to many cities and rural homes. Since 1930 several other smaller electric companies have supplied electrical power to rural communities and small villages. Today there are only a few areas in Michigan where electrical power cannot be had.

Michigan's largest industry today is the manufacturing of automobiles and automobile parts. But, although Michigan is the center of the automobile industry, the automobile was not invented in Michigan. One of the first types of power tried in early automobiles was steam power. As early as 1886-1887 Ransom E. Olds, of Lansing, built one of the first steam-driven cars. Several steam cars, such as the White, Stanley Steamer, and Locomobile, later appeared on the market, but steam power was not the answer to power needs for automobile transportation. Before the owner of a steam car could drive, he had to wait ten or fifteen minutes for steam to generate. Once the steam had formed in the boiler, the car moved easily and with no need to shift gears. But at the end of thirty miles or so the driver had to stop, hunt for a water supply, and get up steam again. Then, too, boilers froze on frosty nights, and the owner of a steam car had to see that the boiler was drained if the car was left to stand for any length of time. One interesting feature of these early steam cars was that they had whistles in place of horns to warn people of their approach.

Courtesy of the Henry Ford Museum, Dearborn, Michigan

An early steam buggy

Another type of power tried in early cars was electric power. Large batteries were placed under the seat, and the batteries ran a motor. These cars started easily and one did not have to shift gears, but the life of a battery was short, and it had to be taken out and recharged every little while. This meant that one could not drive very far from a place where batteries could be charged again.

From France and Germany, in 1875, came an engine for which engineers had long been searching. The engine used coal gas for fuel which was made to explode inside a cylinder by means of a spark. Here was the basic principle: If the little engine could be made to explode time after time, this would give it power—power to really drive a carriage. This engine would not have to depend on water and fire, nor, like the first attempts at an electric carriage, would it have to depend on batteries. It could carry its power wherever it went.

But coal gas was too expensive. A cheaper source of explosive material had to be found before the gas engine could become practical. The search for a better gas was soon on, and it was finally found in gasoline. The petroleum industry had already begun to develop. Refineries were taking petroleum and heating it and making refined kerosene. Up to 1900 the main use made of petroleum was to make kerosene for lamps. While petroleum was being heated to make kerosene, it gave off a gas that was highly explosive. It was found that this gas, now called gasoline, could be used to run the new engines. What before had been a waste product now began to be sought after as a motor fuel. These gasoline motors that were developed at the turn of the century furnished a new kind of power. A tank full of gasoline would carry one much farther than one could go on a boiler full of water. About this time, too, new finds of petroleum in Texas promised an abundant supply of power fuel.

With the coming of the gasoline engine it was only natural that carriage makers would try putting the new engines into wagons and buggies. In fact, the first automobiles were called auto-buggies and auto-wagons. Several automobile companies, like Studebaker at South Bend, Indiana, grew from the carriage industry. Only a few gasoline-driven vehicles were built before 1900. In 1894 Mr. R. E. Olds built his first gasoline-driven automobile and began driving it about the streets of Lansing, much to the displeasure of most people who saw in it only a public danger and a death trap for Mr. Olds. In 1895 he began to produce his cars for sale. For some years Mr. Olds was the most successful of the early car makers. In 1896 a young man in Detroit, named Henry Ford, built his first gasoline-driven car. This car can be seen today in the Henry Ford Museum at Dearborn. Mr. Ford's gasoline motor was a two-cylinder engine made from pipe that he had bought from the Detroit Edison Company where he was then employed. Around his little engine he built his first car. It was five feet in length. For wheels he used four bicycle wheels. At first he planned that the car would be driven by the front wheels, but he soon found that this made the little car steer too hard and that the back wheels were of little use in steering it. The car had just two speeds, one forward and one backward. In 1898, the chambered spark plug was invented by a Michigan lumberman named Frank W. Canfield. This was a great advance in the development of the gaso-

Courtesy Ford Motor Co.

The first Ford car

line engine because one could now regulate the time when the gasoline would explode.

Several car manufacturers soon began offering automobiles for sale. By 1899 there were already twenty-five firms manufacturing automobiles. The early auto manufacturers numbered almost a hundred. Many of these early auto companies did not last long. A few like Mr. Olds and Mr. Winton began to make cars by the thousands. Most of the first cars were very expensive, and there were as yet no good roads on which to drive them.

After 1900 many other car manufacturers began making cars. In 1902 the oldest car company still making cars in Detroit was formed. This company is now the Cadillac Motor Car Company. In 1903 the present Ford Motor Company came into being. To house the new Ford Motor Company, a building on Mack Avenue was rented. The new Ford car was to be an assembled job. The motors were to be made by the Dodge brothers, who at that time manufactured bicycles and ran a machine shop in Detroit. The wheels were to be bought from one firm and the bodies from another and the tires from still another.

Flint was also a pioneer in the automobile industry. In 1900 David Buick was running the Buick Manufacturing Company located there and making stationary farm engines. Mr. Buick became interested in the new automobile and built a car for himself. In 1904

Mr. Buick joined with the Flint Wagon Works and formed a new company to manufacture the Buick car. Later William Crapo Durant, who was already well known as a member of the Durant-Dort Carriage Works, joined the Buick company.

Many companies were formed between 1900 and 1925. Several of them did not last long. By 1920 many of the early companies had passed away. Today the names of such cars as the Jackson, Maxwell, Cartorcar, Randolph, Rebacne, and Earl seem unknown to us. Packard cars were first made at Warren, Ohio. In 1902 Henry B. Joy and some other men from Detroit became interested in the Packard car, which was then selling under the name of the Ohio Auto Company. They added three more cylinders to the little car, named it the Packard, and moved the factory to Detroit in 1903. In that same year Mr. B. T. Fetch drove the "Old Pacific," a Packard car, from San Francisco to New York on the first automobile trip across the continent. Fitch made this trip in fifty-five days. The Reo car first appeared in 1904. Hupmobile appeared in 1908. Hudson and Chevrolet cars came on the market in 1909. For several years the Hudson Motor Company made a little six-cylinder car called the Essex. Among the other early automobiles appearing before 1930 were Oakland, Winton, Saxon, Maxwell, Huroon, Paige, Rickenbacker, and Willis Sainte Claire. The Huroon cars were made at Wayne. The Willis Sainte Claire was made at Marysville. The Paige, Maxwell, and Saxon cars were made at plants located in Detroit and Dearborn.

One of the best known and most popular of the early cars was the Model T Ford. The Ford Motor Company began production of this car in 1908. The new car was a great change in the automobile industry. The car was strong and light. The motor was made of vanadium steel. It had a block of four cylinders which was cast all at one time instead of putting four separate cylinders together. The motor also had a removable head. This was a new development that made it possible to repair a motor with much more ease. Because traffic in America keeps to the right and not to the left, Mr. Ford changed the steering wheel to the left side of the new car. The Model T created a sensation. It was cheap enough for even the common man to buy. Thousands of people rushed to see it. Over one thousand of these new cars were sold the first week. By 1908 the Ford Motor Company was making one hundred cars a day. This was four times as many cars as any other manufacturer was making at that time.

About this time the method of making cars changed in the automobile plants. The old method of taking cars around the plant to the parts was changed for a newer method now known as the "assembly line." The parts were to be brought to the cars as they passed slowly along. As each car passed a man, he was to do one thing toward making each of the finished cars. Side conveyors would bring the parts to each man, and he in turn would place the parts into the cars.

Up to this time each mechanic had found it necessary to fit every part to each motor or car. This had caused much useless delay and extra expense. Car manufacturers now began to make each part exactly alike. These identical parts are now called standard, or interchangeable, parts. They will work on one car just as well as on another, and there is no need of fitting each separate part to the machine. To do this the automobile makers had to introduce precision measurement into their parts manufacture. This system of production has now come to be called mass production. It was not developed in the automobile industry but was adopted by the early car makers. Today it is used in many other lines of manufacturing.

Many people saw little use in buying the new cars. There were few roads on which to drive them. In some of the cities there were a few streets that had wooden block pavement or were covered with macadam, but country roads were almost impassable for automobiles. Motorists who attempted to drive on these roads often got stuck in the sand or mud. When they did get stuck, they were often greeted by passers-by with the comment, "Better get a horse." The first mile of cement road in Michigan was built in the year 1908. By 1917 there were only a few miles of paving in the state. Michigan Avenue, US 112; Grand River, US 16; and Woodward Avenue, US 10, were all gravel roads at that time. None of the highways were marked as they are today. But people demanded more and more roads, and the owners of both automobiles and bicycles wanted better roads to ride on.

Early cars were a great annoyance to people having horses. Horses in the fields would become frightened at the horseless carriages putt-putting down the road. Even cattle were disturbed, and farmers said that they did not give their usual quantity of milk. Farmers did not keep their chickens penned up, and many chickens were killed by the automobiles. People riding in wagons and buggies were especially annoyed when they saw one of the early cars coming down the road. Many times horses became frightened at the noisy, ill-smelling cars and ran away, smashing wagons and buggies and sometimes injuring the people who were riding in them. Often a man would get out of his buggy and put his coat over his horse's head and lead him past the car. But as the years passed and more and more cars appeared on the roads, the horses became more used to them and often disregarded them altogether. This was especially true of the younger horses.

General Motors Company came into being on September 16, 1908. This company was succeeded by the General Motors Corporation on October 13, 1916. This corporation was a combination of many early auto manufacturers and various producers of auto parts. Buick was taken in in September, 1908. Olds was added to the corporation in December, 1908. Oakland and Cadillac were taken in in June, 1910. Chevrolet was added in 1918, and in 1919 the Fisher Body Company became a member of the growing corporation. In 1919 General Motors began the building of their general office building in Detroit. This new building was fifteen stories high and was occupied as their general offices in 1921.

In July, 1913, the Dodge brothers decided to build a car of their own, and gave the Ford Motor Company notice that they would not continue to make motors for them after July, 1914. From the time that Mr. Ford had started to make cars to that date the Dodge brothers had built all the motors used in Ford cars. In 1914 Cadillac pioneered in a new field and brought out the first V-eight high-speed motor. In that year Mr. Ford startled the world by increasing the wages of his employees from an average of $2.34 a day to a minimum of $5.00. At the same time, Mr. Ford changed the working day for his men from nine hours to eight hours. By making the working day one of eight hours, he made it possible to work his men three shifts in place of two.

In 1915 ground was broken for a new and larger Ford plant to be located on the River Rouge in Dearborn. As the plant on the River Rouge in Dearborn grew larger and larger, the river was deepened so that boats loaded with coal and iron ore could come up the river and bring their cargoes to the factory. During World War I the Rouge Plant supplied eagle boats, tractors, cars, tanks, as well as liberty motors for airplanes. After the war the Rouge Plant became the center of the Ford industries.

All the auto industries did much to help the United States win World War I. The Dodge Brothers used their plant to manufacture needed war supplies. The Packard Motor Car Company designed and built the first liberty motor. During the war the Packard Plant built more of these motors than did any other company. Each auto plant in Michigan helped in some way to aid in winning the struggle against Germany.

In January, 1924, the first Chrysler car appeared. This corporation soon purchased the Dodge plant. The rise of this corporation has been rapid, and today it ranks as one of the "big three" in the production of automobiles.

During World War II the auto plants again aided in making war materials, and the skilled craftsmen together with the available machinery made Michigan really an arsenal of democracy. From their plants poured a steady stream of supplies for the fighting forces.

Following World War II, the Kaiser-Fraser Corporation occupied the Willow Run Bomber Plant, where bombers were made during World War II, and for a few years Kaiser and Fraser cars were made there.

During the past fifty years much progress has been made in automobile making. Up to about 1925 nearly all automobile bodies were made of wood and covered with metal. Today all automobile bodies are made of welded steel parts. Up to 1920 only a few of the most expensive automobiles had a hard top and windows in the sides. People of that time jokingly said they would not care to ride in one of those glass showcases. All other models were open models with a collapsible top and side curtains that could be put up in case of rain. At first there were no garages, and cars were usually kept in horse barns. Repair parts were hard to get, and everyone had to be his own mechanic.

Many standard features that we now take for granted when buying an automobile were not included on those early models. Such features as a gasoline gauge, oil pressure gauge, self starter, accelerator, windshield wipers, automatic choke, heater, and radio all came later. All the early cars were cranked by hand. The first electric lights ran directly from the generator, and the brightness of the light depended on the speed of the motor. When one needed light the most, one had the least of it. Cars today have over ten times the horsepower of the early cars.

Today automobiles not only are well engineered but are works of beauty and comfort as well. The automobile has become, in just fifty years, a necessary part of our American way of life. Hundreds of them roll off the factory assembly lines each day. Our streets and highways are filled with automobiles carrying people to and from work, on necessary errands, and on pleasure trips. Distance is less of a handicap than it was up to 1900.

Soon after the automobile appeared, the first trucks also appeared. At first these trucks were used mostly as delivery wagons on city streets, but by 1925 large trucks that could be used for hauling coal, gravel, limestone, or sand had appeared. Gradually they took over some of the work that had been done by horses up to that time. Today all kinds of trucks, little ones used by farmers and mechanics, heavy ones to haul huge loads of soil, and long "haul-away" trucks, are a common sight on our streets and highways.

For many years farmers had been looking for a source of power to use on their farms. Steam power had been tried but found to be successful only in threshing machine engines. The new gasoline engine offered a strong source of power in a light machine that would not bog down in muddy ground. Soon auto manufacturers, such as Mr. Ford, were experimenting with new farm machines called tractors. These early experiments proved successful, and now each year hundreds of tractors come off our production lines. With the coming of the tractor the farmer's life was made easier. Not only that, but the amount of work he could do was greatly increased. Since the coming of the tractor the number of horses in the state has greatly declined.

Today automobile manufacturing is Michigan's largest industry. Not only are there large plants in Pontiac, Lansing, Flint, and Detroit devoted to the manufacture of automobiles, but there are hundreds of smaller plants scattered all over the state which make parts that find their way to the assembly lines in the huge automobile plants. These plants give to thousands of men living in Michigan their regular daily employment.

In the early twenties radio first appeared. WWJ, The Detroit News, was one of the first commercial broadcasting stations. Soon hundreds of people had radio sets in their homes. In the following decade television also appeared. Again hundreds of people purchased these sets for their homes. The manufacture of radios and television sets as well as the parts for these sets now employs hundreds of men and women here in Michigan.

With the coming of the gasoline engine and electrical power at the turn of the century, many mechanical appliances such as washers, ironers, sweepers, electric refrigerators, and toasters appeared on the market. Some of these appliances were developed here in Michigan. Today industries making these appliances are scattered over the state.

As the automobile industry and the manufacturing of electrical appliances developed, there grew a greater and greater demand for more and more steel. About the time Captain Ward's Eureka Iron and Steel Company closed down, mines opened in Minnesota and great quantities of iron ore, as we have seen, began coming down the lakes. Nearly all of it for thirty years sailed right past Detroit's front door to the receiving ports on the south shore of Lake Erie. This is no longer true, for Michigan today produces large quantities of iron and steel for heating units, automobiles, and other manufactured products. Large rolling mills and huge blast furnaces standing along the Detroit river have replaced the crude furnaces and mills of seventy-five years ago.

In 1902 a blast furnace was built on Zug Island at the mouth of the River Rouge. A second blast furnace was built on the island in 1909. These furnaces produced what was known as merchant pig iron that was sold to foundry companies. Later Mr. Ford began producing some steel at his Rouge Plant. Today Ford's steel mills annually produce well over half a million tons of steel. Even this amount is only part of that which is used by the Ford Motor Company.

Mr. G. R. Fink, a sales representative for an eastern steel firm, saw the need for steel to be produced here in Michigan and in 1922 organized the Michigan Steel Corporation. Mr. Fink then built a plant on the Ecorse River. This new steel plant rolled its first steel in July of the following year. At first this company did not smelt iron but bought rough steel from the Pittsburgh area and rolled it into sheets and desired shapes. In 1929 the Michigan Steel Corporation was enlarged, and it became the Great Lakes Steel Corporation. It is now a division of the National Steel Corporation. The site for the new plant was a swamp beside the Detroit River. One hundred thousand piles were driven into the ground to support the new plant. After long months of hard work the new steel mill started production in August, 1931. Other plants including the blast furnaces on Zug Island were brought into the new corporation. A new blast furnace was added in 1938 and another was built on Zug Island in 1953. To these former steel-making facilities were later added 130 coke ovens, a by-product plant, and docks and storage space for coal, iron ore, and limestone. Since that time both hot and cold mills have been added to roll steel. Today Great Lakes Steel is the largest producer of steel in the state. Much of the steel it produces goes into the making of automobiles.

The Detroit Steel Corporation was formed in 1923. In 1944 this corporation was merged with the Reliance Steel Division. In 1953 this company produced 450,000 tons of coke, 504,000 tons of pig iron, and 1,290,000 tons of steel ingots.

In 1934 Donald B. McLouth formed the McLouth Steel Corporation. In 1935 this company rolled its first hot-rolled steel. Cold rolling mills and blast furnaces have since been added. The McLouth Steel Corporation has its plant in Trenton.

That gas and oil exist in Michigan has been known from the earliest days of settlement. Early settlers found oil and gas escaping in Montcalm, Wayne, and Monroe counties. Sometimes films of oil appeared on streams and ponds. This oily film was sometimes so thick that stock refused to drink the water.

The first real oil well was struck at Port Huron in 1886. This well produced only two barrels of oil a day. From this oil a small local industry made greases for greasing axles of buggies and wagons. About this time, while drilling for salt, oil and water were struck at Manistee. The oil and water were under such pressure that it shot upward with a strong enough force to wreck the derrick. Between 1889 and 1914 several very shallow wells, going about 600 feet in depth, were drilled. The most important of these were drilled at Port Huron, but even these were soon out of production.

In 1912 several test wells were drilled in a large circle around Saginaw. Unfortunately, all of these wells were drilled around the edge of what later proved to be the Saginaw oil pool. Some of these wells at first produced around eighty barrels of crude oil a day, but soon their flow had dropped to only two or three barrels a day. Very little gas was found in these wells. In 1925 the Saginaw pool was discovered lying within the circle of wells that had been drilled. The first well was only a twenty-five-barrel producer, but soon over one hundred wells had been drilled in the area. Michigan's real oil development had begun. The boom of the Saginaw pool, however, was short-lived for it lasted only until 1928. Too many wells were sunk within a small area. When the pressure on the pool was released, the crude oil ceased to flow. Only a few of these wells are producing today.

In 1927 oil was discovered in the Muskegon field near Muskegon.

More than five hundred wells were drilled by 1929. Again too many wells were drilled. Much natural gas was lost and thus the pressure was reduced. For a time this area ranked second in oil production in Michigan. Some of these wells are still producing. In 1928 the state passed a law to prevent waste and regulate the number of wells that could be drilled in a given area.

About this time studies were made of the drillings that had been made by the Dow Chemical Company in its search for salt deposits. These drilling cores showed the presence of crude oil in the area. On March 31, 1928, a well giving thirty barrels a day was struck in Greendale Township in Midland County. That same year oil was struck ten miles east of Mt. Pleasant in Isabella County. The wells in this area in general produce from one hundred to three hundred barrels a day. They have been better spaced than were the earlier drillings. Not much natural gas has been found in this area.

The following year, 1929, oil was struck at the Leaton Pool in Isabella County. The wells in this area range all the way from dry holes to some which produce over five hundred barrels a day. In the same year gas was struck in the Bloomfield Township Pool and in the Vernon Township Pool in Isabella County. In the Vernon Township Pool, oil as well as gas was found. In 1931, oil was struck in the Porter Township field in Midland County. In 1933 some gushers were struck that produced fourteen thousand barrels a day.

In 1933 the Jasper Field in Midland County was located. This field has been the largest producer to date. Shallow wells have also been located near Grand Rapids. In 1940 the Reed City field was located. In 1946-1947 new fields were discovered north of Muskegon. Crude oil is produced in fourty-one counties.

In 1954, crude oil was found near Northville and Clinton. In 1958, the Albion-Pulaski-Scipio field was developed in the Trenton-Black River formation. In 1959, there were 108 wells in this new field and the production for that year was 2,046,600 Barrels.

The following table shows how Michigan's crude oil production has increased and decreased.

1925	4,000 barrels	1938	18,745,000 barrels
1927	439,000 barrels	1939	23,462,000 barrels
1929	4,529,000 barrels	1940	19,764,000 barrels
1932	6,900,000 barrels	1948	16,870,000 barrels
1936	11,928,000 barrels	1957	10,740,000 barrels
1937	16,628,000 barrels	1959	10,438,000 barrels

To 1948, Michigan had produced 289,903,000 barrels of crude oil. Michigan has also produced much natural gas as well as crude oil. In 1947, 38,300 million cubic feet were produced.* Up to 1948 all gas stored in Michigan was Michigan natural gas, but in 1948 a twenty-four-inch pipeline was completed that connected Detroit with Texas. Since that time much natural gas has come into Michigan from Texas, Kansas, and Oklahoma. Much of this gas is used as soon as it arrives, but some is piped to old gas fields and stored against any future need. To care for this crude oil and natural gas, pipelines have been built from the southern part of the state into the oil-producing areas in the central part of the Lower Peninsula.

Each day Michigan produces about 40,000 barrels of crude oil, refines about 100,000 barrels, and consumes about 275,000 barrels. Therefore, much of it must come into the state from other sources. At present there are some fifteen small independent refineries in Michigan. Refineries are located at Alma, Bay City, Carson City, Detroit, Flat Rock, Grand Rapids, Kalamazoo, Midland, Mt. Pleasant, Muskegon, Reed City, Trenton, and West Branch. At first Michigan gasoline did not rank with gasolines produced outside the state, but in 1938 the Leonard Company at Alma introduced the world's first midget unit to carry out the cracking process. Other companies kept pace with the Leonard Company and today Michigan-made gasoline is of as high a quality as any other gasoline.

Today Michigan has 1,260 miles of petroleum pipelines not counting the one that comes down from Edmonton, Canada, and crosses Michigan to Sarnia, Ontario. Most of these lines are located in the central and western part of the Lower Peninsula. On the Great Lakes there are twenty oil tankers that, during the summer shipping season, carry some 200,000 barrels of oil a day. The Standard Oil Company of Indiana has the largest fleet of oil tankers on the Great Lakes. Five of these boats have each a capacity of 60,000 barrels. These boats carry only the finished product. Most of it is brought from the Toledo area to the Detroit area and from Chicago to cities on the west coast of Michigan.

Prospecting for oil in Michigan is difficult because of the glacial drift that covers the state and hides from view the folds of the rocks that lie hidden underneath. But as new drillings are made, more is becoming known about Michigan's underlying rock formations.

*In 1957 only 9,900 cu. ft. was produced.

Further deposits of oil will no doubt be found. Deeper drillings may also open deposits of oil not yet discovered.

Michigan's second largest industry today is her tourist industry. Because of the fact that Michigan touches four of the five Great Lakes, has many lovely inland lakes, has many pretty streams, and has gently rolling hills, it is visited by hundreds of people who come here each year to spend their vacation. Thousands of cottages, motels, hotels, and clubs are scattered all over the northern country. Each summer the people living in these areas are busy caring for the people who come here to spend their vacations. Winter sports are also becoming more and more popular. Several recreation areas cater to those who like to ski, toboggan, and ice skate. Hundreds of others like to hunt and come to Michigan's hunting areas each fall. As people travel along our highways or stay at motels or cottages, they spend much money. This money helps today to keep many of the smaller northern communities alive.

Thus we see that Michigan has many and varied industries. Most of them are based on the geography and geology of Michigan. Few states in the Union have the varied resources that Michigan has. However, we must learn to use these resources wisely if Michigan is to remain a strong industrial state.

Courtesy Leonard Refineries, Inc.

Making gasoline and other useful products, Alma, Michigan

Chapter XVII

AGRICULTURAL DEVELOPMENT IN MICHIGAN

Michigan's first farmers, as you learned in Chapter Three, were the native Indian women. Because the Indians had only a few very crude tools with which to work they could not easily clear away the forests. The crops they raised, therefore, were only such as could be grown in open places where a little sunshine filtered into the forest. They grew their crops of beans, squash, pumpkins, maize, and tobacco even as far north as Sault Ste. Marie. But the Indians were a people who lived more by hunting and fishing than they did by farming. As they had no tame animals, except their dogs, the wild animals of the forest and the fish from the lakes and rivers furnished their entire meat supply.

Only a very little farming was done in the area during the years that France held the Great Lakes Region. The French were more interested in their missions and the fur trade than they were in developing agriculture in New France. What is more, France tried to set up a feudal system in New France. Land was not given, or sold, to settlers like it was in the English colonies, but rather it became the property of local lords, called seigneurs. Frenchmen wishing to farm had to get the right to farm the land from some seigneur. Then, too, the Great Lakes area was far from any good market, and canoe transportation was too slow and costly to permit carrying farm products to the French settlements back east along the St. Lawrence River.

After 1700 a few French farmers were to be found in Michigan but they grew crops only for their own use or the very limited local market. They found the soil rich and easily able to supply food for their families. Their farms were small strips of land about a block wide that ran back into the country from the Detroit River or the St. Mary's River. Usually they were cleared only a little way back from the settler's cabin, for the Frenchmen saw little use in the hard work of clearing land if it was not needed for immediate use. The French farmers had a few cows and some horses which were really only ponies. These ponies they hitched to little two-wheeled carts. These little carts and canoes were the Frenchmen's only means of transportation. Near each French farmer's house there was usually a garden. Near the garden was often an orchard in which grew peach trees and apple trees. These trees furnished fresh fruit that was then considered of little value, but the juices were made into brandy for the Indian trade.

During the years that England controlled this area, the few French farmers who were still in the locality kept on working on their farms. A few English farmers moved into Michigan but England did not encourage the development of agriculture in Michigan. The Proclamation of 1763 forbade settlers from taking up lands west of the mountains until the land could be taken from the Indians by treaty. Michigan was still Indian country, and title to any of the land was hard to secure.

After the War of 1812 the first surveys in Michigan by the United States Government gave the settlers their first real chance to take up farm lands in Michigan. A settler could then purchase a definite area of land which could be easily located. As we saw in Chapter Eight, settlers came in large numbers into Michigan after 1830 and by 1860 the area south of Bay City could be called a settled area.

The system of land survey used by the United States Government affected the system of farming in Michigan in two ways: First, Michigan farms were laid out in definite lines running north and south along the lines of survey. These section survey lines also later became roads and thus in many parts of Michigan these roads cross each other every mile and thus form square blocks of land one square mile in area. This is why so many of Michigan's roads run straight north and south and east and west. Second, as the land passed from government ownership to individuals, settlers set up the practice of each family living on its own farm. In Europe, China, and India, the peasants often live in little villages and go out to their farms each day. The French farmers had lived in little houses that sat in one long line on each side of the St. Lawrence and Detroit rivers. As each settler who came to Michigan built his cabin on his own land he was often a quarter of a mile, or even more, from his nearest neighbor. Usually a settler built his house not far from the section line that was to be used as the road. Thus today our farmers live in houses scattered here and there along the roads that spread across Michigan.

Michigan's real agricultural development began less than one hundred and fifty years ago. When the land was opened for settlement, people came to Michigan from New England and from the states of Indiana and Ohio. Many of these people from Indiana and Ohio were from families which before that time had lived in the South.

Along with these early settlers who pushed west from the older settlements came many people from Europe. Just at the time Michigan was being settled there was much unrest in Europe. Many Germans who had seen the revolutions of 1830 and 1848 fail left Germany and came to the Lake Region to take up farms. Some came for political reasons. Some came because of their religious beliefs. Others came because a good farm was to be had in Michigan for much less money than in Germany. Still others came to escape the compulsory military training that Germany then required. Sometimes these people came in groups and formed rural settlements of Lutherans, Roman Catholics, Moravians, or United Brethren. Nearly all the Germans who then came to Michigan settled in southern Michigan.

The coming of the Dutch to Michigan was already discussed in another chapter. All of these immigrants coming from Europe brought new ideas of farming not known by the settlers coming from New England or the South.

Michigan's agricultural development was encouraged in the early days by the new means of transportation that were then developing. The opening of the Erie Canal made it possible for men to start farming in southern Michigan. The new railroads that spread across the state opened large areas to settlement. By 1837, the area around Detroit was a large wheat producer. It has been estimated that about one million bushels of wheat were produced in Michigan in that year. By 1840, wheat production had increased to about two million bushels, and by 1850 it had reached about five million bushels. The Erie Canal also made it possible to ship much of this wheat and other farm produce such as chickens, pigs, and cattle to the eastern markets that were then growing very rapidly. As people in the East, and in England, left their poorer lands and began working in the growing factories, they came to depend more and more upon the western farmers for food for their tables.

Though transportation by rail and water had grown better, local transportation was still very poor. Some main roads leading out from

Detroit had been built, but these roads were not well made. Often they were little more than lanes cut through the forest. They were poorly graded and drained. In wet weather they became muddy and slippery. During dry weather they were hard and bumpy.

In 1844 a charter was granted for the building of the first plank road in Michigan. It was to run from Detroit to Port Huron. In 1848 the state legislature passed an act known as the Plank Road Act. Plank roads were to be eight feet wide and three inches thick. These roads were made possible because of the improvements in sawing lumber and because of the vast amount of hardwood that was near at hand. A plank road was built between Detroit and Pontiac. Another ran from Detroit to Howell. One was also built from Flint to Saginaw. Anyone who used a plank road had to pay for its use. A two-horse wagon paid two cents a mile. A one-horse wagon paid one cent a mile. To take twenty cattle one mile cost two cents. Plank roads were never very successful. The planks rotted rapidly and wore away with use as hoofs and wheels passed over them. When new planks were put in to replace the old ones, they were higher than the worn ones and thus made the road bumpy. Some boards warped out of shape. Horses often got slivers in their feet.

Until about 1880, the only roads in Michigan besides the toll roads were township roads. These highways were supposed to be cared for by the people living along the road. Each taxpayer was expected to work out part of his tax by working so many days on the road or paying cash for his share of the tax. People who were not taxpayers were to give one day's work or pay a man's wages for one day's work. But the roads were poorly kept. This lack of good highways hindered cultural and economic development.

Up to 1850 ox teams were more used than horses. Although they were slow, the settlers liked them better to use in clearing the land and plowing up the tough sod. Then, too, their meat could be used to supply food for the family table. Wagons pulled by oxen provided the main means of transportation on the farms and from the farm to the village. A man with a team of oxen was regarded as being well off, for many early settlers had to do all their own work and carry provisions from town on their backs.

At first the farmers of Michigan were known as self-sufficient farmers. That is, they supplied almost all of their needs from their own farms. Sheep were raised for their meat and wool. The wool was used to make clothing. Hogs, cattle, grain, and vegetables supplied the family table. Wood cut on the farm wood lot kept the cabin warm and provided heat for cooking the meals. But before long wheat and wool became the leading cash crops that the farmers sent to market to get cash to buy the things they needed which their farms could not produce.

Settlers pushing into Michigan brought with them the first real horses. They also brought cattle, sheep, hogs, and poultry. At first, meat for the settler's table often came from the forest, but as the forests were cut and the game killed or driven away, the settlers came to depend more and more upon their animals for their meat supply.

Work on these early farms was all hard toil. Farmers and their sons worked long hours, from dawn to dusk. The ground, at springtime, was turned by a spade or a crude heavy wooden plow. A tree branch often served as a drag to break the earth into fine pieces. Sometimes it was pulled by oxen but in many families the father, mother or sons dragged the tree branch over the ground. Sowing was done by hand. During the summer, crops such as potatoes, corn, and vegetables had to be hoed. In the fall all the grain had to be cut by hand. Sickles and scythes were used. Grain was threshed with a flail and winnowed in the open air. Often the tools with which they worked, such as rakes, hoes, spades, plows, and pitchforks, were made of wood by the farmer who used them. All the milking was done by the farmer's family.

By 1870 the four lower tiers of counties in Michigan had been settled. Between 1870 and 1885 there was a rush of settlers into the northern part of the state, and by 1900 almost all the farm land in the northern part of the state had been taken. Some of this land the settlers bought from lumber companies, some of it they bought from railroad companies that had been given land grants to help them build their railroads, some of it they bought on school sections that had been set aside to build up the Primary Fund, and some of it was settled under the Homestead Act of 1862. This act made it possible for the head of a family to claim, free of cost, one hundred and sixty acres of government land if he would settle on it and live there for five years. Some three million acres of land were thus claimed in Michigan.

Many of the people who settled northern Michigan were sons and daughters of earlier settlers in southern Michigan. Many of the men were veterans of the Civil War who had gone north to find work in the lumber camps.

Another group of settlers in this area were the Finns. These people found their way to Michigan to work in the woods and mines. Many of their children are now found on farms in the Upper Peninsula and in the upper part of the Lower Peninsula where the soil, the lakes, and the climate are in many ways similar to those of their native Finland. These hardy, industrious people make farming profitable where others of less sturdy stock would fail. So many of these people have come to Michigan that about one fourth of all the Finnish people in the United States now live in Michigan.

One other race from northern Europe has helped to develop Michigan's agriculture. These people are the Swedes. Like the Finns, the Germans, and the Dutch, they are hard working and thrifty.

As the settlers spread across the state they soon learned that Michigan's soils and variations in climate changed quickly from place to place. Because of this many crops are now grown in Michigan. Perhaps no other state presents the variations in soil and climate as does Michigan. Michigan is a large state bordering on four large bodies of water. From south to north it reaches across six degrees of latitude. Although most of the state is low, gently rolling land, some of it in the High Plains Area of the Lower Peninsula and in the western part of the Upper Peninsula reaches a height that is high enough to affect crops, especially by the shorter growing season.

Because of the way the land of Michigan was formed, it is today a land of varied soils. As was shown in Chapter One, all of the soil of Michigan is glacial till that was pushed south by the glaciers. Since that time, the crushed material, which the glaciers brought here and deposited on the limestone saucers, has been affected by the weathering agents that have been at work upon it. Rivers have carried away the finer pieces and made deposits of clay. Rains have soaked into some areas, and the down-running water has carried the minerals from the land. In some areas, decaying vegetation has formed muck lands. Some of these black muck lands are of good quality, while others, looking equally black and good, are practically useless for farming.

Good soil to farmers means good land having the necessary qualities for good plant growth. Michigan's land varies all the way from loose, shifting sand, like the sand dunes along the Great Lakes or the barren sandy plains of the High Plains Area, to heavy clays that bake hard under the warm summer sun. Some of the sandy areas drain too easily while other clay areas scarcely drain at all. The humus, organic matter that is necessary for good plant growth, varies from place to place. Some areas are rich in humus while other areas have very little.

What is more, there is no regularity in the soil in the amount of elements such as minerals, lime, or nitrogen. Because it was a forest land, most of the soils were podsol; that is, they were high in acid content.

Often a farm of just a few acres has several kinds of soil, and extensive changes in soil take place within just a few miles. One can notice this as one drives along our highways. At one point one may be passing beautiful farm homes and barns, and a few miles farther along the road the farms are gone and only brush land lines the highway. A few miles farther on and one may again be passing through farm lands.

Good crops require not only good soils but also a favorable climate. By climate is meant the minimum and maximum temperature, the number of frost-free days, the degree of cloudiness, the amount and length of sunshine, the amount of rainfall and snowfall, and the effect of the prevailing winds. Over an area as large as Michigan with bodies of water on all sides one finds many variations in climate. To help you better understand the forces that make up climate, each of the above phases will be discussed.

In order for plants to grow they must have enough moisture. Fortunately for Michigan, the heaviest rainfall, in the Lower Peninsula where the farms are the most numerous, comes in May, June, and July when the plants are growing. Rains are less frequent in the fall when the crops are ready for the harvest. Droughts are not uncommon but they are usually local and do not often affect wide areas. The same area seldom is affected by drought two years in a row. Most of Michigan has an average rainfall of about thirty-one inches a year. This rainfall varies from about twenty-eight inches in the drier parts of the state, such as the Thumb area and the eastern half of Mackinac County in the Upper Peninsula, to about thirty-six inches in the areas of heaviest rainfall. Michigan's heaviest rainfall lies in the area where Michigan touches Indiana.

Crops usually mature in a definite number of days. Therefore, the number of days from the last killing frost in the spring until the first killing frost in the fall often determines what crops can be grown. In Michigan the number of days free from killing frosts varies all the way from one hundred eighty days in the eastern half of Berrien County, in the southwest corner of Michigan, to only ninety days in the area just north of Iron River in the Upper Peninsula and in Crawford County in the Lower Peninsula. In some places in Michigan spring frosts occur as late as June 10. Some areas have warm days but very cool nights. These cool nights retard growth in some plants.

The length of the growing season in the various parts of Michigan is affected by the altitude, the latitude, and the effect of the Great Lakes upon the land. Of the four Great Lakes that touch Michigan, Lake Michigan, because of its size and shape, has the most effect on Michigan's agricultural development. Lake Michigan is some one hundred miles wide and spreads north along the entire west side of the Lower Peninsula. The prevailing westerly winds that blow across it onto the Lower Peninsula are affected by the temperature of the water in Lake Michigan.

That water is capable of absorbing much heat can readily be seen in the length of time it takes to boil water in a teakettle or a pan. During the summer, when the sun shines down upon the Great Lakes, the water absorbs heat and tends to warm. But even in the summer the winds coming from the drier lands farther to the west are cooled as they pass over Lake Michigan. Not only that, but they pick up moisture on their way and that increases the humidity of the air blowing onto the land during the growing season. These winds bring a more even, cooler summer climate to the area lying along the western side of the Lower Peninsula. The days are not so warm or the nights so cool as they are farther inland. Western Michigan during the summer has more sunshine than most other areas because the land is warmer than the water and winds bringing moisture do not condense and form clouds. This sunshine is good for the ripening fruit.

When fall comes, the inland areas tend to cool more quickly. But the autumns along Lake Michigan's shore are long and mild. During October and November Lake Michigan is fifteen or twenty degrees warmer than the cooling land. During this season winds blowing in from Lake Michigan bring warmth from the lake to the land. This gives the area along the eastern shore line of Lake Michigan some twenty to fifty more frost-free days than are found in the more inland areas. During this period the summer's growth on the fruit trees has time to harden and this helps to protect the new growth from the winter's cold. During the fall months this area has less sunshine than any other part of the country for when the warm air coming in from Lake Michigan strikes the cooling land the moisture which it carries condenses and forms clouds.

During the winter, Lake Michigan slowly gives up the warmth it has stored during the summer. The water of the lake often freezes solid for some ten miles or more out from the shore line where the water is less deep. When spring comes, the increasing sunshine during the daytime quickly warms the land farther inland from the lakes, but at night killing frosts often occur. Such frosts often do much harm to growing plants and trees. This is especially true of fruit trees, and that is why Michigan's fruit belt is limited to the eastern shore of Lake Michigan from Indiana to Petoskey. Along the Lake Michigan shore the winds blowing in from the cooler lake keep the land from warming too rapidly. This retards the opening of the buds on the fruit trees until the danger of killing frosts is usually past. Some years, however, the fruit trees even in this area are frosted and the fruit is destroyed as soon as it begins to form.

Lake Huron, because of its location on the eastern side of Michigan and the prevailing westerly winds, has far less effect on agriculture. Lake Superior, also because of its location and the direction of the winds, has little effect on much of Michigan.

Lake Michigan, however, has another effect on Michigan's climate. Hail storms are frequent in the southeastern part of Michigan but nearly unknown in the western and upper part of the state. The lake seems to stop the development of air currents that result in violent storms.

Sunshine is an important factor in growing crops. As stated above, western Michigan has much sunshine during the summer. The Upper Peninsula being farther north has longer days during the summer months. The days there are about forty-five minutes longer in the summer than they are in southern Michigan. The opposite is true in the wintertime. Then there is less sunlight than there is in southern Michigan. The longer summer days give the Upper Peninsula the extra sunlight needed for growing crops.

Markets and economic conditions are two more factors of major importance to farmers. A farmer must not only be able to grow crops but also must have a market for his crops after they are grown, or else there is no use in producing more than his family needs. If a farmer is to buy the needed items his farm cannot produce, he must have a market for at least part of his crops.

At first Michigan's farms were nearly all general farms: they raised a variety of crops and were generally self-sufficient like the New England farms from which so many of the settlers had come. But before long, some of them, closer to the routes of transportation that led to markets, began raising what are known as cash crops. One of the first cash crops, as you have seen, was "propeller wood" and wood for the trains. Another cash crop was wheat. The heavy clay soil of the southeastern counties was well suited to wheat growing. Wheat kept well, could be easily hauled to market on the new railroads and the Erie Canal where it could be sold in the newly growing cities in the East and in Europe. Where the spreading city of Detroit now stands, and in the many smaller cities adjoining Detroit, there were, one hundred years ago, large fields of waving grain. So new and rich was the land that many bushels of wheat were produced to the acre. Michigan at that time was one of the major wheat-producing areas of the nation. Wheat from Michigan and from the area around and west of Chicago formed the first bulk shipments of freight on the Great Lakes.

As the railroads spread across the state they gave the farmers a means of getting their produce to the market. But long transportation often consumed a major portion of the profit. What is more, perishable products, until recently, could not be carried for long distances. Michigan's best farming lands in general are in the southern part of the Lower Peninsula below the Bay City-Muskegon line. Some three million people live in this area and perhaps twice as many live in the nearby area in Ohio, Indiana, and Illinois. Today this area is well supplied with both roads and railroads, and farm produce can be easily and quickly shipped to market. Because of this easily accessible transportation, many of Michigan's farmers specialize in such products as milk, fruits, vegetables, and poultry.

The farmers of northern Michigan are today farther from the markets and must face the extra cost of transportation over longer distances to markets. Up to 1900 they had local markets, for the lumber and mining industries brought hundreds of people into northern Michigan. These people, living in lumber camps, sawmill towns and mining communities, required a large amount of farm produce. After 1900, this market greatly declined in volume.

Modern refrigeration, rapid transportation, and canning have brought great changes in modern farming. Fruits and vegetables are now shipped over long distances to market. This brings new areas into competition with the older areas closer to the cities. Meat packing plants and modern laws regarding sanitation of foods make marketing more standardized than it was fifty years ago.

After the Civil War great changes began to come into the farmer's way of life. Iron plows began to be used more. Obed Hussey and Cyrus McCormick each patented a reaper in 1833. Soon reapers were being used on Michigan farms. By 1850, mowing machines had been developed. By 1860, grain was commonly cut by a reaper, but it still had to be bound by hand. Steam threshing machines had been tried. Steel plows soon replaced iron plows. By 1870, corn planters and corn cultivators were being used. Small tools such as hoes, rakes, and pitchforks began to be made from steel rather than wood. Improved drags and harrows made of wood and steel began to be used. In the 1880's the twine binder appeared.

Courtesy of the Henry Ford Museum, Dearborn, Michigan

An early reaper

By 1900, windmills, seed drills, manure spreaders, hay loaders, and hay forks had come into common use. The new kerosene lamps had appeared in nearly every farmhouse, and kerosene lanterns were used as the common light in barns.

All of these machines that had been developed by 1900 had made the farmers' work easier and greatly increased the amount of produce each farmer could raise. But as yet little power had been developed to replace the muscle power of mules, horses, and men. Steam had been tried but steam tractors were too heavy and large. The only successful development in the way of steam power for farm use was the steam threshing engine that was used at the turn of the century to run threshing machines. These machines, the steam engine and the threshing machine, were taken from farm to farm each fall so that each farmer's grain could be threshed.

Today less than half of the land in Michigan is classed as farm land. Michigan had her largest number of farms in 1933. In that year there were 200,000 farms in the state. They averaged ninety-two acres per farm. That was a slight decrease in size from the one hundred and one acres per farm in 1930. The amount of land in farms seems to have been the highest during the years 1935 and 1936 when about 18,500,000 acres were under cultivation. In 1959, only 16,467,000 acres were being cultivated. That means that over two million acres have been taken out of cultivation since 1936. In 1959 the number of farms had dropped to only 132,000 but the average size had risen to 129 acres per farm.

For many years hay* was Michigan's first crop in terms of value. But, since hay makes poor food for cattle and as the number of horses has decreased each year, less and less hay is grown. Today Michigan's hay crop ranks third in value as a farm crop, being surpassed by wheat and corn. The spring rains are favorable to hay crops, and the hot days of early summer permit the farmers to cure it before it is placed in barns for winter use as stock food. Most hay is used near where it is grown but some is bailed and shipped to other areas which need more feed for their stock. Hay is grown all over the state, but the southern counties are the largest producers. Sanilac is the leading hay-producing county. Other large hay-producing counties are Washtenaw, Lapeer, Hillsdale, Kent, and Ingham. Alfalfa is grown mostly in the Lower Peninsula and in Dickinson, Menominee, and Delta counties in the Upper Peninsula. In 1958, Michigan ranked fourteenth among the states in the production of hay. In that year Michigan farmers harvested 2,063,000 acres and produced 3,176,000 tons of hay.

Oats grow best on the heavier soils that hold moisture. Most of the Michigan crop is grown south of Bay City and Muskegon. The leading counties in oat production are Lenawee, Sanilac, Huron, and Tuscola. Oats are a good feed for livestock and are very good to use in crop rotation. Since 1925, the number of horses has grown smaller. With the decline in the number of horses there has also been a decline in the amount of oats produced. In 1959 Michigan ranked eighth among the states in oat production.

1948-57 average	47,625,000 bushels
Production 1957	40,882,000 bushels
Production 1958	53,856,000 bushels

Michigan, in 1958, ranked tenth among the states in the production of rye with 975,000 bushels, nineteenth in barley with 3,960,000 bushels, and fourth in buckwheat with 192,000 bushels.

Wheat, as has been shown earlier in this chapter, was one of

*Alfalfa, timothy, clover, etc.

Michigan's early cash crops. By 1880, Michigan ranked in fourth place as a wheat producer. During the years between 1880 and 1890 nearly two million acres were planted in wheat each year. During each of those years Michigan harvested about 30,000,000 bushels of wheat. As more and more wheat was produced in the western states, Michigan's crop for some years declined. During the past few years more wheat is again being grown in Michigan. Most of Michigan's wheat is now grown in the south central and southern part of the state and is what is known as winter wheat. It is sown in the fall, in areas where it is not apt to be killed by the cold of winter, and harvested late the following spring. Because of the colder winters, spring wheat is grown in the upper part of the Lower Peninsula. Spring wheat is sown in the spring and harvested in the fall.

(Winter)	Average	1948-57	32,935,000 bushels
	Production	1957	28,739,000 bushels
	Production	1958	41,800,000 bushels

When the settlers came to Michigan they found the Indians raising corn for a winter food. The settlers soon began planting better grades than the Indians had been growing. They were yellower and harder and had better keeping qualities. From the days of the first settlers in Michigan, corn has been an important crop. Corn was and is an important stock food. In the early pioneer days corn bread, or johnnycake as they called it, and mush were important food items on the settlers' tables.

Corn now is grown all over Michigan but does best, except in some local areas, in the area south of Clair County. To grow corn there must be at least 170 frost-free days. Corn does best where the nights are warm and humid. Michigan's southern counties are on the northern edge of what is known as the "Corn Belt." Lenawee, Hillsdale, Washtenaw, and Monroe counties are Michigan's leading corn-producing counties. Most of the crop is harvested as a grain. The stalks are often made into silage and used with the grain as a stock feed during the winter months.

Although corn is a valuable crop, it, like potatoes, tobacco, and cotton, is often a soil destroyer. Before any of these crops are planted, the ground is carefully plowed and prepared. Then the corn is planted in hills equal distances apart. After the corn begins to grow, it is carefully cultivated to keep the soil soft and free from weeds. Soil in this loose state is easily carried away by running water. The sudden thundershowers which come during the summer months flood the land faster than the water can seep into the soil. The excess water runs away, and as it goes, it carries some of the loose soil with it. Much of what was fine farm land a few years ago is now almost useless because of the fertile soil having been washed away from the surface. Grass crops such as wheat, oats, clover, timothy, and alfalfa are far better crops for soil conservation. Not only do they put valuable plant food elements into the soil, but their soddy roots also help to keep the fertile soil in place.

In 1958, Michigan ranked in ninth place among the states as a corn producer. Michigan is a large producer of popcorn.

All Corn

Average 1948-57	81,781,000 bushels
Production 1957	91,278,000 bushels
Production 1958	106,344,000 bushels

Another crop that was grown by the Indians was beans. It is now one of Michigan's leading crops. The fertile soil and temperate climate found in some areas of Michigan make it possible for Michigan to be a leading bean producer. Winter freezing kills the bean weevil. Most of the beans grown are navy beans but other kinds are grown as well. Huron and Tuscola counties are the largest producers of beans. Red kidney beans are grown in the largest amounts in Newaygo and Oceana counties. Bean acreage varies from year to year, and so does the yield per acre. Beans are very subject to weather changes. Wet springs cause the beans to rot. Rains during the ripening season often cause the beans to discolor and thus they lose their market value. Beans are grown throughout the state but mostly in the Thumb and Saginaw area. Saginaw has the largest bean elevator in the world.

Field Beans (clean)

Average 1948-57	4,105,000 bushels
Production 1957	3,508,000 bushels
Production 1958	5,199,000 bushels

Soybeans

Average 1948-57	2,668,000 bushels
Production 1957	5,192,000 bushels
Production 1958	6,095,000 bushels

Sugar cane was grown in Michigan up to and for a few years after the Civil War. Like most of the other crops it grew best in the lower part of the Lower Peninsula. From the crushed cane, the early settlers secured a syrup that took the place of sugar and added to the limited supply of maple syrup. Later developments in transportation and the cultivating of sugar beets have placed cheap sugar on the market, and sugar cane is no longer grown here.

In 1881 the state offered a bounty of two cents a pound for all sugar made from beets or cane grown within the state. In 1890 the Michigan State Agricultural College bought 1,760 pounds of beet seeds in Europe, where sugar beet growing had already developed on a large scale, and distributed the seeds to farmers who would plant the new crop. More seeds were later distributed. Now Michigan is one of the leading states of the union in the production of sugar beets.

The soft, sandy soil of Michigan, in some areas, is well adapted to the growing of sugar beets. Because the soil is soft, the growing beets can easily push it aside as they grow larger. In clay soils the earth sometimes bakes quite hard, and the growing beets cannot easily expand in size. Few beets are grown in the Upper Peninsula except in the area near Menominee.

To produce sugar beets requires not only good soil but also much labor. The small plants have to be thinned and weeded with care. To do this work many people are brought to Michigan beet fields

Courtesy Michigan State University

Storage piles of sugar beets (1937)

each year. Over the past years many of these people have come from central Europe and Mexico. Many of them are migrant laborers. Some have remained and added new nationalities to our rural population. Many of these people who came to Michigan as laborers, or their children, now own farms within the state.

Most of Michigan's sugar beets are grown in the Saginaw River Valley and the Thumb district. Tuscola, Huron, Saginaw, and Bay counties are the leading producers.

Michigan is not only a producer of sugar beets but also a producer of sugar as well. Michigan's first sugar beet refinery was built at Bay City in 1898. Today sugar beet refineries are located at several places in the southern and eastern part of the Lower Peninsula. Each of these refineries uses the beets that are raised near it. Beets are usually brought to the refineries by trucks but sometimes they are shipped in by train in large hopper cars. The pulp that remains after the sugar has been taken from the beets is used for stock feed.

Sugar Beets

Average 1948-57	718,000 tons
Production 1957	907,000 tons
Production 1958	1,112,000 tons

Leading Counties in 1958

Tuscola	269,610 tons	Bay	194,150 tons
Huron	218,750 tons	Saginaw	218,880 tons

Potatoes are a native plant of South America. Early colonists there sent the plant to Europe and from Europe it was brought back to the English colonies. Michigan's sandy loams, especially in the Upper Peninsula, are well adapted to potato growing. Potatoes, therefore, are one of Michigan's principal crops. In 1935, Michigan ranked third among the states as a potato producer, being surpassed only by Maine and Minnesota. Since that time, however, because of a potato blight, Michigan's potato production has declined. Each year, thousands of bushels of potatoes find their way from Michigan's farms to the cities of the nation. Unfortunately, potatoes, like corn, because they have to be cultivated, tend to let the sandy soil wash away.

Potatoes do best where the growing season is cool and moist and a soft loamy soil allows the growing potatoes to push the soil aside as they grow. The short growing season of the Upper Peninsula does not keep that area from being a potato producer. In fact, potatoes are an important cash crop in the Upper Peninsula as well as elsewhere in the state. In 1958 Michigan produced 8,745,000 hundredweight of potatoes and ranked tenth among the states.

Average 1948-57	7,564,000 Cwt.
Production 1957	6,660,000 Cwt.
Production 1958	8,745,000 Cwt.

Leading Counties in 1958

Montcalm	1,537,000 Cwt.	Presque Isle	474,000 Cwt.
Bay	840,000 Cwt.	Houghton	665,000 Cwt.

One of Michigan's special crops is mint. Peppermint was first set out on White Pigeon Prairie in St. Joseph County about 1835. For many years after that date the southwestern part of Michigan was the leading peppermint producer of the world. Mint has been found to grow well on the muck lands of Clinton, Shiawassee, and Van Buren counties. Spearmint and peppermint are grown and harvested in much the same way as hay. The freshly cut plants are taken to a small local distillery where the plants are placed in vats and put through a steaming process which releases the oil. The pulp, when dried, is used as a stock food. The oil is used to flavor medicine, chewing gum, candy, and cake icings. In 1958, Michigan ranked fifth among the states in the production of peppermint and second in spearmint oils.

Another of Michigan's special crops is chicory. Most of the chicory crop of the nation is grown in Michigan. Chicory as a plant looks much like the sugar beet and also does well in the same climate. The plant top grows from three to six feet tall and is used as a stock food. The large root is dried, roasted, and then ground. The ground root is sometimes used with coffee to give it a deep-brown color, a better aroma, and to make the flavor last longer. Most of the chicory is grown in the thumb district and the Saginaw Valley.

Small fruits and vegetables have, from the early days of settlement, always been a part of the crop produced on most farms. Because transportation was poor and these crops spoiled easily unless carefully cared for, each farmer grew these crops for his own family use. During the summer and early fall, fruits and vegetables were taken from the orchard and garden and eaten while still fresh. These were the only fresh fruits and vegetables most people ever got. As fall advanced, fruits and vegetables were carefully stored away in root cellars where they would be kept cool but not allowed to freeze. Some fruits, such as apples, plums, peaches, and berries, were dried and thus kept for use during the winter and early spring. Later, canning in glass jars with rubber rings and metal tops became a family task in most homes.

But as the years passed and the cities grew, there became more and more of a demand for fresh fruits and vegetables to supply the families that were beginning to live in the cities. Farmers found that they could, by using the better means of transportation that were developing, turn their fruits and vegetables into cash crops.

Areas where the soil and climate had special qualities soon began to grow selected crops for market. Most of the vegetables for the market are grown south of Bay City and Muskegon on the soils which are a rich sandy loam. Among the special crops are tomatoes, snap beans, cabbage, celery, asparagus, cucumbers, and berries.

Muskegon is the center for cucumber production. Kalamazoo is known as the celery center. Tomatoes are grown in the largest amounts in Berrien, Bay, Macomb, Wayne, Lenawee, and Monroe counties. Green beans are grown all over the Lower Peninsula. Mecosta, St. Clair, Oceana, and Montcalm counties are the largest producers. Snap beans grown here are canned in local canneries. Many melons are grown near Bay City. Early cabbage is grown by market gardeners in Allegan, St. Clair, Macomb, Wayne, and Monroe counties. Late cabbage is grown in the muck areas throughout the state and sold to sauerkraut factories.

Michigan is one of the leading states in the growing of small fruits such as strawberries, dewberries, blackberries, raspberries, and grapes. Berrien County, with about 180 frost-free days, is the leading producer. Good transportation makes it possible to quickly send the fresh fruit to the large Chicago market. Many grapes are grown in Berrien and Van Buren counties. Here the summer heat is strong enough to allow for the development of sugar in the fruits, which gives the fruit a good quality. The long mild fall lengthens the growing season and gives the grapes time to mature. Local markets for the fresh grapes, juice factories, and wineries give the farmers of the area a ready market for their crops.

Wild strawberries are a native crop in Michigan and grow in many parts of the state. They grew in such abundance, especially on the oak openings in the southwestern part of the state, that the feet of the settlers' cattle often were stained red from tramping on the bright red berries. About 1860, tame strawberries began to be grown near St. Joseph and Benton Harbor. The berries grew well

COURTESY HENRY FORD MUSEUM

With the coming of telephones many people were soon employed as switchboard operators. This early switchboard is from the period about 1900.

COURTESY HENRY FORD MUSEUM

These men are grinding grain at the Loranger Gristmill at Greenfield Village. The grain passes through the hopper and is ground into flour between the two burr stones.

COURTESY HENRY FORD MUSEUM

This is a typical kitchen in the 1890 period. Note the wood range for cooking, the small cistern pump for water, the wooden dishes and coffee grinder on the table, and the kerosene lamps sitting on the shelf. How does this kitchen compare with yours today?

Extracting peppermint oil along US-27 near St. Johns. Mint is one of Michigan's special crops. Photo 1939.

Another of Michigan's special crops is onions. This picture taken in 1939 shows an onion farm on US-27 a few miles north of Lansing.

This photo taken in 1910 shows how farmers at that time harvested their hay. Note the sling hanging in the front of the wagon for carrying the hay up into the barn, and also the hay loader drawn along behind the wagon.

Today tractors furnish much of the power used on farms. This photo, taken in 1957 near Mecosta, shows how modern farmers bale the hay in the fields before it is hauled into the barn.

Courtesy of Traverse City Chamber of Commerce

Cherry orchard in blossom

in the soil of that area. At first the ripe berries were shipped by boat to Chicago. This ready market for the ripe, fresh fruit caused a large increase in the acreage. Today Berrien and VanBuren counties are one of the leading strawberry-producing areas of the nation, but because of modern freezing and shipping methods many berries and vegetables are also shipped into the state, in the early spring, from Florida, Georgia, and Texas.

Peaches and pears are grown in the southwestern part of the state along the shore of Lake Michigan, in the area around Ionia, and the east side of the state from Monroe County to Macomb County. In Washtenaw County and Oakland County, fruit does well especially on the south side of slopes where the summer sun can ripen the fruit. The rolling country lets the cool air of late frosts in the spring settle to the bottom of the valleys and thus keeps the blossoms from being killed. Farther north, around Manistee, is the center of apple production. Still farther north around Traverse City is the center of cherry production. The highest cherry production is in the Grand Traverse region. Old Mission Peninsula is well known for its cherry orchards. This area is one of the largest producers of cherries in the United States.

The strip of land along the eastern shore of Lake Michigan is known as the fruit belt. Most of the fruit belt is a sandy loam and not very good for most crops. Beneath the loam lies a clay. Fruit trees push their way through the loam and into the clay.

Little fruit is grown on the High Plains Area. Here the late frosts of spring often damage the buds or blossoms. Some fine fruit is grown in the Upper Peninsula in Delta County, but most of that area is not suited to fruit production. The winters are cold, and killing frosts in the late spring often destroy the crop.

Fruits 1958

	Bushels	Rank		Tons	Rank
Apples	12,200,000	3	Plums	7,800	2
Peaches	3,200,000	5	Cherries (sour)	49,500	1
Pears	1,400,000	4	Cherries (sweet)	13,500	3
			Grapes	50,500	4

Commercial Vegetables Produced in Michigan

	1949-56 Average	1958	Rank
Asparagus (fresh mkt.)	20,600 Cwt.	21,000 Cwt.	5
Asparagus (processing)	6,201 Tons	6,600 Tons	2
Snap beans (fresh mkt.)	77,000 Cwt.	84,000 Cwt.	5
Snap beans (processing)	10,925 Tons	11,200 Tons	10
Lima beans (processing)	1,662 Tons	880 Tons	8
Red beets (processing)	7,362 Tons	8,400 Tons	4
Cabbage (fresh mkt.)	750,000 Cwt.	874,000 Cwt.	3
Cantaloupes (fresh mkt.)	262,000 Cwt.	234,000 Cwt.	1
Carrots	693,000 Cwt.	529,000 Cwt.	3
Cauliflower (fresh mkt.)	181,000 Cwt.	228,000 Cwt.	2
Sweet corn (fresh mkt.)	762,000 Cwt.	1,015,000 Cwt.	3
Celery, summer (fresh mkt.)	410,000 Cwt.	396,000 Cwt.	2
Celery, early fall (fresh mkt.)	536,000 Cwt.	468,000 Cwt.	1
Cucumbers (fresh mkt.)	65,000 Cwt.	60,000 Cwt.	4
Cucumbers (processing)	3,062,000 Bu.	4,145,000 Bu.	1
Lettuce, head (fresh mkt.)	145,000 Cwt.	208,000 Cwt.	4
Onions (fresh mkt.)	2,319,000 Cwt.	1,918,000 Cwt.	4
Green peas (processing)	4,417 Tons	6,300 Tons	13
Tomatoes (fresh mkt.)	704,000 Cwt.	722,000 Cwt.	1
Tomatoes (processing)	60,437 Tons	94,000 Tons	9

Number of trees and production of Michigan fruit for the year 1958

Number of trees bearing		Total Production
Apples	2,470,000	12,200,000 bushels
Peaches	1,746,000	3,200,000 bushels
Pears	745,000	1,400,000 bushels
Sour Cherries	3,420,000	49,500 tons
Sweet Cherries	380,000	13,500 tons
Plums	269,000	7,800 tons
Grapes (vines of bearing age)	8,800,000	50,500 tons

When the early settlers came to Michigan they brought with them horses, cattle, hogs, sheep, and poultry. At first it was hard to keep these animals from wandering away into the woods or from being killed by bears or wolves. But as time passed, farmers built barns and stump or split-rail fences to protect their stock and keep them from wandering away. Progressive farmers soon began developing better grades of cattle. After the Civil War, herds of Herefords, Aberdeen Angus, Holsteins, Jerseys, and Guernseys were all found on Michigan farms. The coming of the barbed wire fence in the 1880's made it easier to keep stock on the farms. Today electric fences are widely used by farmers to keep their stock confined.

During the period to 1900 most milk was locally used. Even village people often kept a family cow so that they would have a milk supply. Because milk spoils quickly and the means of transportation was slow, butter was often made at home or in a local creamery. Each family usually made their own butter in a home churn. This was slow, hard work. As better means of transportation developed, people began to depend more and more upon creameries to supply butter.

Beef cattle are found all over the state, especially in the area south of Bay City and Muskegon where the cost of feed during the shorter winter is less. In the upper half of the Lower Peninsula cattle tend to be greatest in numbers along the shore lines of the Great Lakes. Only a few cattle are found on the High Plains Area.

Many farmers, especially those in the southern part of the state, have developed large herds of dairy cattle to supply fresh milk for city use. The Detroit area alone uses well over one million quarts of fresh milk every day. To supply this large demand for fresh milk requires thousands of cattle and many people to care for them. Dairying in Michigan is therefore a large industry. Farmers living in the

Courtesy Michigan State University

Hauling milk and cream to a Michigan creamery (1937)

more remote districts of the state send their cream in cans to a nearby creamery where it is made into butter. Much milk is also made into evaporated milk.

Some of Michigan's milk is made into cheese. Once many small cheese factories were scattered over the state. Cheese making has remained a local industry. To develop a large cheese industry means standardization, and this is difficult in cheese making because the various areas produce various stock feeds, and these in turn cause a change in the flavor of the milk and thus of the cheese also. In 1958, Michigan produced 31,187,000 pounds of American cheese, 51,887,000 pounds of creamery butter, 131,795,000 pounds of evaporated milk, 29,162,000 gallons of ice cream.

Sheep were once more numerous in Michigan than they are today. Wool, besides being used in the home, was one of the leading cash crops one hundred years ago. At one time there were many small woolen factories in Michigan. Sheep today are found mostly in the central part of the state below Isabella County. Washtenaw and Lenawee counties are good sheep producers. In 1933 there were 1,035,000 sheep in Michigan, but by 1958 this number had declined to 424,000 head. In 1958 there were 332,000 sheep shorn, and Michigan produced 2,585,000 pounds of wool.

1947-58 average	432,000 head
1958	405,000 head
1959	424,000 head

Because hogs multiply quite rapidly, the early settlers depended upon them for much of their meat supply to replace the diminishing game of the forest. Hogs were often allowed to run in the woods so that they could feed on the mast beneath the trees. Fencing was a problem because they could usually root under any pioneer fence. The early varieties of hogs were usually of poor quality, being rather thin and tough from much wandering. But during the last one hundred years, new and better types have been developed.

Hogs are not raised in large numbers in Michigan because Michigan is not a large corn-producing state. The largest numbers of hogs are found in Lenawee, Hillsdale, and Monroe counties where corn production is the highest. Most of Michigan's hogs are grown in the two southern rows of counties. In 1959 there were 719,000 hogs in Michigan.

Horses first came to Michigan with the French settlers, but they were of the pony type and not the large work horses of the last century. Farmers moving in to settle the area brought the larger breeds from the East. After 1850, horses began to replace oxen on the farms for draft animals. From then until 1920 they provided most of the power used on farms. They were used for plowing and hauling. Specially bred driving horses were used on buggies for transportation to and from town.

The number of horses in Michigan reached its peak in 1917 when there were about 680,000. By 1930, after the coming of the tractor, truck, and automobile, the number had dropped to 381,357. By 1959 the number had dropped to only 33,000.* Because of this decline in the number of horses, many acres of land that once were used to grow feed for horses have been used to grow feed for cattle and other crops.

Bees are important to crop production because of the fact that they help in pollination. Honey bees, as we know them, were not native to Michigan but were brought here by the early settlers. In 1958, Michigan produced 8,525,000 pounds of honey.

Many chickens, ducks, geese, and turkeys are raised in Michigan. City markets create a demand for poultry and eggs. Poultry production is centered in two areas. One is close to Detroit in the Hillsdale, Lenawee, and Monroe county area. The other is in the Allegan,

* Horses and mules.

Courtesy Tractor and Implement Division, Ford Motor Company

Ford 10-foot self-propelled combine. Its 78-hp Ford six-cylinder engine allows rapid threshing of heaviest crops under all conditions. (1961)

Courtesy Massey-Ferguson, Inc.

MF 35 S P Combine. (1961)

Ottawa, Kent county area. Poultry production is closely linked with the growing of suitable poultry feed. Because of the lack of grains north of Bay City, few chickens are raised in the upper part of the Lower Peninsula or in the Upper Peninsula.

Livestock

	1947-57 Average	1959
All cattle	1,864,000	1,829,000
Milk cows (two years and over)	924,000	820,000
All hogs	771,000	719,000
Horses and mules	81,000	33,000
Sheep and lambs	432,000	424,000
All chickens	10,761,000	9,683,000
All turkeys	106,000	105,000

To provide better roads, the state legislature passed the county road act of 1893. This act made it possible for a county to create a road system. Better equipment could be bought. By 1890 there were only about two hundred miles of stone or macadam roads in Michigan. All the remaining roads were still mud or sand.

By 1900 there were many bicycles and a few automobiles. Those that owned bicycles and automobiles wanted to ride in the country and this meant that better roads had to be built. But better roads would cost money and that meant that the people of the cities would have to help pay for their cost. Bicycle clubs and automobile clubs began to work to get better roads for Michigan.

In 1905 the Michigan State Highway Department was started. Those who owned automobiles were required to register them. A state-wide system of highways began to be planned. By 1913 some sixty thousand autos were registered. In order to help pay the cost of building better roads, cars were to be taxed on their horsepower and their weight. A three-thousand-mile main trunk-line system was set up. In 1916 the Federal Government passed a Road Aid Act to help states build roads. As late as 1918, even main highways like US 16 and US 10 were still only gravel roads.

In 1925 a tax was placed on gasoline to get more money to build and keep in repair state trunk lines. Since 1934, this tax has been the main support of the state trunk-line system.

Today a system of state trunk lines spreads across the state. Each highway is designed, as well as it can be with limited funds, to carry the flow of traffic. Some are four-lane roads and still others are four-lane divided highways. These later highways carry traffic fastest and safest. Most of the main trunk lines lie south of Bay City and Grand Rapids.

The legislature in 1951 increased the gas tax for the purpose of financing the building of new highways and repairing those already built. The weight tax was also increased.

Rapid and easy transportation is now a part of our modern way of life. Today we have come to depend more and more upon our state system of highways. Each day hundreds of gallons of fresh milk are carried by special trucks to cities and creameries. Over our roads go the men in cars and trucks to carry on the work of delivering mail to people scattered all over the state. Today there are fewer Rural Free Delivery routes than there were in 1920 but their length has more than doubled. Rural Free Deliveries in Michigan alone cover some fifty-five thousand miles each day.

One of the main reasons for the decline of the railroads during the past thirty years has been the rapid advance in highway building. Today much freight is hauled by trucks. Millions of dollars are invested in the trucking industry. Modern manufacturers use trucks for shipping their goods to market and for bringing raw materials to their plants. Cement, drugs, salt, paper products, chemicals, automobiles, and furniture are hauled to market in trucks. This type of shipping can be handled by padding and the expenses of crating and repeated handling are eliminated. Trucks can go almost anywhere, even to the consumers' doors. These main highways also serve the farmers living in the state. Perishable products can be hastened to the market.

The farmer, as well as the manufacturer, has found that better all-year hard-surfaced roads have become a part of his way of life. Nearly all farmers own cars and most of them own trucks as well, especially in the fruit and vegetable growing districts where perishable products must reach the markets quickly. More and more of Michigan's livestock is going to market by truck. In this way a farmer can sell his stock quickly and take advantage of fattening and market prices.

Migrant laborers use highways to go from job to job as the seasons pass. Better fire protection is possible because better equipment can be hurried to the fire. All-weather roads have brought better police protection and education as well. Each day, during the school year, nearly seven thousand school buses pass over Michigan's highways, carrying Michigan's rural children to consolidated schools.

The Industrial Revolution has changed not only the farmer's means of marketing but also his manner of farming as well. Today, a modern farm represents a large investment not only in land but also in machinery. Most of Michigan's farms have electricity. This means that farm homes can have electric lights, radios, television, electric stoves, washing machines, ironers, sweepers, and electric pumps. Most barns in Michigan today have electric lights. To aid in his work, the modern farmer uses: barn cleaners, which carry the manure automatically from the barn and dump it into a manure spreader; mechanical milking machines, hydraulic hoists, tractors, grain combines, bailers, corn pickers, potato harvesters, sugar beet harvesters, electric water pumps, and silo fillers. These machines have increased the farmer's output 111 per cent in the past forty years. The Michigan farmer of today has most of the advantages of city life, and his children are getting an equal opportunity with city children for an education.

One of the many problems facing Michigan farmers today is soil conservation. When the forests were cleared from the land much of it, because it was hilly, began to quickly erode. Erosion was aided by poor farming methods. Fire, wind, and water have also destroyed much of Michigan's crop and forest land. But today farmers are becoming aware of this soil loss problem and are doing much to check it. New methods, such as contour plowing, check dams, cover cropping, strip cropping, reforestation, and setting out wind breaks, have done much to check erosion and to restore the land. Because of a better knowledge of soils and soil usage, farmers today are putting more elements back into the land. In 1958, Michigan farmers used 647,449 tons of fertilizer on their land. But this is still not enough. Some means must be developed where city wastes of sewage and garbage can be returned to the soil. More study must also be made on the effects of soil bacteria on plant life.

Some land not suited to agriculture has been returned to private forests known as tree farms. Many of these tree farms have been started here in Michigan and are already providing a large percentage of our Christmas trees. The trees help hold moisture in the ground and also provide shelter for birds and other animals that help the farmers in many ways. In the future these tree farms will help supply lumber to our children.

Michigan farmers today have the help of many organizations to aid them in their work. Michigan State University, located in East Lansing, teaches young farmers scientific agriculture, helps to develop better breeds of stock and crop varieties, carries on experimentation in soil fertilization, and carries on a large educational extension program throughout the state. In all of its program, it works closely with the United States Department of Agriculture.

The State Department of Agriculture was set up in 1921. Several former state agencies were then put under this new department. Since 1945 this department has been run by a five-man commission which is appointed by the governor.

Most counties in Michigan have a county agent who is a member of the extension division of Michigan State University. From him, farmers can get advice as to crops, soil, stock, and such services as the state and nation provide.

In 1875 the state legislature provided for the founding of the Michigan Grange or, as it is called, the Patrons of Husbandry. The Michigan State Grange operates as a part of the national organization. Many counties have a branch of this state organization. The Michigan Farmers' Union is also another farmers' organization.

In 1917 the United States Government started the 4-H club movement among young people living on farms. Today this movement in Michigan is directed by the extension service of Michigan State University in cooperation with the county governments. The 4-H clubs do much to teach young people about rural life in Michigan.

The Future Farmers of America is another national organization. It is made up of farm boys who are interested in studying agriculture. The Future Farmers of America carries on local, state, and national activities.

Many farm journals, including the *Michigan Farmer* which was first published in 1843, carry the latest farm news and reports into the farmer's home. Daily quotations on the radio give the farmers the latest prices and warn of the dangers of frost.

It is less than one hundred and fifty years since Michigan was a vast wilderness. In that time Michigan's farmers have changed much of that wilderness into farm land that gives Michigan one of her three largest occupations. In 1958 the principal crops and livestock grown in Michigan had a total value of $714,118,000. Government payments amounted to $25,592,000. In 1958 Michigan farmers thus received $739,710,000.

Chapter XVIII

CULTURAL AND POLITICAL GROWTH SINCE 1875

By 1875 many social changes had begun to appear in the way of life of the people living in Michigan. Ten years had passed since the Civil War had ended. People were beginning to forget the war and were becoming more and more interested in the new machines that were then beginning to be made. Most of the good farm land had been taken by this time, and people began leaving the farms and going to the cities where the men in the family could find work in the growing factories, and the wives and children could enjoy some of the new comforts that machines were bringing into people's lives. For many centuries there had been little change in the way people lived and did things. Now the new machines began to change people's lives both on the farms and in the cities. More and more machines were beginning to do much of the hard work that had before been done by men and animals. Steam engines were running

Courtesy of the Henry Ford Museum, Dearborn, Mich.

Visiting the country store about 1875

boats, trains, sawmills, gristmills, and factories. The new sewing machines began to relieve the women from the long hours they had spent in sewing. Men's clothing began to be machine-made and men began buying their clothing at the stores rather than having it made at home. Machine-made shoes began replacing shoes made by the local cobbler. The Civil War, with its standardized guns, shoes, and uniforms, had helped to bring this change about. Hundreds of patents were applied for at the United States Patent Office as inventive men and women developed new ways of doing things. Among the many inventors of this period was Thomas Alva Edison, who became known as the "Wizard of Menlo Park."

Thomas Edison was born in Milan, Ohio, in 1847. When he was seven years old his parents moved to Port Huron. In all his life Edison attended school for only two months. His mother, Nancy Edison, taught him to read and write. Then she let him follow his own interests. By the time Edison was ten years old, he was reading some of the best of the world's books. At this early age he became very much interested in science. He read many books on science and spent all the money he could earn buying chemicals with which to experiment.

To get more money for his experiments, Edison began to sell newspapers and candy on the Grand Trunk passenger train that ran between Port Huron and Detroit. During his spare time at Detroit, he visited the Young Men's Society and read many of the books in their reading room. Mr. Edison became especially interested in the progress then being made in the fields of chemistry and electricity. In the baggage car of the train, where he kept his papers and candy, Edison set up a chemical laboratory so that he could work on experiments such as those about which he had been reading. One day as the baggage car lurched, some of his chemicals were spilled. His newspapers and other things caught on fire. The fire was put out, but the disgusted crewmen of the train dumped Edison and his materials at the next station, which happened to be Smith Creek. This old railroad station now stands in Greenfield Village in Dearborn where Mr. Ford had it placed in honor of his friend, Mr. Thomas Edison.

One of Mr. Edison's first inventions was an automatic vote recorder. He also made improvements in the method of sending telegraph messages. Another early invention was a machine to be used in stock markets to record the sales that were made in stocks.

In 1876, Mr. Edison moved from New York, where he was then

living, to Menlo Park where he built a new experimental laboratory. In this little wooden building and its adjoining machine shop, Mr. Edison and his men, in the years that followed, made many inventions that have greatly changed our way of life. One of his first inventions at Menlo Park, made when he was just thirty-one years old, was the victrola or phonograph. At first his voice was recorded on a piece of tin foil wrapped around a metal cylinder that was turned by hand. Later thick flat discs made by Mr. Edison were used as records. A megaphone was added to the new machine to increase its sound volume. For the first time in history a sound could be recorded and reproduced.

In 1878 Mr. Edison began working on the electric light. After many trials he finally made a usable one. In 1881 Mr. Edison and his men successfully wired and lighted one square mile in New York City. Gas lights slowly gave way in the cities to the newer, safer, and better electric lights.

Mr. Edison also was the first one to invent motion pictures. His first motion picture was made in 1887. In 1889 he actually showed

Courtesy of the Henry Ford Museum, Dearborn, Mich.

Thomas Edison's experimental laboratory at Menlo Park, now at Greenfield Village. The light to which the arrow points was made by Mr. Edison on the fiftieth anniversary of the electric light. The chair is fastened to the floor just where Mr. Edison left it on that night in October, 1929.

a talking picture by working a motion picture machine and a phonograph at the same time. Mr. Edison also invented or improved upon the typewriter, telephone, and telegraph.

Other inventors, too, were finding out many things in the field of science and making new machines. People liked the new inventions that brought pleasure into their lives or saved them time and labor. The World's Fair which was held in Chicago in 1893 called people's attention to these new inventions.

If you visit Greenfield Village in Dearborn you can see the buildings in which Mr. Edison and his men worked at Menlo Park, for Mr. Ford had these buildings restored. Even the red ground on which these buildings sat while in New Jersey has been brought to Greenfield Village. Inside Mr. Edison's old laboratory can now be seen many of his first inventions as well as old tools and broken bottles that Mr. Edison once used in his work. Many of these relics were dug from the pile of waste that was thrown from the laboratory when it stood at Menlo Park.

Just as these new inventions were beginning to demand more steel, new discoveries of iron ore in Michigan and Minnesota made possible an abundant supply of the metal. Better boats, as we have seen, brought down an increasing supply of iron ore while trains, with their tracks now stretching across the nation, brought raw materials to the new factories and carried the new products to the growing nation.

Larger railroad engines and better coaches began to replace the little trains of the period before the Civil War. The earlier coaches had been made of wood and were heated by a stove that sat in the middle of the car. Those seated near it suffered from the heat while those nearer the doors suffered from the cold and drafts. The newer coaches were heated with steam coming from the engine's boiler, and they were thus heated more evenly. At first the railroad coaches had been lighted with candles, then with oil lamps, then with gas lamps; but with the coming of electricity they, too, soon had electric lights.

The railroads of this period had fences along their right-of-way. At the road crossings, metal cattle guards kept the cattle and horses from straying onto the tracks. At some of the most dangerous crossings, viaducts began to be built to reduce the number of accidents and to save life. Later, at other crossings, electric signals were installed to warn people of a train's approach.

At first the cars of a train were coupled together with huge chain links that slipped over a pin standing upright at each end of the car. These large chain links were heavy, and to couple or uncouple a car a brakeman had to step in between the cars. Often while uncoupling or coupling cars brakemen were injured or killed. To provide a better way of fastening cars together, the automatic coupler was invented. Each coupler fits into one on another car like the bent fingers of one hand hooked into the bent fingers of the other. Couplers are now made so that when an engine pushes one car against another the couplers automatically fasten together without someone having to step between the cars. A coupler can be unfastened by means of an iron rod that runs from the coupler to the side of the car. The automatic coupler has thus done much to reduce railroad accidents and provide better service.

Another improvement in railroading was the coming of the air brake. The first trains had had only hand brakes. When an engineer wanted to stop, he blew his whistle as a signal for brakes. Then a brakeman climbed over the tender and set the brakes on the first three or four cars. While he was doing this, another brakeman set the brakes on the last four or five cars. This was a slow and dangerous way to stop a train. Today the air brake has become standard railroad equipment. With the air brake, compressed air is carried from car to car by means of a hose. When the air is let out of the hose, it sets the brakes on every car on the train.

To keep the tracks clear of snow in the wintertime was often a huge task. In places where snow drifted deeply, snow fences made of boards were built to keep the snow from drifting onto the tracks. After a blizzard, huge snowplows, called "jumbos," pushed the snow from the tracks so that the trains could get through.

Surprising changes were also made in railroad engines. The first ones were crude machines having little power. These were followed by huge engines, weighing many tons, that were able to pull long strings of loaded freight cars at a high rate of speed. Whereas the early engines often had names, the engines of this period were given numbers. During the past ten years, most of these steam engines have been taken out of service and replaced by the newer diesel engines.

From the simple little cars of a century ago have grown many types of railroad cars to meet the changing needs of transportation. Boxcars, flatcars, gondola cars, drop-bottom gondola cars, hopper cars, stock cars, tank cars, poultry cars, refrigerator cars, sleeping cars, sight-seeing cars, chair cars, and baggage cars are all common on our railroads today.

Car ferries on the Detroit River presented many problems. They slowed up traffic and were often delayed because of ice and bad weather. To remedy this, the railroad engineers began to look for another way to get trains across the river. The river was too large to build a railroad bridge at that time. The land on both sides was too flat and low to provide height enough for a bridge that would allow the passage of the large lake boats. So, soon after 1870, work was begun on a tunnel that would let trains pass under the river. The workers had not gone far before they ran into sulphur, water, and quicksand. The work of building the tunnel was then stopped. In 1906 the Michigan Central again tried to build a tunnel. Using newer methods, the work was this time a success and the tunnel was completed on July 1, 1910. Today many trains running between New York and Detroit pass under the river through the tunnel.

In place of trying to bore a tunnel beneath the river bed, the railroad tunnel was built in a new and different manner. First a huge ditch was dredged across the river bottom from shore to shore. Into this ditch were then placed sections of a huge steel tube reaching all the way across the river. The tube was then covered with concrete. Since the building of this railroad tunnel, a tunnel and a suspension bridge, known as the Ambassador Bridge, have been built for auto traffic crossing the Detroit River.

The development of railroads in Michigan had two effects. With better transportation, natural resources were more easily moved to market. With the coming of the railroad, new markets were opened for farm crops. In the days of wagon transportation any farmer living a few miles from the lakes was cut off not only from supplies but also from any large market for his goods. Because of the railroads, farmers living in the interior of the state were able to market their crops not only in their own neighborhood but hundreds of miles away.

Michigan's longest mileage of railroad tracks was in the year 1916. Autos, trucks, and buses have, of late, cut into the railroad traffic. Today our railroads are undergoing still greater changes to meet this new competition. Little branch lines, that were run to lumbering towns, which now have lost most of their people or disappeared altogether, have been abandoned, and the tracks have been taken up. New rolling stock consisting of lighter cars with better bearings have also been produced. These changes have kept the railroads in their position as the main bulk carriers for land transportation.

Steamboats and trains were good for carrying heavy loads for long distances. However, there grew up a need for better transportation to various parts of a city and from city to city. To meet this need, street cars and interurbans were developed. At first, street cars were small and were pulled by horses. In 1886 the first street car line in Michigan and the third in the United States was built in Port Huron. This line was about one mile long.

In 1890 an interurban line was built between Ypsilanti and Ann Arbor. The builders of this line saw the growing need for personal transportation that was developing. They saw, too, that the number of young men attending the University at Ann Arbor was far larger than the number of young women, while at Ypsilanti there were far more young women than there were men attending the Normal College. The promoters of the line said that five hundred persons a day could be carried between the two places. This number was not idle fancy, for soon interurban cars were carrying over six hundred people each day between Ann Arbor and Ypsilanti.

The first ride over this line was a gala affair. City officials from Ypsilanti and Ann Arbor boarded the steam car at Ann Arbor and rode to Ypsilanti. The car and passengers arrived safely at Ypsilanti and only one farmer's barn had been set on fire. At first the interurbans were driven by steam but soon electricity was used as the source of power.

In 1895 an electric road was built from Mt. Clemens to Detroit. In 1899 an interurban line was run from Grand Rapids to Muskegon. The line from Ypsilanti to Ann Arbor was later extended until it ran from Detroit to Jackson, Battle Creek, and Kalamazoo. Most of the interurbans in Michigan ran out from Detroit to other cities such as Toledo, Jackson, Lansing, Saginaw, Bay City, and Port Huron. There were, however, lines in other parts of the state, with some built in the Upper Peninsula. In 1918 there were 1,747 miles of interurban lines in operation in Michigan.

The street car and interurban had their day and gave a much needed service to the people. They ran on regular schedule. Interurban cars ran every hour or two during the day and late into the night. This regular service from city to city made it easy for people

Courtesy of the Henry Ford Museum, Dearborn, Mich.

Cars changed the lives of farmers as well as city people. This picture was taken about 1914.

to go from one city to another. Many people left the city and went to live in the country. Each day, the bread winner of the family would go to the city on the interurban in the morning and return to his home on it at the end of his day's work. People who could not otherwise have gotten to the cities to trade came by means of this interurban service. This aided the development of the business sections of the cities.

Street cars* and interurbans thus rendered a service that roads and railroads could not give to the people. There soon came, however, a new means of transportation that was to drive the interurbans out of business and also take much of the passenger traffic from the railroads. This new means of transportation was the automobile and bus, made possible by the gasoline motor.

The automobile enabled the people of both city and country to go when they wished, where they wished, and as fast as they wished. Today the interurban lines and all the streetcar lines have been replaced by buses. From our cities stretch miles and miles of paved road over which each day run thousands of automobiles, buses, and trucks carrying people and freight from place to place.

During the years from 1875 to 1900, many changes came in the field of education. As Michigan grew in population and wealth,

* The last street car in Michigan ran on Woodward Avenue in Detroit on Sunday afternoon, April 8, 1956.

more colleges were started, more courses were offered, and more and better grammar schools were established for children. During the years from 1875 to 1915 the University of Michigan grew rapidly and several new colleges were added. The first to be added was the College of Dentistry in 1875. A College of Pharmacy was started in 1876 and a College of Engineering in 1895. In 1894 the University of Michigan offered its first summer school courses. In 1912 it opened its graduate school.

The Jesuit order of the Catholic Church founded a Jesuit college in Detroit in 1877. This college later became the University of Detroit. For many years this University was located on East Jefferson Avenue near Woodward. But by 1927 the University of Detroit had outgrown its buildings on Jefferson and six new buildings were built on a large new campus on the corner of McNichols Road and Livernois in Detroit. In 1881 the Detroit Normal College was started to train teachers for the Detroit Public Schools. In 1921 the name of this college was changed to the Detroit Teachers College.

Left: An early schoolhouse in Northern Michigan. This building sits a few miles south of Lovells. Right: An early schoolhouse near Hillman, Michigan. This picture was taken in 1928.

As lumbermen and settlers pushed into the upper part of the Lower Peninsula and the eastern part of the Upper Peninsula, grammar schools were started in the rural areas and the villages. Most villages of any size also had a high school. But, because of the migratory nature of the lumber industry, few colleges for higher learning developed in the area. At Big Rapids, however, Woodbridge N. Ferris started the Ferris Institute in 1884. For sixty-five years the Ferris Institute was run as a private school. Hundreds of young men and women, mostly from the upper part of the Lower Peninsula and the eastern half of the Upper Peninsula, came to the

Ferris Institute to finish their high school education, to take commercial training, or to prepare to go on to a college or university. In 1949 the Ferris Institute was offered as a gift to the state if the state would continue running it and did not change its name. This offer was accepted and on July 1, 1950, the Ferris Institute began to be operated by the state. Today it is a leading college in the field of pharmacy.

Because of the growing mining industries that were developing in the Upper Peninsula, the Michigan Mining College was started at Houghton in 1886. In 1897 the name of this college was changed to the Michigan College of Mines and in 1927 it was again changed to Michigan College of Mining and Technology. This college is located on a campus that covers one hundred and twelve acres. It also has a branch at Sault Ste. Marie. The program offered by this college is largely one of science and engineering. Located as it is in the heart of the mining region, Michigan College of Mining and Technology has become one of the best known colleges of its kind in the world. Alma College was also founded in 1886. Much of Alma College's support comes from the Presbyterian church.

Detroit during the period before 1900 was known for salt, seeds, oils, and the manufacture of railroad cars, carriages, parlor organs, stoves, drugs, and paints and varnishes. Michigan's largest city then boasted of having four miles of asphalt pavement. Passenger boats were running between Detroit and several lake ports. Day excursions to Walpole Island or Sugar Island were very popular especially among the young people of that time. By paying the ten-cent fare one could ride all day on the Detroit-Windsor Ferry, or the Belle Isle Ferry, if one cared to do so, and many did, especially on warm summer days.

Many large homes were built in Detroit and the other urban centers during this period. Some of these homes were made of bricks, but most of them were built of lumber which could then be easily bought from any one of Michigan's many sawmills. Houses of this period can usually be told by their size, their wide porches, their high ceilings, and their fancy windows and ornate trim. These were homes that were built by men who had made money in farming, lumbering, mining, or in the new growing industries.

Some of these houses had furnaces, but most of them had several stoves here and there about the house. Upper rooms were often heated during the winter by vents in the floor or ceiling so that

Courtesy of the Henry Ford Museum, Dearborn, Mich.

A typical living room of 1890. This is the living room in Henry Ford's birthplace now in Greenfield Village.

the warm air from below was allowed to rise to the upstairs rooms. Every house of any size had a parlor. The parlor was an extra living room which was used only on very special occasions. Usually the furniture in the parlor was stiff and uncomfortable. Here, on a table, one usually found a fancy-bound family album which was filled with pictures of members of the family. Often under the table on a shelf could be found a basket full of stereoptican views that were supposed to furnish entertainment to guests. There were few pianos during this period but nearly every parlor had one of the foot pump organs that were common in that day.

The living room, or sitting room as it was also called, often had a large false fireplace that had a marble front, but a stove was usually set up in the winter to heat the room. Often in these houses there was a large dining room in which one quite often found a large massive dining room furniture suite such as was then being manufactured. The best of the houses had a plate rail running around the dining room. On this rail, made of wood, the lady of the house placed her choice hand-painted china. The kitchen was the most used room in the house. It still had a large wood range but gas was beginning to be used in some cities. Here one found such new inventions as egg beaters, gas toasters, and iceboxes.

People had found that iceboxes kept their food from spoiling much longer. The cutting of lake ice in the wintertime became a major occupation in some communities. The ice was cut and then stored in large sheds where it was placed in sawdust. With the coming of summer, the peddling of this ice became a daily task in many communities. It was also used to ice railroad cars. Thus fresh frozen meats began to be shipped from packing houses to city markets. Later artificial ice was made and used. By 1930, mechanical refrigeration was beginning to replace lake ice and artificial ice as a means of preserving food.

Up to 1890 it was very common for men to wear beards. During this period, however, beards became less common. Men's suits were all made of wool and these suits were worn both winter and summer. Black or dark blue was the usual color. Derby hats were then the style. Shirt collars and cuffs were heavily starched and thus were very stiff. Socks were heavy, and shoes were quite pointed. The well-dressed man wore a vest and across the front of it, from one pocket to another, usually hung a heavy gold watch chain. From the chain was often suspended an emblem of some lodge or club to which the wearer belonged.

Young ladies of this period never went out alone or with a gentleman friend. They were always chaperoned whenever they appeared at a restaurant, theatre, ball game, party, or at the races. Even in their own living rooms someone had always to be present whenever a gentleman called.

Ladies' dresses were long and often dusty at the bottom, especially during bad weather. Stockings were black and shoes were high. Ladies' dresses had high collars of satin, linen, or lace. Often women wore tightly laced corsets that made them as thin around the waist as possible. Even when swimming, they were fully clothed. But dresses for women began to change with the coming of the bicycle. Bicycles soon put an end to bustles and also long full skirts that swished along the ground.

Monday was wash day. A few city folk were getting water from city water systems, but most women were still pumping it from a well. Clothes were often soaked overnight so that they could be washed more easily. Early on Monday morning women got up and began the task of washing. Washing was then all done by hand. Up and down the clothes were scrubbed on the hand washboard. A few hand-powered washers were beginning to appear, but as yet they were not successful, and they had to be worked by hand.

Tuesday was ironing day. Flat irons were heated on the cook stove in the kitchen. As fast as one would cool it was replaced by another that had been heating on the stove. Ironing, especially on warm days in the summertime was a hot, tiring job.

On Wednesday the women usually did their "darning" and mending. Thursday was somewhat of a rest day. Friday was house-cleaning day. With a dust cap on her head and a broom in her hands, mother or daughter swept the house. Most homes had carpets which were stretched tight and tacked on all four sides near the wall. Sweeping brushed off the top dirt but it also pushed some of the dirt through the carpet onto the floor. Once each year the carpet tacks were pulled and the carpet taken up. The floor was then cleaned.

It was in Detroit, in 1909, that the vacuum cleaner industry started. Fred Wardell, in that year, organized the Eureka Vacuum Cleaner Company. At first women did not like the new machines, but soon they learned that they did not stir up the dust like brooms did and soon many vacuum cleaners were being sold. After sweeping came the dusting. Then, too, there was always the stove to polish.

Saturday in most homes was baking day. Each housewife usually made enough bread to last her family during the following week. Some bread was then beginning to be sold in cities, but usually it was not thought to be as good as home-baked bread. Saturday night was bath night. After supper, as the evening meal was then called, water was heated on the kitchen stove. At bedtime a tub was brought into the kitchen, and into it was poured the heated water. The small children were usually bathed first. Then came the older children in their turn. Mother and dad came last. Bathrooms were beginning to appear in some city homes and new bathtubs with white enamel on the inside were coming onto the market. Inside toilets were beginning to be put in some homes.

Few foods bought at the store were wrapped. Sugar, coffee, and crackers came in barrels and were sold by being weighed out to each customer. Spices also came in bulk and usually had to be ground at home. Cookies came in cookie boxes and were usually handled by the storekeeper as he sold them to the customer. More and more food was beginning to be packed in tin cans.

In the period around 1900 there was a marked difference in the lives of people. Some had grown very wealthy and lived in large homes. They had many servants and rode in the finest carriages. Many of them began to travel in Europe and in other ways show that they were people with money. But many of them were people of little education. Though they had money, they lacked the true culture that comes with education, and often they showed poor taste in style, home furnishings, and in speaking. Operations were becoming more common, and many a person who had had this new experience entertained her friends by going into all the details of her operation.

Whereas a few grew rich, most of the people were poor. Many of them were newly arrived immigrants that had just come from Europe. Men worked ten to twelve hours a day and often received little pay for their work. City slums developed in the newly growing industrial areas. In the rural areas many families lived in poorly built homes. There was no social security or workmen's compensation. When men were injured or died, their families got along as best they could.

Courtesy of the Henry Ford Museum, Dearborn, Michigan

Two types of early bicycles. Bicycles like these were ridden about 1890. These men are resting their feet on a stone watering trough for horses.

Bicycles became common during the period from 1890 to 1900. Many of the first bicycles had one large front wheel and one small wheel in back. The rider usually rode on top of the large wheel, which he turned by pedals which were fastened to its center. Only young men rode these bicycles, but about 1895 the low, modern bicycle, known as the safety bicycle, with two wheels the same size, came on the market. Soon these new bicycles were being made for women as well as men. Workers, mail carriers, physicians—all rode bicycles.

Between the years 1890 and 1910 Michigan was in the bicycle age. Bicycles were then almost as common as autos are today. Men and women rode bicycles to and from their work and on week ends for pleasure. Bicycles were made by the hundreds at that time. Various sizes and shapes could be bought. Some were made for men while others were especially designed for women. Ladies' bicycles had special guards to keep their skirts from catching in the chain or in the rear wheel. Still other bicycles were made for two persons. Then there were yet others that could carry four, five, or six. A few were made that could carry as many as ten people. These bicycles were provided with a pedal arrangement for each person, although there was only one steering bar at the front end. On Sundays and holidays groups of people went cycling together into the country. They did not travel so far as people do today but they had, no doubt, just as much fun. But a bicycle had to be pedaled by the rider and that was hard work. Soon they were replaced by a new means of transportation, the automobile.

Comic strips were beginning to appear in the papers. Theatres were beginning to open for Sunday shows. In 1896 the first real movie was shown in the Detroit Opera House. It was a picture of a Mexican bullfight. Basketball also was played for the first time that year. Roller skating and croquet were both popular, and the people were also beginning to show some interest in baseball. Telephones began to be installed in more and more business places and in homes. In 1889 the ten-story Hammond Building, one of the largest buildings of the time, was built of masonry and was the wonder of Detroit. The coming of structural steel meant that larger buildings could be built. In 1897 the Bankers-Equitable Building was built around a steel frame. Inside were fireplaces to heat the rooms. These two buildings were torn down in 1955 to make way for the new National Bank of Detroit.

In the small villages and rural areas, life did not change as fast as it was changing in the growing cities. Sometimes a group of theatrical players stopped for a night or two and put on "Uncle Tom's Cabin," or some similar performance, in the town hall. But rural people and village people found most of their amusement in dances, bob-sled parties, ice skating, singing, clambakes, barbecues, and Sunday school picnics.

Life in the rural areas was still hard. The homes did not have the new conveniences that were coming to the cities. Most of the homes were still lighted by kerosene lamps. City stores were far away. But most farmers began to receive the Sears-Roebuck and Montgomery Ward catalogs and from them the farm families selected many of their needs, such as hats and dresses for the mother and the daughters, work clothes and Sunday clothes for the father and the sons, harnesses for the horses, and tools for working in the fields. Farmers also started receiving daily mail deliveries with the coming of the Rural Free Delivery that began to spread across the country at this time. Rural telephone lines also brought the farmers and village people closer together.

In 1891 the Detroit College of Law opened and the Y.M.C.A. began offering vocational classes. The Y.M.C.A. now runs a college in Detroit which is known as the Detroit Institute of Technology. Michigan's second teachers college was started at Mt. Pleasant in 1894 as a state normal school. In 1958, the state legislature changed its name to Central Michigan University. Michigan State College of Agriculture and Applied Science has also made many advances since 1875. In 1896 a School of Home Economics was started. A School of Veterinary Medicine was begun in 1909. Today this university has one of the best known colleges of veterinary science in the United States. Two other departments, Hotel Management and Police Administration, have also been added. In 1955 this college became Michigan State University. Today the campus of this university is one of the most beautiful in the United States. Several experimental farms are scattered over the state so that studies of crops, soils, and climate can be made. In 1958-59 over 22,000 students attended this university. Each year some fifty thousand people attend short courses or conferences sponsored by the university. Because it has an agricultural college, it runs on the basis of three terms each year.

In 1896, Suomi College was started in Hancock. This is the only Finnish Lutheran college in the United States. Northern Michigan College of Education was started at Marquette in 1899. Today this college campus covers some eighty acres. St. Joseph College and Academy at Adrian was started in 1900 and is taught by the Sisters of St. Dominic. Western Michigan University was started in Kalamazoo in 1904.

In 1917 the Detroit Junior College was formed when the first two years of college work were added to the high school program at Detroit Central High School. Soon many students were attending the new junior college. In 1923 the Detroit Junior College became the College of the City of Detroit and in 1925 this new college graduated its first class. More and more students came to the college especially for afternoon and evening classes.

In 1927 the Detroit City Law College was started and in 1928 the College of Pharmacy began. In 1934 the Detroit Teachers College, the Detroit College of Medicine and Surgery, the College of the City of Detroit, the Detroit City Law College, and the College of Pharmacy were all brought together as Wayne University. In 1956 it passed from Detroit to state control and is now known as Wayne State University. At the present time its full and part-time student body numbers well over twenty-five thousand.

After 1900 great changes took place in Michigan's system of education. More and more girls continued their education above the eighth grade. School programs began including courses in homemaking and industrial arts. Less attention was paid to the older classical subjects. In 1903 a law was passed allowing school districts to tax so that transportation to a high school could be given to pupils not having a qualified school in their district. In 1909 such districts were required to place this tax. In 1905 a law was passed requiring all children from the ages of seven to sixteen to attend school for nine months each year. In general the city schools were better than the village and rural schools.

Since 1900, higher qualifications for teachers have brought better-prepared teachers into Michigan's classrooms. During the years from 1900 to 1950 adult education became a large part of the educational program in many communities. More and more people began to further their education by attending these evening classes. Many people have attended evening classes so that they might qualify for citizenship. Others have taken industrial or hobby courses. Hundreds of students attend Wayne University and other urban colleges each evening so that they can earn a degree. Extension classes are conducted by several institutions of higher learning at villages far distant from their campus.

Since 1915 the junior college movement has expanded in Michigan. Junior colleges spread across the state make it possible for high school graduates to continue their education for two more years before attending a senior college. This movement has made it possible for many more people to get two more years of education and still live at home. If present trends continue, more junior colleges will be started, and more and more young people will avail themselves of this chance to further their education for at least two years after high school.

Michigan's schools have been paid for from several tax sources.

Local school districts have always been taxed for the support of schools. To this money has been added the district's part of the Primary School Interest Fund. Since 1946, one-sixth of Michigan's three-cent sales tax has been set aside to help support public schools. This money has been divided among the districts according to a plan adopted by the state legislature. The plan aims to give special help to those districts in most need. To these funds are added special grants from the state legislature. The Federal Government grants some special funds for industrial and homemaking teachers. In the school year of 1952-53 Michigan's schools received $468,517,000. The cost per pupil in the school year 1957-58 was $370.45. In that year Michigan had over one and one half million pupils in school. To teach these pupils, the state of Michigan hired 58,254 teachers. Education is the largest business of Michigan state government.

As Michigan has grown, many changes have come into her government. In 1908 the voters of Michigan adopted the third constitution for the state, and under its provisions and added amendments Michigan is governed at present. In 1920 the nineteenth amendment, permitting women to vote, was added to the Federal Constitution. Since that time, women have played an ever-increasing part in local, state, and national government. As Michigan's government grew, the old capitol building became too small to house the offices of the state government and another building called the Lewis Cass building was completed in 1928. This building now houses many of the governmental agencies.

As the settlers spread across southern Michigan and pushed in behind the lumbermen in northern Michigan, only a few gave any thought as to what kind of a land they were leaving for their children. Farmers often got all they could from the soil. Good crops meant plenty to sell on the market. Miners dug deeper and deeper into the copper and iron mines and measured their profits in pounds of copper and tons of iron ore shipped out. Lumbermen cut the forests but planted no trees to replace the ones they had taken.

Only a few people foresaw the results of this wanton destruction. One was Professor Kedsie of Michigan State University. As early as 1867 he warned against the "reckless and violent destruction" that was already going on. But such warnings were easily disregarded. Michigan was still a young state. Her population was small. There was still room for expansion and far more than enough for all.

The years from 1875 to today have witnessed the rapid exploitation of our natural resources in land, fish, forests, copper, iron, and petroleum. But slowly people have become aware that conservation of our natural resources is becoming more and more necessary. In 1873 the State Board of Fish Commissioners was established. The office of Game and Fish Warden was established in 1887. Our first state park appeared in 1895. By this time our forests were nearly gone and people were beginning to see the need of forests and parks for recreation as well as timber. In 1899 the state established a Forestry Commission and in 1903 our first State Forest was established. Thousands of acres of once virgin timber land, now stripped of its trees and its humus burned from the soil, were turned back to the state as useless land. Today, in our state there are 6,000,000 acres of state and national forest land. In this area the soils are again being slowly built up and new forests of second-growth trees, protected from damaging fires, are now growing on the land.

In 1908, President Theodore Roosevelt became interested in conserving the natural resources of the nation. The influence of President Roosevelt was felt in every state, and people began to be more conservation-minded. They slowly began to see that conservation does not mean hoarding our resources, but rather wise planning and use of our natural resources so that we as a nation can get the greatest use of them.

A State Park Commission was established in 1919. Our present State Department of Conservation was begun in 1921 when the state legislature combined the various commissions already established into the State Department of Conservation. At the present time the Department of Conservation is divided into several divisions. They are the Education Division, Field Administration Division, Fish Division, Forest Division, Game Division, General Operation Division, Geological Survey Division, Lands Division, and Parks and Recreation Division.

The work of the Education Division is to tell the people of Michigan of the need for conservation and what can be done about it. This is done by means of pamphlets, lectures, motion pictures, and radio programs. Special units on conservation are taught in the schools. Thus people are made aware of the need to keep our forests and streams clean for their own benefit and for the benefit of others, and of the danger and the ease of setting forest fires.

The Fish Division checks on fishermen to see if they have their licenses. They also see that fish are not caught out of season or that not more are caught than the law allows. The Conservation Department also operates several fish hatcheries where fingerlings are raised until they are large enough to plant in streams and lakes. Lake and stream improvements are also carried on under this division.

The Forest Division cares for our state forests. Today there are twenty-two state forest districts in Michigan. There are also five national forests. Once our forests were badly burned by forest fires, but today, because of public education and better means of fighting forest fires, damage is much less. Two million three hundred acres were burned in the year 1908. In 1954 only 3,384 acres burned. In 1958 nearly twelve thousand acres burned. Such forest fires are a tragic loss of timber resource for the state. Michigan uses the most modern

Courtesy of Michigan Department of Conservation

The Mayfield fire tower—one of Michigan's many fire towers

methods to fight forest fires. Fire towers are located throughout the forest areas. At the Forest Fire Experimental Station, at Roscommon, new methods for fighting forest fires are developed. There are 107 state forest camp grounds and seventy national camp grounds located in the state and national forest. Hundreds of people use these camp grounds each summer. The Forestry Division runs three tree nurseries where little seedlings are grown and then sold to people who wish to plant them. These nurseries are located at Manistique in the Upper Peninsula and at Higgins Lake near Roscommon, and west of Wolverine in the Lower Peninsula. Each year these nurseries grow some thirty million trees and shrubs. Two nurseries are also operated by the United States Forest Service in Michigan. One is the Chittenden Nursery located at Wellston. The other is the J. W. Toumey Forest Tree Nursery at Watersmeet.

The Game Division makes surveys of the amount of game in the state and recommends laws that will keep the game from being overhunted. Studies are made to see how game can be helped to live so that it can be harvested by trappers and hunters.

The Geological Survey Division is the oldest division in the department. It was set up in 1837. This division keeps a record of test drillings so that we will know more about the rocks underlying the state. It also aids in the use and conservation of our mineral resources.

The Parks and Recreation Division cares for our many state parks. There are more than sixty state parks and recreational areas in Michigan today.

To help in training people for the work of the Conservation Department a training school was set up at Higgins Lake in 1941. The work of the Conservation Department is paid for by money granted it by the state legislature and by fees collected for licenses for fishing, hunting, and trapping.

We have just finished fighting the greatest war in all human history. It has cost us much in lives, property, and natural resources. This victory was made possible because of our vast resources and our huge industries. To waste our resources not only takes them from future generations but also weakens our power as a nation. Minerals are not replaceable. Worn-out land can be partially restored, but mines remain as holes, silent, vacant reminders of minerals gone forever. In the days of our expansion and development there may have been some excuse for what now seems useless waste. But today the Conservation Department is helping us to better use our fast shrinking and much abused resources.

Courtesy Marquette County Historical Society

A group of iron ore miners around an air drill. Notice the boxes of Aetna dynamite. The men are wearing carbide lamps. This picture was taken about 1927 at the Barnes-Hecker mine in Marquette County. (1961)

This man controls all the trains underground in an iron ore mine. On the table in front of him is a map of the mine. He has small magnets he moves on the map to show the location of all of the trains all of the time. Contact with the trains is maintained by radio (in box behind man's head). Contact with the foremen up in the subs is by telephone (one he is talking on). Contact with surface plant, other levels, hoistman, etc., is by mine dial phone (hanging up on wall behind man's head—mouth and ear piece visible). (1961)

Courtesy Pickands Mather & Company

The Seul Choix lighthouse stands at the top of Lake Michigan, near Manistique in the Upper Peninsula, to warn boats coming north on Lake Michigan. Photo 1957.

Many canneries like this one at East Jordan prepare Michigan's fruits and vegetables for market. In these canneries asparagus, beans, cherries, tomatoes as well as other crops are prepared for your table. Photo 1957.

Part of the beneficiation plant at Republic. Today the steel companies are spending millions of dollars in building plants like this one to get iron from the lower grades of ore bearing rock. Photo 1957.

Portage Lake Ship Canal between Hancock and Houghton. This canal lets boats cross the Keweenaw Peninsula during periods when storms sweep across Lake Superior. Photo 1957.

COURTESY "STEELWAYS"

This is a picture of the jet piercer that is now used to make blasting holes in the hard low grade ore beds. It cuts much faster than a diamond drill.

This is a picture of the gypsum plant at National City. Gypsum, a mineral similar to salt, is used for making plaster and plasterboard. Photo 1957.

At Alabaster gypsum is carried off shore to the loading dock in these buckets. From the dock it is carried in freighters to plants where it is made into plaster and plasterboard. Photo 1957.

Making coke at the Ford River Rouge Plant. Natural resources and waterways like this one have made Michigan a leading industrial state. Photo 1956.

Chapter XIX

THE UPPER PENINSULA TODAY

South of Lake Superior and north of both Lake Michigan and part of the state of Wisconsin stretches a vast land known to us today as the Upper Peninsula. Once it was the homeland of the Chippewas. Today it is home to many peoples: Cornish miners, Scots and Scots-Irish, Finns, Swedes, Poles, and French Canadians. From this vast area, during the past one hundred years, has come much wealth from its lumber, copper, and iron ore. Although these resources still come from the Upper Peninsula, much of the wealth of the region has already been taken from it. Unfortunately for the Upper Peninsula, only a small part of the money that was made from its vast resources has remained in the Upper Peninsula.

The entire Upper Peninsula is today a huge vacation land, and each year hundreds of people come here to rest, play, fish, ski, or hunt. Tourists enjoy the clear streams, pretty lakes, and forest lands. They also like to visit the sites of former lumber camps, sawmills, and copper and iron mines. People coming to the Upper Peninsula usually enter it by way of one of four cities: Ironwood, Menominee, Sault Ste. Marie, or St. Ignace. Most people visiting the Upper Peninsula cross over to St. Ignace from Mackinaw City. From 1921 to 1957 the State Highway Department ran auto ferries across the Straits of Mackinac and all auto and truck traffic used these ferries. In November, 1957, the new Mackinac Bridge, one of the largest bridges in the world, was opened to auto traffic and the ferries ceased to run. Today auto and truck traffic quickly passes from one peninsula to the other. Each year hundreds of people come to Mackinaw City to cross over this huge bridge.

The Eastern Part of the Upper Peninsula

The eastern part of the Upper Peninsula is flat or gently rolling land. Like the upper half of the Lower Peninsula, it is a land of mixed soils and suited to agriculture in only local areas. Most of it is sandy plains, swamps, or marshlands. On much of the sandy soils there once grew spreading stands of pines that, as we have seen, drew the timber cruisers to the Upper Peninsula. For a few years this area was a busy lumber center, but when the forests were gone the people moved on to other areas. Just a few years ago this area was a cut-over, burned-over wasteland with scattered farms and declining villages. Today much of this area is state or national forest land, and new green timber stands are spreading across much of the land. Some of it is still farm land. Hay, grain, and the dairy industry are best adapted to the climate and soil of this locality. Few fruit trees are found in the area.

Between Big Bay de Noc and Munising spreads the Hiawatha National Forest. West of Whitefish Bay is the Lake Superior State Forest. South of it is the Mackinac State Forest that touches Lake Michigan from Brevort to Naubinway. South of Whitefish Bay and reaching down to St. Ignace is the Marquette National Forest.

Upper Tahquamenon Falls (1950)

In this area, along the south shore of Lake Superior, the Cambrian layer of sandstone, that underlies most of Michigan, comes to the surface. Rivers spilling over this rocky shelf make several pretty waterfalls such as the Tahquamenon Falls. Flowing eastward and northward into Whitefish Bay is the Tahquamenon River. This river is known as Hiawatha's river. In the Indian language Tahquamenon means "black waters." Before reaching Whitefish Bay this pretty river, running through extensive swamps and wooded lands, falls over the Cambrian rock ledge and gives to Michigan her largest waterfall. There are two falls, the Upper Falls and the Lower Falls. They are about three miles apart. The Upper Falls has a drop of some fifty-two feet and a width of two hundred feet.

Two main highways run east and west across the eastern part of the Upper Peninsula. M 28, a state highway, runs west from Sault Ste. Marie through the cut-over lands to Munising, on Lake Superior. Most of the way M 28 runs through what are now state and national forests. US 2, a national highway running west across the United States, runs southwest from Sault Ste. Marie to St. Ignace. From St. Ignace US 2 goes west across the eastern part of the Upper Peninsula through Manistique to Rapid River on Little Bay de

Noc. Much of the way US 2 follows the northern shore of Lake Michigan, and from it a traveler catches many beautiful views of the blue water and sandy beaches of Lake Michigan that spread for miles and miles along the way.

ST. IGNACE is today the major point of entry into the Upper Peninsula. Up to November, 1957, auto ferries and railroad ferries steamed across the Straits of Mackinac carrying automobiles, trucks, and railroad cars.* With the opening of the new bridge the auto ferries were retired from service. Today all autos and trucks use the new bridge in going between the Upper and Lower Peninsulas.

When one arrives at St. Ignace he sets foot on ground that has been trod by many Indians and famous Frenchmen, for to this place came Marquette, Cadillac, Tonty, Allouez, Joliet, DuLhut and many others when this area was a part of New France. Father Marquette founded a mission here at St. Ignace in 1671. St. Ignace, therefore, is the second oldest settlement in Michigan. After Marquette had founded his mission, the French became aware of the important location of St. Ignace and soon built a small fort here which they named Fort du Buade in honor of Governor Frontenac. To this area, called Michilimackinac, came the French *voyageurs* with their Indian friends in large, bark trading-canoes from across the blue waters of the Straits of Mackinac. Located as it was on the north shore of the Straits of Mackinac, Fort du Buade was for many years the major French outpost in the lake area.

Two hundred years have now passed by since the French traders and soldiers gathered for the last time at the little post. Not far from the shore, Marquette lies buried on the site of the little mission he once founded in the northern wilderness. The old French fort has disappeared, but memories of the past still linger and give a quaint charm to this busy little city in the Upper Peninsula. Where once the large French trading-canoes came quietly up to the sandy beach with their valuable loads of furs from the forest wilderness, for many years auto ferries came steaming silently into port from Mackinaw City across the straits. As soon as a ferry had docked, a steady line of autos, filled with happy people visiting one of America's best-known vacation lands, came off the lower deck of the ferry. When the last auto had left the ferry, others, which had usually been waiting in line, were driven onto the ferry. These huge ferries usually held about eighty or ninety autos. Again filled with a load of autos and people, the ferry slipped noiselessly, except

*Railroad ferries still carry railroad cars across the straits.

for a deep blast or two of its whistle, from dock. Soon its white form was seen against the deep-blue waters of the straits as it hurried south to Mackinaw City to pick up another load of waiting tourists.

During the lumbering days St. Ignace was a port city for the lumber trade. At one time iron smelters were also located here, but they closed down in 1900. Many of the people living at St. Ignace are the descendants of Indians or the early French settlers. For many years some of the people living here were engaged in commercial fishing. Near the city are farm lands where potatoes, hay, and dairy products are produced. Just east of St. Ignace can be seen Mackinac Island, while farther to the northeast are the pretty Les Cheneaux Islands.

Courtesy Upper Peninsula Development Bureau

Mackinac Island

MACKINAC ISLAND is one of Michigan's most beautiful islands. It is located in the Straits of Mackinac a little east of St. Ignace, and people crossing the straits on the new Mackinac Bridge can get a good view of the island. Mackinac Island, sometimes called "The Fairy Isle," is now a state park and is well known as a summer resort. Because of its historic interest, its beauty, and the fact that it is surrounded by miles of pure water, many people visit the island during the summer and early fall. People wishing to go to the island usually go by ferry from either Mackinaw City or St. Ignace.

Automobiles are not allowed on the island. Horse-drawn vehicles are the only means of transportation. Everything is moved just as it was in the days before automobiles. Horse-drawn sight-seeing wagons carry hundreds of tourists to the points of interest on the island each day during the busy summer tourist season. Several hotels care for summer visitors. Only a few people live on the island all year round.

Cut River Bridge on US 2 west of St. Ignace (1952)

Perhaps the most important tourist attraction on Mackinac Island is old Fort Mackinac which was built by the English at the time of the Revolutionary War. In 1781 the English moved their garrison from the old fort, at what is now Mackinaw City, to their new fort on Mackinac Island. It was this fort that the Americans occupied in 1796 when the island became American. It was here that the English surprised the Americans and captured the fort during the War of 1812.

There are many other points of interest on the island. The Grand Hotel, one of the best-known summer hotels in the country, is located here. For many years Mackinac Island was a fur-trading center, and today the old Astor fur warehouse, with its unusual large wheel for raising and lowering bundles of furs from the first to the second story, stands as a silent reminder of the days when furs were Michigan's major export. The restored Beaumont house keeps fresh in the minds of tourists the work that Dr. Beaumont did in studying the action of the human stomach. Dr. Beaumont was one day called to the fur warehouse to attend a trader who had accidentally been shot in the stomach at close range. When the trader's stomach wound was healed, a strange flap that never closed made it possible for Dr. Beaumont, for the first time in history, to look into a human stomach and observe the manner in which it functioned. Other points of interest on the island are Arch Rock Natural Bridge, Sugar Loaf, Skull Cave, Fort Holmes, and the oldest Protestant mission still standing in the Northwest.

NEWBERRY, in the Tahquamenon Valley, was once a lumber community. Some logging still continues, and lumber and wood products are still made. There are farm lands nearby. The Newberry State Hospital is located here.

From Newberry a hard-surfaced road leads to the Upper and Lower Tahquamenon Falls and from there on to Paradise on Whitefish Bay. East of Newberry is Soo Junction. From Soo Junction the "Toonerville Trolley" carries tourists, during the summer and early fall, over an old narrow-gauge logging railroad through forest lands to the Tahquamenon River. Boats then carry tourists down the Tahquamenon River to the falls. From Hulbert, just east of Soo Junction, the river trip can also be taken. The boats follow the winding river through the forest land of Hiawatha.

Northwest of Newberry on M 77 is Grand Marais. Many sand dunes line the shore of Lake Superior about one mile to the west. These dunes run along the shore for about seven miles. A Coast Guard station is located here.

West of Newberry on M 28 is the little town of Seney. During the lumbering days Seney was a busy sawmill town. South and west of Seney is the "Seney Federal Migratory Waterfowl Project." South of Seney on M 77 is Blaney Park, a well-known summer resort.

SAULT STE. MARIE is located on the St. Mary's River not far from Lake Superior. Before the white man came, this spot was a well-known meeting place for Indians who came here to fish in the rapids of the river for whitefish and trout. This area was first visited by Frenchmen in 1641, although Etienne Brulé or other fur traders may have been here before that date. In 1668 the Jesuits founded a mission here, and thus Sault Ste. Marie is not only the oldest settlement in Michigan but perhaps the oldest in the United States west of the Allegheny Mountains.* It was here that Simon Francois Daumont took possession of the entire Lake Region in the name of the king of France in May, 1671.

In 1823 the Americans built a fort here named Fort Brady. The settlement, however, remained small until the St. Mary's Falls Ship Canal was opened in 1855. Since that time it has grown to be one of the largest communities in the Upper Peninsula. Across the river, in Canada, is Sault Ste. Marie's sister city Sault Ste. Marie, Ontario. A ferry runs across the river between the two cities.

Each year during the shipping season, hundreds of tourists visit the "Soo" locks to see the many freighters pass through the busy locks. In the daytime one can see the huge 600-foot freighters as they steam

*See page 53.

along the St. Mary's River. At night their twinkling lights and the deep-pitched blasts from their noisy whistles give a new charm to the river so filled with memories of the days of the French missionaries and *voyageurs*.

Sault Ste. Marie has some industries. Hundreds of cottages line the nearby shore of Lake Superior and the St. Mary's River. A tannery makes fine grades of leather. Another industry produces carbide. A woolen mill makes mackinaws and clothing for hunters. The largest sawmill left in the Upper Peninsula is located here.

DETOUR is a small village located at the far eastern end of the Upper Peninsula on Detour Passage. Detour is the leading bunker port on the Great Lakes. Lake steamers, unlike ocean freighters, carry only a small supply of coal, as they are never far from a coaling station. This allows them to carry a larger paying cargo. Detour has been for many years a bunkering port at which passing freighters have refueled. From Drummond Island to the east across Detour Passage come shipments of limestone.

MUNISING is located on the south shore of Lake Superior about half way between Sault Ste. Marie and Hancock and Houghton. The high hills along the shore line, together with the deep-blue waters of Lake Superior, give Munising one of the most beautiful locations to be found in Michigan. A completely land-locked harbor provides a good port.

Just north of Munising lies Grand Island in Lake Superior. This island is kept as a game reserve. Large herds of deer and elk can be seen from along the wooded drives and paths that wind through the untouched forest lands.

The Pictured Rocks are located on the shore of Lake Superior about five miles east of Munising. They extend along the lake in a northeasterly direction for more than twenty-seven miles. These rocks are composed of Cambrian sandstone, and their present formations are the result of the ice action and wave action of Lake Superior. Oxide deposits have stained the rocks many hues that give them their beautiful reddish-brown color. Each summer hundreds of people take boat trips along the shore of Lake Superior to see these rock formations. Perhaps some day a state park can be made here so that more tourists can enjoy the unusual beauty of the Pictured Rocks.

Near Munising can be found nine waterfalls which are formed by streams spilling over the ancient rocks as they near Lake Superior. Unfortunately, better roads will have to be built nearer to them

Courtesy Pickands Mather & Company

This is a new experimental drill machine built by Ingersol-Rand & Company and paid for jointly by Ingersol-Rand and Pickands Mather & Company. The idea of the machine is to drill out a pattern of holes from one level in the iron ore to the next level (150′ to 250′). The holes would then be loaded from the top level, and a raise could be blasted out between levels without having to send men and machines up into a raise for each segment of advance. Plan on shooting up to 10′ of hole per blast. Holes are 4″ diameter. Machine drills 6″ per minute in granite. Photo taken in the Geneva Mine. (1960)

and better viewing conditions developed before some of the falls will be the tourist attraction to Munising that they should be.

Local industries in Munising now produce stationery paper, plastic-coated board, wax paper, box and crate material, and other wood products.

MANISTIQUE began in 1860 as a lumber sawmill town and port. From the large, spreading forests nearby, pine logs were floated down the Manistique River to the busy sawmills. At one time sawmills, docks, and booms extended several miles along the stream, but by 1900 even the hardwoods had been cut and the sawmills had nearly closed down.

Northwest of Manistique lie Indian Lake and the Big Spring, Kitch-iti-ki-pi. The Ojibway Indians called this spring "The Mirror of Heaven," "The Evening Star," and "The Boiling Cauldron." This spring is four hundred feet across and about forty feet deep. Each year many people stop at the state park located here and visit the Big Spring. A large raft, with an open well in the center of its deck, carries people out over the surface of the spring. Once over the moving water, one can see through the crystal-clear, cold water forty feet to the bottom of the spring and watch the icy water as it comes bubbling up from the sandy bottom, and thrill at the large trout as they swim lazily about the raft in the cold spring water.

Schoolcraft county has over 340 lakes. State forests and the Hiawatha National Forest spread north across the peninsula to the shore of Lake Superior. Today the remaining timber and the nearby stone deposits form the main basis of local industry. Newsprint, wallpaper, furniture, handles, brooms, and crushed stone are produced.

East of Manistique on the shore of Lake Michigan is Port Inland from which limestone is shipped. There is no community at the port. Most of the workers live in Manistique or Gulliver. Just south of Port Inland is Seul Choix Point, on which is Seul Choix Lighthouse at the top of Lake Michigan. Southwest of Manistique lies the Garden Peninsula with its pretty rock formations along the shore.

The Western Part of the Upper Peninsula

The western part of the Upper Peninsula is higher and rockier than the eastern part. Most of the land is covered by glacial till, but underneath lie the remains of the Killarney Mountains from which have come vast quantities of copper and iron. The outcroppings in this area of Michigan are one of the few places in the world where one can see and actually walk on rock that is millions of years old, for in most places it lies deeply buried under later land formations. The highest point in the state is in the Porcupine Mountains where at one point the land reaches to a height of 2,023 feet above sea level. East of Keweenaw Bay lie other highlands known as the Huron Mountains.

Much of the land is still covered by hardwood forests and some coniferous trees. Some sections, especially in the south from Iron Mountain and Gladstone south to Menominee, have developed into dairy regions, but the major industries of this part of the Upper Peninsula are still mining and lumbering. From Iron River north to Lake Superior spreads the huge Ottawa National Forest, the largest national forest in Michigan. Many pretty lakes—the largest of which is Lake Gogebic, the largest lake in the Upper Peninsula—are scattered throughout this area.

Throughout the western part of the Upper Peninsula stand many ghost mining towns near abandoned copper or iron mines that are now filled with water. The high-grade hematite iron ore has long since been dug from many of the pockets in which nature deposited it millions of years ago. Only a few of the iron mines are still in operation today. These mines are producing a high-grade ore which is often mixed with the lower grades of ore coming from the huge open-pit mines of Minnesota.

During the last century, iron ore from Michigan and Minnesota has supplied about seven eighths of all the iron ore used in the United States. This ore, together with the coal from the East, has made it possible for the people of the United States to live in the steel age that has become our modern way of life. But extensive as these deposits were, they are now nearly gone. Modern methods of mining and bulk handling of the ore are quickly depleting the remaining supply of high grade ore. Only a few years' supply remains to be mined and even this ore now has to be especially treated to meet the present standards of smelting. Every pound of ore passes through some treatment process today. With this rapidly diminishing iron ore supply in Minnesota and Michigan what, then, is the future of Michigan's iron ore region?

Hematite is a high-grade concentrate of almost pure iron ore. This is the type of iron ore that has been mined. Throughout Michigan's mining region, in Minnesota, and spreading northward into Canada north of Lake Superior, are vast quantities of a low-grade iron ore called "taconite."* This ore is found in very hard rock that was laid down during the Huronian Period and is known as the mother lode. It was from this lode, by a leaching process, that nature formed the

* Or "jasper" in Michigan.

deposits of hematite. This mother lode extends over hundreds of square miles around the western end of Lake Superior. It is about 25 per cent iron and lies in a layer 175 to 300 feet deep, and from it in future years must come our domestic supply of iron ore unless new high-grade deposits of iron ore are discovered.

Until recently, prospecting for iron ore deposits has been discouraged because mine owners were taxed on known reserves even though the reserves were not being mined. In 1947 the state legislature passed the Lindquist Bill which now exempts owners of mineral deposits from such taxation for ten years after its discovery or until the mine is in operation. This has encouraged diamond drilling, and no doubt new deposits of iron ore that do not come to the surface will be discovered in this manner.

But most of tomorrow's supply of iron ore mined in the United States must come from taconite. Mine owners, realizing this, began experimenting with this low-grade ore as early as 1916. Their success in freeing the iron ore from the hard rock was very poor, and about 1924 the experiments were stopped. World War II cut deeply into our already fast fading reserves, and again in 1942 experiments on taconite began. In 1943 the first black pellets of iron ore were made from taconite. Experimentation in developing a process to make it possible to use taconite has already cost the mining companies millions of dollars.

Courtesy "Steelways," published by American Iron and Steel Inst.

Taconite pellets

The mother lode is near diamond hardness, and ordinary drills cut into it very slowly. Today, however, a new drill called the "jet piercer" has been developed. The jet piercer burns a mixture of oxygen and kerosene and throws a hot jet flame at the rate of 6,000 feet per second. In an hour this flame can burn a nine-inch hole twenty to thirty feet deep into the hard rock of the mother lode. The principle used is the same as the Indians used in heating rock and thus causing it to chip off or flake. The hot flame from the jet piercer causes the heated rock to chip, and as it does, hot steam, forced into the hole with the flame, flushes away the flakes of rock as they break from the mother lode.

After holes twenty to thirty feet deep have been made, the rock is shattered by blasting. Then the shattered pieces of rock are crushed to the fineness of flour and thus the iron particles held in the mother lode are freed from the rock. If the iron ore is magnetic it can easily be gathered by magnets from the crushed rock. However, most of Michigan's iron ore is of a nonmagnetic type called "jasper." The iron particles are freed from this crushed jasper by a flotation process in which air bubbled through oil picks out the little pieces of iron ore. In this way a high-grade concentrate can be made from the vast low-grade mother lode.

The ore thus secured is formed into small balls, called pellets, about the size of a walnut. These pellets can be charged into a blast furnace. In 1948 the first pig iron was made by using only these taconite pellets.

In Minnesota large sums of money have already been spent in developing taconite processing plants. Here in Michigan work is being carried on at an old mine at Randville, twelve miles north of Iron Mountain; at the Ohio mine, two miles west of Michigamme; and at Republic, a few miles west of Ishpeming and Negaunee. The Michigan College of Mining and Technology is playing a leading role in this low grade ore research.

Already taconite is being used, but how will this new success in using low-grade iron ore affect the iron mining region? The answer to this question lies in the cost of production. It is now an expensive process to produce taconite pellets. Vast new deposits of iron ore have been uncovered in the Ungava district of Labrador. For the past few years mining companies have been building a new railroad, 300 miles long, through the hard old Canadian Shield from Seven Islands to the new mines. The high-grade iron ore is now coming south in ore cars to Seven Islands on the St. Lawrence River. At present it is being shipped to Atlantic seacoast ports. The new St. Lawrence Waterway now makes it possible for ore carriers to bring this rich Canadian iron ore from Seven Islands to the furnaces south of Lake Erie. Much of this iron ore will also find its way to the new smelting centers near Philadelphia. Another vast deposit of high-grade iron ore has been discovered in Venezuela, in South America.

Ore from Venezuela is now coming to the United States. New metals, too, such as titanium, aluminum, and magnesium hold unknown possibilities for the future.

But Canadian and Venezuelan deposits, vast and rich though they are, are foreign deposits and can be cut off from us in time of war. Most of our future domestic supply must come from taconite, and in that knowledge iron mining companies are spending millions of dollars to get the taconite mills in operation. Taconite is opening a new future for Michigan's iron mining district. Another unknown in the region is uranium. Traces of it have been found in mines at Champion and Gwinn. Some of this ore may some day be mined in the Upper Peninsula.

The Keweenaw Peninsula, known as the "Copper Country," juts northward seventy-five miles into the largest fresh-water body in the world and is one of Michigan's most scenic areas. In the upper part of the peninsula one can see the remains of the Killarney Mountains, which are now well-worn by glaciers and time. M 26 leads along the shore of Lake Superior past many pretty sand dunes. Farther toward the upper end of the peninsula the ancient rocky crags still stand against the rolling, pounding waves of Lake Superior.

Far out across the clear blue waters of the lake, like a phantom ship, can be seen on clear days the country's only island national park, Isle Royale. This island was discovered by Frenchmen and named after the king of France. Except for the damage caused by forest fires, little has been done to change the island from its native state. On the island is a large herd of moose that has increased under government protection. No automobile has ever been here. Its twenty lakes and streams are as pure today as they were when the Frenchmen first visited the island looking for furs and copper.

Prehistoric man once came to this island to dig copper from the rocky land. On the hard rocky surface of the island can still be seen the ancient pits from which copper was once taken. Many persons visit Isle Royale each summer to see these Indian copper mines. In the ancient pits can still be found many of the native stone hammers with which the aborigines once pounded out the copper they found wedged between the rocks.

Once, many copper mines along the Copper Range of the Keweenaw Peninsula were bringing copper from deep under the ground. Today only a few of these copper mines are still in operation. The busy days of the copper mines have passed. Today the Keweenaw

Peninsula is a beautiful vacation land. From the clear blue waters of Lake Superior come fresh, cool breezes free from dust or pollen. Driving into the peninsula, one passes old abandoned mines marked only by signboards which locate the scenes of the once-busy copper mining days.

State highways wind in and out through the forests that now cover most of the rocky land. At the top of the peninsula is the restored Fort Wilkins. Nearby is Lake Fanny Hooe with its tree-lined rock shore. Brockway Mountain Drive runs along the crest of a hard old mountain ridge. From a turn-out on Brockway Mountain Drive near Copper Harbor one can look far out across the deep-blue waters of Lake Superior and perhaps see in the distance a smudgy plume of smoke from a freighter as it pushes slowly across the lake with a load of wheat or iron ore.

Today, as we have seen in an earlier chapter, a few of the copper mines on the Keweenaw Peninsula are still mining copper, but the busy days of the copper mines have passed. World War II demanded vast quantities of copper, and prices rose. Some of the copper mines are now being dewatered and may again be put into operation. To pump the water from one of these copper mines often takes two or three years of steady pumping. Six miles south of Silver City is the White Pine Mine which was first opened by the Calumet and Hecla Company in 1906-1907. Later it was sold to the Copper Range Company. During the past few years the new White Pine Company, a subsidiary of the Copper Range Company, made the necessary arrangements to again open the mine. The White Pine Copper Company spent seventy million dollars to develop the mine, mill site, and town. Fifty-seven million dollars of this money was loaned to the company by the national government through the Reconstruction Finance Corporation. Fifteen million dollars of this money was used for building the new village.

During the past twenty years, many test borings with diamond drills have proven that much copper still remains in the Copper Range, but what the future of the copper towns will be is uncertain. Copper at present can be more cheaply produced from the low-grade ores dug in the open-pit mines of the West than it can be in Michigan's deep shaft mines. Price ceilings have kept the price of copper down, and it has been imported from Chile and Africa rather than being mined here in the state. At present a few mines are still in operation, and others are reworking the tailings that were thrown out many years ago. New processes of crushing the rock now make it possible to reclaim copper from rock once discarded as useless. Much of this discarded tailings is being raised from the bottom of Lake Linden near Calumet.

Perhaps some day, if the price of copper again makes copper mining profitable, other mines will be pumped free of water and again be operated, and newer mines in which copper is not so concentrated as in the older mines may be opened.

MENOMINEE is at the meeting point of the Menominee River and Green Bay. It is just a little above the 45th parallel which is half way between the equator and the North Pole. Across the river is Menominee's twin city, Marinette, Wisconsin. The Menominee River for some distance forms the boundary between Michigan and Wisconsin. Menominee is an Indian word meaning "wild rice." In Indian times the area near Menominee was well known for its wild rice and good fishing. Once it was the homeland of the Pottawattomie Indians before they moved to the southern end of Lake Michigan. When they left, the Menominees moved into the land. The Menominees left the area in 1854 and are now living on the Wolf River in Wisconsin. What few Indians there are in the area are again mostly Pottawattomies.

As early as 1796 a fur trader, Louis Chapee, built a fur trading post at the mouth of the Menominee River, but by this time the fur trading era was coming to an end. In 1832 the first sawmill in the area was built. Not long afterwards the Menominee River, the largest river in the Upper Peninsula, became the scene of huge log drives, and the city of Menominee was for a time the largest lumber shipping port in the Upper Peninsula. To its harbor came the lumber schooners, and from its sawmills went a steady supply of lumber for the market. In 1871, Menominee was partly damaged by the great Peshtigo fire which did much damage in Wisconsin, but like many other lumbering towns it was soon rebuilt.

Menominee is the most southerly city in the Upper Peninsula. Like St. Ignace, Sault Ste. Marie, and Ironwood, it acts as one of the gateways into the Upper Peninsula. Because of Menominee's location it is a meeting point of roads, railroads, and lake shipping. It is the western terminus for the Ann Arbor Railroad, which runs ferries across Lake Michigan and brings trains from Frankfort in the Lower Peninsula. Menominee is the natural distribution center for much of the Upper Peninsula and northern Wisconsin.

With the passing of the forests Menominee turned to other industries besides cutting lumber. Nearby are forest areas from which material is secured to make furniture, paper, boxes, containers, boats, paper board, wood products such as spoons, book ends, and novelties. The surrounding farm land produces a large yield of high-grade potatoes. Milk, butter, and eggs are also products of the local farms. In Menominee is located a factory which makes metal and wood furniture. Menominee also produces sawmill machinery, sugar, maple flooring, clothing, and toys. Like the other centers of the "Northland," Menominee is also a resort center. Many people from Wisconsin and Illinois come here to spend their vacations or pass through it on their way to other vacation centers of the Upper Peninsula.

ESCANABA takes its name from an Indian word which means "The land of the Red Buck." Escanaba is favored by a splendid location on Little Bay de Noc. Not only is it located on one of the best natural deep-water harbors on the Great Lakes, but it is also at the intersection of two highways, US 2 and US 41.

Lumbermen looking for pine came to Escanaba as early as 1830. For many years it was a lumber center, but in 1864 it became an iron

Courtesy Republic Steel Corp.

Iron ore may be taken aboard through as many as eight or more hatches at a single time. When the ore pockets in the dock are emptied, the ship is moved either forward or backward to permit a new set of ore chutes to be lowered into place and the pockets emptied. (Escanaba, Michigan)

Courtesy Ford News Bureau

Ford operations at Iron Mountain, 1948

port when iron ore from the mines of the Marquette range began coming to the port. Trains have for many years brought the iron ore to be loaded on the ore boats. Escanaba and Marquette are the two iron ports of Michigan. At one time Escanaba was called the "Iron Port of the World."

For sometime Escanaba was called the "Bird's-Eye Maple Veneer Capital of the World," for nearly all the bird's-eye maple used in making furniture came from near Escanaba. This industry was made possible by the fact that nearly all the world's supply of bird's-eye maple is located within one hundred miles of this city. Escanaba is also the home of the Upper Peninsula State Fair. This fair was started in 1928. It is held near the last of August each year. The usual agricultural displays, livestock exhibits, horse-pulling contests, 4-H Club contests, together with birling contests and other forms of entertainment make the Upper Peninsula State Fair an outstanding attraction for Escanaba.

GLADSTONE is just north of Escanaba. It was founded in 1887. Once it was a lumber town. It is now a woodworking center making hardwood flooring, veneer, and plywood. Hunting and sports equipment are also manufactured.

IRON MOUNTAIN was an iron mining and sawmill town. With the discovery of iron ore on the Menominee range, the Chapin Mine made Iron Mountain a booming town after 1879. Today most of the nearby timber is gone, and the high-grade iron ore is greatly diminished. The deep underground mines have nearly all closed. The Chapin Mine is now filled with water. Today Iron Mountain is an industrial town making engineering equipment, gray iron castings, and sportswear. Nearby is Fumee Falls, and Schultz Rapids and Piers Gorge in the Menominee River.

Here at Iron Mountain, on Pine Mountain, is located the highest all-artificial ski scaffold in the world. The tower is 156 feet high. Iron Mountain is a winter sports center. Every winter a ski tournament is held. The present distance record is 316 feet—made by Jim Brennan in 1960.

KINGSFORD is a very close neighbor of Iron Mountain. In 1921 Mr. Henry Ford began buying forest lands near Iron Mountain to get timber to make auto bodies. For some time the Ford Motor Company operated a sawmill and chemical plant at Kingsford. All the Ford and Mercury station-wagon bodies were made here. The Ford Motor Company sold its holdings at Kingsford in 1951. East of Iron Mountain and Kingsford lie the mining towns of Norway, Vulcan, Loretto, and Quinnesec. Quinnesec is the oldest village on the Menominee range. At one time iron ore was hauled from it to Escanaba in wagons and sleighs.

IRON RIVER developed after the discovery of iron ore in the nearby region in 1851. Because of the low quality of the iron ore, lumbering for several years remained the major industry. Northwest of Iron River on US 2, on the west side of Golden Lake, is Camp Filibert Roth, the University of Michigan School of Forestry and Conservation. Near Iron River are located the mining centers of Mineral Falls, Stambaugh, Caspian, Gaastra, and Crystal Falls. Farther west of Iron River on US 2, in a heavily forested area, is Watersmeet. From this point the run-off rain water drains into Lake Michigan, Lake Superior, or the Mississippi River.

IRONWOOD is located farther to the west on the far western edge of Michigan where US 2 crosses over into Wisconsin. It is the largest of several mining towns located on the Gogebic range. As one drives about these mining towns, one can see the old shaft-houses where the skips used to dump the ore that they had brought up from far below the ground, and the large trestles that carried the ore cars out to the stock piles. Mining was begun here in 1885. Because of the deep shafts in the steeply titled mines, very expensive machinery was necessary and much underground tunneling was required. The first iron ore from this region went to Erie, Pennsylvania, by way of railroad to Milwaukee, Wisconsin. In 1885 the Milwaukee Lake Shore and Western extended its line to Ashland, Wisconsin, and completed an ore dock at Ashland. After that date all ore from the area moved to Ashland, Wisconsin.

Courtesy Michigan Conservation Department

These men are loading powder into holes drilled up through the back of a slice in an iron ore mine. The man you can see has both hands on a piece of flexible plastic tube which has been pushed up through the lagging and void above it and on into the drill hole. Without this tube the second man—holding a piece of powder on the end of a charge stick—could not get the powder into the hole. (1961)

IRONWOOD is a wholesale center for the area. Some lumber is still produced. Many pretty waterfalls are found along the Black and Presque Isle Rivers as they flow over the rocky area toward Lake Superior. West across the Montreal River is Hurley, Wisconsin. US 2 passes on west of Ironwood through northern Wisconsin to Duluth, Minnesota, and then on west across the United States.

East of Ironwood are the old mining centers of Bessemer, Ramsey, and Wakefield on the Gogebic Range. At Bessemer woodworking plants turn out varied products. At Wakefield one can now see the old open pit mine that is now abandoned and partly filled with water

MARQUETTE, one of the largest cities in the Upper Peninsula, is located on a good harbor on Lake Superior. It became a village in 1859 and was named after the French missionary Father Marquette who had visited the region nearly two centuries before. In 1868 a fire destroyed much of the little town, but its location as a shipping center was favorable and the town was soon rebuilt.

Marquette's location on Lake Superior makes it a natural shipping center. For over a hundred years the red iron ore from the nearby mines at Ishpeming and Negaunee has come to its ore docks. When the opening of the St. Mary's Falls Ship Canal made it possible to ship iron ore direct to the lower port cities, the little trickle of ore that had found its way to the port at Marquette on wagons and sleighs greatly increased in volume. Railroad cars were soon bringing the ore to the dock by the trainload. Each shipping season, some iron ore still goes rumbling down the huge chutes of the ore docks into the empty holds of waiting freighters. There are two huge ore docks at Marquette. The dock of the South Shore Railroad is in the lower harbor while the dock of the Lake Superior and Ishpeming Railroad is in the Upper Harbor. Today these huge docks can load about 18,000 tons of iron ore into one of the huge ore boats in a few hours. To this port also come each year a half million tons of coal from the coal fields south of Lake Erie. During the winter season a heavy snowfall covers the area and Lake Superior freezes, but with the coming of spring another busy shipping season begins.

Marquette is also a college town. Here is located Northern Michigan College. Some of the buildings are made of brownstone that was quarried at L'Anse in 1914. Presque Isle public park is a local tourist attraction. Here at Marquette is also located the Upper Peninsula branch of the Michigan State Prison. This prison cares for about eight hundred prisoners. The Cliffs Dow Chemical Company, a branch of the Dow Chemical Company of Midland, is the world's largest producer of charcoal products. Local industries also produce foundry machinery, women's clothing, dairy products, core and diamond drills, and mining machinery.

ISHPEMING and NEGAUNEE are the two oldest iron mining towns in Michigan. Both of these mining centers are named from words in the Indian language. It was near here that Mr. Burt's surveyors first discovered iron ore on the Marquette range in 1844. Here on the Marquette range has been mined some of the most valuable high-grade iron ore in the world. The range has given us much of the ore that has done so much to make the United States a great nation. Both shaft mines and open-pit mines have been operated in this area. The Mather A shaft at Ishpeming is the largest underground iron mine in the United States. Each year over one million tons of high-grade ore are shipped from this shaft alone. Two miles away in Negaunee is the Mather B shaft. Shaft B has not been

Courtesy "Steelways," published by American Iron and Steel Inst.

Rod mills at Ishpeming

as well developed as shaft A, but shaft B is expected to increase production in the next few years.

The nearby forests are still being lumbered. The agricultural products of this region are potatoes and milk. The snowfall here is very heavy, and this community has become a winter sports center. Ishpeming's ski-jump, "suicide hill," is the scene of an annual ski meet held by the National Ski Association.

M 28 runs west from Munising to Ironwood. Many good views of Lake Superior can be seen from the highway as it winds through the forest lands. Just south of Marquette, M 28 is joined by US 41. At Marquette the highway turns inland from the lake and passes near the iron mining towns of Ishpeming and Negaunee. Then it pushes west along the Marquette range. Just west of Ishpeming and Negaunee is Humboldt, where a plant has been built to make taconite pellets. Farther west is Champion, Lake Michigamme, and the old mining center of Michigamme. To the north of the highway can be seen the Huron Mountains that so far have not been crossed by a state highway. West of Michigamme, M 28 goes west to Ironwood. US 41 turns north and runs through pretty wooded country to L'Anse and Baraga at the southern end of Keweenaw Bay.

L'ANSE is located on L'Anse Bay, a part of Keweenaw Bay. The Celotex Corporation has a large plant here that now uses large quantities of pulpwood that is cut in the nearby area.

BARAGA is named after Bishop Baraga who did parish work among the whites and missionary work among the Indians about a hundred years ago. Baraga County once produced slate and brownstone. It was formerly a lumbering area with mills at L'Anse, Baraga, Skanee, and Pequaming. A few years ago much of the standing timber was owned by the Ford Motor Company, which ran sawmills in the area. The company, however, has now sold its interests and moved out of the area. Nearby, there are many small farms. On leaving Baraga, US 41 runs north along the west shore of Keweenaw Bay and then swings inland along Portage Lake to Hancock and Houghton.

HANCOCK and HOUGHTON are twin cities, each one standing on one of the steep hillsides along the Portage Canal. These are two old copper mining centers, and today one can see the old shaft houses of the abandoned copper mines that spread deep down under the two cities. Between the two cities runs the Portage Lake Ship Canal. During stormy weather on Lake Superior many ore carriers use this waterway rather than go around the dangerous rugged shore of the

Courtesy Copper Country Vacationist League

Milling plant at the Calumet and Hecla mines when the copper mines were being worked in the Calumet area.

Keweenaw Peninsula. At Houghton is located the Michigan College of Mining and Technology. This college is one of the best of its kind to be found anywhere in the world. Near Hancock, at Ripley, tourists can explore an old copper mine. The Arcadian Mine there is the only one in which tourists are allowed to see any of the old underground workings. North of Houghton and Hancock the Keweenaw Peninsula pushes out into Lake Superior.

CALUMET and LAURIUM were once well-known copper mining cities. Here one of the richest strikes in the copper range was made. Farther north are the little villages of Eagle Harbor, Eagle River, and Copper Harbor. At the top of the peninsula stands the restored Fort Wilkins which was built in 1844. As one drives along the highway through the woodlands of this pretty peninsula, one passes by many abandoned mines from which copper was once dug far underground.

The Keweenaw Peninsula is one of Michigan's prettiest summer playgrounds. The air coming from across Lake Superior is nearly free from pollen and is pleasantly cool. From the highway and at the copper port towns one gets pretty views of Lake Superior, "The Shining Big Blue Water." Lake Superior is crystal clear and varies less than five degrees in temperature from winter to summer.

South of Houghton, on M 26, one goes south along the southern end of the copper range. Here in this wooded country one finds the old mining centers of Greenland, Mass, and Rockland. Turning northwest on US 45, one comes to Ontonagon.

ONTONAGON is on the south shore of Lake Superior at the mouth of the Ontonagon River. It was from this river that the Ontonagon Boulder was raised. Here also the first copper mine in the Upper Peninsula was started. Much copper from the mines to the southeast once passed through Ontonagon. West of Ontonagon is Silver City. This village was the center of the silver mining activity of the early 1870's. South of it today is the White Pine Mine and Lake Gogebic, the largest lake in the Upper Peninsula. From Silver City the highway, running along the pretty shore of Lake Superior, leads west to the Porcupine Mountains. Much of this area is still covered with virgin forests that spread across the rolling mountains. Here in the Porcupine Mountains State Park many footpaths lead through the virgin forests. Not far from where one parks his car on the shore of Lake Superior one finds the remains of the old Carp Lake Mine and the Lake of the Clouds, which is the highest lake to be found in Michigan.

Chapter XX

THE CHANGING NORTHERN PART OF THE LOWER PENINSULA

Sixty years ago only wealthy people took vacations and visited the newly developing resort areas in northern Michigan. In those days their personal things were carefully packed into a large trunk or two and the trunks hauled by a horse-drawn dray to the village depot. The vacationers then took a train to a northern resort hotel that was usually a large wooden building with wide porches that were trimmed with fancy woodwork. It stood near one of the larger lakes and not far from the railroad tracks. Once there, there was little for the vacationers to do and hardly any place for them to go, for as yet there were no automobiles or good roads. Of course they could sit on the cool front porch and rock and visit with the other guests who were also staying at the hotel. If they grew tired of this, they could walk through the village or along the beach. Then there was bathing—that is, if one were properly clothed in a long heavy bathing suit. Only a few of the more hearty ventured closer to nature and went tenting overnight or for a few days.

The new changes in modern transportation that have come since 1900 have had much effect on the northern part of the Lower Peninsula and on the Upper Peninsula. Men do not work as many hours now as they did fifty years ago. Many people are given one, two, or three weeks' vacation each year. People today like to spend their free time in traveling or at a summer vacation area. Each year hundreds of people from other states come here to see our industries, Great Lakes, freighters, mines, and forested lands. Each year many people leave Michigan to travel in other states.

Our modern automobiles, highways, and motels make it possible for people to travel long distances and see many of America's scenic spots. People can come and go when and where they please. They can start when they want, stop when they wish, and when they get where they are going they have their car for local transportation. Trunks, to the modern tourist, are as out of date as the old one-horse dray that pulled them to the village station fifty years ago. Automobiles make it possible for many people to get away from the hot cities even on week ends during the summertime. Each week end during the summer the roads of the upper part of the Lower Peninsula are lined with cars filled with happy people going to the "Northland" to spend a few days, and with cars carrying people home from a holiday in northern Michigan.

Michigan's industries, mines, and agriculture are centered in somewhat local areas, but the tourist industry is one that is shared by all of the state. Today the tourist industry is Michigan's second largest industry. It is the largest industry in the upper part of the Lower Peninsula and in the Upper Peninsula.

Each year hundreds of people come to the area between the three cities of Bay City, Muskegon, and Mackinaw City to spend their vacations. The short distance of this area from the large cities in the southern part of the state and in northern Ohio, Indiana, and Illinois, where millions of people live, makes it possible for many of these people to spend a week end here or to come for all of the summer.

Several good highways run north and south throughout this area. US 23 follows the shore of Lake Huron from Bay City to Mackinaw City. M 33 runs north from Alger through state and national forests to Cheboygan. US 27 runs north from Mt. Pleasant to Mackinaw City. This highway passes near four of Michigan's largest lakes: Houghton Lake, Higgins Lake, Burt Lake, and Mullett Lake. Much of the way it runs through cut-over lands that are now state forests. M 66 runs north from Ionia to Charlevoix. People traveling this road pass through the old lumber towns of Lake City, McBaine, Kalkaska, and Mancelona. US 131 runs north from Big Rapids through Cadillac and Petoskey to Cross Village. From the highway near Cross Village one can see, on a clear day, Beaver Island, North Fox Island, and South Fox Island lying some thirty miles to the west in Lake Michigan. Much of the drive from Petoskey to Cross Village is through a hardwood forest area and is thought by many people to be one of the prettiest drives in the state. US 31 runs north from Muskegon. At some points it touches Lake Michigan. From Traverse City north it follows the fascinating shore of Grand Traverse Bay and Little Traverse Bay. In this area it passes by three of Michigan's largest lakes: Elk Lake, Torch Lake, and Lake Charlevoix. Several highways run east and west across the state. Hundreds of picnic tables are set in pretty spots along the highway or in roadside parks. During the busy days of summer they are usually used by people who pack picnic lunches to eat along the way.

From early spring to late fall, especially on week ends, hundreds of cars speed along these highways carrying happy people into Michigan's vacation lands. Many new motels, cottages, and resorts care for the hundreds of people that visit the area each year. Because these highways are kept free from snow and ice in the wintertime, this area has become an all-year-round recreation center. There are many reasons why people come here each year. Some come because of the cooler weather. Some enjoy swimming, fishing, and canoeing. Others like to hike through the forest areas and perhaps take pictures of the animals they find there. Each fall many come to hunt. Winter brings its snow and cold weather, and hundreds come to ski, snowshoe, and toboggan.

Sixty years ago the upper part of the Lower Peninsula was a land of dying lumber towns and burned-over forest waste lands. The hundreds of lakes and many miles of streams were seldom visited because it was not easy for people to get to them. Today this area is a green forested area. Because of the work of the Department of Conservation, new second-growth trees have taken their stand in the old cut-over areas and spread along the highway as far as the eye can see.

Along the shores of the lakes and along the banks of the many clear, cold streams that run down from the High Plains Area to the Great Lakes now stand hundreds of cottages and cabins where people spend their vacations. These cottages, cabins, and motels have greatly increased the taxable property of the area and replaced the economic loss suffered with the passing of the forests. Vacationers also spend much money in the area. This money passes from person to person and helps to bring good times to communities that were declining after the timber was cut. Many little towns that were once sawmill towns are scattered through the area. Today they are resort centers. In this area there are also many camps for boys and girls. Some of these camps are privately owned. Others are run by church groups, Boy or Girl Scout organizations, the YWCA, or the YMCA. State parks, county parks, and city parks provide camping places and recreation areas.

In the springtime people come to the area to see the fresh, soft green colors of the forest lands and the hundreds of wild flowers that spring up in the damp soil. When school is out there is a rush of people into the area. Many pass through it on their way to more distant places, but hundreds stay all during their vacations. Some swim or sun themselves on sandy beaches, go surfboard riding, yachting, or sailing. Others fish, golf, play tennis and shuffleboard, or go horseback riding. All enjoy the natural beauty of the woods and waters and the cooler temperature. The wildlife of the woods attracts others. Canoe trips and float trips bring pleasure to those who enjoy wooded streams. Others like to drive through the rolling forest lands and enjoy the pretty sunsets of the long summer evenings. Some like to pick wild berries.

When fall comes, nature seems to quickly tire of her green summer colors. The frosted or aging leaves of the hardwood forests suddenly take on their brilliant fall colors. Then the rolling hills are radiant with flaming reds, oranges, and yellows that stand out against the lasting darker green of the evergreen trees. Hundreds of people visit this area on week ends in the fall just to see the brightly painted forests. Fall also is the hunting season, and many come at this time to hunt deer, fox, bear, ducks, and geese.

Winter brings its snow and cold. Most of the summer cabins stand deserted, but cars still roll along the highway bringing people who like to ski, snowshoe, skate, or fish through the ice of the frozen lakes. Special trains bring people to the winter sports' centers during week ends. Others like to hunt the large snowshoe rabbits. Some come here to hunt bob cats. This sport is becoming more and more popular as a winter sport.

The Saginaw and Bay City Area

Once the homeland of the Sauk Indians from whom the city of Saginaw takes its name, the Saginaw Valley became during the early lumbering days one of Michigan's leading lumber producing areas. After the forests had been cleared from the land, many of the workmen who had saved money from the lumber industry invested it in the fertile farm land they found in the river valley. This valley, known as "The Garden Spot of Michigan," with its low, flat, rich land is one of the most productive farming areas in the state, and some of Michigan's best farms are to be found in this locality. Many farms produce sugar beets while others specialize in truck gardening, navy beans, or small grains. The many small streams that flow into the Saginaw River drain the central part of the state. Nearby is Saginaw Bay. The twenty-one-foot-deep channel of the Saginaw River makes it possible for some lake freighters to reach Bay City and Saginaw. For many years Bay City and Saginaw were busy shipping centers sending huge quantities of fresh-cut lumber to market.

Today these two cities act as receiving ports for the area. This is especially true of Bay City. To it come shipments of coal, limestone, gasoline, and fuel oil that are used in the nearby area.

BAY CITY was once a busy sawmill town. When the local supply of timber was cut, hardwoods were, for many years, shipped into the city to keep the sawmills running. But as the timber to the north disappeared, Bay City took on a more general industrial character. One of its earliest and best-known industries manufactured bicycles. Bay City now produces railroad equipment, industrial cranes, steel freighters, luxury yachts, auto parts, magnesium castings, electric furnaces, welding machines, power shovels, wood products, and cement. One hundred fifty-four vessels were made here for the navy during World War II. The local sugar beet refinery is one of the largest east of the Mississippi River. A meat-packing plant processes meat that has been produced in the Saginaw Valley and on the farms lying farther to the north. Textiles and ladies' hose are manufactured. The nearby sandy shore of Saginaw Bay provides an excellent setting for bathing beaches, cottages, and camping grounds. Many people come to this area each summer season. While many people find Bay City a resort center, others, from farther north, find Bay City a convenient retail center.

SAGINAW, during the last ten years, has been one of Michigan's most rapidly growing cities. Today it is a city that has many industries and produces many different products. General Motors Corporation has plants here that produce parts for General Motors cars. The Lufkin Rule Company manufactures rulers and measuring devices.

Although Saginaw is a city of diversified industry today, it has a long and varied history. Before the white man came to Michigan, it was the homeland of the Sauk Indians. When the Frenchmen came here, they found Chippewas living in the area. In 1816 Louis Campeau built a fur trading post here so that he could trade with the Indians for their furs. It was Mr. Campeau's friendship with the Indians that helped Governor Cass make the Treaty of Saginaw with the Indians at Saginaw, in 1819, that opened a large tract of land in this area to lumbering and settlement. In 1822 the United States Government established a small fort on the west side of the river. In 1834 a Mr. Todd built an inn and began running a ferry across the Saginaw River. In that same year Mr. Harvey Williams built the first sawmill in the Saginaw Valley. For many years there was much rivalry between East Saginaw and West Saginaw. Finally in 1889 the two cities, on the opposite sides of the river, united to form the present city of Saginaw.

For several years Saginaw was a leading producer of white pine lumber, but by 1885, when the pine in the river valley was almost gone, Saginaw turned to cutting hardwood and manufacturing articles made from it.

Each year much beet sugar is manufactured from the beets grown in the nearby fields. The Saginaw Valley is also well known for its bean production. The largest bean elevator in the world is located here. About one third of the nation's bean crop is handled at Saginaw. For many years Saginaw was a producer of salt. Refuse from the busy sawmills was used to evaporate the water from the salt brine that was pumped from underneath the city. Today little use is made of this salt brine except in the Midland area.

At one time coal was produced in this area, but today all of the coal mines have ceased operation. No commercial coal has been mined since 1946. Now only local noncommercial mines are used.

The Eastern Side of the Upper Part of the Lower Peninsula

Just north of Bay City the good soil of the Saginaw River Valley changes to sand and swampland. Most of the upper half of the Lower Peninsula is a land of light soils. Farms are scattered throughout the area on the better soils, but most of the land is forest land. In the area along the shore of Lake Huron from Bay City to Cheboygan are many old sawmill towns. Today limestone and gypsum form the basis of the major industries. One railroad, the Detroit and Mackinaw, passes through this area. Alabaster and National City are centers where gypsum is now quarried.

TAWAS CITY, EAST TAWAS,* AU SABLE, and OSCODA were once sawmill towns. Au Sable and Oscoda, at the mouth of the Au Sable River, cut and shipped more than a million board feet of lumber. But when the logs stopped coming down the river, the twin towns declined. In 1911 a forest fire swept in upon the towns. It took several lives and burned most of the buildings.

West of Oscoda, on a high bluff of the Au Sable River at an old rollway where pine logs once went splashing into the river, now stands the Lumberman's Memorial which is dedicated to the memory of the lumbermen who once made Michigan a leading lumber producer. It is composed of three figures: a riverman holding a peavey in

*In 1958 a new dock was built by the National Gypsum Co. at East Tawas so that gypsum can be shipped by that company.

his hand, a woodsman holding an ax and a crosscut saw, and a land looker, or timber cruiser, studying his map.

Today dams on the Au Sable River produce electric power for the nearby area and for cities farther to the south.

ALPENA is the largest city in the northeastern part of the Lower Peninsula. This city, like others on Michigan's shore line, owes its location to a natural, partly landlocked harbor, a rich forest hinterland, and the mouth of a large river. Later, spur railroad lines made it possible to transport the heavier hardwoods to Alpena's sawmills. Today pulp and paper industries make paper products from the pulpwood secured from the nearby forest area.

Four times Alpena was almost destroyed by fire, but each time new sawmills and houses were built on the ashes of the old, and lumber continued to be cut and shipped away. As the timber supply declined, new occupations developed. Farmers found the local clay and loam productive and developed farming areas. Today hay, potatoes, raspberries, and strawberries are the major crops.

Where once the local forests supplied the main raw material for

Courtesy Michigan Limestone, a Division of United States Steel Corporation

This is the stone processing plant of Michigan Limestone. Here the quarry stone is crushed, screened and washed and separated into the various sizes required by customers ranging from a fine sand-like product to the 5½ by 11-inch stone used by steel mills in open hearth furnaces. (1961)

the area, today limestone is the basic raw material for the major local industries. Several limestone quarries are now found near Alpena. One of these quarries is over a mile long and one and one-half miles wide. Large privately owned docks from which limestone and cement are shipped are located east of Alpena on Thunder Bay. Here also coal shipments are received for use in the local area. Shipments of limestone from Alpena began as early as 1903. By 1914 the amount of limestone and cement shipped had reached as high as one million tons a year. The Wyandotte Chemicals Corporation of Wyandotte secures much of its limestone from this area. Much limestone is also shipped away to be used in refining iron ore and making chemical products. Shale is quarried a few miles west of the city. Limestone and shale are used to make cement. Here at Alpena, the Huron Portland Cement Company operates one of the largest cement plants in the world. Lake shipping makes it possible to ship the cement to other lake ports, and thus greatly reduces the cost of transporting this heavy commodity.

Alpena also manufactures cement blocks, gray iron castings, rustic fences, leather, air hydraulic cylinders, and cotton and woolen goods. The National Guard air base is located here. Each year members of this force spend two weeks here in training.

Nearby are several large lakes: Black Lake, Hubbard Lake, Long Lake, Grand Lake, and Fletcher Pond. These lakes and many smaller ones, together with the rivers, the shore line of Lake Huron, and the Alpena State Forest of nearly twenty-four thousand acres, make the area a busy resort and recreation center.

To the west are located the two former lumber towns of Atlanta and Lewiston. To the northwest lie Millersburg, Onaway, Posen, Metz, and Hawkes. All of these towns helped to make Michigan's lumber story. In 1908, when huge forest fires swept this northeastern area, Hawkes, Metz, and Posen were completely destroyed. North of Millersburg is the Ocqueoc Falls in the Ocqueoc River. East of Onaway is also found Rainy River Falls. In this entire area the winter hunting of snowshoe rabbits, fox, and bobcats has become a major sport.

Just east of Rogers City, at Calcite, high-grade limestone is being quarried by Michigan Limestone, a Division of United States Steel Corporation, for use in blast furnaces and chemical industries. Limestone is used in the manufacturing process of many things, such as steel, paper, glass, leather, soaps, and paints. Crushed limestone also acts as a soil sweetener and is used by farmers to improve their land. Much of this limestone formation is used in the manufacture of cement.

The Northern and Northwestern Cities of the Area

With the passing of the lumber industry, this region turned as early as 1900 into a resort area. Besides the waters of Lake Michigan there were also Grand Traverse Bay, Little Traverse Bay, and many beautiful inland lakes such as Mullett, Burt, Crooked, Walloon, Charlevoix, Torch, and Elk. Railroads, then feeling the decline of the logging era, were pleased to get the new tourist traffic and often ran special trains to resort centers. Lake resort areas near the railroads soon built hotels and cottages to care for the summer guests. Three resort centers developed in the northern and northwestern part of the Lower Peninsula. The first one is the area of Mackinaw City and Mackinac Island. The second one is found around Petoskey and the Little Traverse Bay area. The third one that developed in this section was in the Grand Traverse region around Traverse City. The many lakes of this area, the cool breezes from Lake Michigan, the rolling hills with their hardwood forests, and the pretty sunsets all helped to develop this area into one of Michigan's major resort areas.

CHEBOYGAN was a busy sawmill port town during the days of falling timber and whining saws. In 1890 as many as twenty ships at one time were here loading lumber from its nine sawmills. When the local supply had been cut, much timber was rafted to Cheboygan from the Upper Peninsula and from Canada. But as the supply of timber declined, so did the city. Today Cheboygan is a resort center. Close by are Black Lake, Mullett Lake, and Burt Lake, as well as several attractive streams. Hundreds of cottages and summer homes line their banks. During the summer months Cheboygan is a busy tourist and resort center. Some lake fishing is still carried on. During the summer a ferry runs from Cheboygan to Bois Blanc Island which lies to the north in the Straits of Mackinac.

MACKINAW CITY, on the Straits of Mackinac, lies at the northern tip of the Lower Peninsula. It was here that the Indians captured the fort from the English during Pontiac's Conspiracy. A few years ago a model of the old fort was rebuilt. This wooden stockade, standing just west of the Mackinac Bridge, is now an attraction to many tourists. At one time Mackinaw City was a lumber center. For many years Mackinaw City was the southern terminus for the auto, as well as the railroad, ferries that crossed to St. Ignace in the Upper Peninsula. During the summer tourist and fall hunting seasons thousands of autos left Mackinaw City on the auto ferries for the Upper Peninsula. Ferries from here still carry people to Mackinac Island. Today a new bridge carries autos and trucks between the Upper and Lower Peninsulas. Mackinaw City is the northern point of three railroads: the New York Central, the Detroit and Mackinaw, and the Pennsylvania. Railroad-car ferries carry railroad cars across the straits between the two peninsulas. West of Mackinaw City, on Waugoshance Point, is Wilderness State Park.

PETOSKEY is located on the south shore of Little Traverse Bay. The bay received its name for the French *voyageurs* and means "the little crossing." Petoskey is the distributing center for Charlevoix, Cheboygan, and Emmet counties. It is surrounded by beautiful rolling hills and forested areas. On Little Traverse Bay and on many of the lakes nearby are hundreds of summer homes and cottages. During the summer months the population of this area more than doubles. Besides being a resort city, Petoskey is also a manufacturing center. The cement plant here produces about six million sacks of cement every year. A tannery produces leather. Auto parts, furniture, wooden novelties, butcher blocks, maple tables, radio cases, paper twine, and stampings are also made by local industries.

On Little Traverse Bay, one mile from Petoskey, is Bay View, a well-known summer resort. As early as 1876 Bay View was the site of religious meetings. In 1886 these gatherings became known as the Michigan Chautauqua Assembly. Each summer programs under the direction of the Bay View Assembly are held here. On the programs appear many of the nationally known musicians and speakers. Albion College offers several summer classes here each year.

On the north shore of Little Traverse Bay is located Harbor Springs, one of Michigan's most fashionable summer resorts. From this point a scenic road follows the Lake Michigan shore line of Emmet County through the old homeland of the Ottawa Indians. At some points the road, overlooking Lake Michigan, runs along the top of a two-hundred-foot sandy bluff. The entire area from Little Traverse Bay to Sturgeon Bay is known as L'Arbre Croche from the French, meaning "the crooked tree." It is so called from the fact that at one time *voyageurs* going north from the south shore of the bay headed their canoes in the direction of a large crooked tree that then stuck out along the northern shore.

Good Hart and Cross Village are old Indian settlements. A large white cross now stands on the lake shore at Cross Village at the place where French Jesuits once came to work among the Indians. It is said that a cross has stood on this site for two hundred years.

Northeast of Petoskey is Conway, on Crooked Lake. North of Conway are the old lumber towns of Alanson, Brutus, and Pellston. Pellston often records the lowest temperature in the Lower Peninsula during the winter. South of Petoskey is Walloon Lake, a well-known summer resort since 1900.

CHARLEVOIX was once called Pine River, but its name was later changed to Charlevoix in honor of a French priest of that name. In the early days its location between Lake Michigan and Lake Charlevoix made it a lumber port, but now Charlevoix is an important resort center. Each year nearly five hundred small pleasure craft enter its harbor on Round Lake. From it, a ferry runs to Beaver Island every day during the summertime.

Beaver Island is the largest of a group of islands lying in the northern part of Lake Michigan. On this island a group of people who belonged to the church of the Latter Day Saints once made their homes. These people are often spoken of as Mormons.

About 1850 there were about a thousand Mormons, together with fishermen and woodcutters, living on Beaver Island. James Jesse Strang was their spiritual leader; therefore he was called "King Strang." Strang was an educated leader and for some time the Mormon settlement prospered under his guidance. Little cabins were built and in these the Mormon people lived. A log house served as a meeting place for worship and recreation. The people called their settlement St. James. Although the Mormons were industrious, they were disliked by many people then living in Michigan. After Strang's death the little colony disbanded.

The little town of St. James, on the northern end of Beaver Island, is at present a small village. Fishing was for many years the major industry, but with the coming of the sea lamprey this industry has stopped. Two other things remain to remind us of the earlier Mormon settlement on the island: a road called the King's Highway and a lake known as the Sea of Galilee.

EAST JORDAN is located at the mouth of the Jordan River on the south arm of Lake Charlevoix. It was a lumber sawmill town and shipping center during the years the Detroit and Charlevoix Railroad was running here from Frederic. Dairy farms are located nearby. Much fruit, especially cherries, is grown in the area and canned at the local cannery.

BOYNE CITY also was a lumber center in the days when lumber schooners entered Lake Charlevoix to load lumber for the Chicago market. Today it is known for the smelt runs of early spring. A tannery here makes shoe sole leather. Boyne City also serves as a coal distributing center for the area as large boats can dock on Lake Charlevoix easier than at Petoskey on Little Traverse Bay. A local electric power station supplies electricity for much of northern Michigan. Seven miles east of Boyne City is Boyne Falls. The Boyne Mountain Lodge located here is one of the most popular summer and winter recreation spots in Northern Michigan.

TRAVERSE CITY is located at the southern end of Grand Traverse Bay. The words Grand Traverse, meaning "great crossing," come to us from the French *voyageurs* and no doubt refer to the necessity of paddling canoes from the Leelanau Peninsula to the mainland. This open strip of water had to be crossed if the *voyageurs* wanted to avoid the delay that was necessary in following the longer shore line of the bay.

In 1839, two years after Michigan had become a state, Protestant missionaries sent by Henry R. Schoolcraft, the Indian agent at Sault Ste. Marie, founded a mission on what is now known as Old Mission Peninsula.

About 1846 white settlers began to arrive in the area, and a little village, later called Traverse City, began to appear at the southern end of West Bay near Lake Boardman. In 1847 the first sawmill in the region was built by Horace Boardman on what is now known as Asylum Creek. Not many years later newer and larger mills were built, and the timber harvest of the locality began. The white billowed sails of lumber schooners were often seen against the deep-blue waters of the bay.

As the forests were cut away, settlers pushed in to occupy the better lands where the hardwoods had grown. Potatoes and hay were the leading crops for years, but when other areas began to compete, the farmers of the region turned to more diversified farming. It was discovered by 1905 that cherries could become a very important crop because of the climate. Large cherry orchards were soon spreading across the rolling countryside. Refrigerator trains began to run at night during the picking season to speed the fresh-picked cherries to the large cities of the Midwest. In 1912 a local canning factory began to process the fruit. Other canneries soon were built. In a single year, Traverse City has been known to process nearly thirty-five million pounds of cherries.

The region around Traverse City is now known as the "Nation's Cherry Bowl." Cherries are produced in Antrim, Benzie, Leelanau, Charlevoix, and Grand Traverse counties. From this area each year come over fifty million pounds of cherries. Grand Traverse County has over eight hundred thousand cherry trees and it is the largest producer of the section. Most of the cherries grown are of the Montmorency variety and are red and tart. During the last few years more sweet cherries have been grown than in past years.

From Traverse City comes a third of all the cherries produced in Michigan. Each season, when the cherries are ripe, hundreds of cherry pickers come north and camp in the area and harvest the bright red fruit. They are paid by the lug, a box containing about twenty-eight pounds. During the busy picking season the canning factories run at capacity day and night to keep up with the truck loads of cherries that come rolling in from the cherry orchards. The ripe cherries are carefully washed, sorted, and then pitted by mechanical pitters. They are then placed in cans and steam cooked. Some cherries are brined and thus prepared for the maraschino trade.

In 1924 the first cherry celebration was held. In July, 1928, the first real cherry festival took place. Since that time a cherry festival has been held each year and is now known as the "National Cherry Festival."

Traverse City is also an important distributing center for the area. Because of the many lakes near it, Traverse City is also a busy summer resort center. Old Mission Peninsula is a tourist attraction as well as a cherry-producing area. The 45th degree parallel crosses just north of the peninsula.

Northwest of Traverse City is the Leelanau Peninsula which stretches north between Lake Michigan and Grand Traverse Bay. Leelanau County is the little finger of the Lower Peninsula. In this area one finds several small lakes as well as Glen Lake and Lake Leelenau. Here in the Leelanau Peninsula is also found Sleeping Bear Sand Dune. Each summer many people visit the sand dunes in the Leelanau Peninsula and take a ride on one of the dunemobiles. These are automobiles which have large tires that keep them from sinking into the dry, soft sand.

Southwest of Traverse City is Interlochen. Each summer nearly one thousand high school and college musicians come here to enjoy the northland and to study under well-known music instructors. Musical concerts are given on Sunday afternoons and on many evenings.

The West Coast Cities of the Upper Part of the Lower Peninsula

Long ago Lake Michigan and Lake Huron were larger than they are at present. Although they were larger, their beds were not quite so deep as they are now. But during the ages the winds and waves have been busy, and the lakes have scoured out deeper basins for themselves and receded from the land. The sand washed in by the wave action makes pretty sandy beaches and excellent places to swim, but as it dries, the winds blow it inland where it is piled along the shore in the form of sand dunes.

Sand dunes reach from Benton Harbor along the east shore of Lake Michigan to Mackinaw City and from there southward along the west shore of Lake Huron to Tawas City. These dunes often reach a height of between two and three hundred feet. The largest and most active sand dunes are now found along the east shore of Lake Michigan. These huge piles of sand are slowly growing larger as the winds carry the dry sand inland from the beach. Nature is ever trying to conquer them and cover them with grass and trees. Sometimes they are conquered, but often they slowly creep inland, killing grass and trees as they cover them with the ever-shifting sand. Some of these dunes have been made into parks so that tourists may see these huge sand ridges that have been made by the waves and winds.

The west coast port cities were well located for the lumber trade. The rivers that flow into Lake Michigan usually have a large lake located near their mouths just before they enter Lake Michigan. The lakes are large in size and are separated from Lake Michigan by large sand dunes. These dune-locked lakes have been formed by the dune action of the area and the sedimentary deposits brought down by the rivers. Once the sand bars were removed from the river mouths, these sheltered lakes made good harbors for the lumber boats and booming places for the logs. The high dunes also protected the cities from the winds of winter that blew from Lake Michigan. From these good harbors the boats had an open road to the busy lumber port at Chicago. Today only three of the old port cities carry on an active commerce. They are Frankfort, Ludington, and Muskegon.

When the lumber had been cut from this area, much of the area, because of its nearness to Lake Michigan, became a fruit-growing region.

FRANKFORT, which was founded in 1850, lies just south of the Leelanau Peninsula on the shore of Lake Michigan. Nearby are Crystal Lake, Platte Lake, and the Fife Lake State Forest. Frankfort is an important summer resort city and fruit market. It is located in the heart of the cherry-producing region of Michigan. Several canneries for the caring of the fruit are located in or near the city. In its early days Frankfort was an important lumber center. At one time an iron foundry was located here. Frankfort now produces sash, doors, clothing, tools and machine parts, and truck bodies.

Frankfort has the northernmost ice-free harbor along the west shore of the state. The Ann Arbor Railroad was the first railroad to operate car ferries across Lake Michigan, and it began this ferry service from Frankfort in 1892. Today Frankfort is the home port for the Ann Arbor Railroad car ferry fleet.* From this port railroad-car ferries, carrying railroad cars, automobiles, and tourists, run to Manitowoc and Kewaunee in Wisconsin, and to Menominee and Manistique in the Upper Peninsula of Michigan. This freight and passenger service across Lake Michigan is carried on even in the wintertime. The ferries have cabins, staterooms, and dining rooms to care for the needs of the passengers. This ferry service across Lake Michigan is really an extension of the railroad and saves many miles of travel around Lake Michigan.

MANISTEE is located on the eastern shore of Lake Michigan at the mouth of the Manistee River. The city lies between Lake Michigan on the west and Lake Manistee on the east. Nearby are Portage Lake and Bear Lake. The Manistee River is now known as one of the best trout streams in the state, but during the last half of the past century it was known for the pine logs it brought to the sawmills at Manistee. Every spring it ran brown with some of the finest cork pine that ever grew in Michigan. This fine saw timber, together with the booming possibilities of Manistee Lake, made Manistee one of Michigan's well-known sawmill centers. The first sawmill at Manistee was built in 1841. On October 8, 1871, the year of the big fires, a fire from an old chopping, fanned by a strong wind, set the town on fire. The town was soon destroyed, but a new one sprang up on the old site.

As Manistee's lumber industry declined, Manistee was fortunate in being able to turn to other industries. Salt was discovered at Manistee in 1882. Today Manistee is a large salt-producing center. Salt wells

*The dock is at Elberta across the Betsie River from Frankfort.

reach down into the ground some two thousand feet to vast deposits of salt. Water is pumped down pipes into the salt bed. There the water dissolves the salt and forms a brine, which is pumped to the surface. Then the water is evaporated from the brine. This is done in huge vacuum pans that are as large as a three-story house and hold as much as twenty-two thousand gallons of salt brine. When the water is evaporated, cubic salt crystals are formed. About four hundred thousand tons of salt are produced in this manner each year. Much of this salt is made for cooking and table use. Salt for industrial uses and for animal feeding is also made.

Later drillings have revealed a salt brine heavier in chemical content than that to be found in any other salt deposit in the state. Because of this, new chemical industries have developed which now produce bromine and chlorides.

Other industries have also developed in Manistee. Manistee's industries now produce drop forgings, chemicals, clothing, shoes, maple furniture, iron castings, speedboats, paper boxes, paper, rotary pumps, and oil burners.

Besides being a resort center, Manistee is located in the heart of the western fruit belt. Manistee County is a large producer of fruit. Both apples and cherries are grown. The annual yield places the county in the top brackets of production for the state.

Extending to the south and eastward lies the large Manistee National Forest which covers thousands of acres and extends through several counties. At Wellston, east of Manistee on M 55, is the Tippy Dam on the Manistee River and the Chittenden Nursery, where young trees are grown for replanting in forest areas.

LUDINGTON is located at the mouth of the Pere Marquette River, on the shore of Lake Michigan and Pere Marquette Lake. Originally the city was called Marquette, but the name was later changed to Ludington after James Ludington, an early lumberman. Between Pere Marquette Lake and Lake Michigan, on a narrow strip of duneland, stands a large cross marking the spot where Father Jacques Marquette died on May 18, 1675.

In 1849 a small sawmill was built at the north end of Pere Marquette Lake. The splendid harbor, together with the logs that could be floated down the Pere Marquette River, soon made Ludington a busy, growing lumber town. Where once the lumber hookers came into port, to this Lake Michigan harbor now come the Chesapeake and Ohio Railroad car ferries. Among the car ferries running from

Ludington are the Spartan and the Badger, which are two of the finest car ferries of their type. The latest type of tourist accommodations are provided on them. Each year many tourists cross Lake Michigan on these car ferries and thus save time and many

Courtesy of Michigan Department of Conservation

Weighing, packing and counting pine transplants to be shipped to schools, clubs, and other agencies for reforestation. Picture taken in 1950.

miles of driving. These ferries run to Kewaunee, Manitowoc, and Milwaukee, Wisconsin. About two thirds of the freight moving across Lake Michigan from the three car ferry ports is incoming freight from the west. It consists of lumber and grain and other bulk commodities.

Along the shores of Lake Michigan and the smaller nearby lakes, hundreds of cottages have been built. East of Ludington is the Manistee National Forest. North of Ludington along Lake Michigan is Ludington State Park, in which stands Big Sable Lighthouse. In this park is found the site of Hamlin Village, a lumber town founded in the middle of the nineteenth century. Hamlin is remembered for a tragic flood which occurred in 1888 when a dam burst and released nine miles of backed-up water down upon the village. The flood destroyed the village and also a large number of logs which were carried out into Lake Michigan and lost.

Besides being a port and resort center, Ludington is also an

Courtesy Dow Chemical Company

Experimental plants are grown under this stainless steel hood in the Spectroscopy Laboratory of The Dow Chemical Company. By the use of radioactive isotopes, studies are made in the effects of various agricultural chemicals on plant tissues. (1961)

Shown here is the Van de Graaff accelerator used by The Dow Chemical Company as a source of nuclear radiations for research. The installation was one of the first in industry. Here a Dow scientist is preparing an experimental chemical reaction for activation by electrons from the machine. (1961)

Courtesy Dow Chemical Company

Courtesy Hooker Chemical Corporation

Caustic soda final filter test. Hooker Chemical Corporation, Montague, Mich. (1961)

Automatic can line inspection of Morton Salt. Port Huron, Michigan. (1961)

Courtesy Morton Salt Company

Three continuous strips of paper, the middle one coated with hot asphalt, are fed onto a mandrel, forming a laminated tube. This tube is cut into sections to form cans for containing salt. (1961)

Courtesy Diamond Crystal Salt Company

The slurry containing salt crystals is drawn from the pan into a centrifuge which extracts most of the moisture. (1961)

Courtesy Diamond Crystal Salt Company

Courtesy Buick Motor Division, General Motors Corporation

Looking like toys are these cars on an overhead assembly line in Buick's new assembly plant in Flint. Cars are assembled entirely on this overhead conveyor which is 3,700 feet long and will hold 125 units. Cars are shown moving down from the second floor to the reliability inspection area on the first floor where they are given a water test and run on a dynamometer before being released for shipment. (1961)

Testing a car on the four-wheel dynamometer. Electric instruments check noise level inside the car, vibration of various components and the torque output of the engine. Designed to duplicate actual operating conditions on the highway, the dynamometer can simulate climbing a steep hill, coasting down a hill or a ride over a bumpy road. (1961)

Courtesy Buick Motor Division, General Motors Corporation

industrial community having some thirty-nine diversified industries. Here are made cement products, chemicals, castings, boats, fruit crates, brooms, wood products, watch cases, canvas goods, clothing, printers' equipment, and auto parts.

HART, located south of Ludington, is in the center of a large fruit and vegetable growing area. Two large canneries here run from early June to late October to prepare choice canned products. Rides up and down the huge sand dunes along Lake Michigan in specially built dunemobiles can be taken from Silver Lake.

MUSKEGON was for many years one of Michigan's leading lumber producers. Its location at the mouth of the far-reaching Muskegon River, whose headwaters reached into large pineries, and the presence of Muskegon Lake made Muskegon an ideal sawmill center.

Today Muskegon is the largest city in western Michigan. Busy industries have replaced the forty-seven noisy sawmills that once stood along the shores of Muskegon Lake. Among Muskegon's many products can be listed tools and dies, motor blocks, combustion engines, auto parts, foundry products, office equipment, refrigerators, paper, wire, coil springs, electric cranes and hoists, bowling and billiard equipment, sanding machines, metal awnings, and buses. Two refineries process about ten thousand barrels of petroleum a day.

Car ferries run across Lake Michigan from Muskegon to Milwaukee, Wisconsin, carrying mail and railroad cars. The car ferry tonnage from this port is about forty per cent of the total tonnage carried across Lake Michigan. The tonnage that passes through this port is about one million tons annually. The Milwaukee Clipper, a passenger boat, runs between Muskegon and Milwaukee, Wisconsin, during the summer months. It carries passengers and automobiles. Another boat carries new automobiles to Milwaukee, Wisconsin. Muskegon is the one port of western Michigan that has lake freight traffic. Being in the industrial area of the state helps in these freight shipments. Oil, coal, cement, and pulpwood account for most of the incoming tonnage, while molding sand taken from Muskegon Lake accounts for much of the outgoing shipments.

Besides being a port and an industrial center, Muskegon is also a resort and agricultural community. Northeast lies the Manistee National Forest. Much fruit is grown nearby. The area is a large producer of apples, celery, and small fruits.

Muskegon Heights is a residential area. North of Muskegon are located Montague and White Hall on White Lake, both well-known resort centers.

FREMONT lies northeast of Muskegon. The Gerber plant here was the first to pioneer in the manufacture of baby foods. Today the

Courtesy Hooker Chemical Corporation

Storage of raw brine after pumping from brine wells, Montaque, Mich.

Gerber plant makes a large percentage of the total baby foods produced.

The Inland Towns in the Upper Part of the Lower Peninsula

Most of the inland towns in this area are located on the sandy High Plains Area. All of them had their beginning, and many their end, in the lumber industry. For many years after the timber was gone these towns declined, but with the building of better roads in the area and the rise of the tourist traffic, many of these towns have again grown in size. Some farming in scattered areas is carried on, but most of the area is now covered by second-growth timber stands. The clear, swift, shallow streams of the area and the many pretty tree-lined lakes with their sandy beaches make this area today a popular place for people to spend their summer vacations. Many of the older buildings in the little villages that were built during the lumbering days are still standing, while others have been torn down. Newer, more modern stores and homes are replacing the older buildings. Along the busy highways many new attractive motels have been built during the past ten years to care for the hundreds of people that come to, or pass through, the area each year.

CADILLAC is located just east of two beautiful lakes, Lake Mitchell and Lake Cadillac. Cadillac began as the village of Clam Lake, but in 1877, during the lumber era, it was incorporated as the city of Cadillac in honor of Antoine de la Mothe Cadillac, the French commandant who founded Detroit in 1701. With the coming of the railroad, Cadillac became a lumber producer, but with the passing of the pine and hardwood forests, Cadillac was forced to turn to other industries.

Unfortunately for Cadillac most of the land surrounding the city is a sandy loam unsuited to agriculture. A few better strips of soil, where once hardwoods grew, have become farm land.

Cadillac has succeeded in making a new adjustment, and today it is an industrial community making dairy products, cement blocks, aluminum and brass castings, canvas products, gray iron castings, hardwood plywood, toys and novelties, pleasure boats, temperature control equipment, furniture, and potato flour.

Cadillac is the center of a summer and winter recreation area. It is well known for its painted forests in the fall of the year when the first frosts have turned the hardwoods into brilliant displays of gaudy colors. Nearby is the Manistee River, well known for canoeing and fishing. Between Cadillac and Traverse City is located the Fife Lake State Forest. Because Cadillac is located in a hollow saucer on top of the highest land in the Lower Peninsula, it often is the coldest spot in the state.

Sixteen miles west of Cadillac is Caberfae, a well-known winter sports area which is operated under a permit from the Forest Service of the United States Department of Agriculture. The heavy snowfall of the high area makes this a good winter sports area. As many as fifteen hundred skiers come here on some week ends during the wintertime. Caberfae has rope ski tows, several cross-country trails, two ski jumps, and seventeen ski runs. Northwest of Cadillac at Mesick is the Briar Hill ski area. Here is located one of the longest ski jumps in the Lower Peninsula.

MANTON lies north of Cadillac. It was settled in 1871 and was for some years a lumber center.

REED CITY and BIG RAPIDS lie south of Cadillac. Reed City was settled by German immigrants after 1848. Big Rapids, located on the upper Muskegon River in what used to be a pine forest area, was settled shortly after 1850. During the lumbering days it prospered. Much of the nearby land is unsuited to agriculture, but oil has been discovered. Around 1880 Mr. Woodbridge N. Ferris, later governor of Michigan and also senator from Michigan, started a private school here known as the Ferris Institute. For many years this institute was the leading educational center in northern Michigan. Today the Ferris Institute has been taken over by the state and is now run as a state college. It is now well known for its college of pharmacy.

MIDLAND, the county seat of Midland County, is located on the Tittabawassee River. One hundred years ago this area was an important lumber region. At Averill, the lumberjacks piled logs along the river bank each winter. In springtime the river was filled with large pine logs drifting downstream to Bay City and Saginaw.

Today Midland, the home of the Dow Chemical Company, is a busy

Courtesy Dow Chemical Company

Part of the Dow Chemical Company's Midland Division plant at Midland, Michigan, as it appears today. The Midland operation, with more than 500 buildings covering approximately 1,000 acres, is one of the largest chemical plants in the country. (1961)

industrial town. The Dow Chemical Company located there is one of the largest chemical companies to be found in the country. Nearby are oil wells which are some of the best producing wells in Michigan.

MOUNT PLEASANT was once a lumber town having five sawmills. It was given its name in 1863 by David Ward, one of Michigan's best-known lumbermen. In 1864 a treaty with the Indians permitted them to settle permanently in the region. The United States Government started an Indian industrial school here in 1892. This school is now used as one of the state hospital units. Since 1930 many of the Indians have lived on an Indian reservation located east of Mount Pleasant.

Mount Pleasant is pleasantly situated amid the farm lands of Isabella County where general farming is carried on. The principal crop of the area is sugar beets. Some industries, such as refining gasoline, making auto parts, drying chicory, milling flour, and condensing milk, are located in Mount Pleasant. Mount Pleasant, however, is primarily a college town. It is the home of Central Michigan University, which was founded as a normal college in 1895. The university has grown rapidly during the past few years.

GRAYLING was named after the grayling fish that once lived in large numbers in Michigan's rivers but have now become extinct. Their place has been taken by brook trout, which were first planted in Michigan in the Au Sable River at Frederic in 1884. At one time Grayling was a busy sawmill town, but the passing of the lumbering era left Grayling without an important industry. Nearly all the nearby land, which has little agricultural value, has been taken over by the state and is now in state forests. North and northwest of Grayling is the Au Sable State Forest. South of it lies the Higgins Lake State Forest. In this area oil has been discovered. East of Grayling lies the Huron National Forest. The entire area, with its clear, fast-flowing rivers, clear lakes, and sandy soil, is an ideal summer playground. Hundreds of people come to the nearby forested areas each year to spend their vacations. Grayling is the starting point for people who take canoe trips down the Au Sable River. Grayling is also a winter sports area. Special trains from Detroit bring people to the area each winter.

Seven miles northeast of Grayling is the Hartwick State Park. Each year many people visit this park to see the few remaining pine trees that are still left standing from Michigan's original pine forests in the Lower Peninsula.

Four and one-half miles from Grayling is the Hanson Military Reservation comprising some eighteen thousand acres of land. In this reservation on the shore of Lake Margrethe is located the camp site for the Michigan National Guard. Each August the Michigan National Guard spends about two weeks in training in this area. During this period the National Guardsmen go through various military maneuvers necessary to preserve order and defend the state.

The National Guard is an integral part of the defense structure of the United States and is our answer to state and national security without maintaining a large professional standing army in time of peace. The present strength of the organization is a little over twenty-four thousand men.

The Michigan National Guard, though called by other names, had its beginning even before Michigan became a state. As early as 1812 a militia of two hundred men was enrolled to help defend the territory. In 1832 it defended the territory against Black Hawk and his Indian followers. In 1835 it helped in the so-called "Toledo War." In 1838 it became known as the State Guards, and in 1848 it sent several companies to the Mexican War. In 1861, at President Lincoln's call, the Guards were some of the first to respond. In every major conflict of the Civil War, Michigan men took part. About thirteen thousand five hundred men from Michigan were killed in that war. The total number of men from Michigan who took part in the Civil War was nearly ninety-one thousand.

In 1870 the name was changed to the Michigan State Troops. In 1891 the name was again changed to the Michigan National Guard. With the coming of the Spanish-American War five regiments were sent and three left the states for Cuba. The National Guard was made a part of the Army of the United States in 1916.

During World War I, Michigan Guardsmen joined those of Wisconsin to form the 32nd Infantry Division which arrived in France in February, 1918. Michigan soldiers were among the first of the United States soldiers to go into active service. As part of the "Red Arrow Division" they continued in active service until the close of the war. Some of Michigan's soldiers were sent to Russia and were known as the "Polar Bears."

During World War II, Michigan sent over eight thousand National Guardsmen into the Federal service, and they served in the Middle East, Africa, Europe, the Aleutians, and the South Pacific. Again the 32nd Infantry wrote heroic pages in our nation's history.

The tradition and glory of the old 32nd Division is now carried on under the post-war reorganization by the present 46th Division. Today, as in the past, the National Guard stands ready to be called to serve the state or defend the nation.

ROSCOMMON is the center of some of the work of the Department of Conservation. Here experimental shops produce fire-fighting equipment. Nearby, on Higgins Lake, is located one of the state nurseries where thousands of white pine seedlings are grown each year for replanting in the forest areas. Here also is located a camp where meetings on conservation are held. On the southeast shore of Higgins Lake, eight miles southwest of Roscommon, is Higgins Lake State Park.

Courtesy Michigan Dept. of Conservation

Higgins Lake State Nursery

OTHER INLAND TOWNS in the area are Wolverine, Vanderbilt, Gaylord, and West Branch. Near Wolverine is a hardwood nursery. Vanderbilt, once a lumbering center, was named after the Vanderbilts of the East. Gaylord is one of the largest centers in the inland part of the northern area of the Lower Peninsula. Once it was a lumbering center. It is now an agricultural and resort community. East of Gaylord is a winter sports area. West Branch got its name from being on the west branch of the Rifle River. Once a lumber town, it is now a recreation and agricultural center. Some farm land is found in this area. Oil is also produced. Indian River is the recreation center for the area around Burt and Mullet lakes.

Chapter XXI

THE CHANGING SOUTHERN PART OF THE LOWER PENINSULA

Only one hundred and fifty years ago, the southern part of the Lower Peninsula was still a forest-covered land. But soon after 1800, as we have seen in an earlier chapter, the southern part of the state was quickly settled. By 1860, or just one hundred years ago, southern Michigan could be called a settled area. Where once hardwood forests had stood, farm lands then spread across the countryside. Many communities were already growing into the cities and villages we know today. From the land each summer and fall came agricultural products. Up to about 1900 there were only local industries in the area.

As time passed and the farmers prospered, the earlier log cabins made from round logs cut from the forest gave way to block houses made from hand-hewn logs. These were later replaced by homes made of lumber or brick. Many of these houses built before 1900 are still standing, but the earlier log cabins of the frontier days are nearly all gone.

Most of Michigan's population and industry is found in the area south of Bay City and Muskegon. Half of the entire population of the whole state lives in the little industrial area that will be discussed in the next chapter.

The land is more fertile in this part of Michigan, and much of it is now farm land. The summers are longer here, and warmer too. The winters are not so cold. These factors of climate aid the agriculture of this area. Many of the villages have remained small agricultural communities, but others have grown larger. Some have become large cities and are now industrial communities from which comes a variety of industrial products.

Much of the Thumb is low, flat land, but most of the remaining part of this area is gently rolling land now covered with farms and patches of second-growth hardwood. The highest areas are found in the Irish Hills and in Oakland County. Though greatly varied, the soils here are generally better than those found farther to the north. Because of the varieties of soil, many different crops are grown. The nearby centers of population provide a large, close market for much of the farm produce. Part of the crop is marketed at the farms to city folks who drive into the country with their cars. Because milk, a highly perishable product, can be quickly shipped to the cities from the local farming areas, dairying is one of the major types of farming in the area.

Many good highways lead through this area. US 25 runs from Toledo, Ohio, north through Detroit to Port Huron. From there it follows the sandy shore line of Lake Huron and Saginaw Bay to Bay City. US 10 runs north from Woodward Avenue, in Detroit, through Pontiac, Flint, and Saginaw to Midland. US 16 is the old Grand River Road. It runs out Grand River Avenue, in Detroit, through several rural villages to Lansing. From Lansing, US 16 runs west to Grand Rapids and Grand Haven. US 12 follows the old Territorial Road and runs west through the second tier of counties. It passes through Ann Arbor, Jackson, Marshall, Battle Creek, and Kalamazoo, to Benton Harbor and St. Joseph on Lake Michigan. US 112 is the old Chicago Road. It runs out of Detroit on Michigan Avenue and passes through Ypsilanti, Jonesville, Coldwater, Sturgis, and Niles and runs to New Buffalo on Lake Michigan. US 23 runs north from Dundee to Bay City. US 27, the main highway north through the central part of the Lower Peninsula, comes north from Indiana, passes through Coldwater, Marshall, Charlotte, Lansing, and then goes on north through Mount Pleasant. US 66 runs north from Battle Creek. Several of these main trunk lines, as you have read in the last chapter, continue north through the northern part of the Lower Peninsula. Several main highways besides those already mentioned lead east and west across this area. M 46 runs west across the state from Port Sanilac to Muskegon. M 21 runs west across the state from Port Huron through Flint, Ionia, and Grand Rapids to Holland.

All these highways are now trunk lines. Over them pass not only passenger cars but much freight that is hauled in large trucks. This spreading network of highways not only provides rapid transportation from city to city but also provides access to ready markets for the farmers in the area. Along these highways, as along those farther north, picnic tables are placed in wooded spots or in pretty wayside parks. During the summer these picnic tables are much used by people who stop to eat and rest as they drive from city to city or stop on their way to, or from, a vacation area.

PORT HURON is located at the source of the St. Clair River where Lake Huron spills its overflow waters into the channel that carries the run-off water to Lake Erie. This is the most easterly point in the state of Michigan and is some fifty miles nearer Buffalo, New York, and the eastern seacoast than is the city of Detroit.

At the center of Port Huron, the Black River empties into the St. Clair River. This was once the meeting place of Indian trails that led from Michigan into Canada. When the French became interested

Courtesy East Michigan Tourist Association

Blue Water Bridge crossing the St. Clair River from Port Huron to Sarnia, Canada

in this area, Daniel DuLhut, in 1686, built Fort St. Joseph just north of where the Blue Water Bridge now crosses into Canada. As early as 1782 French fishermen and trappers began to live in this locality, but it was about 1790 before real settlement began. This area was further opened to settlement when the Fort Gratiot Turnpike was built from Detroit in 1826. The Americans built Fort Gratiot on the site of the old French Fort St. Joseph to protect the American settlers from the English and the Indians. The fort was abandoned in 1879 and dismantled in 1882. The region along the St. Clair River was for many years an important boat-building center. From 1840 to 1870 lumbering was the major industry of the district.

Many farms are located in the nearby area. Tuscola and Huron counties are well known for their bean production. Sanilac County is noted for its dairy cattle. Lapeer, St. Clair, and Macomb counties produce much beet sugar as well as fruits and vegetables. In this vicinity are located the agricultural communities of Imlay City, Lapeer, Marlette, Vassar, Sebewaing, Bad Axe, and Sandusky. At Lapeer is located the Lapeer State Home and Training School.

Port Huron is one of the three Michigan cities to have sister cities in Canada. Across the St. Clair River from Port Huron is the Canadian city of Sarnia which, because of the salt underlying it and the oil that is now being piped to it from western Canada through Michigan, is destined to become one of the major industrial cities of Canada. Auto ferries for many years carried traffic across the St. Clair River, but now the auto and truck traffic uses the Blue Water Bridge which crosses the river not far from Lake Huron. The Blue Water Bridge was paid for by the United States Government and the Canadian Government. Its total cost of construction was over four million dollars. It is 8,021 feet long. It rises one hundred and fifty feet above the St. Clair River so that the large freighters on the Great Lakes can pass under it. It was opened for traffic on October 10, 1939. The Grand Trunk Railroad Tunnel, one of the longest submarine tunnels in the world, carries railroad traffic between the United States and Canada under the St. Clair River.

At Port Huron are located some eighty-four diversified industries, some of which produce salt, copper wire, automobile parts, pulp products, farm and road machinery, cement, speedboats, hardware, and paints. The salt plants turn out many carloads of salt each day. At Port Huron, terminal shops are maintained by the Grand Trunk and Pennsylvania railroads.

Port Huron is the Thumb's largest city and trading center. The entire Thumb shore line all the way from Lake St. Clair to Bay City is a summer playground. Thousands of cottages have been built along the St. Clair River, on the islands in the river, and on the shore of Lake Huron and Saginaw Bay. Below Port Huron are found Marysville, St. Clair, Marine City, and Algonac. These cities are small industrial centers but primarily resort communities.

North of Port Huron spreads the clear, blue water of Lake Huron, and along the shore line are several villages which are resort communities: Lakeport, Lexington, Port Sanilac, and Harbor Beach. Near the tip of the Thumb stands the abandoned community once known as Grindstone City where grindstones were made from the Marshall sandstone that comes to the surface there. Today one can see the old deserted quarries from which the sandstone was taken. Farther to the west lie Pointe Aux Barques, a summer resort, and the village of Port Austin.

FLINT lies on M10 about sixty miles north of Detroit. In 1819 a fur trader built a post at the place where the Saginaw trail then crossed the Flint River. The first family to settle at what is now the city of Flint was that of John Todd, who arrived from Pontiac in 1830. Mr. Todd ran a tavern and also a ferry across the river. Three years later the new road from Detroit to Saginaw reached Flint, and soon many settlers began building in the area. At first the settlement was called Grand Traverse, but in 1855 it was incorporated as the city of Flint. For some years lumbering was the major industry of the area, but as the forests were cleared away, farmers took over the land.

Flint today is the second largest manufacturing city in Michigan. It ranks next to Detroit as the most important vehicle city in the world. In the city there are over one hundred manufacturing plants. Here are found the large plants of Buick, Chevrolet, Fisher Body, and A. C. Sparkplug. Flint has no raw materials in its vicinity to give it commercial advantages, nor has it any special location favorable for transportation. In spite of these handicaps the leadership and vision of the men in Flint's industries have made the city of Flint a leader in the automobile field.

Flint is the third largest city in Michigan. From its factories come automobiles, trucks, automobile finish, upholstering for cars, carburetors, motors, spark plugs, pressed metal parts, speedometers, trailer coaches, and many automobile accessories.

At Flint are located the Flint Junior College, General Motors Institute, and the Michigan School for the Deaf.

OWOSSO was named after a Chippewa Indian chief named Wasso, who lived with his tribe in the area. Owosso is located in one of the state's best farming and grazing areas. Once the forests were cleared from the area, settlers occupied the farm lands. Some turned to furniture making. Owosso is the home of the late James Oliver Curwood who wrote many interesting novels. Some of them were written at his castle on an island in the river. Owosso is also the former home of Thomas E. Dewey, the Republican candidate for President of the United States in 1944 and 1948.

Courtesy Massey-Ferguson, Inc.

MF 35 Special Tractor and MF 66 Moldboard Plow. (1961)

The Fluid Manufacturing Department of the Upjohn Company. (1961)

Ezra Stoller Photo. Courtesy Upjohn Company

ANN ARBOR, Mich.—Organic Chemist Robert W. Fleming (R.), and his associate, Yvon L'Italien, develop compounds for testing as ultimate nervous system control drugs such as stiumulants and depressants. The laboratory in which the pair is working is one of 93 such rooms contained in the new Parke, Davis & Company research facilities here. (1961)
Courtesy Parke, Davis & Company

Extraction unit separates useful antibiotic from crude fermentation mixture.
Ezra Stoller Photo
Courtesy Upjohn Company

Among the items manufactured here are dairy products, stampings, furniture, electric goods, concrete products, sugar, abrasives, castings, tanks, and boilers.

LANSING is located where the old Grand River trail crossed the Grand River. It was settled in 1837 when the site was chosen for a dam across the Grand River to develop water power. Settlers moving into the area from New York State named it after their former home, Lansing, New York. When the state capital was moved from Detroit in 1847, Lansing was chosen because of its central location.

In January of each year the state legislature begins a new session in the capitol building. Here the laws that govern our state are made. Among the points of interest in Lansing are the Michigan State Library, the Michigan Historical Museum, the Michigan School for the Blind, and the Michigan Vocational School for Boys.

With the coming of the railroad, Lansing, situated in the center of a rich industrial and agricultural peninsula, soon became an industrial center as well as the state capital. Ransom E. Olds was the city's first leading industrialist. At first he made the Oldsmobile and later the Reo cars. Today many industries are located in Lansing. Among the plants are Oldsmobile, Motor Wheel Corporation, Reo Motors, Duplex Truck Company, and Fisher Body Corporation. Among the many other things made at Lansing can be named aircraft instruments, dairy equipment, concrete products, chemicals, mattresses, tools and dies, refrigerator units, beet sugar, conveyor belts, rubber stamps, tents, and boilers.

EAST LANSING is a residential community. It has no industries. It is the home of Michigan State University. This university, founded in 1855, is the oldest land grant college in the United States. During the past few years many new buildings have been added, and the university enrollment has grown rapidly. Today it ranks tenth in size among the universities of the United States. Its present enrollment is about fifteen thousand students.

ALMA is on US 27, just west of Saginaw. Here is located Alma College, which was founded in 1886. At Alma are also located a large oil refinery and the Masonic Old People's Home.

IONIA, located where M 66 now crosses the Grand River, is in a good farming and fruit-growing area. One of Michigan's prisons, known as the Michigan Reformatory, is located here. Ionia also has a state hospital. Just west of Ionia is Lowell, which is well known for its "Show Boat" that hundreds of people come to see each July.

GRAND RAPIDS is Michigan's second largest city in population. It is well known throughout the nation as "The Furniture City." Grand Rapids was first settled in 1827 when Louis Campeau founded a fur trading post here. As early as 1836, as has been told in another chapter, William Holdane began making furniture at Grand Rapids. After 1854, Grand Rapids became a lumber center, and for several years the whining saws ripped into lumber the logs that came floating down the Grand River. It was from this supply of lumber from Michigan's forests that the first furniture makers at Grand Rapids chose their materials. Later trains brought in the fine hardwoods from the Grand River Valley.

Some years ago the furniture manufacturers at Grand Rapids started the Grand Rapids Furniture Exposition so that customers could come to Grand Rapids and see the fine furniture they were producing. Shown at these expositions is not only fine furniture made in Grand Rapids but also quality furniture made by other furniture manufacturers. Twice each year, in January and July, buyers of furniture visit this leading market for fine furniture and buy for the nation's markets.

Not only does Grand Rapids make fine furniture for home use, but it is also the world's largest producer of school, church, and theater seats. Many of the factories have acres of floor space devoted to displays where one can, at any time, see the furniture they are making.

Here at Grand Rapids is located the only museum in the world in which only furniture is shown. This museum is known as the Grand Rapids Furniture Museum and was opened on January 1, 1938, in what had once been the home of T. Stewart White, a wealthy Michigan lumberman. At one time this museum had been the home of Gilbert White, the artist; Roderick White, the musician; and Stewart Edward White, the author. Among Stewart Edward White's books, two were written on lumbering in Michigan. *The Riverman* tells of the problems of driving logs on one of Michigan's larger rivers. *The Blazed Trail* tells of life in a Michigan lumber camp. Today this former home, now known as the Grand Rapids Furniture Museum, is one of the show places in Michigan. All of the furniture is arranged according to history, design, and use.

The Ryerson Library, in downtown Grand Rapids, has a collection of some four hundred thousand books. Its collection on furniture design and manufacturing is one of the best in the United States. In an upper hallway of this building is a large wood carving made by Hans Berg, a furniture craftsman. Into this large piece of wood Mr. Berg has carved several scenes showing the major periods in Michigan's history. The Michigan Room in the Ryerson Library has over sixteen thousand volumes on Michigan and the Great Lakes Area.

Other places of interest in Grand Rapids are: Michigan Veterans Hospital, Calvin College and Seminary, the Grand Rapids Public Museum, the Grand Rapids Art Gallery, the Kendall School of Design, and the large Civic Auditorium. Outside Grand Rapids along Grand River and Plaster Creek one can see gypsum plants where gypsum is mined from the ground and made into plaster.

Although furniture making is Grand Rapids' major industry, many other products are also made. Among the products made here can be named radio and electrical equipment, chemicals, textiles, paints and varnishes, carpet sweepers, business machines, refrigerator cabinets, auto bodies, and auto parts. Grand Rapids is also a center for printing and photoengraving.

Grand Rapids is the leading trading center in western Michigan. Nearby are several smaller cities and good farm land from which come potatoes, vegetables, fruits, and dairy products. Grand Rapids, although it has local recreational areas nearby, is also known as "The Gateway to the Nation's Playground," as many people pass through it on their way north into Michigan's vacation lands.

GRAND HAVEN is located west of Grand Rapids at the mouth of the Grand River. The Grand Haven, Ferrysburg, Spring Lake area is a summer resort and vacation area for people living in southwestern Michigan and the Chicago area. The mineral waters also make it a health center. The area, like that of all western Michigan along the Lake Michigan shore, has pretty sand beaches, sand dunes, and air purified by having passed over one hundred miles of water.

Much celery and many grapes are grown on the farm lands near Grand Haven. Each year about two million dollars' worth of celery and grapes pass through Grand Haven on their way to the Chicago market. Many of the people living in this area are descendants of the early settlers who came from Holland about one hundred years ago.

Grand Haven is an industrial center producing boilers, tools, dies, presses, cutters, hardware specialties, wooden articles, plastic products, aluminum and brass products, and dairy products. A Coast Guard Training School is located here.

HOLLAND was settled in 1847 by immigrants who came here from Holland. The city is located at the mouth of the Black River, on Lake Macatawa, some six miles from Lake Michigan. At first the Hollanders bought one thousand acres of land on which to build their settlement. They found that the rich soil of the region made good farm land. During the years that have passed since the first settlers came, their children have spread over the surrounding area and established other communities. Today the city of Holland, the neighboring centers of Zeeland and Vriesland, and the Hollanders living in the rural sections of the area form the largest group of Hollanders in the United States.

Courtesy Holland Chamber of Commerce
Windmill Park at Tulip Time, Holland

During the early days of the settlement, lumbering formed the major industry, but with its passing the thrifty Hollanders turned the cut-over lands into one of Michigan's best agricultural sections. Many of the Hollanders turned to truck gardening. On the lowlands of former glacial lakes, celery and onions are grown. Flower bulbs are also grown. The poultry industry also forms a major occupation of this area. Each year some fourteen million baby chicks are hatched.

The skilled craftsmen of the community turned to making furniture. A large furniture industry grew in the community, and the products of these early craftsmen helped to make Michigan widely known as a furniture center. Other industries followed. At present Holland makes furniture, cosmetics, beet sugar, leather goods, dyes, auto parts, dairy products, and heating units. One of the largest heating unit factories in Michigan is located here at Holland.

In 1866 Hope College was founded by the Dutch Reformed Church. In 1871, the year of the big fires, Holland lost seventy-six business places and 243 homes.

At Holland is located the Netherlands Museum. Here are preserved such articles as have local historical importance to the people of Holland. The Netherlands government has also supplied it with much rare and valuable material. Lake Macatawa is one of the large sand-dune-locked lakes on the shore of western Michigan. After the sand bars at the mouth of the river had been removed, Lake Macatawa made an excellent harbor. Today the steamships "North American" and "South American" use Lake Macatawa as their winter port.

Many Dutch customs have been kept by these people from Holland. Their Dutch novelty shops are an interesting attraction to tourists. Tulips and wooden shoes (*klompen*) mark their spring festival, and people come to Holland by the thousands each spring at "Tulip Time."

Tulip Time was started in 1930. It is now held each spring at the time thousands of tulips are in bloom. It is a gala occasion that lasts for nine days. On the first day of Tulip Time, many men and women of Holland dress in their colorful Dutch costumes and scrub the streets with large scrubbing brushes. If you visit Holland at Tulip Time, you will see the miles of tulip lanes, and perhaps you will see some of the old men smoking their long pipes in one of the many coffee shops.

ANN ARBOR, located on the Huron River in Washtenaw County, is the home of the University of Michigan. Early settlers coming into the state found this region not only pleasant but also one of good farm land as well. Settlement began in 1824. Other settlers soon arrived, and by 1829 the little village had a newspaper, the *Western Immigrant.* At first the Huron River provided the only highway to other communities, but before long a road and a railroad were cut through the forest to Detroit.

One of the first acts of the new State Legislature in 1837 was to reorganize the state university. Many cities desired that the university be located in them, but it was decided to locate it at Ann Arbor. Buildings were soon under construction, and in 1841 the university was opened.

From this small beginning the University of Michigan has grown until today Ann Arbor is known throughout the United States and the world as the home of the University of Michigan. Many of the leaders of our times have been educated here or have served on the university faculties. In 1870 coeducation, a very progressive step for the time, was adopted.

Today the assets of the university exceed one hundred million dollars. Its libraries have more than one million volumes. The William L. Clements Library possesses many rare books, first editions, maps, and manuscripts on American history up to 1800. Among the places of interest in Ann Arbor can be listed: the University Hospital, the Law Quadrangle, the William L. Clements Library, the Burton Memorial Tower, the Baird Carillon, the Michigan League Building, the Michigan Union Building, the University Museums, the Hill Auditorium, the Botanical Gardens, and the University of Michigan Stadium at Ferry Field which seats over ninety-seven thousand people.

In general, the main occupation of Ann Arbor is caring for the nearly twenty thousand students attending the university. Yet, while primarily a leading educational center, Ann Arbor is an industrial community as well.

At one time watches were manufactured here; and pianos and organs were made here for many years. These early industries have given way to others. Today skilled labor in over seventy industrial plants produces castings, automobile instruments, cameras and supplies, scientific instruments, piston rings, machine parts, duplicating machines, wood products, and books.

JACKSON was settled about 1830 at a point where an Indian trail crossed the Grand River. The good farm land near the city soon attracted settlers. In 1838 the Michigan State Prison was established and located here. In 1841 the Michigan Central Railroad reached the city. Today Jackson is one of the most important railroad centers in the state. Since 1873, when the railroad moved its shops from Marshall to Jackson, the New York Central has maintained a large roundhouse and repair shop in the city.

Jackson was once a carriage-making center. When automobiles first appeared, several early cars, such as the Jackson, Imperial, Briscoe, and the Earl, were made in the city. Though these early cars are no longer made, Jackson is still an important industrial center having some 145 manufacturing plants. Among the products produced in Jackson may be named cushion springs for automobiles, tires and tubes, automobile accessories and parts, furniture, sleeping garments and clothing, lawn mowers, electric dishwashers, and grinding wheels.

Three of southern Michigan's largest rivers rise in Jackson County:

the Grand, the Raisin, and the Kalamazoo. In the county are found sixty-five lakes which add their sparkling beauty to the rolling farm land where general farming, dairying, and livestock raising are carried on.

Jackson is also the birthplace of the Republican party, which was founded here on July 6, 1854.

Until 1930, or for almost a century, the Michigan State Prison was located just north of the main business section in downtown Jackson. In that year it was moved to new buildings and grounds on the north side of the city. The present Michigan State Prison at Jackson is the largest walled prison in the world. Fifty-seven and one-half acres are enclosed inside the prison wall. At the present time the prison houses almost six thousand prisoners. In many ways the prison is self-supporting. It operates a number of farms where food for the prisoners is grown. The prisoners make their own shoes and other clothing as well as uniforms for the guards. They also operate their own cannery. Besides these activities they also make automobile license plates and road signs for the state. Prisoners are paid a small wage for their labor. They have religious, recreational, and educational opportunities.

South of Jackson are Hillsdale and Adrian, two rural communities. Hillsdale College is located at Hillsdale and has the distinction of being the first college in Michigan to grant degrees to women. Near Hillsdale College is Slayton's Arboretum. Will Carleton, Michigan's early poet, lived near here and attended Hillsdale College. Stock's flouring mills, the largest in the state, are located here.

ADRIAN, first called Logan, was founded in 1826 and is one of the oldest settlements in Michigan. It is located in beautiful rolling country where farming is the major occupation. Corn, sugar beets, cattle, sheep, hogs, and truck crops are the major farm products. At Adrian are located a beet processing plant, two canneries, and five milk processing plants which care for the crops and milk produced in the area.

The fact that Adrian is an agricultural community has not hindered its industrial development. Today some fifty products such as castings, farm gates, auto parts, leather goods, and paper products are made here. Adrian is also an educational community. Adrian College, St. Joseph's College, and the Girls' Training School are located here.

COLDWATER lies west of Hillsdale on US 112. Here is located the

Coldwater State Home and Training School. West of Coldwater on M 86 is Colon which is known as "The Magic Capital of the World." Here magicians' equipment is manufactured.

STURGIS is located on US 112, southwest of Coldwater. It is located in a good farming area. Venetian blinds and office furniture are manufactured. An industrial fair is held annually. Sturgis also produces prepared baby foods. North of Sturgis is Centreville, which is noted for its manufacture of children's sleeping garments.

ALBION is in the center of a good agricultural community. It is also a college town. Here is located Albion College, which was founded in 1835 by the Methodists. Several oil wells have been developed in this area in the last few years.

MARSHALL, on the old Territorial Road, was settled in 1831. It was named Marshall after John Marshall, Chief Justice of the United States Supreme Court. It was at Marshall that Rev. John D. Pierce, a missionary of the Congregational Church, and Isaac E. Crary, a Marshall attorney, in 1834 made plans for the Michigan Public School System. The plan set up by Pierce and Crary was adopted by the Constitutional Convention in 1835. This plan has been the pattern for nearly all the states that have entered the union since that date. Marshall was the scene of the famous Crosswhite Case. Marshall is also the birthplace of America's oldest continuous labor organization, the Brotherhood of Locomotive Engineers, which was founded here in 1863.

Marshall has some local industries, but it is primarily the center of an agricultural community. Here is located a large pickle salting station.

BATTLE CREEK, founded in 1831, derived its name from a dispute between a party of surveyors and some Indians. It stands at the meeting place of the Battle Creek and Kalamazoo Rivers. It is one of the larger cities in Michigan and one of the best known. The name of this city has been carried to every state of the Union and every country of the world on packages of various cereal and health foods which are produced here. Battle Creek may claim the distinction of being not only the largest producer of this type of food in the United States, but also the first producer in this field.

Battle Creek was also well known for many years as a health center. People from all over the world came to the Battle Creek Sanitarium to take advantage of the expert medical service here.

The former Battle Creek Sanitarium became the Percy Jones Hos-

Courtesy Kellogg Company

The present large Kellogg plant in Battle Creek where breakfast foods are made. The Kellogg Company also has plants abroad to provide service in over 100 countries. (1961)

More than 75 packages a minute are shaped, lined, filled, and sealed by each of the lines in the packing rooms. (1961)

Courtesy Kellogg Company

Courtesy Post Division, General Foods

Golden streams of freshly toasted Corn Flakes pass over the cooling screens at the Post Division of General Foods Corporation, Battle Creek, Michigan. The lady in the lower right foreground is taking a sample for quality checking purposes. (1961)

Quality Control is highly important in the production of breakfast cereals. Here a laboratory technician at the Post Division of General Foods Corporation in Battle Creek, Michigan, performs an analysis. (1961)

Werner Wolff Photo. Courtesy Post Division, General Foods

pital and was used as an Army hospital during both World War II and the Korean War. Today this large hospital has become the Federal Government's Civil Defense Headquarters.

Just west of Battle Creek is Camp Custer, which was used as a recruiting and training center in World War I, World War II, and the Korean War. Today it is being used to store machines that were used in war production during World War II and the Korean War. This machinery came from southern Michigan and northern Indiana. First the machinery was carefully checked and processed to keep it from rusting. Some ninety-six buildings are thus being used to protect this equipment that might again be needed during war time.

While famous for its work in the field of health and the manufacture of breakfast foods, Battle Creek is also an important manufacturing center. Many industries are located here. Among the products made at Battle Creek can be listed breakfast foods, auto parts, boxboard, cartons, welded ware, agricultural equipment, printing presses, and bread-wrapping machines. Shops of the Grand Trunk Railroad are located here. At one time stoves were made here.

KALAMAZOO is located on the Kalamazoo River about thirty miles from Lake Michigan. It lies midway between Detroit and Chicago. The area for many years was the homeland of the Pottawattomie Indians. At first the area was called Ke Kalamazoo from the Indian language and means "boiling pot."

In 1823 a trading post was located at the meeting place of the Indian trail and the river. The first settler was Titus Bronson, who came to Kalamazoo in 1829. Until 1836 the little settlement was called Bronson, but in that year the shortened Indian name of Kalamazoo was given to the settlement.

In 1847, and in the years that followed, many Dutch settlers came to the city and county. In 1870 these thrifty farmers began to grow celery. Large areas of swampland and marshland were drained, and the rich, black soil was found well suited to the new crop. For many years Kalamazoo was a leading center of celery production. Today the variety of soils in the vicinity makes the area one in which diversified agriculture is carried on.

Kalamazoo is also an industrial center. Several large paper-making plants are located here. All grades of paper, from cardboard for boxes to the finest grades of writing paper, are produced. The Upjohn Company is a large manufacturer of pharmaceuticals. Heating units and auto parts are also produced.

Kalamazoo is also a college community. Here are located Kalamazoo College, the oldest college in Michigan; Nazareth College, a Catholic girls' school; and Western Michigan University. Western Michigan University is the third largest state-supported college in Michigan. Over five thousand college students are enrolled at the present time.

Northeast of Kalamazoo on the shore of Gull Lake is the Kellogg Bird Sanctuary. Each year many people visit this waterfowl refuge to see the birds as they stop there on their way north in the spring and south in the fall.

Lawton, Decatur, and Paw Paw are nearby communities. In this area the making of grape juice is a major occupation. Dowagiac manufactures heating equipment and fishing tackle.

BENTON HARBOR and ST. JOSEPH are twin cities located on opposite sides of the St. Joseph River at the place where it empties into Lake Michigan. In 1679 La Salle visited the area and built a small fort. Mound builders once occupied this vicinity, but the Pottawattomie Indians were living here when the settlers arrived.

The early settlers in the area found the land of southwestern Michigan good for farming and especially well adapted to fruit growing. Today, because of the fertile soil, the effect of Lake Michigan on the climate, and the nearby location of large markets—especially Chicago, which is only sixty miles away—the entire area of Berrien, Van Buren, and Allegan counties has become a leading fruit- and vegetable-producing center.

Because of the longer growing season, southwestern Michigan produces most of Michigan's peach crop. Apples are produced in such volume that the area is considered to be one of the more important apple-producing localities of the country. Plums, pears, grapes, cherries, strawberries, and tomatoes are also important crops. In the spring when the "Blossom Festival" is held, the countryside is fragrant and colorful.

Much of this fruit, destined for the Chicago market, passes through St. Joseph and Benton Harbor, which act as distributing centers. The local open-air fruit market at Benton Harbor is one of the largest open non-citrus fruit markets in the country and each year handles over seven million packages of fruit valued at over five million dollars. Each day during the harvest season trucks bring the fruit and vegetables to the market.

These cities and the nearby shore line of Lake Michigan furnish a recreational area for people from Chicago and northern Indiana and

Illinois. The cities are also known for their sulphur baths. The twin cities are also industrial communities producing auto and aircraft parts, washing machines, pumps, dies, rubber goods, hosiery, canned fruits, jams and jellies.

NILES, on the St. Joseph River, is located on a site where Indian trails once crossed. At one time it was the homeland of mound builders. Later it was the homeland of the Miamis and then the Pottawattomie Indians. During the latter part of Allouez's life this early French Jesuit missionary carried on his missionary work among the Indians in the St. Joseph valley of southwestern Michigan. After spending almost a quarter of a century as a missionary among the Indians of Wisconsin, Illinois, and Michigan, he died and was buried somewhere near Niles in August, 1689. A large granite marker near Niles marks the scene of Allouez's last missionary activity.

Another large boulder marks the site of a French fort first built in 1697 near what today is the present downtown section. After the fall of New France, the English occupied the fort. During Pontiac's Conspiracy, on May 25, 1763, the Pottawattomies attacked and killed the English garrison. Later, during the Revolutionary War, on January 2, 1781, a Spanish raiding expedition from St. Louis made its way overland across Illinois and captured the fort. Because of this Spanish raid, Niles is the only city in Michigan to have been under four flags: French, English, Spanish, and American.

In 1822 Rev. Isaac McCoy founded the Carey Mission to work among the Indians. The next year the first settlers arrived, and in 1832 the mission was closed. When the road was opened between Detroit and Chicago, it passed through Niles. Soon settlers were coming into the region from the East as well as from Indiana to occupy the prairies and fertile woodland.

The industrial city of Niles is located in an area of fertile farm land. Besides producing general crops, it is noted for its apple orchards and its mint and mushroom production.

Niles is also proud of some of its native sons: Montgomery Ward, the founder of Montgomery Ward Mail Order House and retail stores; the two Dodge brothers, who founded the Dodge Motor Company; and Ring Lardner, the noted writer.

The industries of Niles produce dress patterns, architectural metal work used in front entrances of stores, shops, and theatres, auto parts, electrical appliances, telephone parts, tools and dies, spring steel, tanks, furniture, wire, paper, toys, and ventilator equipment.

Chapter XXII

MICHIGAN'S SOUTHEASTERN INDUSTRIAL AREA

Although some of Michigan's industries are scattered over much of the state, a large part of her industries is located in the southeastern part of the state near the Detroit River. This area has developed rapidly, both in the diversity of its industries and in the size of its population, since World War I and the coming of the automobile era in American history. Because of this industrial development, more than one half of all the people in Michigan live in Detroit and the nearby area. Today this section of Michigan also possesses a major portion of the total wealth of the state. So large are the industries of this part of Michigan that they use about ten per cent of all the steel used in the nation. Much of this steel is used in making automobiles and automobile parts.

To this industrial area along the Detroit River, the busiest river in the world, come large lake freighters bringing coal, iron ore, and limestone. Several railroad and truck lines running into this area bring in a variety of other raw materials needed in manufacturing. The railroads and trucks also bring in the vast quantities of food and personal items needed in this highly populated area. From this area goes out each day a large volume of various manufactured products, the most important of which is automobiles.

Here in the southeastern part of Michigan are found the industrial or residential cities of Allen Park, Berkley, Birmingham, Bloomfield Hills, Brighton, Center Line, Dearborn, Detroit, East Detroit, Ecorse, Farmington, Ferndale, Flat Rock, Garden City, Grosse Pointe, Grosse Pointe Farms, Grosse Pointe Shores, Grosse Pointe Woods, Hamtramck, Hazel Park, Highland Park, Huntington Woods, Inkster, Lincoln Park, Livonia, Melvindale, Monroe, Mount Clemens, Northville, Oak Park, Pleasant Ridge, Plymouth, Pontiac, River Rouge, Riverview, Rochester, Rockwood, Romulus, Roseville, Royal Oak, St. Clair Shores, Trenton, Utica, Wayne, Wyandotte, and Ypsilanti.

Some of these centers are residential areas and do not permit manufacturing to be carried on within their city limits. Other communities are made up of residential areas and industrial areas. Nearly all

Detroit skyline with Cobo Hall in foreground. (1960)
Courtesy Detroit Convention and Tourist Bureau
A Detroit Free Press Photo

Curing, or vulcanizing, is begun when the barrel-like tire is placed in a mold. An inflated "shaping bag" is forced inside the tire. The mold gives the tire its permanent shape and tread design. (1961)

Courtesy United States Rubber Company

Looking like a real tire after its curing, tubeless U.S. Royal is removed from "bag-o-matic" mold. (1961)

Courtesy United States Rubber Company

these communities have grown rapidly during the past few years. Automobile transportation has made it possible for people to live in nearby suburban residential areas and to drive each day to the factories and offices in the industrial areas to work. The entire area is covered with villages, cities, farms, parks, and recreation areas. During the past few years, many homes, sitting on wide, deep lots, have been built along the highways. Large parks and bathing beaches have been provided for the recreational needs of the people. In this part of the state there are many small lakes. Hundreds of cottages line their shores.

DETROIT is the oldest city in this area. As you know, it was settled in 1701. For over a century after its founding, Detroit remained a small wilderness fort and fur trading center. Its strategic location was known at the time of its founding, but the real importance of its location became more evident after the opening of the Erie Canal in 1825. Detroit then became one of the leading receiving ports for traffic going west across Lake Erie.

Courtesy Detroit Convention and Tourist Bureau

Detroit's downtown SKYLINE as seen from Windsor, Canada. In the foreground, Detroit's new Civic Center. The huge building in the foreground, dominating the Civic Center, is Cobo Hall, world's largest single convention exhibit building. (1960)

Today Detroit is Michigan's largest city. In 1951 this city, one of the oldest in the state, celebrated its two hundred and fiftieth birthday. But there is nothing left in it now to remind one of its long history since 1701 when Cadillac came here to found a little French fort on the wide river. In fact, there is not much left to remind one of how Detroit looked just a century ago. Today Detroit is a new city, changed and enlarged with the coming of the automobile industry at the turn of the century.

Detroit has had quite a steady growth since the Americans began settling the area after the War of 1812. Every census since that time shows an increase in Detroit's population. In some decades Detroit has even doubled her population. This rapid growth of Detroit is unusual, too, for Detroit has no special geographic advantages that can account for her steady growth. Also there is no major resource in the area to which Detroit's growth is allied. Michigan's early roads and railroads fanned out from this early trading center, and this no doubt brought people and goods to the area, but Detroit's real growth—like that of Flint, Grand Rapids, Kalamazoo, Battle Creek, and many other cities in Michigan—has been the result of the vision, plans, and work of the people living here.

In 1850, Detroit's population was about twenty-one thousand people. But each year after that saw new buildings, such as homes, hotels, stores, churches, and warehouses, being built. After 1850, industries began to grow in Detroit. As men grew wealthy from these industries, many of them built brick homes along some of the city streets such as Woodward Avenue and East Jefferson Avenue. These large brick homes with their spacious lawns easily let it be known that rich men as well as laborers lived in the rapidly growing city of Detroit.

Although Detroit had a normal growth during the years between 1850 and 1900, most of the people coming into the area just passed through it on their way to other places farther north and west. Up to 1900 most of the area around Detroit, where heavily populated suburbs are today, was still used as farm land. On market days the nearby farmers drove their teams of horses to town and sold their farm produce at the open city market. The entire city in 1900 lay within what is now the well-known street called Grand Boulevard. At that time Grand Boulevard formed a half circle around the city of Detroit. On Sunday afternoons people drove their horses and buggies along this spacious boulevard.

Detroit's rapid growth, as well as that of the other cities in the area, can be traced back to about 1900 when automobiles began to be made. Today Detroit is known throughout the world as the Automobile City. Although many auto parts are still made in Detroit, only a small percentage of the total automobiles produced in the area are made in Detroit. Today Detroit has become a city of greatly diversified industries.

About 1900, when automobiles began to be manufactured here, Detroit's population was only a little over one quarter of a million people. It had reached nearly half a million by 1910. By 1920 it had grown to nearly a million. By 1930 it was a little over one and one-half million people. By 1950 it had reached nearly to the two-million mark. In 1850 Detroit was ranked thirty-third among American cities in size, but today it holds fifth place among the cities of the nation. Over three million people now live in Detroit and its nearby suburban area.

From the time of American settlement up to 1880, most of the people coming to the United States were people from the countries of northern Europe. It was these people, or the children of such people, who came to Michigan from New England and settled here. Most of these early settlers belonged to one of the Protestant faiths. After 1880 a great change came in the nationalities of immigrants coming into the United States. More and more people began coming to the United States from southern and eastern Europe. These new immigrants were largely Roman Catholic or Greek Catholic. As there was little frontier land left, these later immigrants settled in America's rapidly growing cities where work could be found in the new and growing industries. After 1900 many of these people came to Detroit to work in the automobile factories. Many people have also come to Detroit and the suburban areas from the southern states. Among this group of people seeking work in Detroit's industries were many Negroes who came north to find work and better living conditions. With the rise of industries in Detroit there has also taken place a change in the nationalities of people that make up the new and rapidly growing city. Thus, there is a marked contrast between the nationality groups of our urban centers and our rural areas today, both as to nationality stock and religious belief.

During the past ten years a still new and different Detroit has been in the making. Hundreds of old houses and warehouses have been torn down to make way for a newer and more beautiful city. Along the waterfront, where passenger steamers docked for over a century, a new Civic Center is now being developed. New city buildings and a green parkway will greet tomorrow's visitors along Detroit's waterfront. New expressways, cut through old residential areas where once stood hundreds of old homes, are already reaching across the city. These new highways have done much to speed up traffic moving from one part of the city to another.

On the south side of the Detroit River, across from Detroit, stands Detroit's sister city, Windsor, Ontario. For over a hundred years little steam ferries carried wagons, buggies, automobiles, and people across the Detroit River from one country to the other. These little white ferryboats, hurrying back and forth across the river, always were of interest to local people as well as to visitors that came to the city. But today these picturesque little ferries no longer run back and forth across the Detroit River. Automobile, truck, and bus traffic moving between the two cities now goes through the Detroit and Windsor Tunnel or over the Ambassador Bridge. One railroad tunnel runs under the river. Much railroad traffic to and from the eastern part of the United States thus moves under the Detroit River. But some railroad car ferries still carry railroad cars across the river. Fast trains run across Canada from Windsor to Buffalo, New York, and from there to Albany on the Hudson River.

Courtesy Detroit Convention and Tourist Bureau

Detroit-Windsor tunnel—this tunnel carries auto traffic between Detroit and Windsor.

Today Detroit is an educational center as well as a manufacturing center. Here are located Wayne State University, the University of Detroit, the Detroit Institute of Technology, Marygrove College, and Mercy College, and also several private schools and colleges.

Among the buildings and places of interest in Detroit the following can easily be listed: the Detroit Public Library, which also contains the Burton Historical Collections, the finest collection of historical material on the Old Northwest to be found in Michigan; the Detroit Institute of Arts; the Detroit Historical Museum; the Detroit Zoological Park; the site of Old Fort Pontchartrain, on West Jefferson Avenue, in front of the new Veterans' Memorial Building; Mariners' Church; the new City-County Building; the Detroit and Windsor Tunnel, which runs between Detroit and Windsor; the Ambassador Bridge; Fort Wayne; the site of old Fort Shelby; the site of Michigan's first capital, where Stevens T. Mason lies buried; Belle Isle, a city park lying in the Detroit River; and the Michigan State Fair Grounds where the Michigan State Fair is held each fall. The salt mine is not open to visitors, but many manufacturing plants take visitors on guided trips through their plants. Each year hundreds of people visit Detroit's industries. During the summer months most people like to watch the huge ore freighters as they push steadily along on the Detroit River past Detroit, busily carrying most of the nation's iron ore from the mines to the blast furnaces.

Courtesy Kaiser-Frazer Corporation

Bombers were made in this plant during World War II. Then it was used by the Kaiser-Frazer Company to make automobiles. Today the plant is used by the General Motors Corporation. Willow Run Airport in the background.

At the present time there are several hundred manufacturing concerns in the Detroit area. Most of them are producers of automobiles or are allied in some way to the automobile industry. However, many other articles are produced in Detroit besides automobiles. Here are located some of the largest drug, varnish and paint, and button manufacturing plans in the world. Detroit is also a salt center for the United States. Among many important products manufactured may be listed: oil burning furnaces, business machines, chemicals, vacuum cleaners, electric refrigerators, electrical equipment, buttons, fertilizer, gelatine, overalls, brass and copper products, books, bolts, nuts, screws, soft drinks, tires, tools, and steel. Detroit also has meat packing plants.

During the past few years Detroit's suburban areas have built more new factories and created jobs faster than has Detroit. No doubt this is due to several factors: land is cheaper in the suburbs; there is more land to be had; and older buildings do not have to be wrecked to make room for new factories. From 1950 to 1953 fifty-five new plants, each employing one hundred men or more, were built in the suburban areas. Many older plants which were once in Detroit have moved to outlying areas, especially north of the Eight Mile Road in Oakland and Macomb counties.

DEARBORN has a long and interesting history. Not including the little French forts which were built in Michigan, Dearborn's history is as old as any community in the state. French settlers made their homes in the forest along the banks of the River Rouge before 1800 and pastured their little ponies where the Ford Rouge Plant now stands. The oldest continuing Protestant church, and the second one built in Michigan, was built near the banks of the River Rouge in Dearborn in 1818.

Settlers began pushing into this area soon after the land was put on sale by the government in 1818. This was before the Chicago Road was built, and these early settlers found their way into the Michigan wilderness along the Old River Road that followed the north bank of the River Rouge. Today what remains of this old road is known as the Ann Arbor Trail. Later hundreds of settlers, in ox-drawn wagons, pushed through Dearborn along Michigan Avenue, in the years between 1830 and 1850, to start new homes in Michigan's wilderness.

Dearborn is known today as the center of the Ford industries. For many years Dearborn was a small village on the old Chicago Road and all the land around it was farm land. After Mr. Ford began building his large plant on the River Rouge in 1915, people settled on the farm land near it, and the little city of Springwells grew up. Later this became the city of Fordson. Present Dearborn is made up of two cities, Dearborn and Fordson, which were joined together into the city of Dearborn in 1929.

After Fordson and Dearborn joined together, Dearborn became the most rapidly growing city in the United States. For some years bricks were made here, but this industry has now ceased to exist. Most of the old clay pits have been filled in, and today they are covered with homes. The Ford Rouge Plant is Dearborn's largest manufacturing plant; in fact, it is one of the largest industrial plants in the world. To it come railroad cars, trucks, and ore and coal boats bringing raw materials to be used in making Ford cars. From this plant each day comes a steady stream of automobiles. The Chrysler Corporation has taken over other older auto plants and now manufactures the DeSoto car here in Dearborn and in the nearby Detroit area. The American Blower Corporation manufactures ventilating equipment. Here at Dearborn are also located Greenfield Village, the Henry Ford Museum, the Ford Experimental Laboratories, the Ford Rotunda, and the General Offices of the Ford Motor Company.

Greenfield Village is an educational project started by Mr. Henry Ford in 1929. The village is built around a green similar to that in many early American villages. Greenfield Village covers about two hundred acres and includes nearly one hundred buildings. Many of these buildings were brought here by Mr. Ford from other places in the United States. Some of them are as old as 1650, but most of them represent the period from 1800 to 1900 and are closely associated with what we call the Industrial Revolution.

At Greenfield Village one can see many interesting buildings and things which are no longer a part of our American way of life. Among the buildings is the Clinton Inn that once stood at Clinton, Michigan, over a century ago and cared for the needs of settlers as they pushed into the wilderness. There are old sawmills which show the early methods of making lumber. The Martha-Mary chapel is a typical church of one hundred years ago. The Cotswold Cottage group was brought here from England to represent life as it was lived in England in 1600. At this group one can visit an old blacksmith shop and see iron products being made just as they were made at the time the Pilgrims settled at Plymouth. The Lincoln Court House is one of the buildings in which Abraham Lincoln practiced law. Menlo Park is the restoration of an experimental laboratory that Mr. Edison built in New Jersey in 1876. In this building Mr. Edison invented the electric light. Today it has many of his earliest inventions on display. You will also find an old-fashioned post office; a tin-type studio where you can have a tin-type picture made of yourself; the Smith's Creek Station where Mr. Edison was thrown off the train; a carding mill that once stood at Plymouth, Michigan; a cooper shop where barrels were once made; a blacksmith shop similar to those in every early community a century ago; and a general store that stood at Waterford a hundred years ago. These and many other things will interest you when you visit Greenfield Village.

Beside Greenfield Village stands what is now known as the Henry Ford Museum. Until Mr. Ford's death this building was known as the Edison Institute. The Henry Ford Museum is devoted to the story of the economic freedom of man. The building itself is a replica of three buildings. The central section is built like Independence Hall in Philadelphia. The building covers nearly eleven acres and is devoted mostly to exhibits showing progress in agriculture, industry, and transportation. The floor of the building covers about 320,000 square feet and is made of teakwood blocks that are placed together without nails. It is the largest single teakwood floor in the world.

Under the roof of this large building Mr. Ford has brought together thousands of interesting things: old binders, reapers, wagons, buggies, chariots, oxcarts, steam engines, sewing machines, automobiles, and many other interesting things that have been developed as man has gradually learned to control better the forces of nature. Here also can be seen exhibits of furniture, silverware, porcelain, and ceramics. There are also many old-time shops such as the shop of a tailor, the shop of an iron craftsman, an early barber shop, a gun and locksmith's shop, and the shop of a violin maker.

HIGHLAND PARK for many years was a northern suburb of Detroit, but now Highland Park is surrounded by Detroit and Hamtramck. After 1910, when the Ford Motor Company moved its factory from Detroit to the newly built Highland Park Plant, the city grew rapidly. For a few years this plant was the main plant of the Ford Motor Company, but with the building of the Ford Rouge plant in Dearborn, the Ford Motor Company moved its main offices to Dearborn. The old Ford Highland Park plant is now used to make Ford tractors and upholstery. During the past few years Highland Park has declined in population. Here at Highland Park are located the Highland Park Junior College and the main business offices of the Chrysler Corporation.

HAMTRAMCK was named after Colonel John F. Hamtramck, the first American military commander at Detroit. The present city is entirely enclosed by Detroit and Highland Park. During the past few years Hamtramck has declined in population as more industries have moved into the area. Perhaps the best-known plant in Hamtramck is the main Dodge plant of the Chrysler Corporation.

MT. CLEMENS is located on Lake St. Clair at the mouth of the Clinton River. The Moravian Indians built the first Protestant church in Michigan at what is now Mt. Clemens when they settled there during the Revolutionary War. White settlers began coming into this area soon after 1800. In 1818, Mt. Clemens became the county seat of Macomb County. At one time it was a center for the manufacture of barrels and boats for the lake trade. In 1862, drillers looking for oil in the area found salt water instead. The salt water was found to be good for baths. In 1873 a bath-house and hotel were built at Mt. Clemens. Since that time Mt. Clemens has been nationally known as a health center. Each year many people come here and stay at the large bath-houses in order to avail themselves of the healing value of the water. For many years caring for these people furnished the major occupation for people living in Mt. Clemens, but today Mt. Clemens is feeling the press of the industrial area and several large factories have developed.

One of Mt. Clemens' major industries is the manufacture of lightweight dinnerware. Hundreds of dishes are made each day at the Mt. Clemens Pottery. These dishes are sold throughout the nation by one of the leading chain stores. Mt. Clemens is also known as the Rose City. Some fifteen million roses, as well as other flowers, are produced here each year. These flowers, which are grown in large greenhouses totaling sixty-five acres covered with glass, are shipped all over the United States. Among the products manufactured here are electric ironers, electric ranges, freezers, air conditioners, and television sets. Mt. Clemens also has several machine shops and die shops.

Three miles north of Mt. Clemens, on the shore of Lake St. Clair, is located Selfridge Field, one of the nation's many air bases. Planes of many kinds including jet-propelled fighter planes are stationed here. This air base is one of the air bases that protect the locks at the "Soo." Mt. Clemens is also a recreational center for many people living in the industrial area. Close to Mt. Clemens on the shore of Lake St. Clair are located St. Clair, Metropolitan and Jones beaches.

YPSILANTI is located where the old Sauk Trail, later the Chicago Road, crossed the Huron River. It was first a trading post on the Huron River and did not get its first settlers until 1823. Ypsilanti was named after a young Greek military hero, Demetrius Ypsilanti, who led the fighting for the freedom of Greece from Turkey. After the coming of the Chicago Road and the Michigan Central Railroad, the area around Ypsilanti settled rapidly. With the increased development of the industrial area, many industries have developed in Ypsilanti. Today, Ypsilanti has some thirty-five manufacturing plants that make auto parts, hardware, soaps, paper, and plastic products. Ypsilanti is also known as the home of Eastern Michigan University, the oldest normal college in Michigan. Here also is located the Ypsilanti State Hospital.

Just east of Ypsilanti is the Willow Run Bomber Plant where bombers were made during World War II. Following World War II this plant was used by the Kaiser-Fraser Corporation to make automobiles. Here is also located the Willow Run Airport, one of the largest airports in Michigan. This port is run by the University of Michigan. Much of the air traffic into and out of the industrial area uses Willow Run Airport. A little farther to the east is Detroit Metropolitan Airport.

PONTIAC is another of Michigan's rapidly growing industrial centers. It lies twenty-five miles north of Detroit. Its first settlers were a group of men from Detroit. These men purchased land in the area and came up the Clinton River to settle in the year 1818. Their little village was named Pontiac after the Ottawa chieftain who had once attacked the little fort at Detroit. Pontiac early turned to the making of wagons from the good hardwood found in the area. One of the best-known wagon companies was the Pontiac Spring Wagon Works. For several years Pontiac was known as a carriage center. Later, when the automobile industry developed, the city's carriage industries began making automobiles. Today the Pontiac automobile is made near the spot where Pontiac buggies were once made. For many years the village grew slowly, but after World War I it began a rapid growth and expanded along with the industrial area.

Pontiac's industries now produce automobiles, General Motors trucks, buses, taxicabs, auto bodies, paints and varnishes, Whizzer motor bikes, grey iron castings, and auto parts.

Pontiac is located in the center of a good farming area. Nearby, in the rolling farm lands, are the old towns of Orion, Rochester, Ortonville, Holly, Oxford, and Highland. These communities are still agricultural centers. The farming area around Pontiac is largely devoted to dairying, the raising of fruits, and truck garden crops. This area is the best fruit-growing area in southeastern Michigan. Pontiac is also a recreational center. The nearby area is some of the most beautiful rolling land in southern Michigan. Some four hundred lakes are located near Pontiac. Thousands of people from the busy cities find rest and relaxation in this area. During the summer they picnic, swim, sail, canoe, and ride in speedboats. In the wintertime they ski, toboggan, and skate.

At Pontiac is located the Pontiac State Hospital. South of the city near Birmingham is located the Cranbrook Foundation, which is a center of art and culture.

"THE DOWN RIVER COMMUNITIES" are several communities that lie along the Detroit River south of Detroit. In this group are River Rouge, Ecorse, Wyandotte, Riverview, Trenton, and Grosse Isle. The future looks bright for the further development and industrialization of this area. It is the center of the alkali industries of this part of Michigan, and heavy industries have also lately moved into the area. Located as they are along the Detroit River, they can easily receive bulk shipments of freight from Great Lakes steamers. Now that the Livingstone Channel leading into Lake Erie has been deepened, these cities can use ocean transportation as well as lake transportation to receive needed raw materials such as coal, limestone, gypsum, and iron ore. These same ships can also carry away many of the finished products. Railroad transportation is also good to the nearby large centers of population in northern Ohio, Indiana, and Illinois. Detroit's automobile and other industries provide a ready market for steel produced in the area. There are still vacant areas for building plants, parks, and residential sections.

RIVER ROUGE was just a small sawmill town of less than two thousand people when it became a village in 1899. It began to grow rapidly after the Great Lakes Engineering Works was started here in 1902. Boat-building was one of River Rouge's first industries. Over 250 Great Lakes boats have been built here by the Great Lakes Engineering Works.* Among these are several of the largest freighters like the "William Clay Ford III" and the ice breaker "Straits of

---

This boat building company closed down in the spring of 1961.

Mackinaw." River Rouge has twenty-one manufacturing plants. One of the largest of these plants is the United States Gypsum Company's plant where gypsum shipped from Alabaster is processed.

Courtesy The Great Lakes Steel Corporation

Great Lakes Steel Corporation, Ecorse, Michigan

ECORSE is known today as the home of the Great Lakes Steel Corporation. Its early history dates back to the time of Pontiac when, in 1764, the Labadie family settled here on the west bank of the Detroit River. For some time Ecorse was called Grand Port. Up until 1942, Ecorse kept her village government and for several years was the second largest village in the United States. With the coming of the Great Lakes Steel Corporation and other industries the area grew rapidly. Today there is little area left in Ecorse for residential expansion. At present Ecorse has twenty industries. Among the products made here can be listed parts for screw machines, stamping machines, folding tables and chairs, electric welded steel tubing, chassis frames for automobiles, rolled and stamped moldings, and toys. The Nicholson Terminal and Dock Company is located here. Large quantities of steel shipments from Chicago, Youngstown, Pittsburgh, Cleveland, and Buffalo are unloaded here as well as other bulk commodities used in industry. Repairs on lake boats and small lake craft are also made here.

WYANDOTTE is named after the Wyandotte Indians who once lived in the area. After the founding of Detroit, the remaining Hurons, sometimes called Wyandottes, came here to live so they would be near the protection of the French at Fort Pontchartrain. The first white settler at Wyandotte was George Clark, who moved into the area in 1817. During the early years of the settlement there was much speculation in land. It was here that Captain Eber Ward built his Eureka Iron and Steel Works just before the Civil War. When these works were destroyed by fire, the town declined until the coming of the alkali industries at the turn of the century.

Today, Wyandotte is the largest of "the down river communities." It is the nation's largest producer of cleaning compounds. The largest bleach plant in the United States is located here. This plant makes bleaching powder or chloride of lime. Among the many chemicals made in this city can be named sodium chloride, soda ash, sodium carbonate, atabrine, caustic soda, and baking soda. These products are made from the salt brine found under the area and from limestone. For many years limestone was quarried at nearby Sibley, but today large carriers bring limestone from the Alpena area

Courtesy Wyandotte Chemicals Corporation

South Plant, Wyandotte, Michigan. (1961)

to be used in manufacturing the products produced at Wyandotte. Wyandotte also produces some half million gallons of paint each year. This paint is used for automobile, industrial, and household finishes.

RIVERVIEW is a newly developing community. Here is located

Sharples Chemicals, Inc., which produces more than sixty products. One of its products is a gas odorant which is put into natural gas to give it an odor so that one can tell when it is leaking from a pipe. Its other products are used in such things as paints, and the average person never sees them although he uses them. The Firestone Steel Products Company produces steel rims, stampings, and steel cabinets. Riverview had an eighty per cent increase in population between 1940 and 1950.

TRENTON is another of "the down river communities" lying along the Detroit River. Just below Trenton a railroad bridge, now a county road bridge, once crossed to Grosse Isle. Another bridge connected the railroad to Stony Island. From Stony Island, trains were for many years ferried across the Detroit River to Canada. At one time the building of a railroad tunnel under the Detroit River at this point was planned, but the rocky nature of the river bottom caused the work to be dropped. For many years Trenton was a boat-building center.

Within the present city limits of Trenton is located one of the largest units of the Detroit Edison Company. It has capacity to produce three quarters of a million kilowatts an hour. This is one of the largest Edison plants in the Detroit area. Each summer, during the shipping season, many boats filled with coal from the mines of Pennsylvania dock at the plant and unload their cargoes of coal. In this day of electrical power one is apt to forget that the source of most of our electrical power is still coal. Coal is turned into steam power at these huge electric plants. The steam power is then turned into electrical power. It is this electrical power derived from coal that is used in the homes and industries of the industrial area.

Nearby is Sibley Quarry. From this quarry limestone was taken to supply the chemical industries of the area. Sibley was annexed to Trenton in 1929. Several large chemical companies are now located in Trenton. These companies use as their basic materials, salt, limestone, sulphur, coal, and petroleum. A gasoline refinery is located here. Trenton is also the home of the McLouth Steel Corporation. Their plant located here has some of the most modern steel-producing equipment in America, such as a modern electrical blast furnace, hot and cold rolled strip mills, and pickling and finishing facilities. The Chrysler Corporation manufactures marine engines, truck engines, and industrial engines here at Trenton.

GROSSE ISLE is a residential community on Grosse Isle in the

Courtesy McLouth Steel Corporation

Electric blast furnace—Trenton Plant (1954)

Detroit River. The island is about nine miles long and two miles wide. Two bridges, one toll and one free, cross from the mainland to the island. At the southern end of Grosse Isle is located a United States Naval Air Station where some twenty-four reserve squadrons, totaling about two thousand reservists, drill on week ends.

MONROE is located in the southeast corner of Michigan between Detroit and Toledo. It was settled in 1784 by some Frenchmen who began a settlement on the River Raisin not far from Lake Erie. For some years the little community was known as Frenchtown. It was here, during the War of 1812, that the massacre at the River Raisin took place. Here also the first American flag to be raised in the area now making up the state of Michigan was flown in 1796.

Monroe is very favorably located for transportation. Several railroad lines and two trunk highways pass through the city. Moreover, it is Michigan's only port on Lake Erie. A United States canal leads from Lake Erie into the Raisin River where a large turning basin of twenty-two acres is located some two miles up the Raisin River. Several lake freighters are docked here each winter. When the new harbor is completed, boats coming up the St. Lawrence Waterway will be able to dock at Monroe.

Several industries are located at Monroe. It is also surrounded by a rich farming area. Large nurseries here produce trees and shrubs for landscaping. For many years Monroe has been one of Michigan's leading paper-producing centers. Paper board, shipping cases, and cartons are manufactured. Among Monroe's many other products can be listed tools, machinery, stokers, automobile parts, office supplies and furniture, crushed stone, aluminum products, and foundry steel. St. Mary's Academy, a school for girls, is located here at Monroe. Sterling State Park is located north of Monroe on the shore of Lake Erie. Here at Monroe is located the Enrico Fermi Atomic Energy Plant. Monroe also has a new cement plant which is one of the nation's largest cement plants.

In December, 1959, a new cement plant, the Dundee Cement Company, opened a new plant at Dundee. Here a very high quality of limestone and clay will provide materials for this new plant for more than one hundred years. The quarry that is to be developed is 1,600 acres in area. Besides the deposit of limestone and clay the spot was chosen because it is only 50 miles from Detroit, 27 miles from Toledo, and only 14 miles from Monroe where the cement can be shipped by boat to ports around the Great Lakes and to other ports by way of the St. Lawrence Seaway. This is one of the largest cement plants in Michigan. Today, cement is Michigan's largest mineral product.

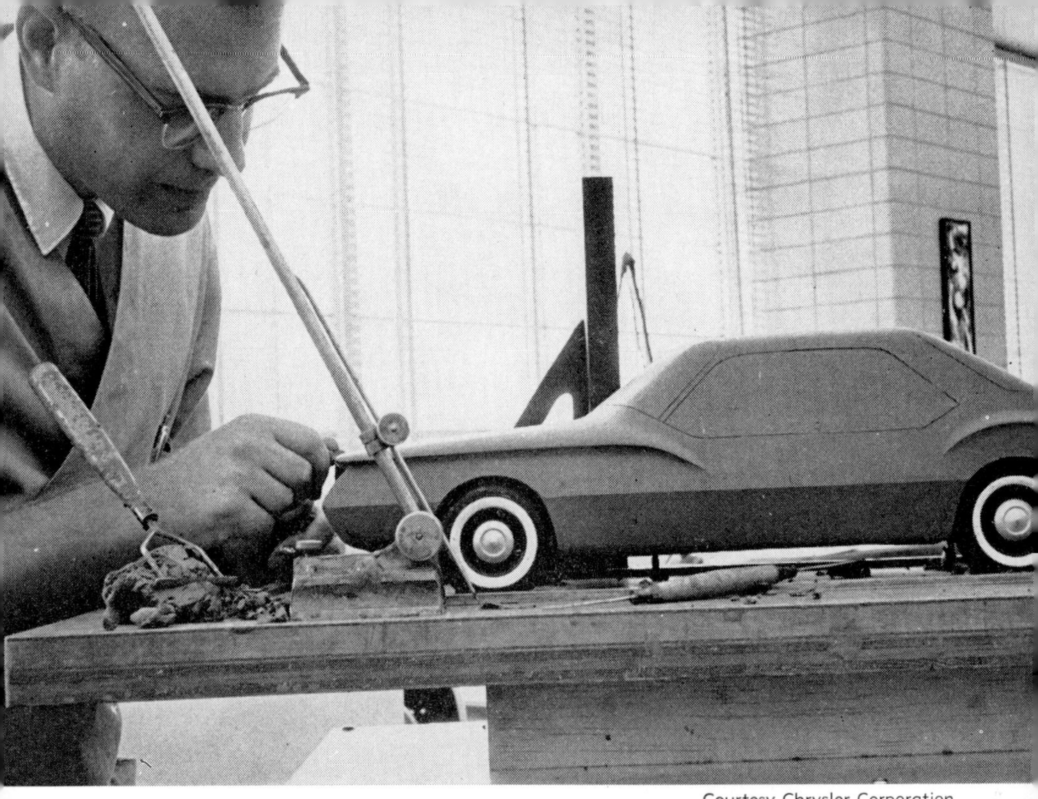

Courtesy Chrysler Corporation

A car stylist at work on the design for a new automobile. (1961)

An assembly line. This picture shows the engine drop in the Dodge Plant. (1961)

Courtesy Chrysler Corporation

Courtesy Ford Motor Company

The body drop station on the final assembly line. (1961)

The fifth wheel shown on this test car is used for concise measurement of gasoline economy. (1961)

Courtesy Ford Motor Company

Courtesy Ford Motor Company

Ore carriers docked at the Ford Rouge Plant in Dearborn, Michigan. (1961)

The Dundee Cement Company's $25 million plant, situated on the outskirts of Dundee, Mich. The plant will have the world's greatest initial rate of production—five million barrels of cement a year. Indicated above are: (1) quarry containing clay and limestone deposits adequated for more than 100 years of peak production; (2) primary crusher which reduces limestone to size suitable for conveyor; (3) cement storage silos 150 feet high with rail and truck loading stations; (4) conveyors and pipelines hauling raw materials and coal; (5) crushed limestone and coal storage area; (6) storage area for 200,000 tons of cement clinker, which will be ground into cement; (7) main plant, housing the five largest grinding mills in the world; (8) two kilns 460 feet long—largest in the Western Hemisphere; (9) electrostatic precipitator area, where more than 99 per cent of all impurities are removed from exhaust before discharge through a stack 350 feet high; (10) main office building. (1961) Courtesy Dundee Cement Company

INDEX